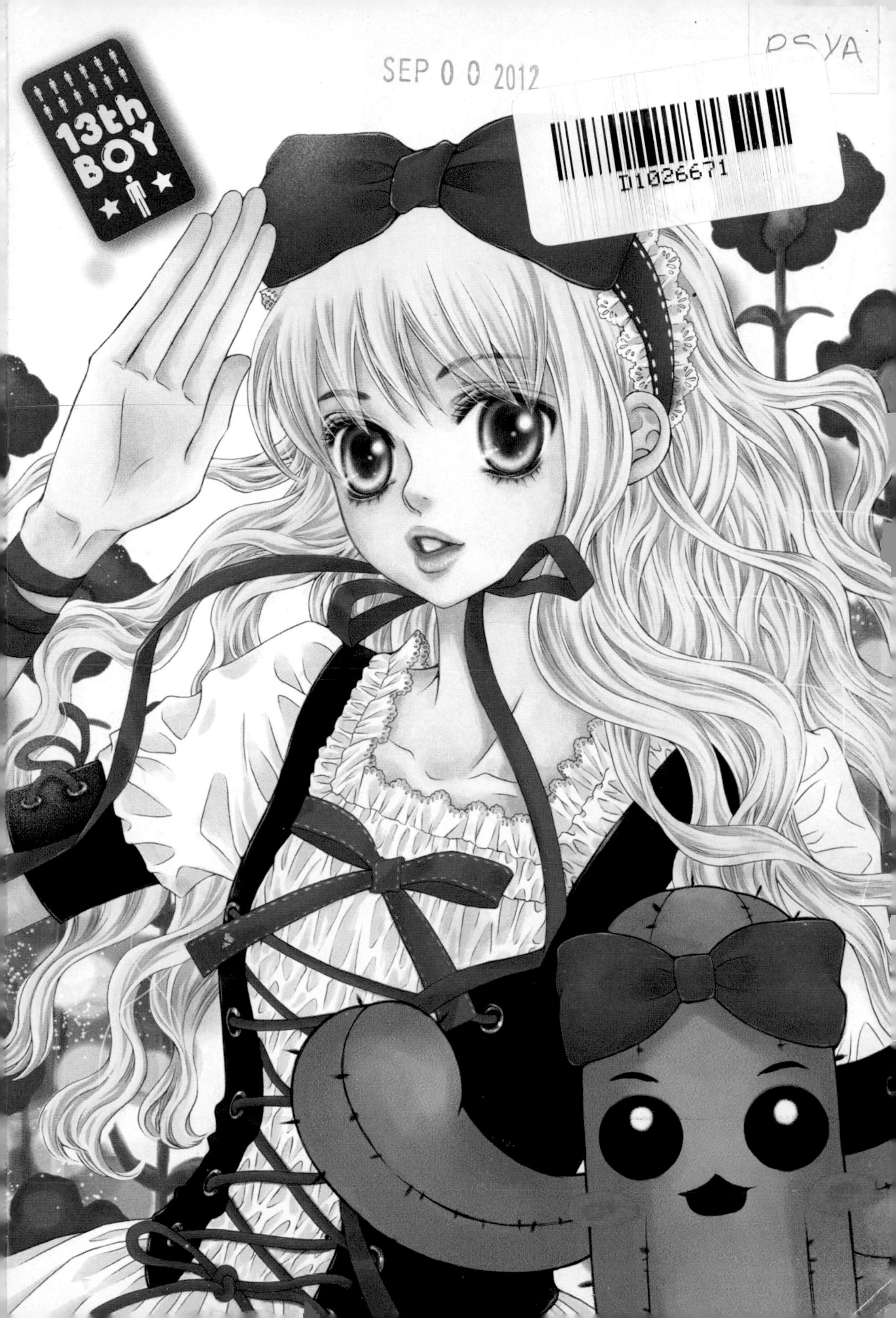
13th
BOY

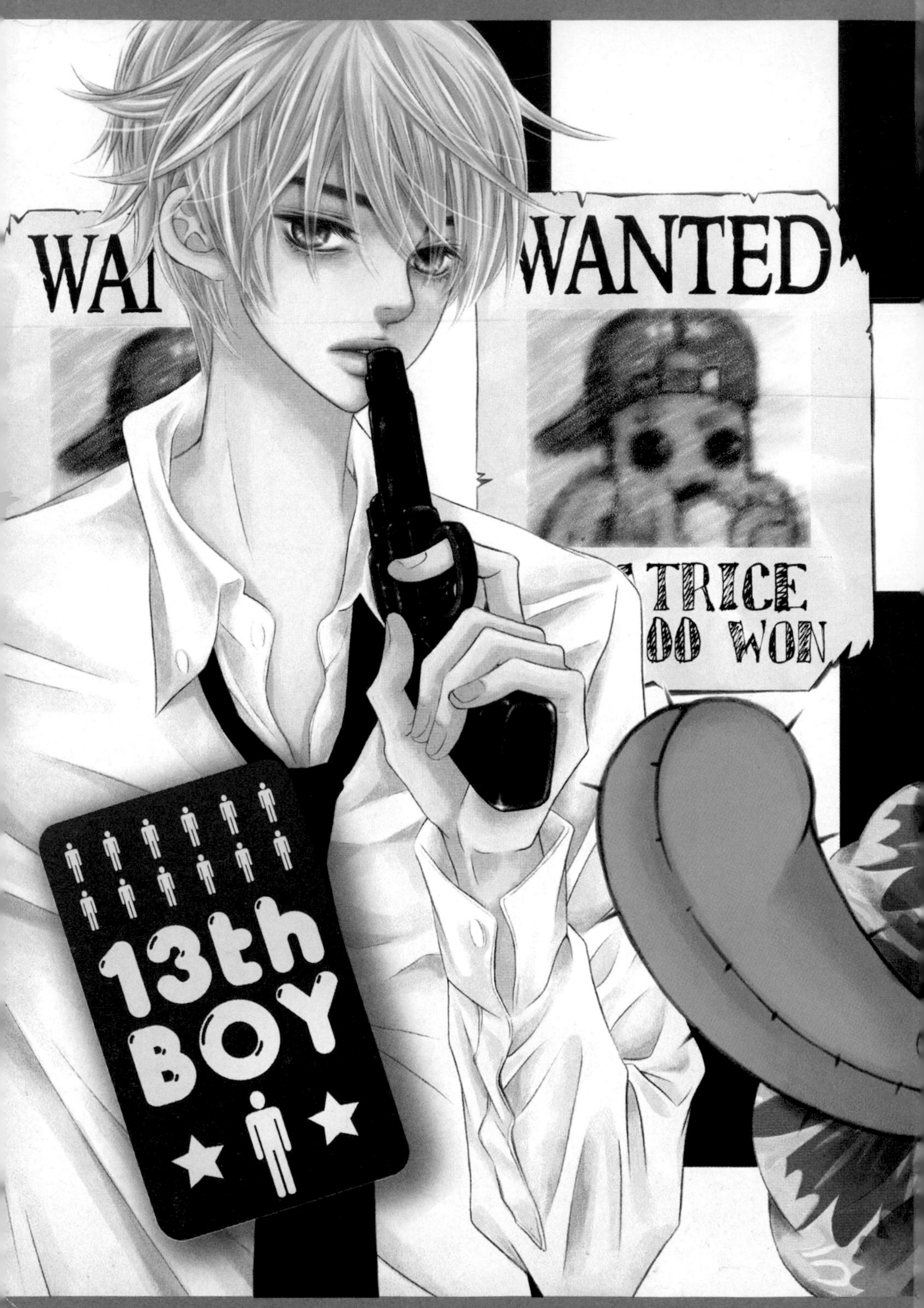
WA
WANTED
TRICE
00 WON
13th
BOY

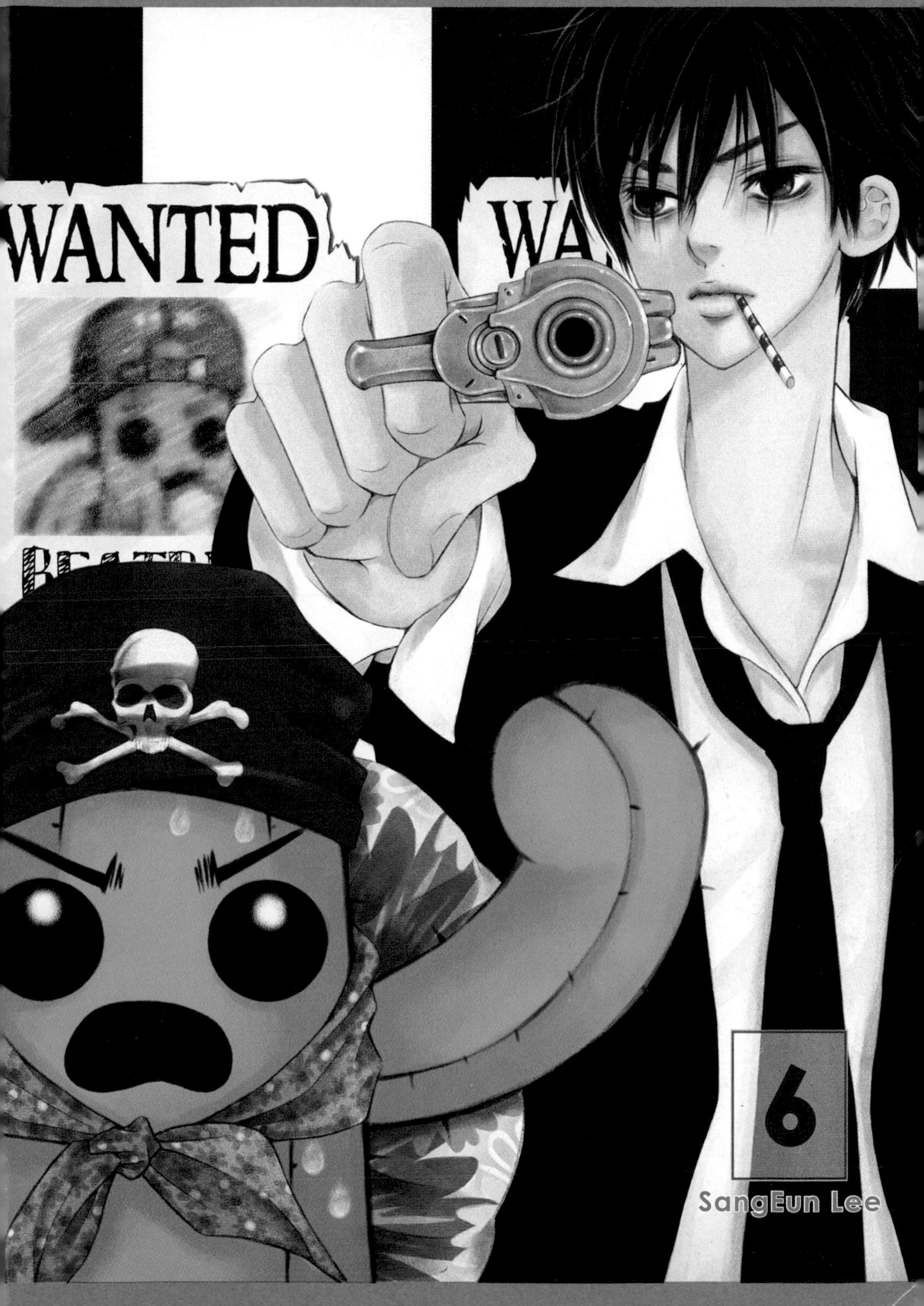
WANTED
6
SangEun Lee

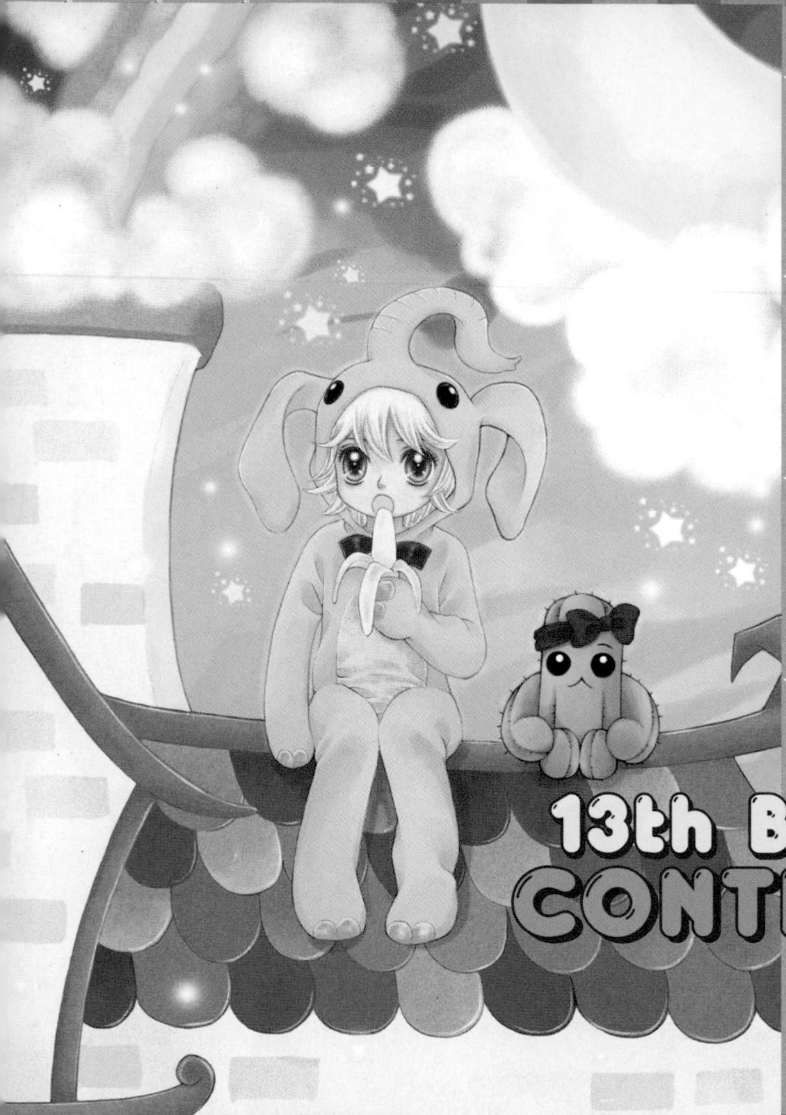

13th BOY♥ CONTENTS

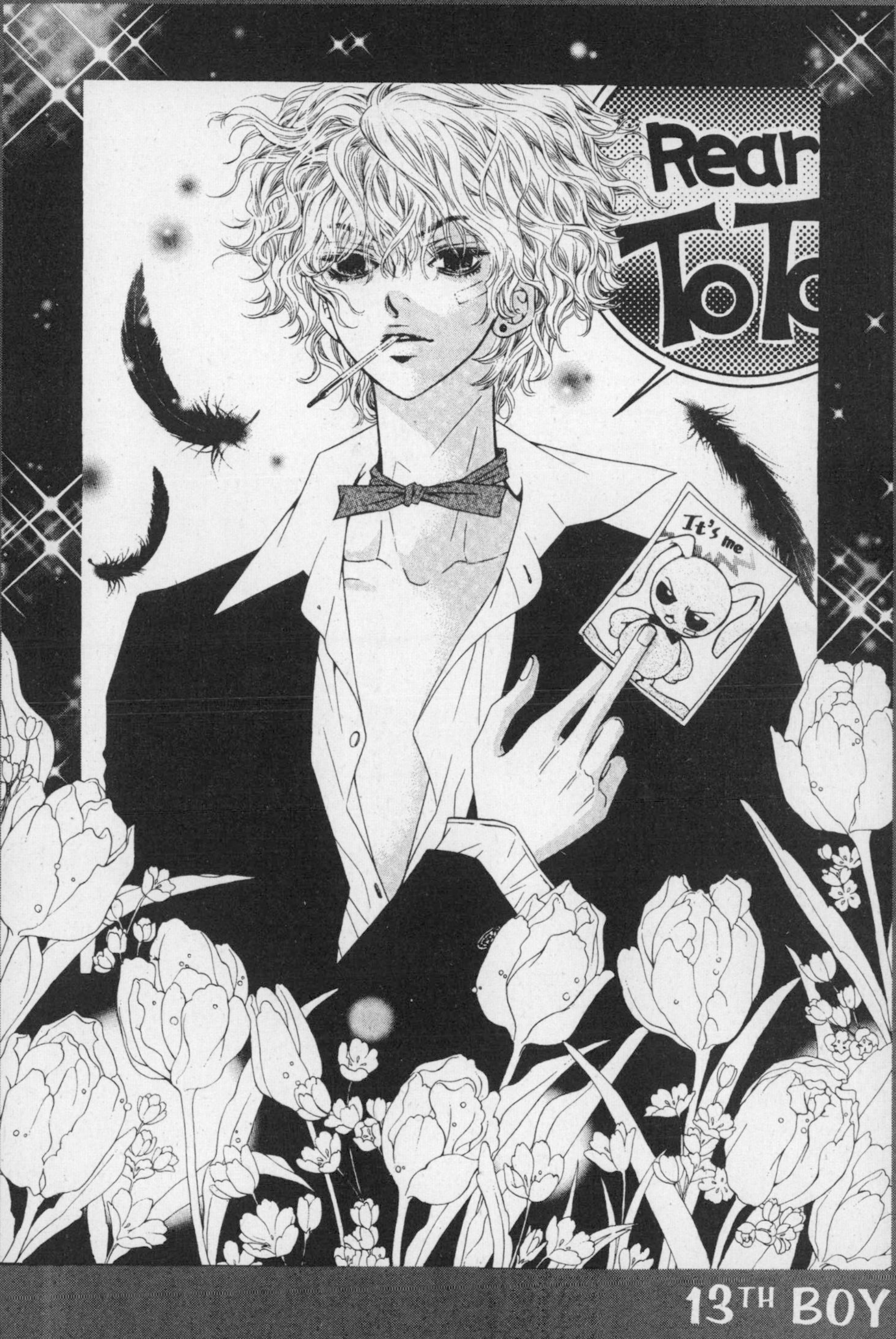
Rear
To To
It's me

13TH BOY

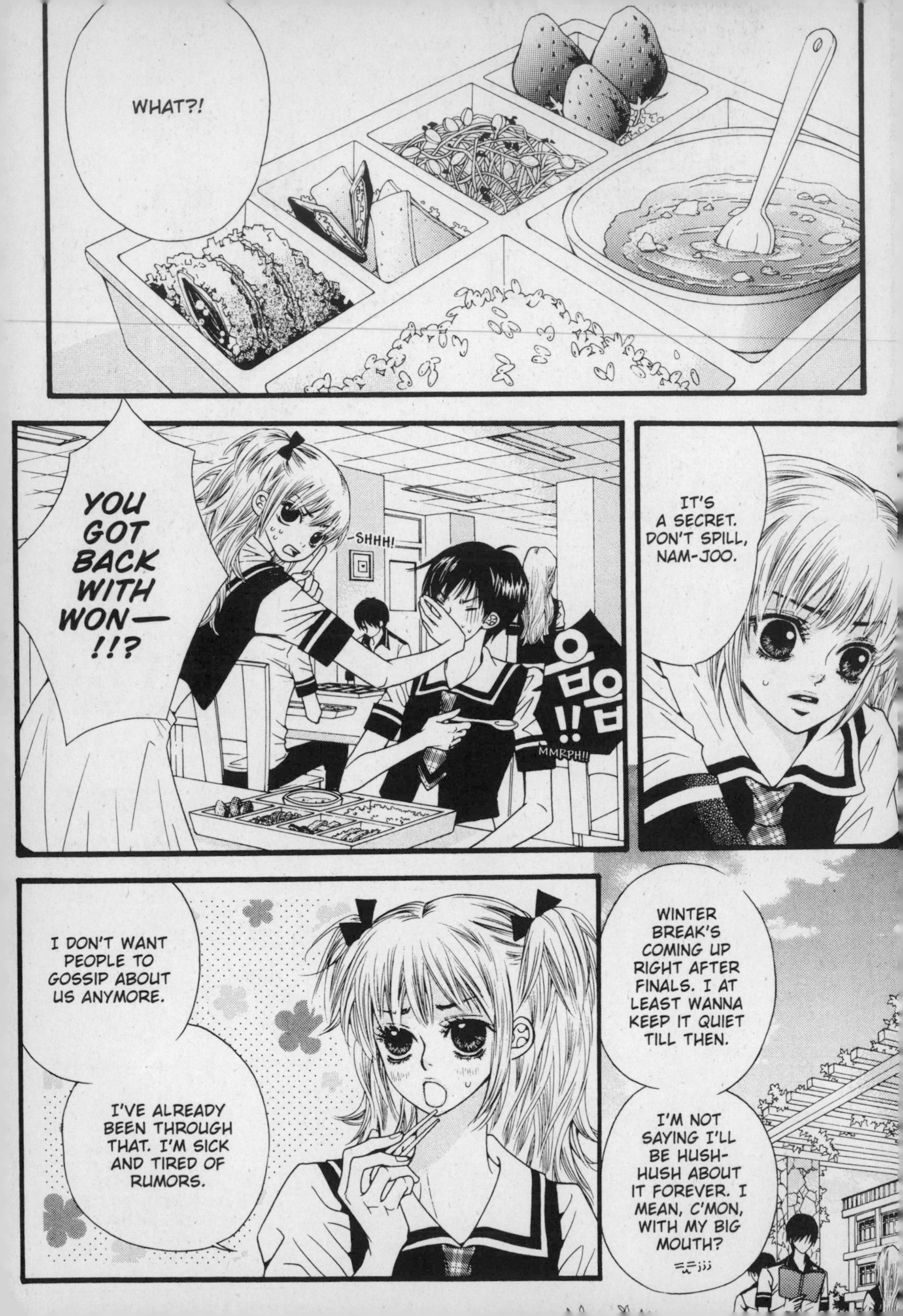

WHAT?!
YOU GOT BACK WITH WON—!!?
-SHHH!
읍읍!!
MMRPH!!
IT'S A SECRET. DON'T SPILL, NAM-JOO.
I DON'T WANT PEOPLE TO GOSSIP ABOUT US ANYMORE.
I'VE ALREADY BEEN THROUGH THAT. I'M SICK AND TIRED OF RUMORS.
WINTER BREAK'S COMING UP RIGHT AFTER FINALS. I AT LEAST WANNA KEEP IT QUIET TILL THEN.
I'M NOT SAYING I'LL BE HUSH-HUSH ABOUT IT FOREVER. I MEAN, C'MON, WITH MY BIG MOUTH?

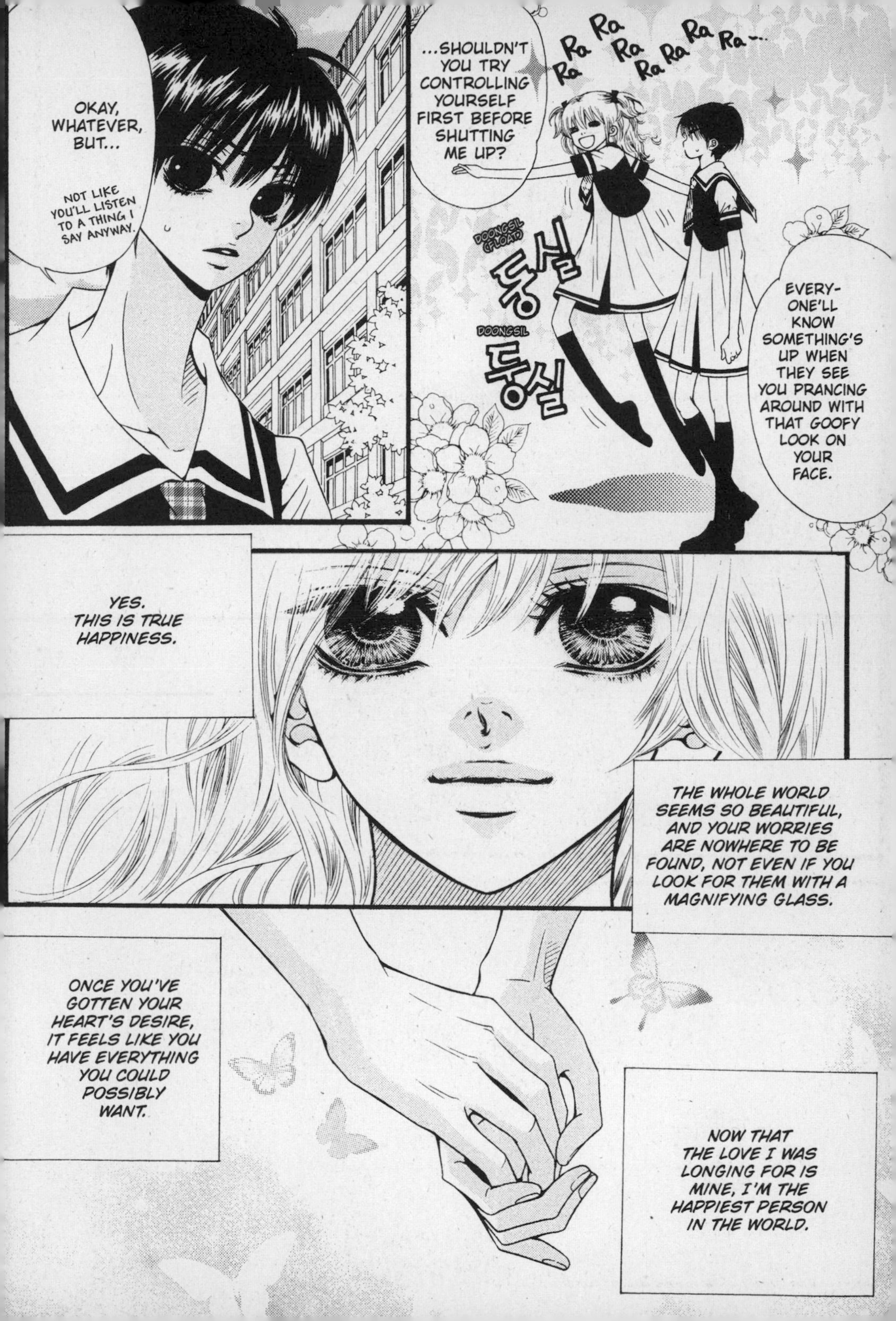
OKAY, WHATEVER, BUT...
NOT LIKE YOU'LL LISTEN TO A THING I SAY ANYWAY.
...SHOULDN'T YOU TRY CONTROLLING YOURSELF FIRST BEFORE SHUTTING ME UP?
Ra Ra Ra Ra Ra Ra Ra Ra~
DOONGSIL (FLOAT)
둥실
DOONGSIL
둥실
EVERY-ONE'LL KNOW SOMETHING'S UP WHEN THEY SEE YOU PRANCING AROUND WITH THAT GOOFY LOOK ON YOUR FACE.
YES. THIS IS TRUE HAPPINESS.
THE WHOLE WORLD SEEMS SO BEAUTIFUL, AND YOUR WORRIES ARE NOWHERE TO BE FOUND, NOT EVEN IF YOU LOOK FOR THEM WITH A MAGNIFYING GLASS.
ONCE YOU'VE GOTTEN YOUR HEART'S DESIRE, IT FEELS LIKE YOU HAVE EVERYTHING YOU COULD POSSIBLY WANT.
NOW THAT THE LOVE I WAS LONGING FOR IS MINE, I'M THE HAPPIEST PERSON IN THE WORLD.

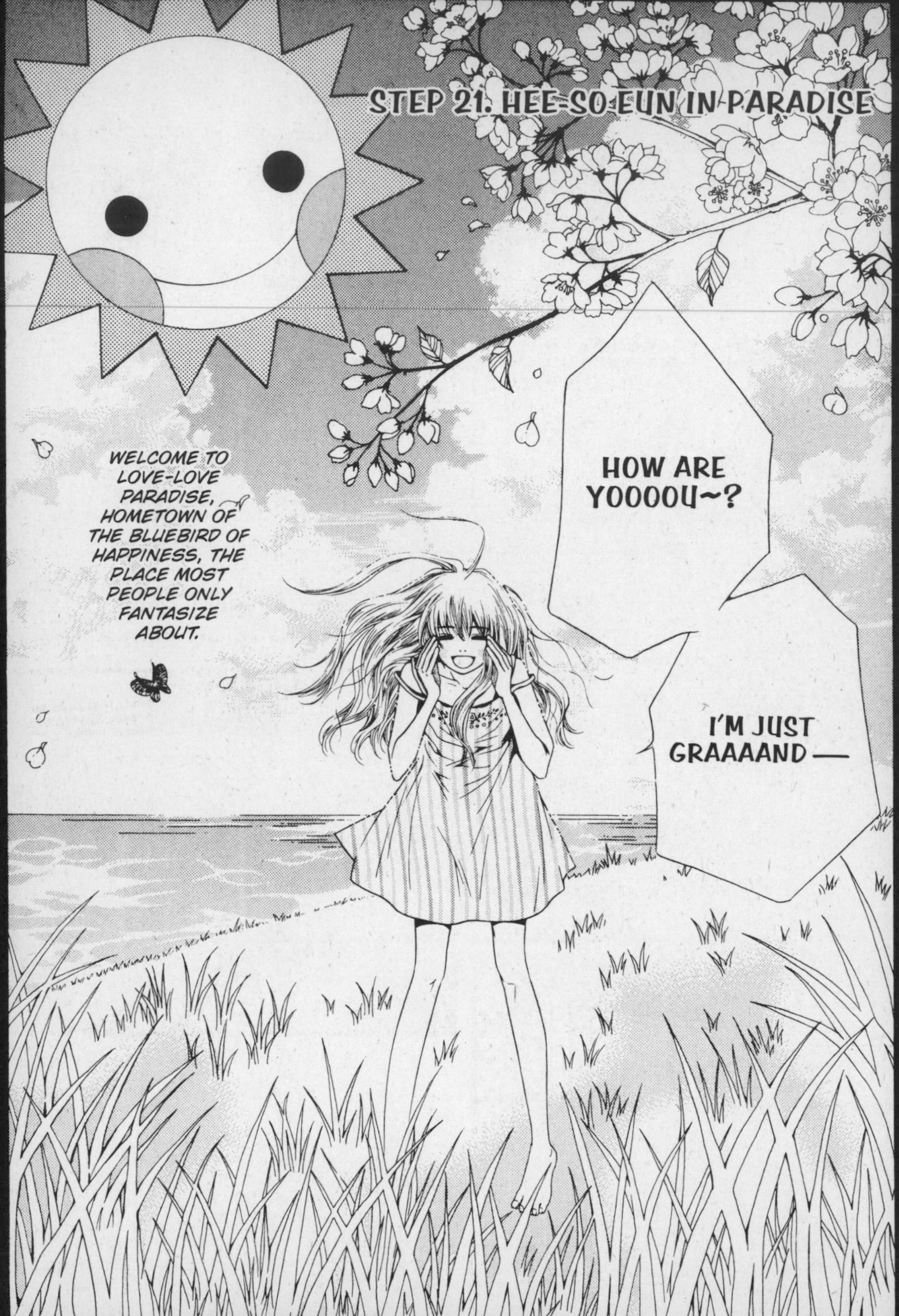
STEP 21. HEE-SO EUN IN PARADISE
WELCOME TO LOVE-LOVE PARADISE, HOMETOWN OF THE BLUEBIRD OF HAPPINESS, THE PLACE MOST PEOPLE ONLY FANTASIZE ABOUT.
HOW ARE YOOOOU~?
I'M JUST GRAAAAND —

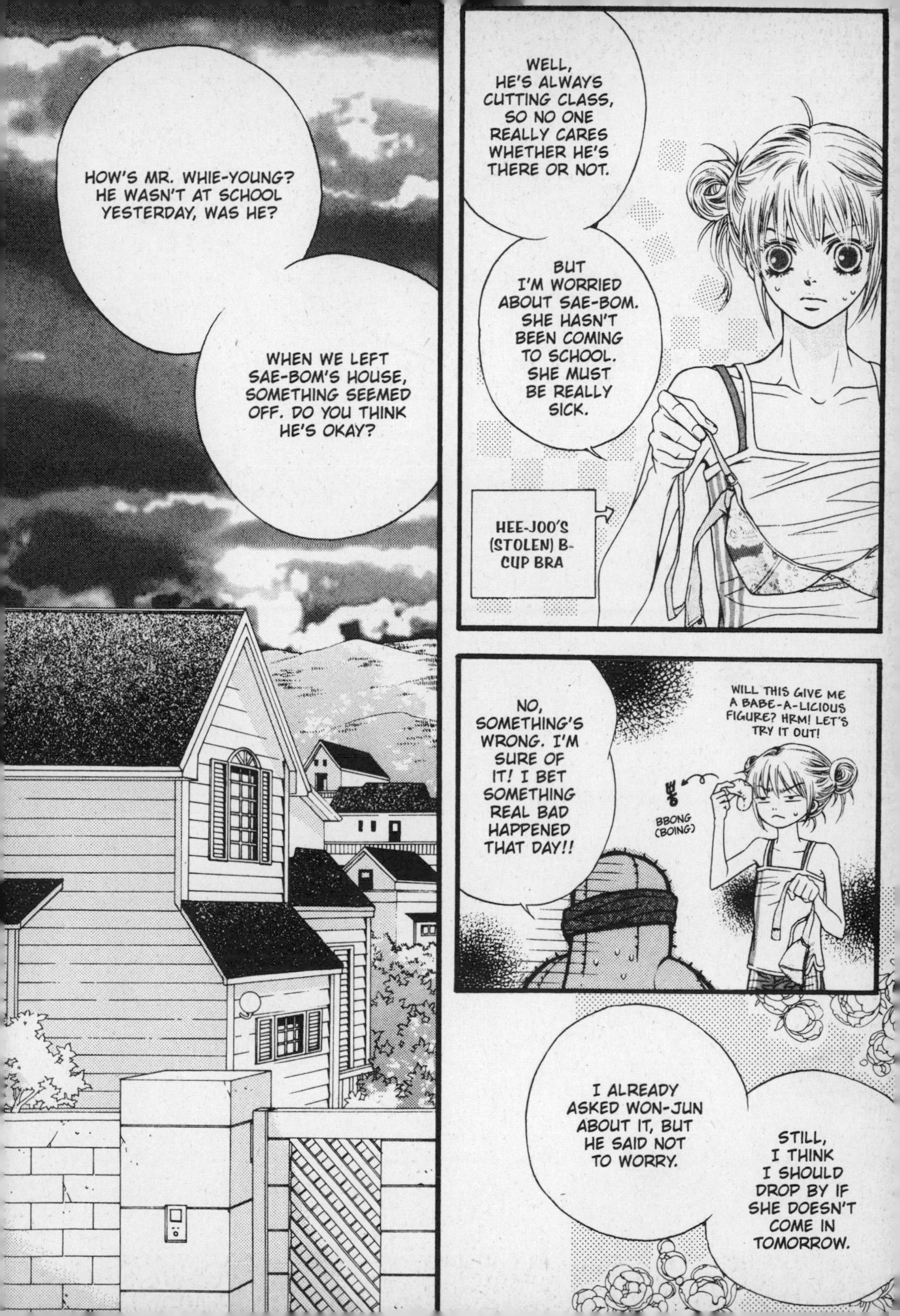
HOW'S MR. WHIE-YOUNG? HE WASN'T AT SCHOOL YESTERDAY, WAS HE?
WHEN WE LEFT SAE-BOM'S HOUSE, SOMETHING SEEMED OFF. DO YOU THINK HE'S OKAY?
WELL, HE'S ALWAYS CUTTING CLASS, SO NO ONE REALLY CARES WHETHER HE'S THERE OR NOT.
BUT I'M WORRIED ABOUT SAE-BOM. SHE HASN'T BEEN COMING TO SCHOOL. SHE MUST BE REALLY SICK.
HEE-JOO'S (STOLEN) B-CUP BRA
NO, SOMETHING'S WRONG. I'M SURE OF IT! I BET SOMETHING REAL BAD HAPPENED THAT DAY!!
WILL THIS GIVE ME A BABE-A-LICIOUS FIGURE? HRM! LET'S TRY IT OUT!
BBONG (BOING)
I ALREADY ASKED WON-JUN ABOUT IT, BUT HE SAID NOT TO WORRY.
STILL, I THINK I SHOULD DROP BY IF SHE DOESN'T COME IN TOMORROW.

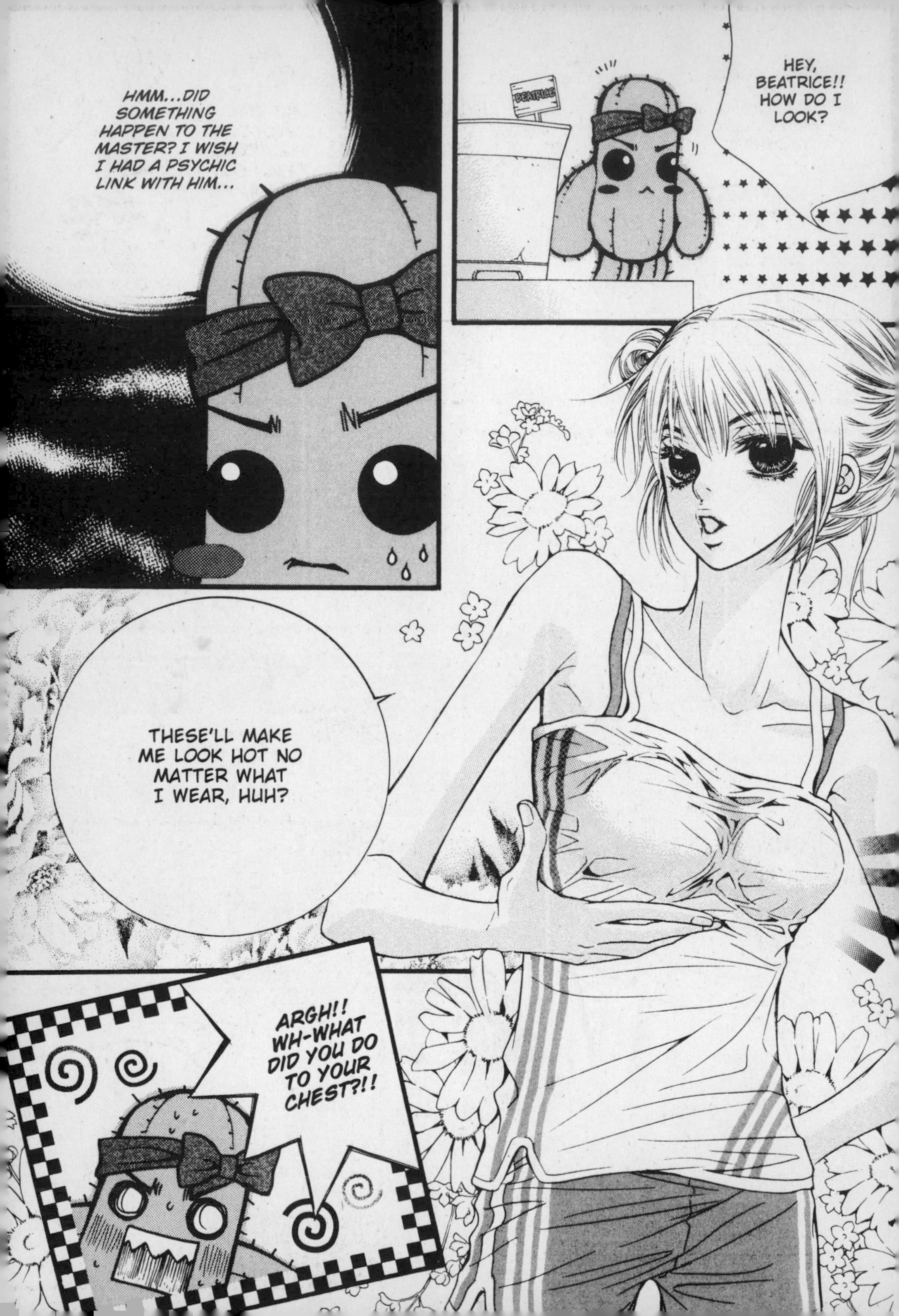
HMM...DID SOMETHING HAPPEN TO THE MASTER? I WISH I HAD A PSYCHIC LINK WITH HIM...
BEATRICE
HEY, BEATRICE!! HOW DO I LOOK?
THESE'LL MAKE ME LOOK HOT NO MATTER WHAT I WEAR, HUH?
ARGH!! WH-WHAT DID YOU DO TO YOUR CHEST?!!

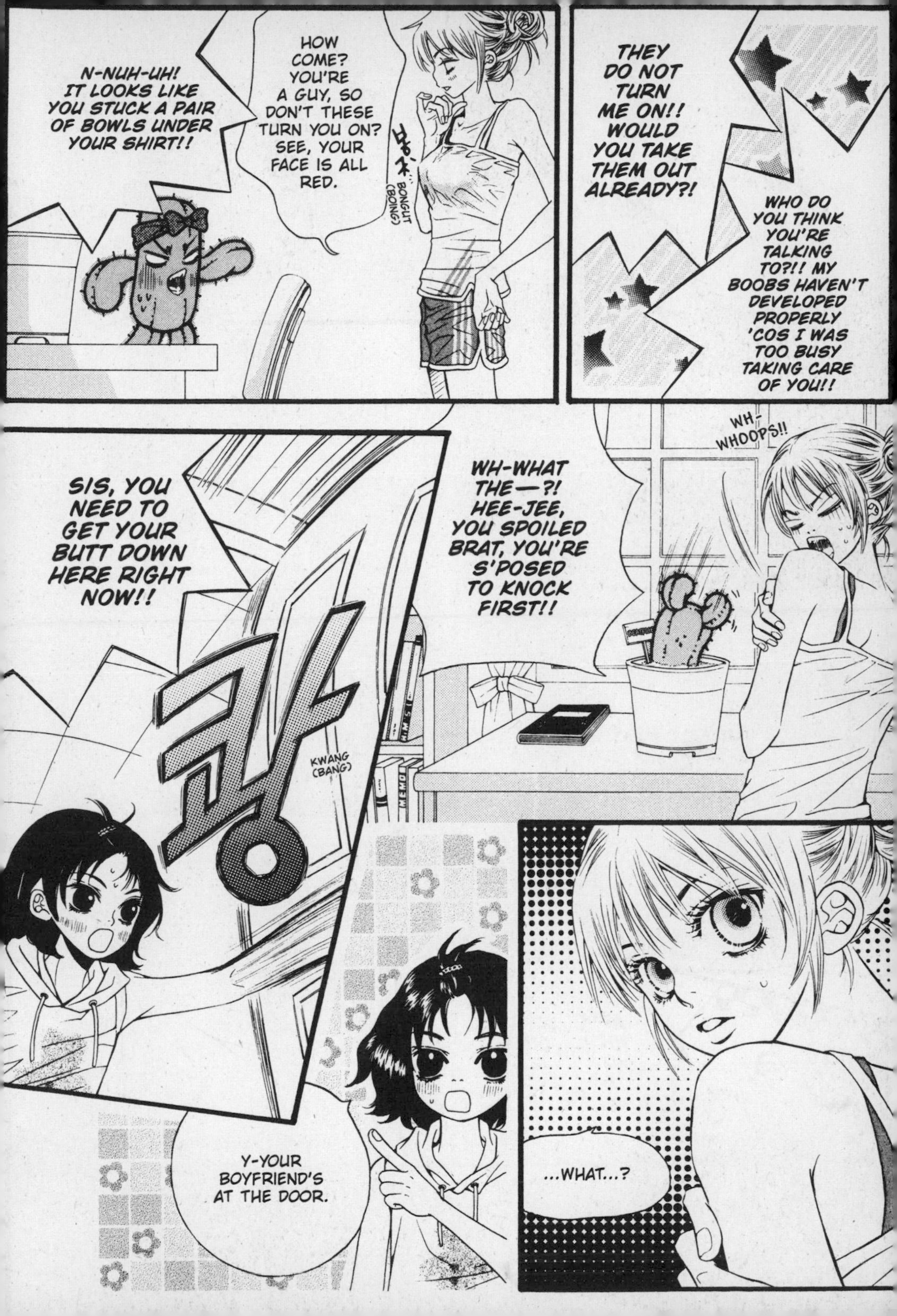
N-NUH-UH! IT LOOKS LIKE YOU STUCK A PAIR OF BOWLS UNDER YOUR SHIRT!!
HOW COME? YOU'RE A GUY, SO DON'T THESE TURN YOU ON? SEE, YOUR FACE IS ALL RED.
봉긋
BONGUT (BOING)
THEY DO NOT TURN ME ON!! WOULD YOU TAKE THEM OUT ALREADY?!
WHO DO YOU THINK YOU'RE TALKING TO?!! MY BOOBS HAVEN'T DEVELOPED PROPERLY 'COS I WAS TOO BUSY TAKING CARE OF YOU!!
SIS, YOU NEED TO GET YOUR BUTT DOWN HERE RIGHT NOW!!
쾅
KWANG (BANG)
WH-WHAT THE—?! HEE-JEE, YOU SPOILED BRAT, YOU'RE S'POSED TO KNOCK FIRST!!
WH-WHOOPS!!
Y-YOUR BOYFRIEND'S AT THE DOOR.
...WHAT...?

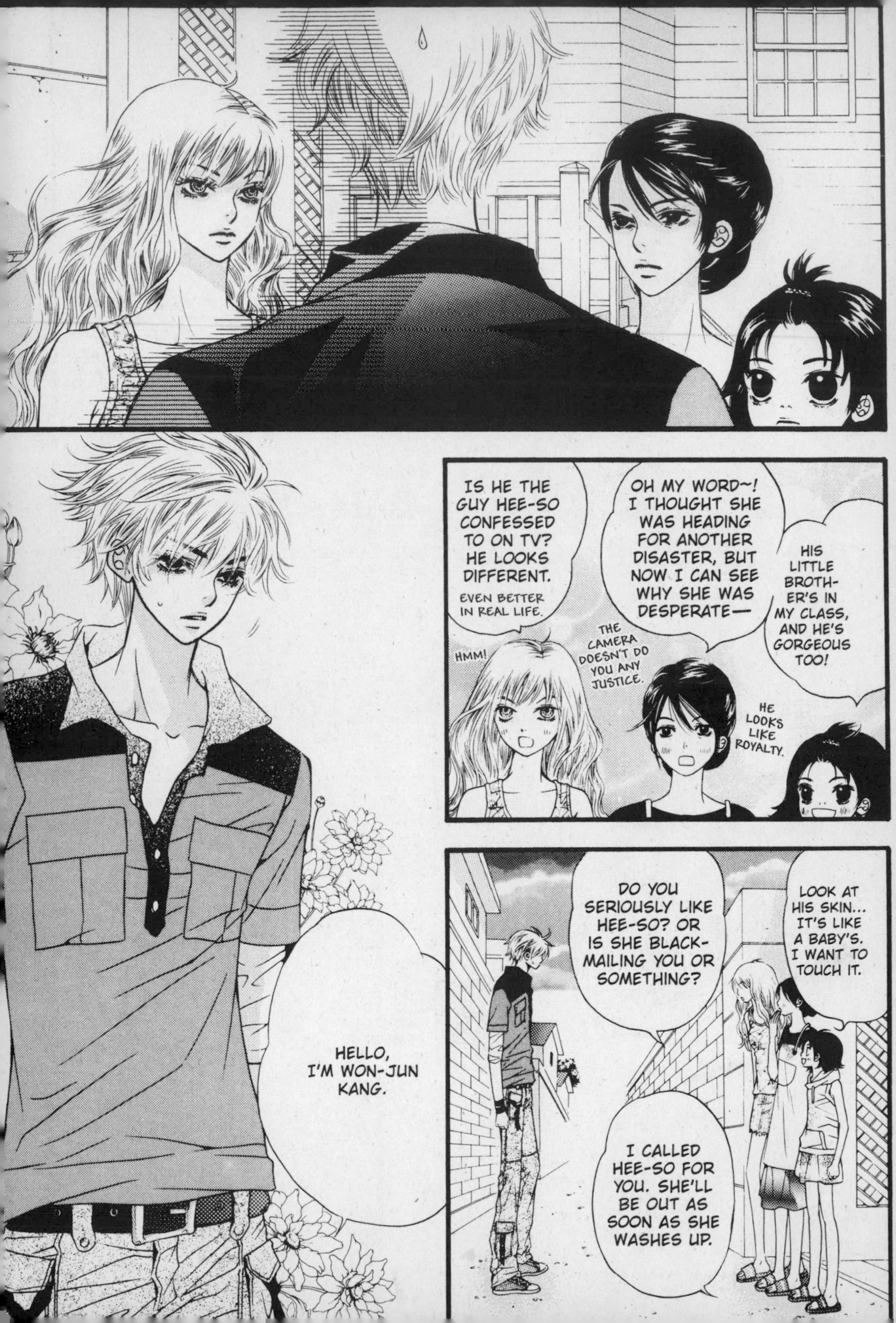
HELLO, I'M WON-JUN KANG.
IS HE THE GUY HEE-SO CONFESSED TO ON TV? HE LOOKS DIFFERENT.
EVEN BETTER IN REAL LIFE.
OH MY WORD~! I THOUGHT SHE WAS HEADING FOR ANOTHER DISASTER, BUT NOW I CAN SEE WHY SHE WAS DESPERATE—
HIS LITTLE BROTHER'S IN MY CLASS, AND HE'S GORGEOUS TOO!
HMM!
THE CAMERA DOESN'T DO YOU ANY JUSTICE.
HE LOOKS LIKE ROYALTY.
DO YOU SERIOUSLY LIKE HEE-SO? OR IS SHE BLACK-MAILING YOU OR SOMETHING?
LOOK AT HIS SKIN... IT'S LIKE A BABY'S. I WANT TO TOUCH IT.
I CALLED HEE-SO FOR YOU. SHE'LL BE OUT AS SOON AS SHE WASHES UP.

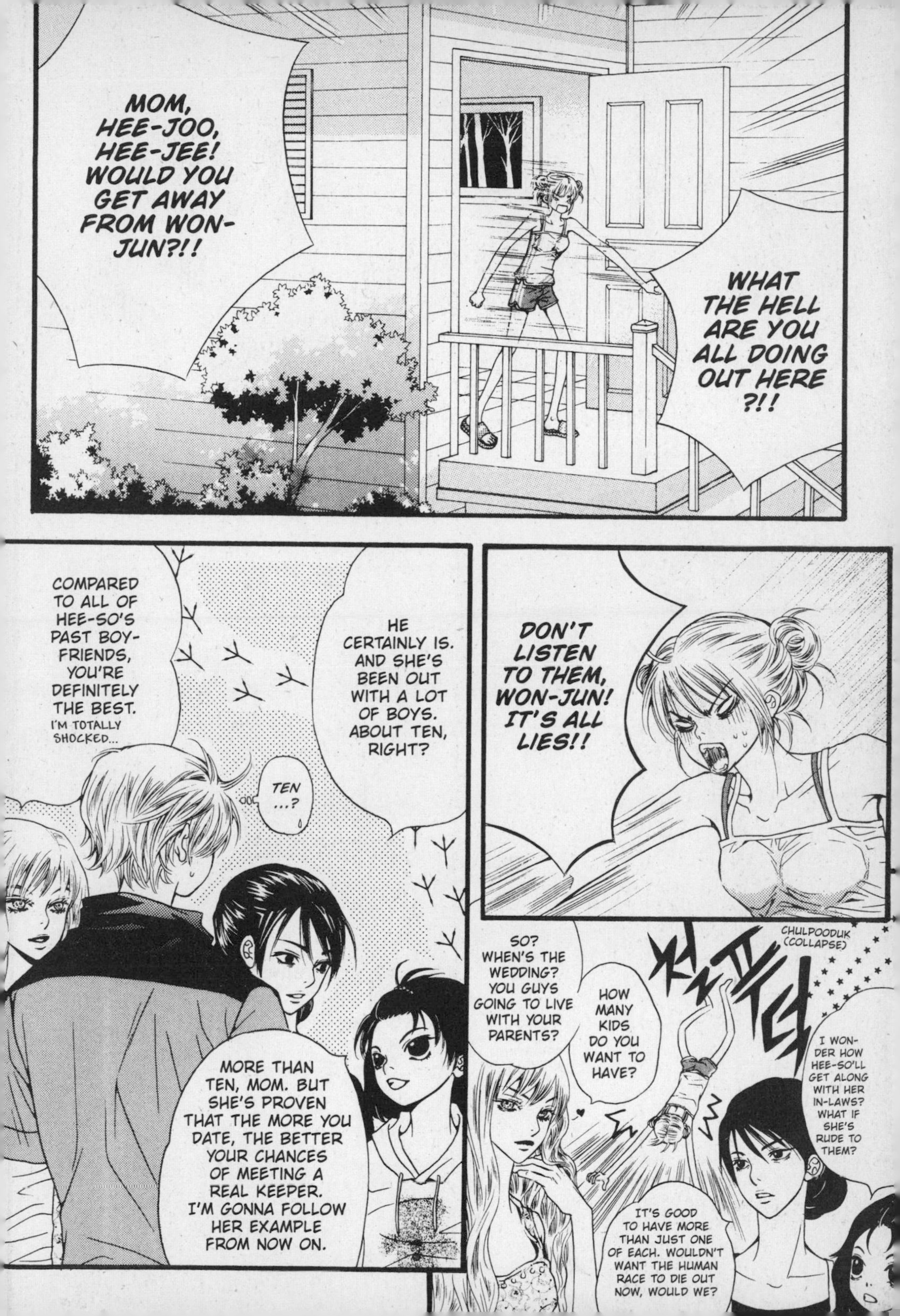
MOM, HEE-JOO, HEE-JEE! WOULD YOU GET AWAY FROM WON-JUN?!!
WHAT THE HELL ARE YOU ALL DOING OUT HERE ?!!
COMPARED TO ALL OF HEE-SO'S PAST BOY-FRIENDS, YOU'RE DEFINITELY THE BEST.
I'M TOTALLY SHOCKED...
HE CERTAINLY IS. AND SHE'S BEEN OUT WITH A LOT OF BOYS. ABOUT TEN, RIGHT?
TEN ...?
MORE THAN TEN, MOM. BUT SHE'S PROVEN THAT THE MORE YOU DATE, THE BETTER YOUR CHANCES OF MEETING A REAL KEEPER. I'M GONNA FOLLOW HER EXAMPLE FROM NOW ON.
DON'T LISTEN TO THEM, WON-JUN! IT'S ALL LIES!!
SO? WHEN'S THE WEDDING? YOU GUYS GOING TO LIVE WITH YOUR PARENTS?
HOW MANY KIDS DO YOU WANT TO HAVE?
CHULPOODUK (COLLAPSE)
I WON-DER HOW HEE-SO'LL GET ALONG WITH HER IN-LAWS? WHAT IF SHE'S RUDE TO THEM?
IT'S GOOD TO HAVE MORE THAN JUST ONE OF EACH. WOULDN'T WANT THE HUMAN RACE TO DIE OUT NOW, WOULD WE?

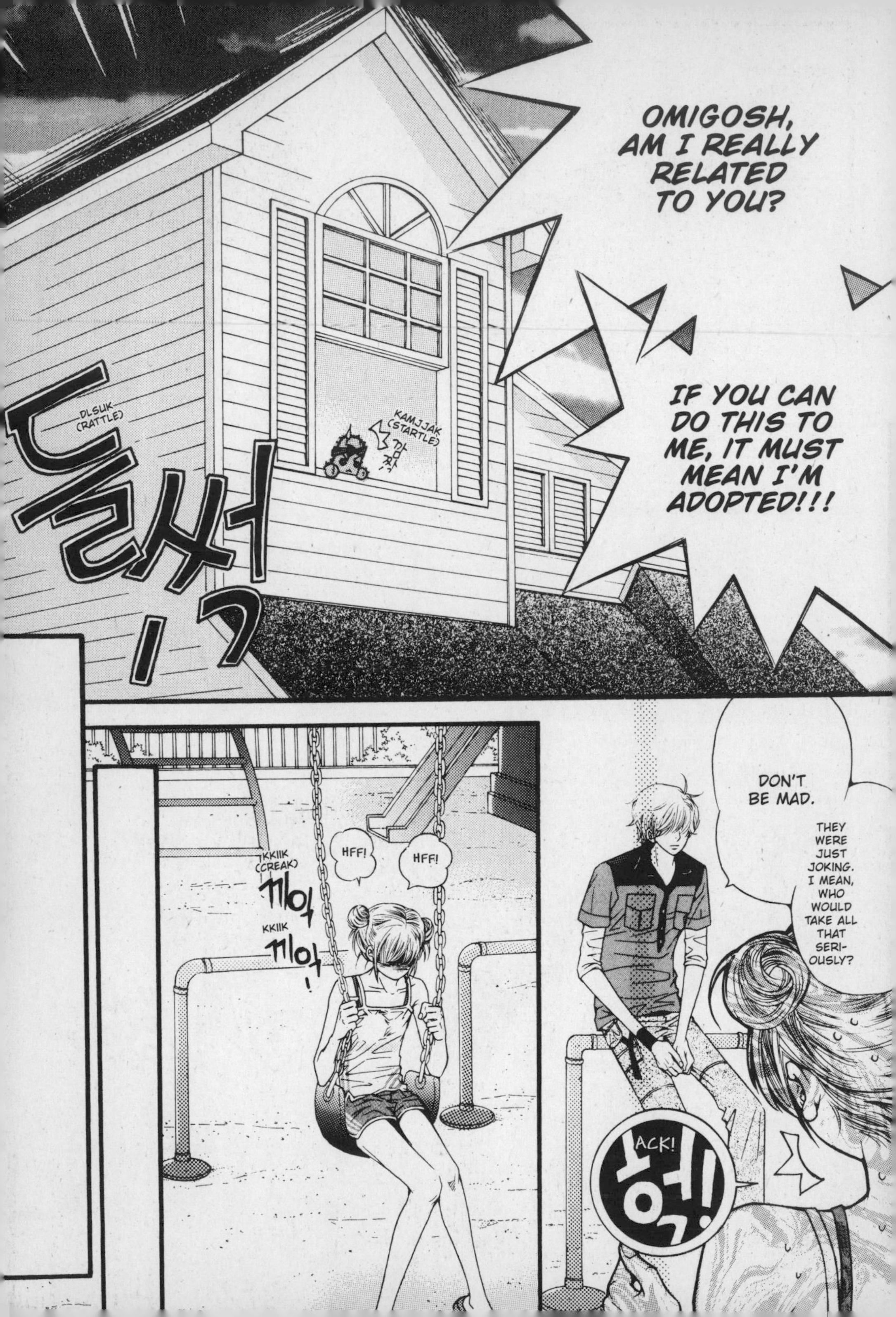

OMIGOSH, AM I REALLY RELATED TO YOU?
IF YOU CAN DO THIS TO ME, IT MUST MEAN I'M ADOPTED!!!
DLSUK (RATTLE)
드르썩
KAMJJAK (STARTLE)
깜짝
IKKIIK (CREAK)
끼익
KKIIK
끼익
HFF!
HFF!
DON'T BE MAD.
THEY WERE JUST JOKING. I MEAN, WHO WOULD TAKE ALL THAT SERI-OUSLY?
ACK!
헉!

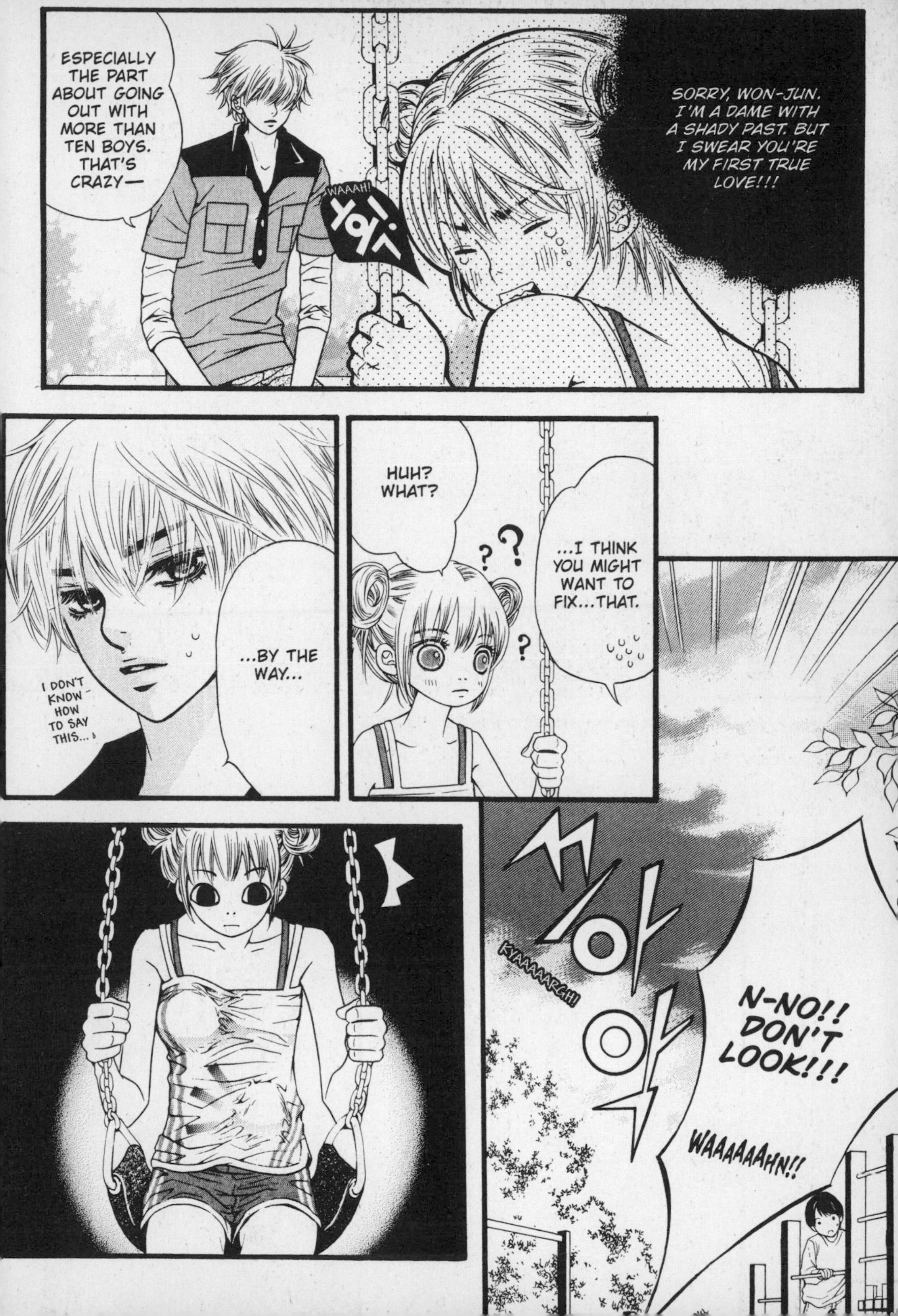
ESPECIALLY THE PART ABOUT GOING OUT WITH MORE THAN TEN BOYS. THAT'S CRAZY—
WAAAH!
SORRY, WON-JUN. I'M A DAME WITH A SHADY PAST. BUT I SWEAR YOU'RE MY FIRST TRUE LOVE!!!
...BY THE WAY...
I DON'T KNOW HOW TO SAY THIS...
HUH? WHAT?
...I THINK YOU MIGHT WANT TO FIX...THAT.
KYAAAAARGH!!
N-NO!! DON'T LOOK!!!
WAAAAAAHN!!

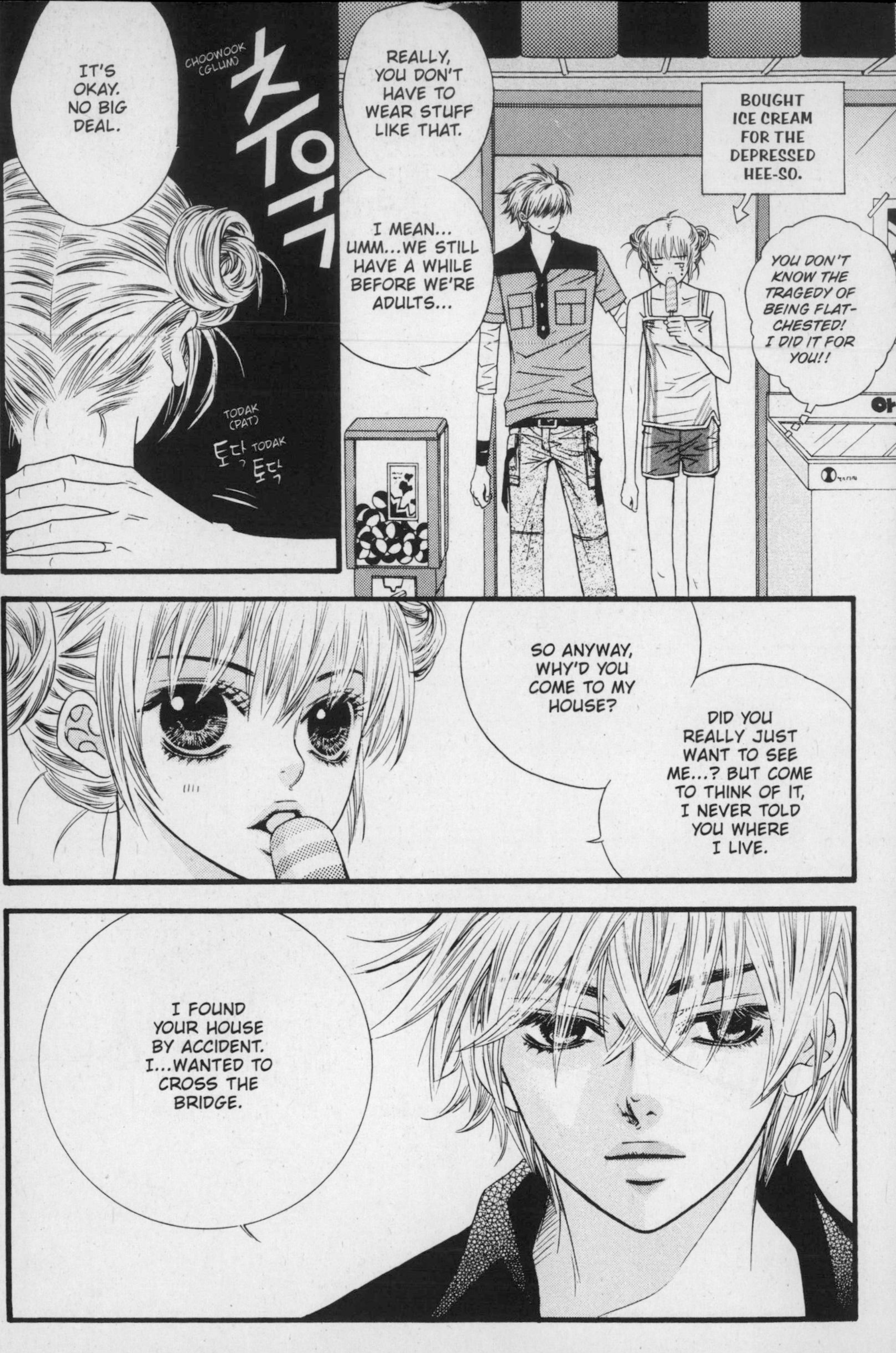
IT'S OKAY. NO BIG DEAL.
CHOOWOOK (GLUM)
TODAK (PAT)
토닥 TODAK 토닥
REALLY, YOU DON'T HAVE TO WEAR STUFF LIKE THAT.
I MEAN... UMM...WE STILL HAVE A WHILE BEFORE WE'RE ADULTS...
BOUGHT ICE CREAM FOR THE DEPRESSED HEE-SO.
YOU DON'T KNOW THE TRAGEDY OF BEING FLAT-CHESTED! I DID IT FOR YOU!!
SO ANYWAY, WHY'D YOU COME TO MY HOUSE?
DID YOU REALLY JUST WANT TO SEE ME...? BUT COME TO THINK OF IT, I NEVER TOLD YOU WHERE I LIVE.
I FOUND YOUR HOUSE BY ACCIDENT. I...WANTED TO CROSS THE BRIDGE.

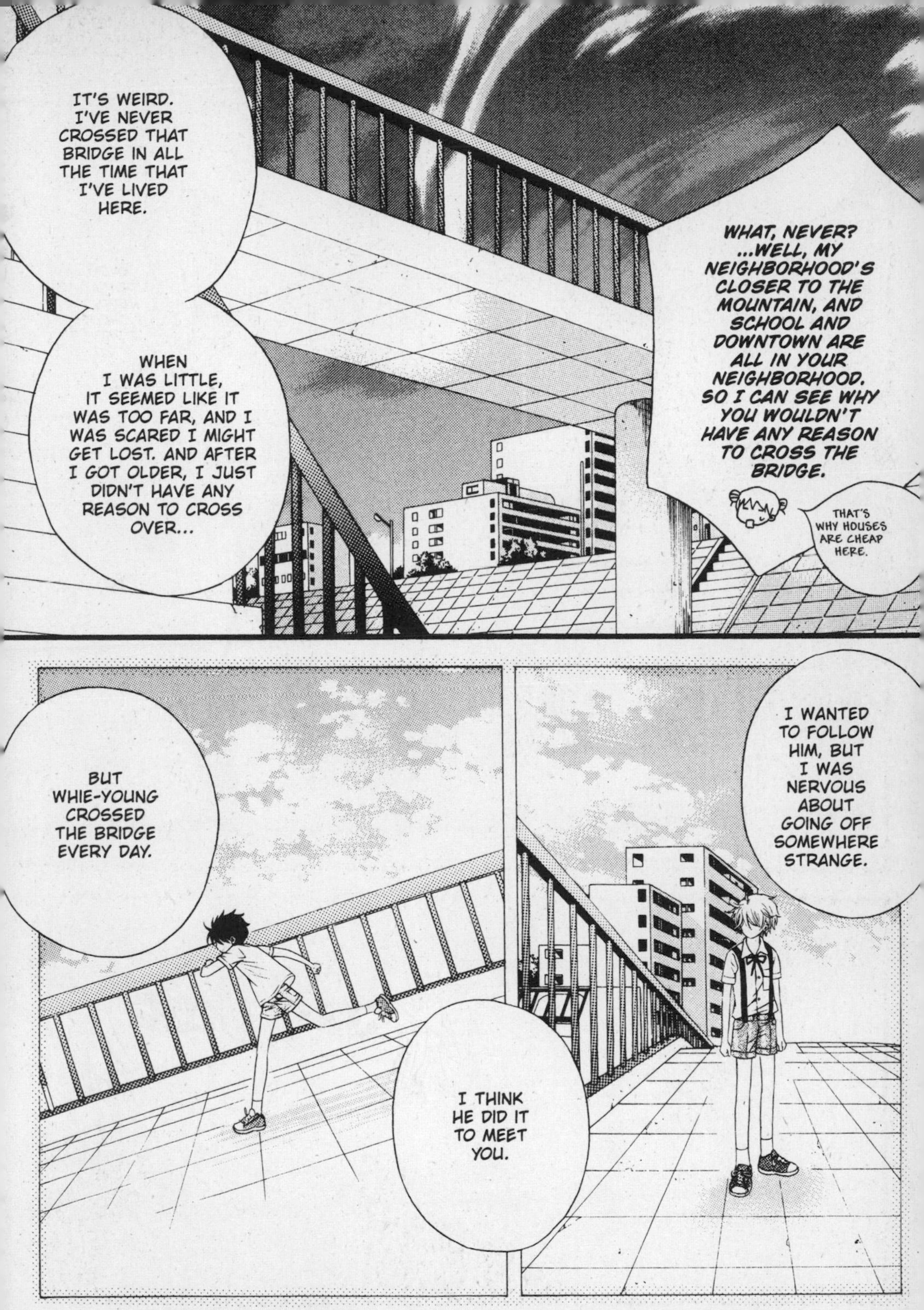
IT'S WEIRD. I'VE NEVER CROSSED THAT BRIDGE IN ALL THE TIME THAT I'VE LIVED HERE.
WHEN I WAS LITTLE, IT SEEMED LIKE IT WAS TOO FAR, AND I WAS SCARED I MIGHT GET LOST. AND AFTER I GOT OLDER, I JUST DIDN'T HAVE ANY REASON TO CROSS OVER...
WHAT, NEVER? ...WELL, MY NEIGHBORHOOD'S CLOSER TO THE MOUNTAIN, AND SCHOOL AND DOWNTOWN ARE ALL IN YOUR NEIGHBORHOOD. SO I CAN SEE WHY YOU WOULDN'T HAVE ANY REASON TO CROSS THE BRIDGE.
THAT'S WHY HOUSES ARE CHEAP HERE.
BUT WHIE-YOUNG CROSSED THE BRIDGE EVERY DAY.
I THINK HE DID IT TO MEET YOU.
I WANTED TO FOLLOW HIM, BUT I WAS NERVOUS ABOUT GOING OFF SOMEWHERE STRANGE.

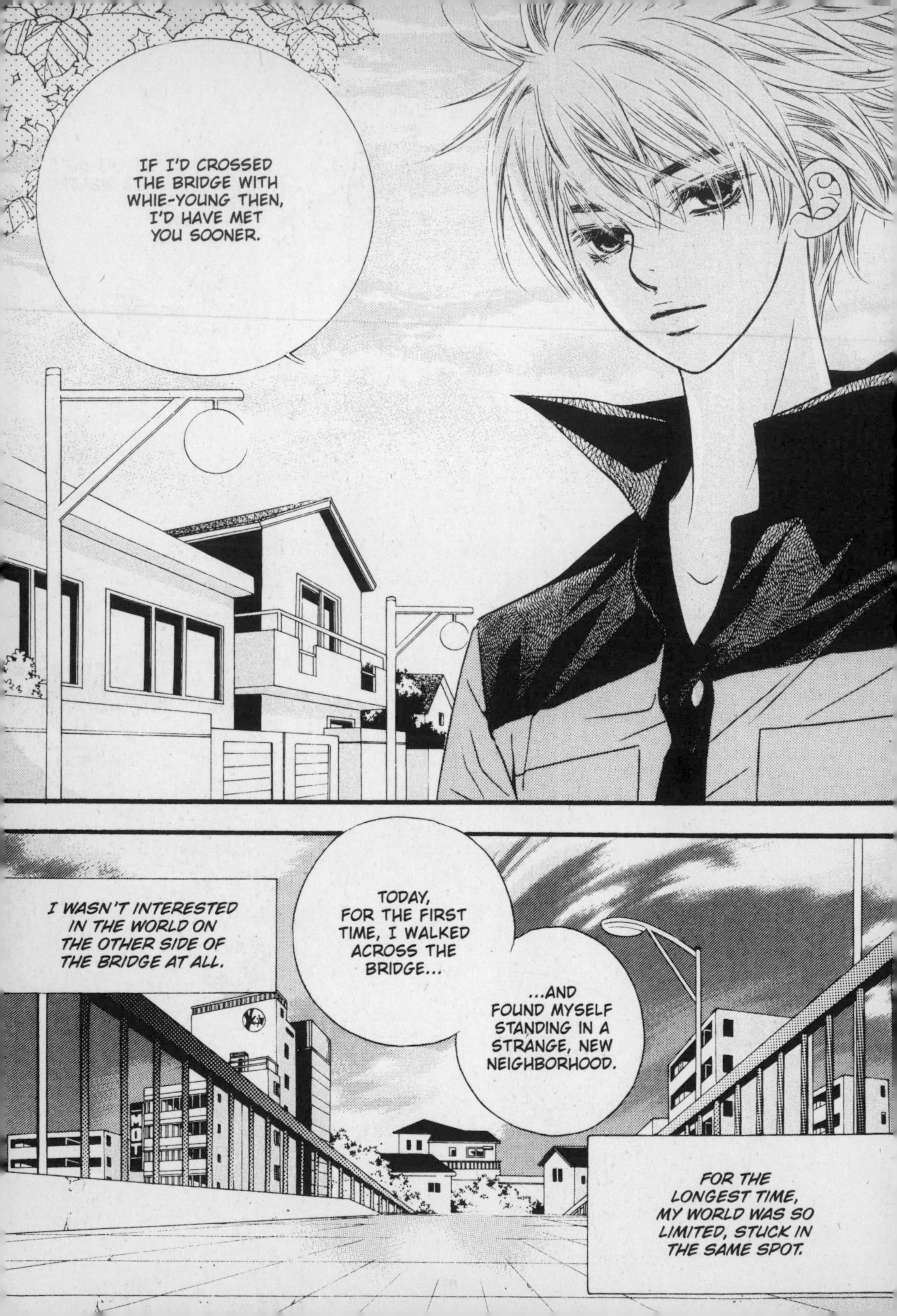
IF I'D CROSSED THE BRIDGE WITH WHIE-YOUNG THEN, I'D HAVE MET YOU SOONER.
I WASN'T INTERESTED IN THE WORLD ON THE OTHER SIDE OF THE BRIDGE AT ALL.
TODAY, FOR THE FIRST TIME, I WALKED ACROSS THE BRIDGE...
...AND FOUND MYSELF STANDING IN A STRANGE, NEW NEIGHBORHOOD.
FOR THE LONGEST TIME, MY WORLD WAS SO LIMITED, STUCK IN THE SAME SPOT.

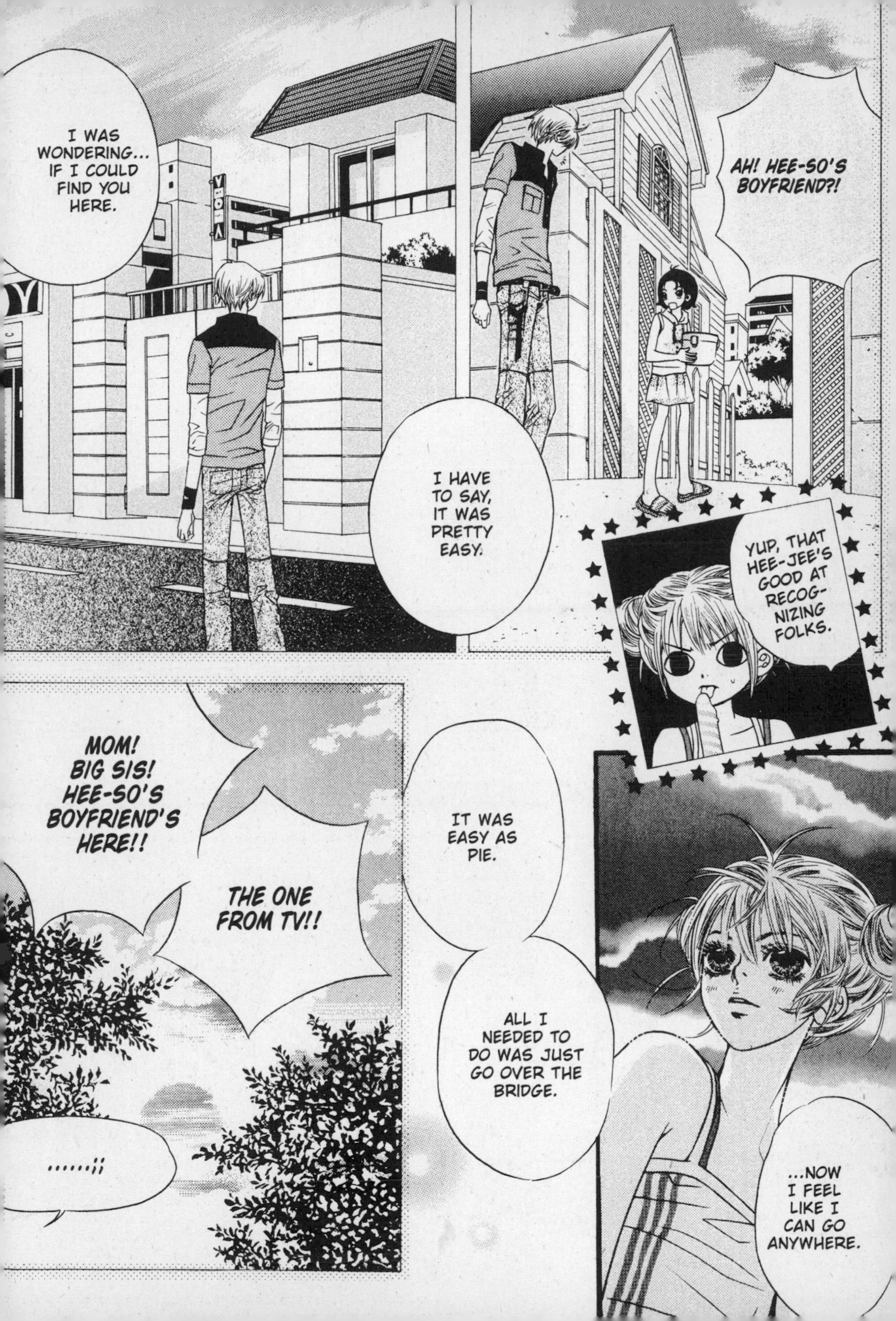
I WAS WONDERING... IF I COULD FIND YOU HERE.
AH! HEE-SO'S BOYFRIEND?!
I HAVE TO SAY, IT WAS PRETTY EASY.
YUP, THAT HEE-JEE'S GOOD AT RECOG-NIZING FOLKS.
MOM! BIG SIS! HEE-SO'S BOYFRIEND'S HERE!!
THE ONE FROM TV!!
......;;
IT WAS EASY AS PIE.
ALL I NEEDED TO DO WAS JUST GO OVER THE BRIDGE.
...NOW I FEEL LIKE I CAN GO ANYWHERE.

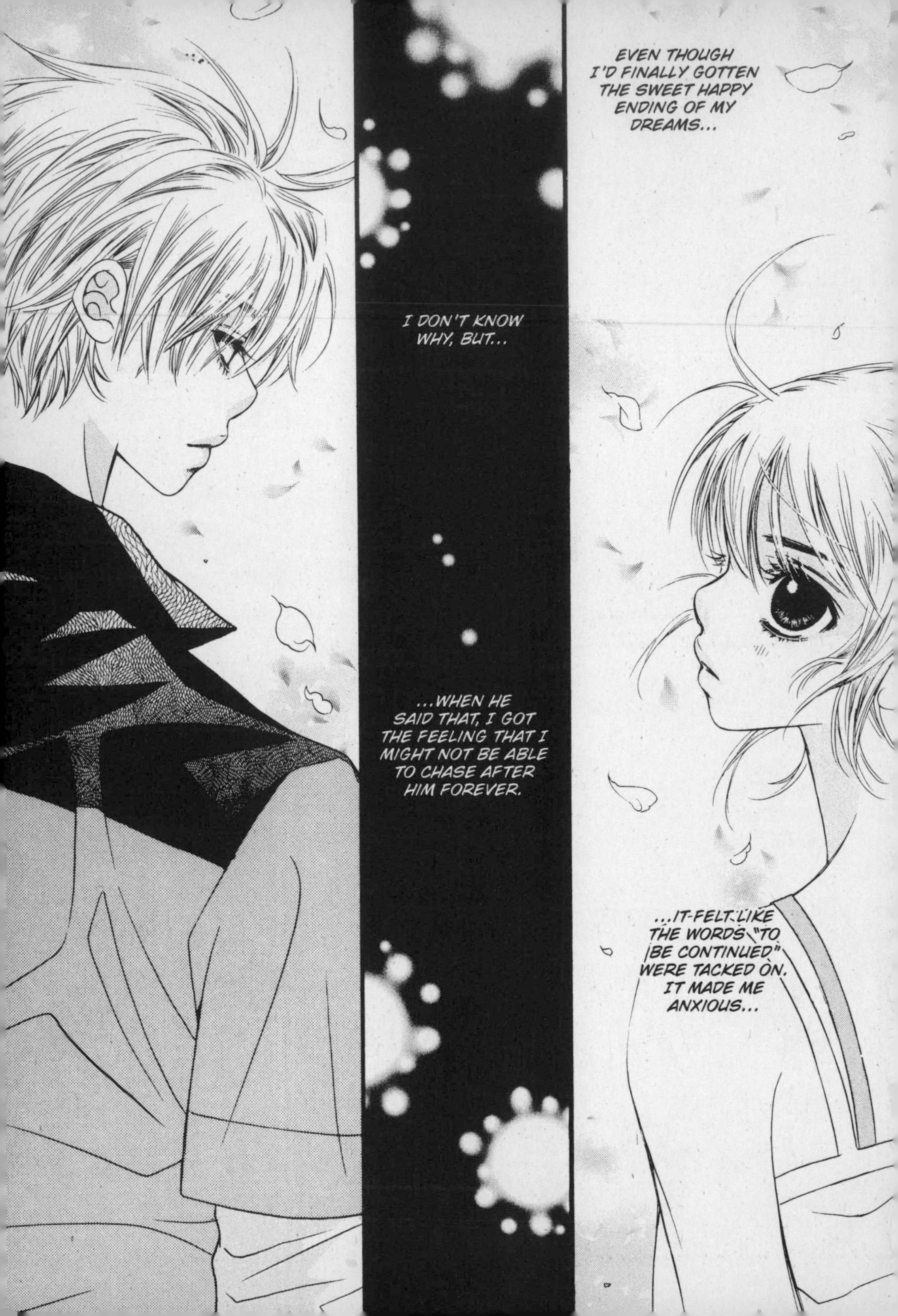
I DON'T KNOW WHY, BUT...
...WHEN HE SAID THAT, I GOT THE FEELING THAT I MIGHT NOT BE ABLE TO CHASE AFTER HIM FOREVER.
EVEN THOUGH I'D FINALLY GOTTEN THE SWEET HAPPY ENDING OF MY DREAMS...
...IT FELT LIKE THE WORDS "TO BE CONTINUED" WERE TACKED ON. IT MADE ME ANXIOUS...

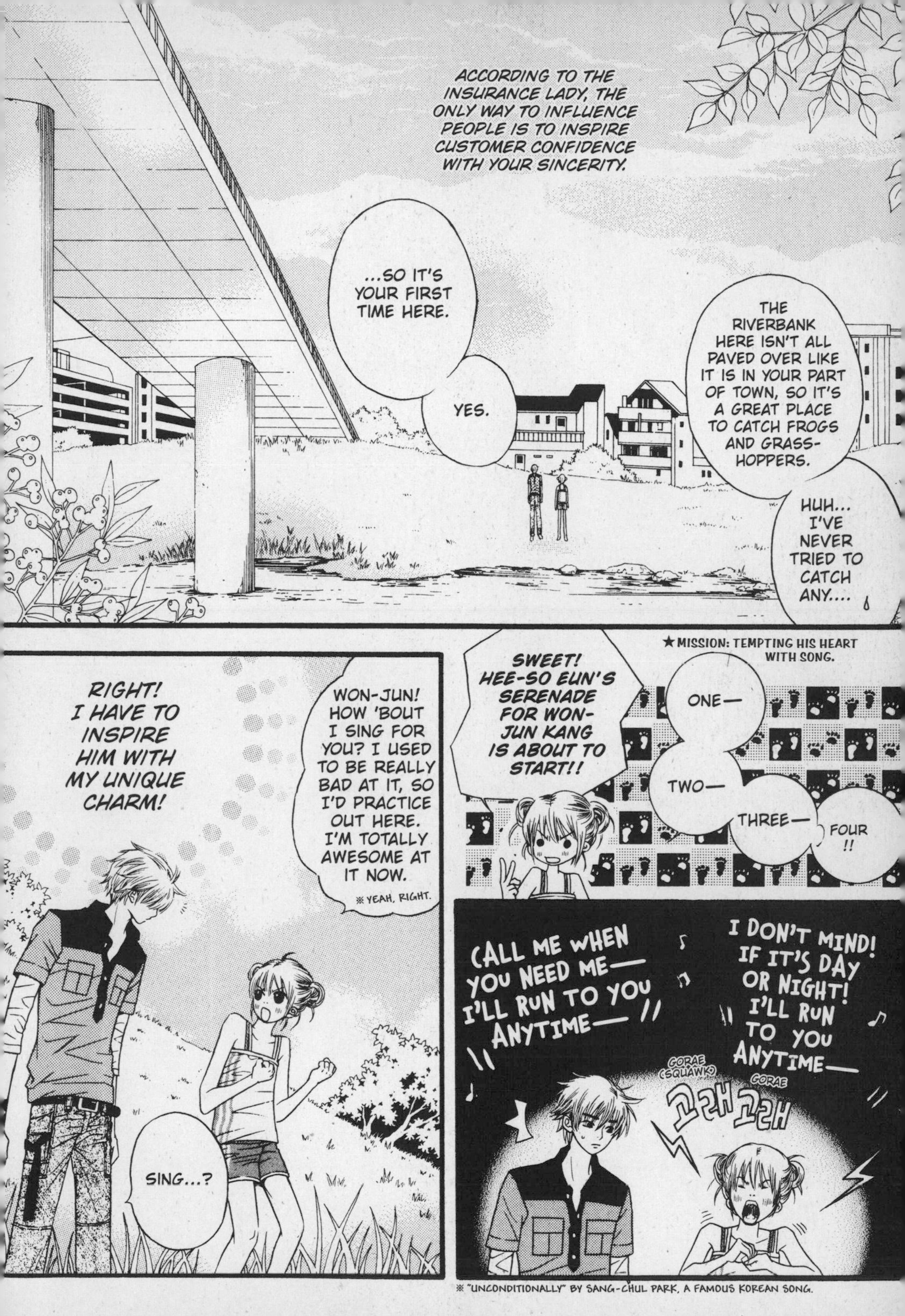
ACCORDING TO THE INSURANCE LADY, THE ONLY WAY TO INFLUENCE PEOPLE IS TO INSPIRE CUSTOMER CONFIDENCE WITH YOUR SINCERITY.
...SO IT'S YOUR FIRST TIME HERE.
YES.
THE RIVERBANK HERE ISN'T ALL PAVED OVER LIKE IT IS IN YOUR PART OF TOWN, SO IT'S A GREAT PLACE TO CATCH FROGS AND GRASS-HOPPERS.
HUH... I'VE NEVER TRIED TO CATCH ANY....
RIGHT! I HAVE TO INSPIRE HIM WITH MY UNIQUE CHARM!
WON-JUN! HOW 'BOUT I SING FOR YOU? I USED TO BE REALLY BAD AT IT, SO I'D PRACTICE OUT HERE. I'M TOTALLY AWESOME AT IT NOW.
※ YEAH, RIGHT.
SING...?
SWEET! HEE-SO EUN'S SERENADE FOR WON-JUN KANG IS ABOUT TO START!!
★MISSION: TEMPTING HIS HEART WITH SONG.
ONE—
TWO—
THREE—
FOUR!!
CALL ME WHEN YOU NEED ME— I'LL RUN TO YOU ANYTIME—
I DON'T MIND! IF IT'S DAY OR NIGHT! I'LL RUN TO YOU ANYTIME—
GORAE (SQUAWK)
GORAE
고래고래
※ "UNCONDITIONALLY" BY SANG-CHUL PARK, A FAMOUS KOREAN SONG.

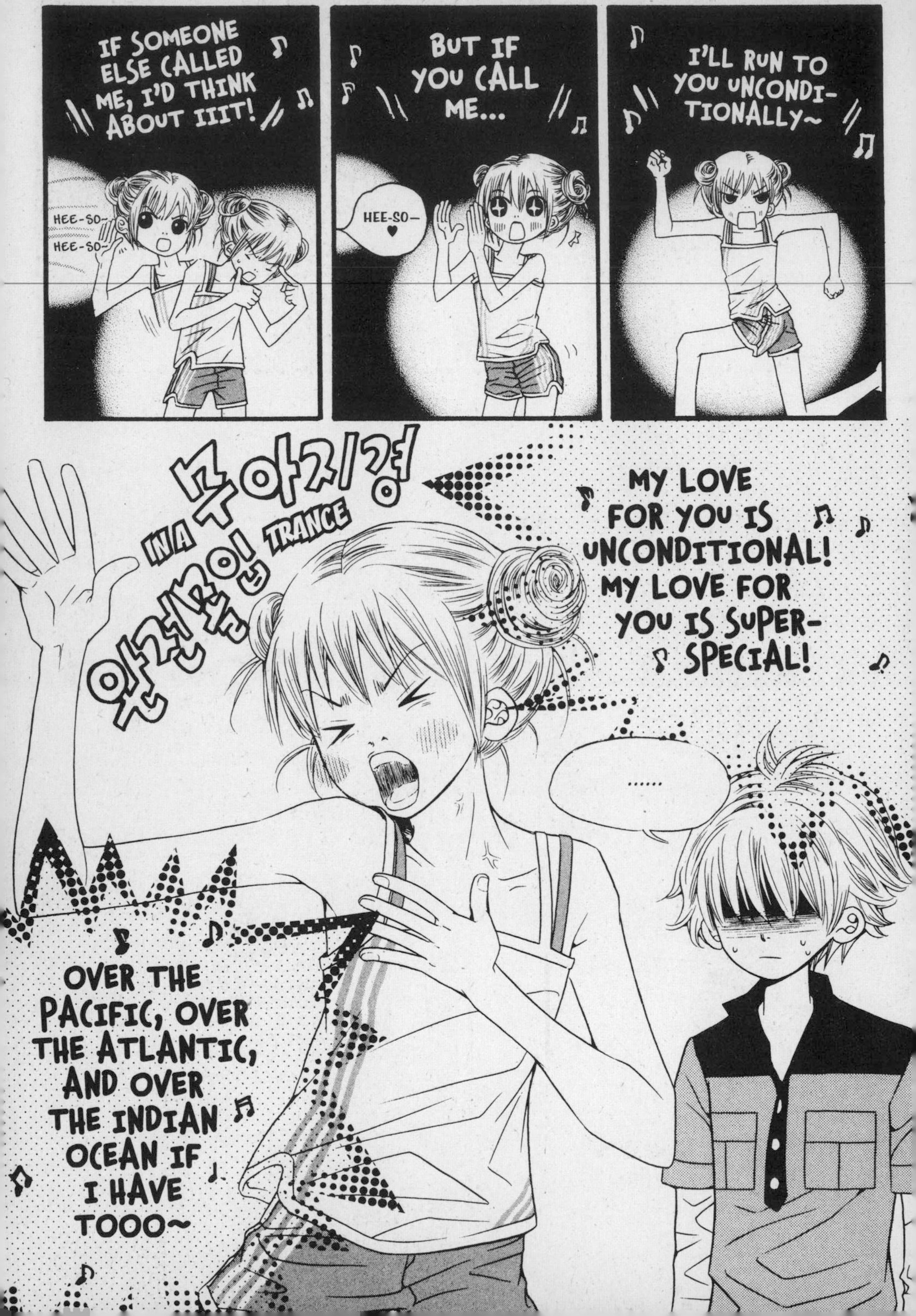
IF SOMEONE ELSE CALLED ME, I'D THINK ABOUT IIIT!
HEE-SO— HEE-SO—
BUT IF YOU CALL ME...
HEE-SO— ♥
I'LL RUN TO YOU UNCONDI-TIONALLY~
IN A TRANCE
MY LOVE FOR YOU IS UNCONDITIONAL! MY LOVE FOR YOU IS SUPER-SPECIAL!
......
OVER THE PACIFIC, OVER THE ATLANTIC, AND OVER THE INDIAN OCEAN IF I HAVE TOOO~

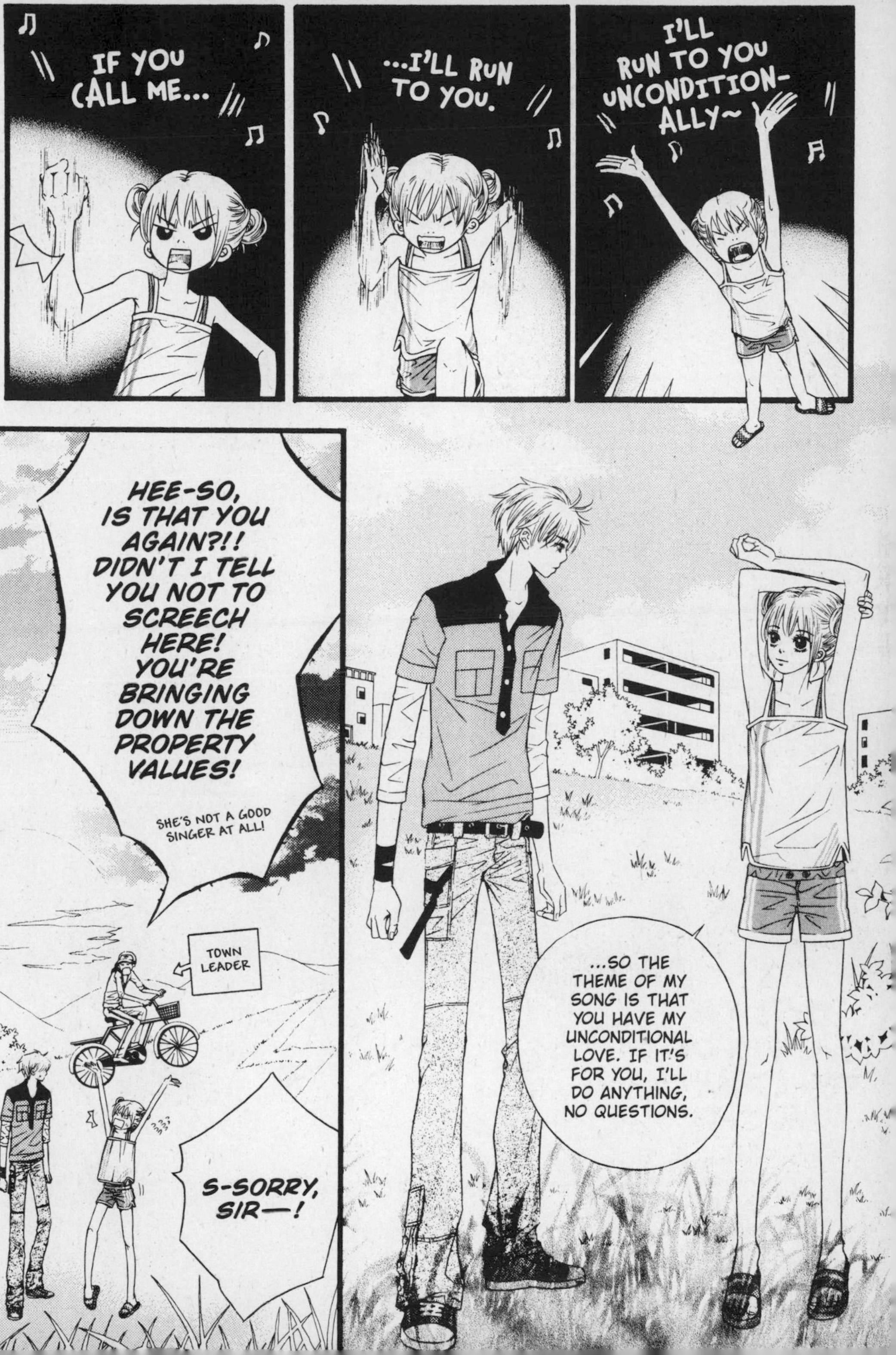
IF YOU CALL ME...
...I'LL RUN TO YOU.
I'LL RUN TO YOU UNCONDITION-ALLY~
HEE-SO, IS THAT YOU AGAIN?!! DIDN'T I TELL YOU NOT TO SCREECH HERE! YOU'RE BRINGING DOWN THE PROPERTY VALUES!
SHE'S NOT A GOOD SINGER AT ALL!
TOWN LEADER
S-SORRY, SIR—!
...SO THE THEME OF MY SONG IS THAT YOU HAVE MY UNCONDITIONAL LOVE. IF IT'S FOR YOU, I'LL DO ANYTHING, NO QUESTIONS.

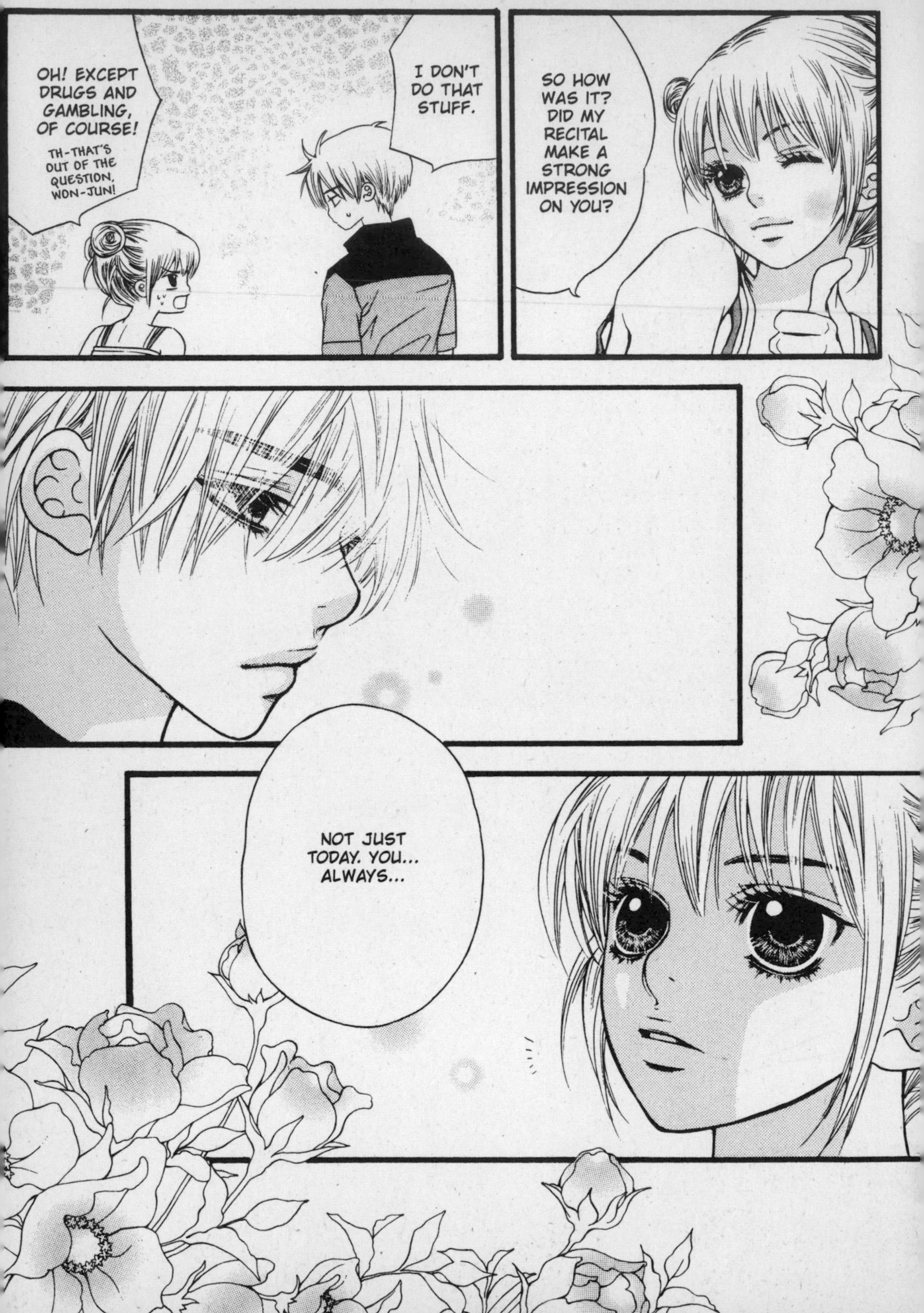
OH! EXCEPT DRUGS AND GAMBLING, OF COURSE!
TH-THAT'S OUT OF THE QUESTION, WON-JUN!
I DON'T DO THAT STUFF.
SO HOW WAS IT? DID MY RECITAL MAKE A STRONG IMPRESSION ON YOU?
NOT JUST TODAY. YOU... ALWAYS...

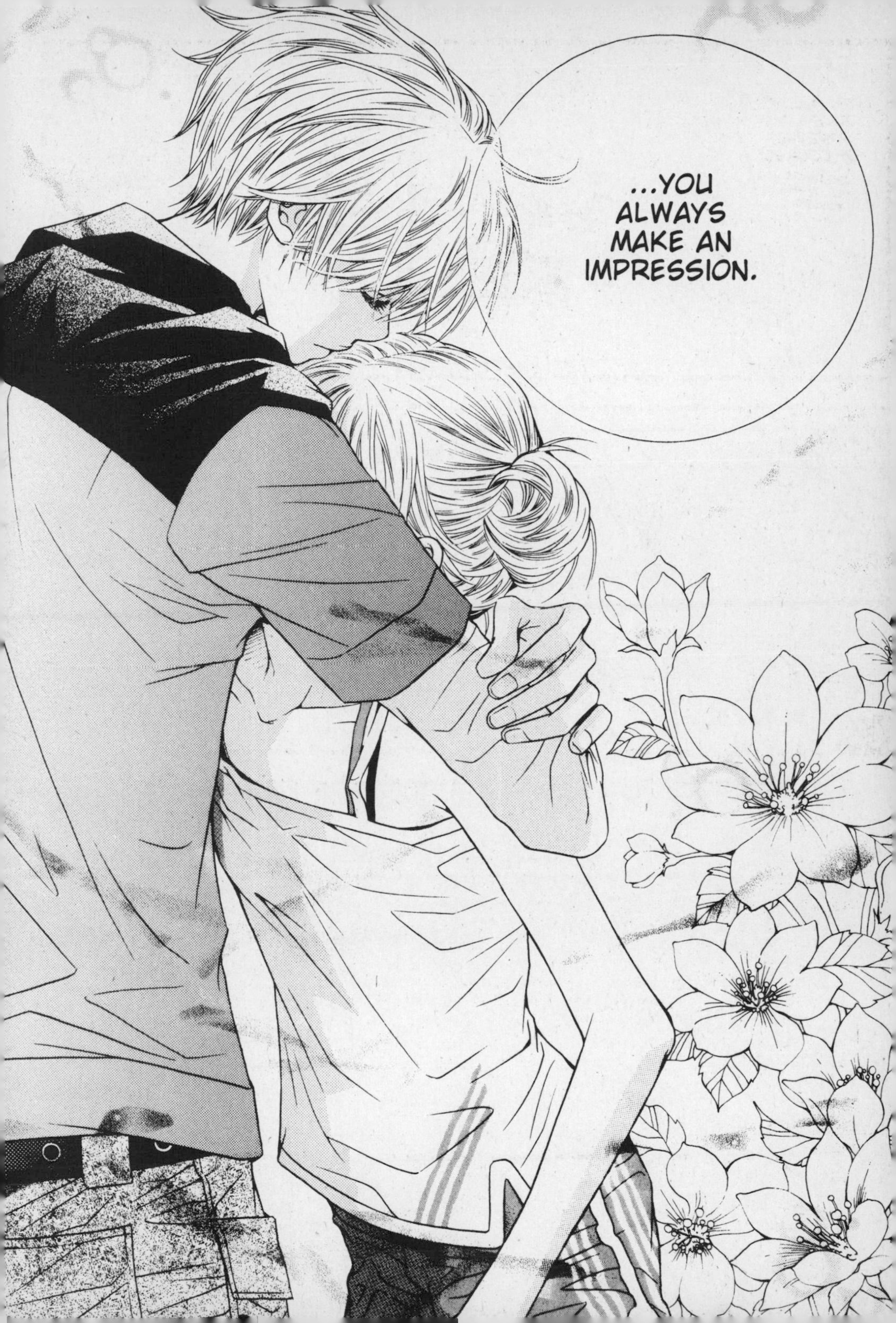
...YOU ALWAYS MAKE AN IMPRESSION.

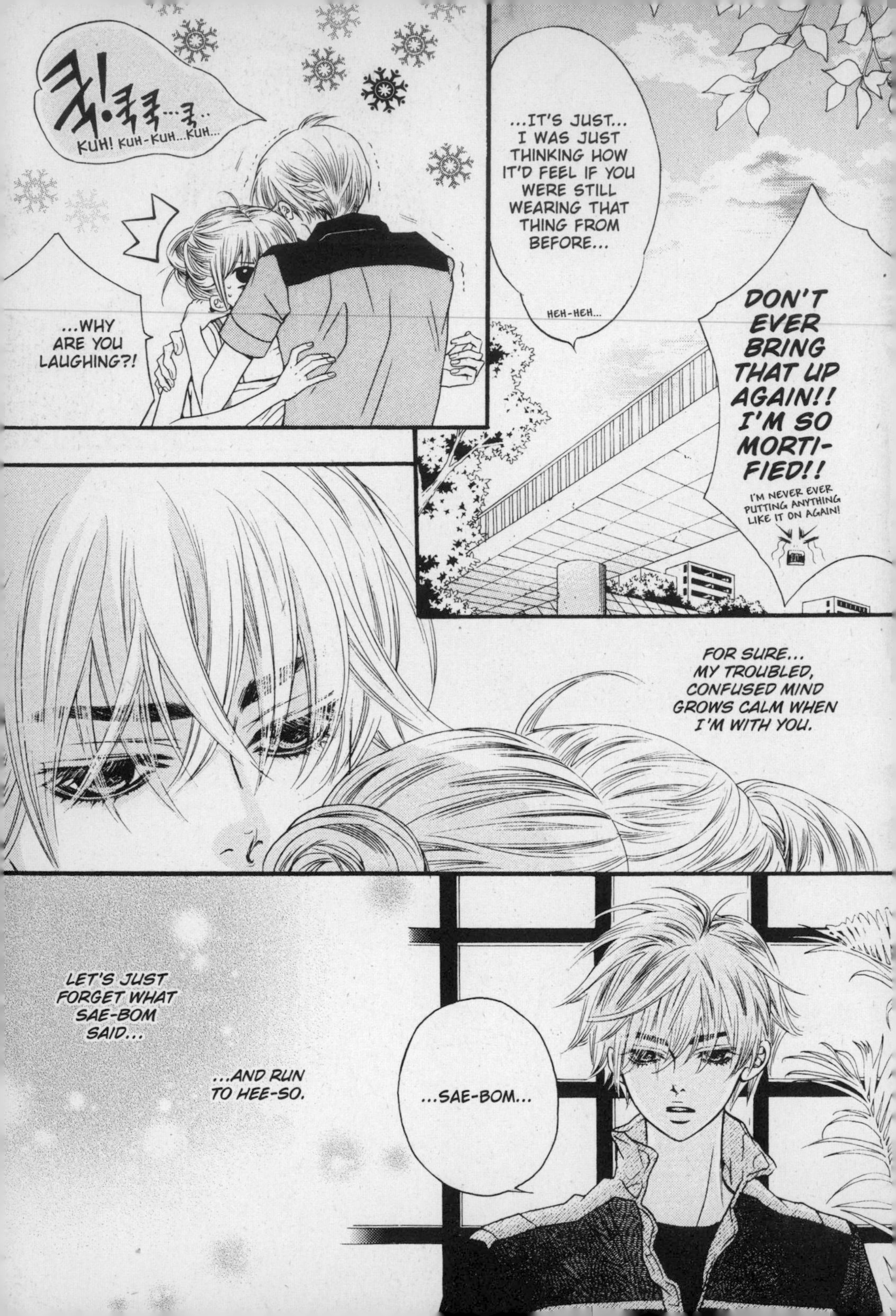

쿡!쿡쿡…쿡..
KUH! KUH-KUH...KUH...
...WHY ARE YOU LAUGHING?!
...IT'S JUST... I WAS JUST THINKING HOW IT'D FEEL IF YOU WERE STILL WEARING THAT THING FROM BEFORE...
HEH-HEH...
DON'T EVER BRING THAT UP AGAIN!! I'M SO MORTI-FIED!!
I'M NEVER EVER PUTTING ANYTHING LIKE IT ON AGAIN!
FOR SURE... MY TROUBLED, CONFUSED MIND GROWS CALM WHEN I'M WITH YOU.
LET'S JUST FORGET WHAT SAE-BOM SAID...
...AND RUN TO HEE-SO.
...SAE-BOM...

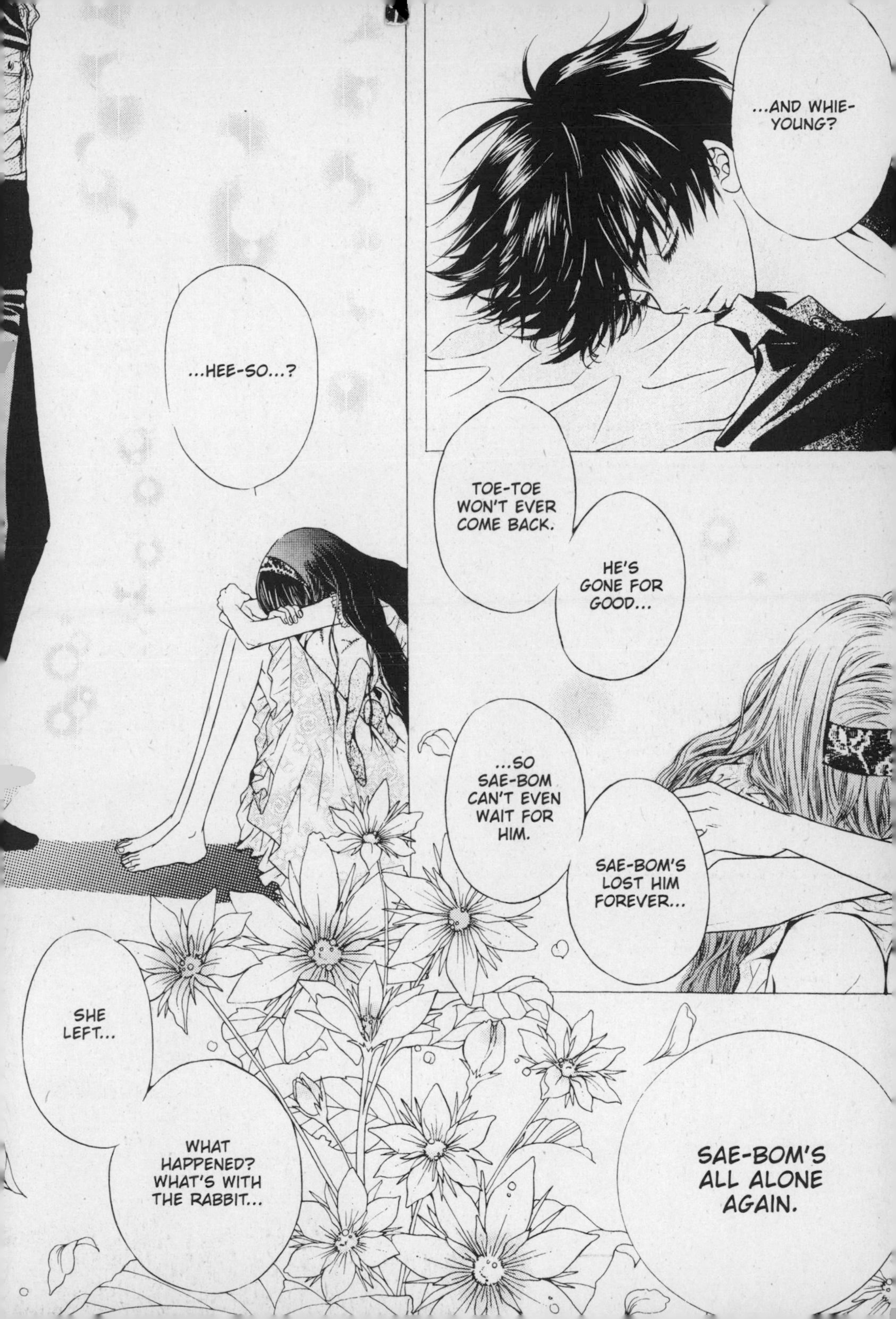
...HEE-SO...?
...AND WHIE-YOUNG?
TOE-TOE WON'T EVER COME BACK.
HE'S GONE FOR GOOD...
...SO SAE-BOM CAN'T EVEN WAIT FOR HIM.
SAE-BOM'S LOST HIM FOREVER...
SHE LEFT...
WHAT HAPPENED? WHAT'S WITH THE RABBIT...
SAE-BOM'S ALL ALONE AGAIN.

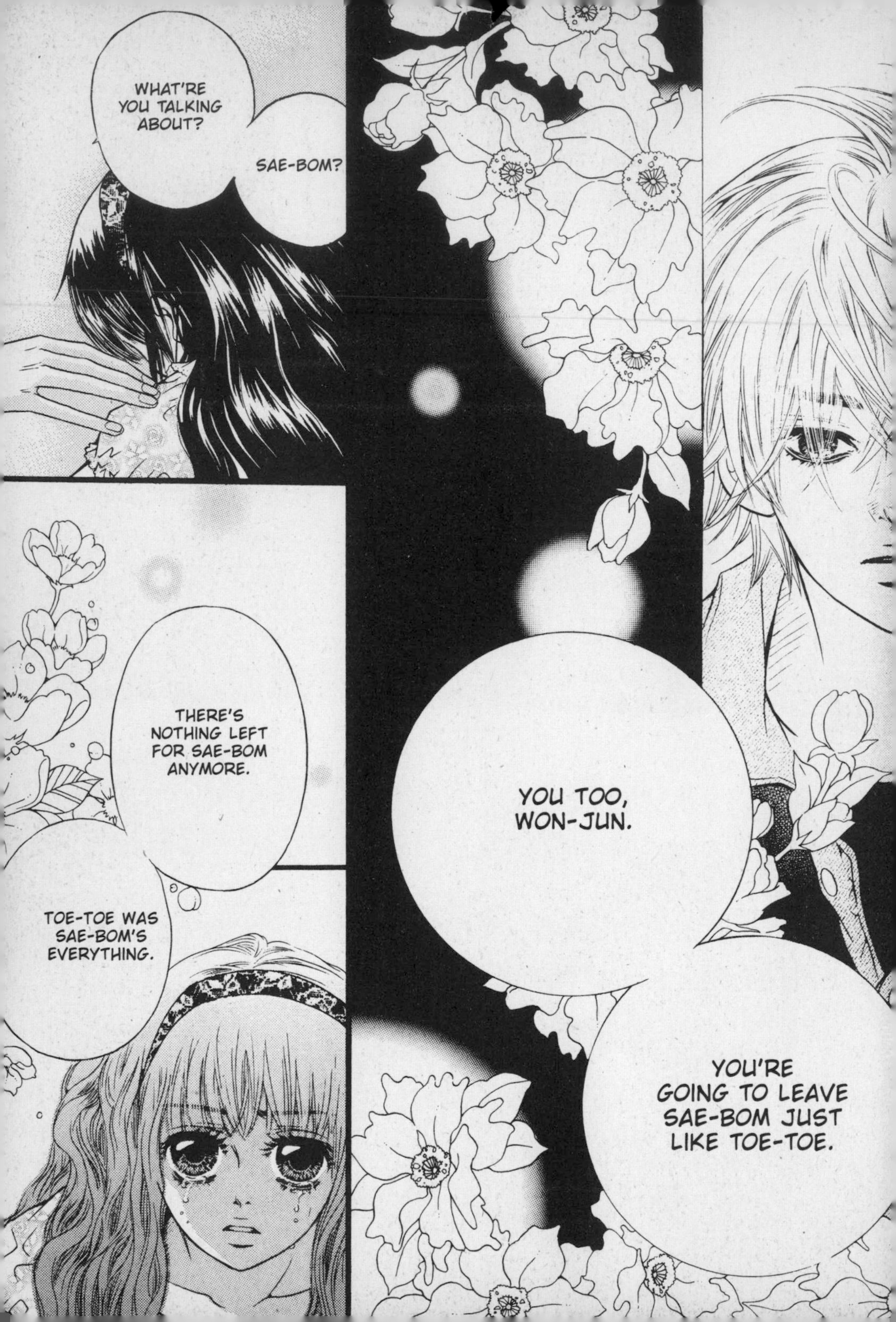
WHAT'RE YOU TALKING ABOUT?
SAE-BOM?
THERE'S NOTHING LEFT FOR SAE-BOM ANYMORE.
TOE-TOE WAS SAE-BOM'S EVERYTHING.
YOU TOO, WON-JUN.
YOU'RE GOING TO LEAVE SAE-BOM JUST LIKE TOE-TOE.

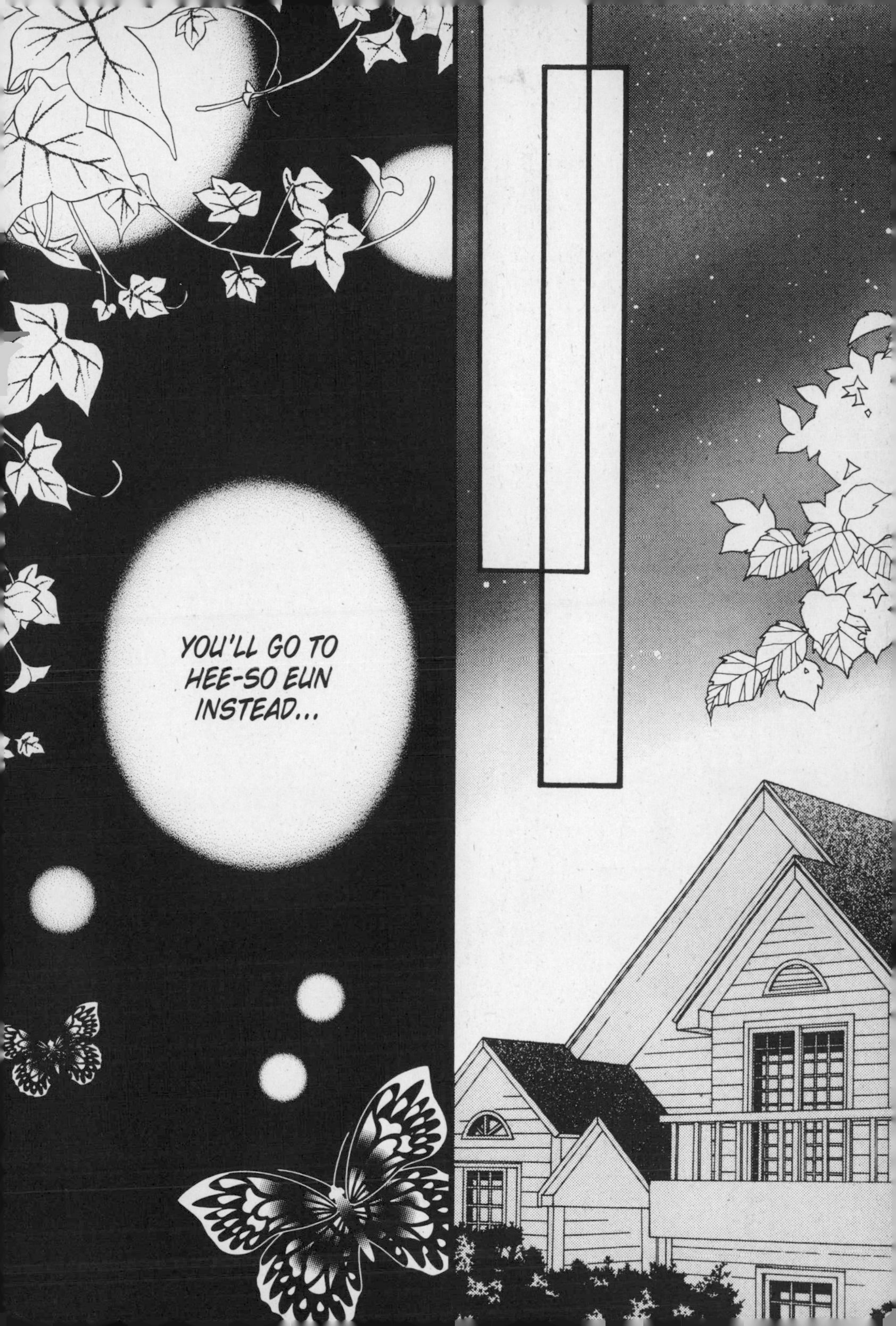
YOU'LL GO TO
HEE-SO EUN
INSTEAD...

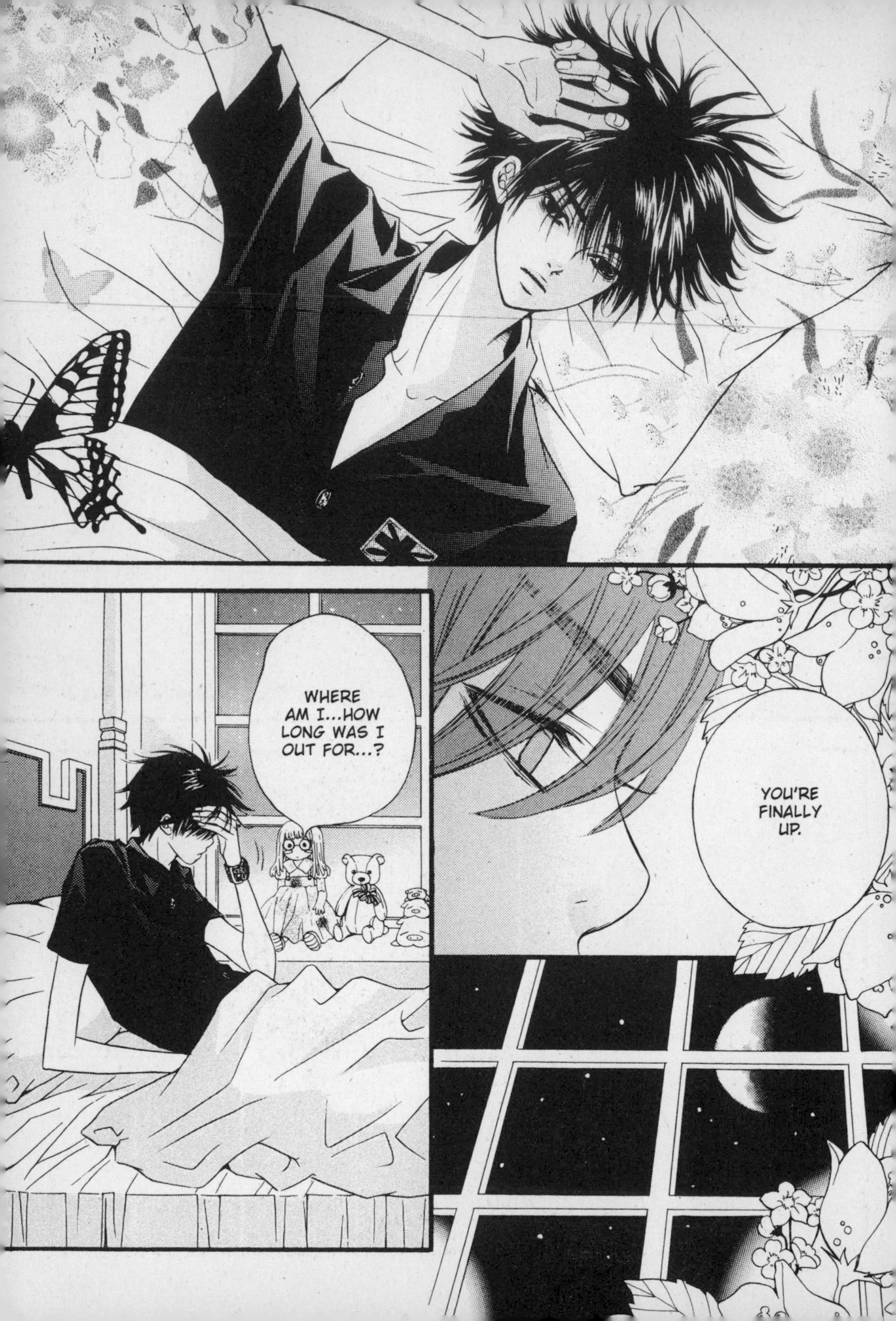
WHERE AM I...HOW LONG WAS I OUT FOR...?
YOU'RE FINALLY UP.

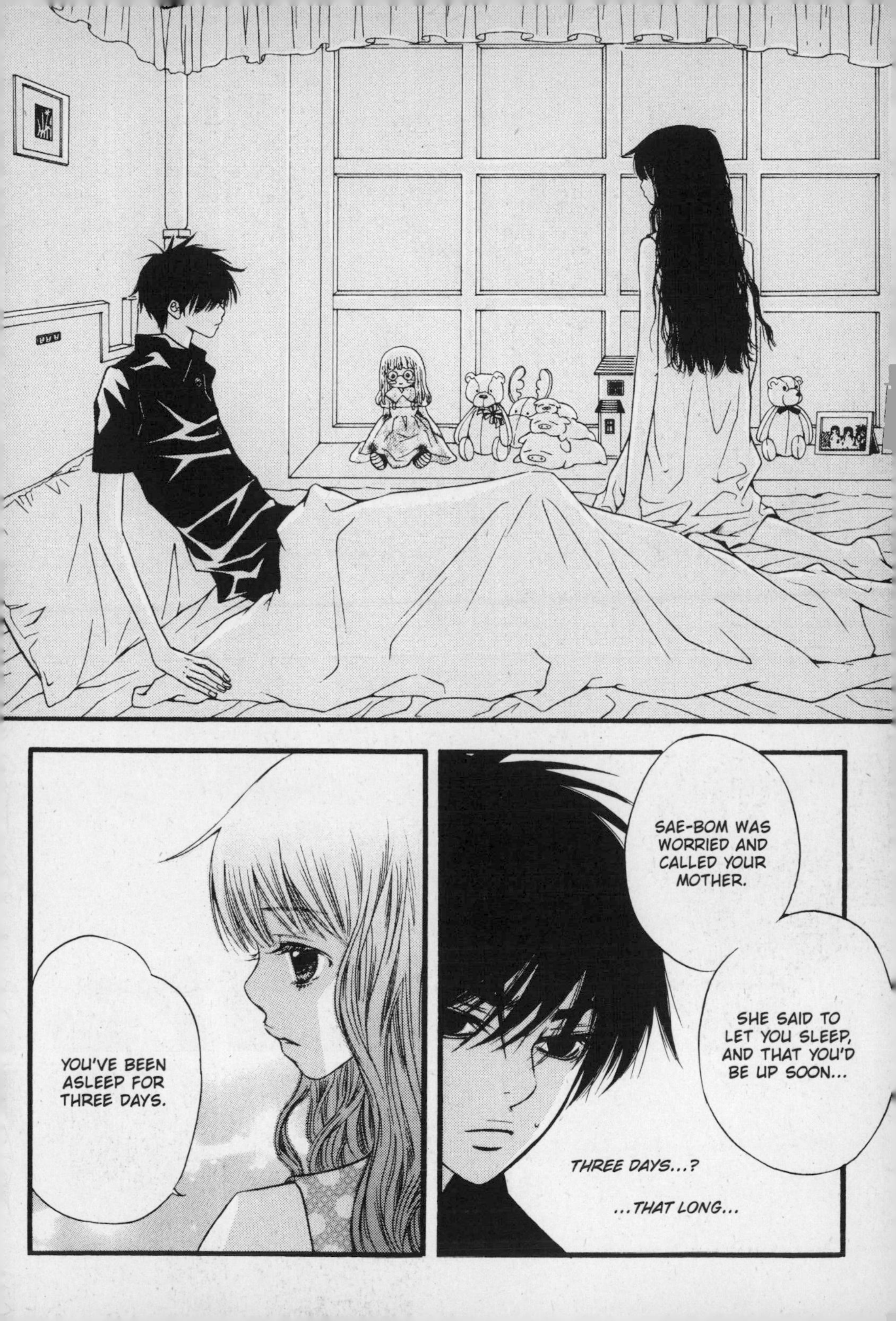
YOU'VE BEEN ASLEEP FOR THREE DAYS.
SAE-BOM WAS WORRIED AND CALLED YOUR MOTHER.
SHE SAID TO LET YOU SLEEP, AND THAT YOU'D BE UP SOON...
THREE DAYS...?
...THAT LONG...

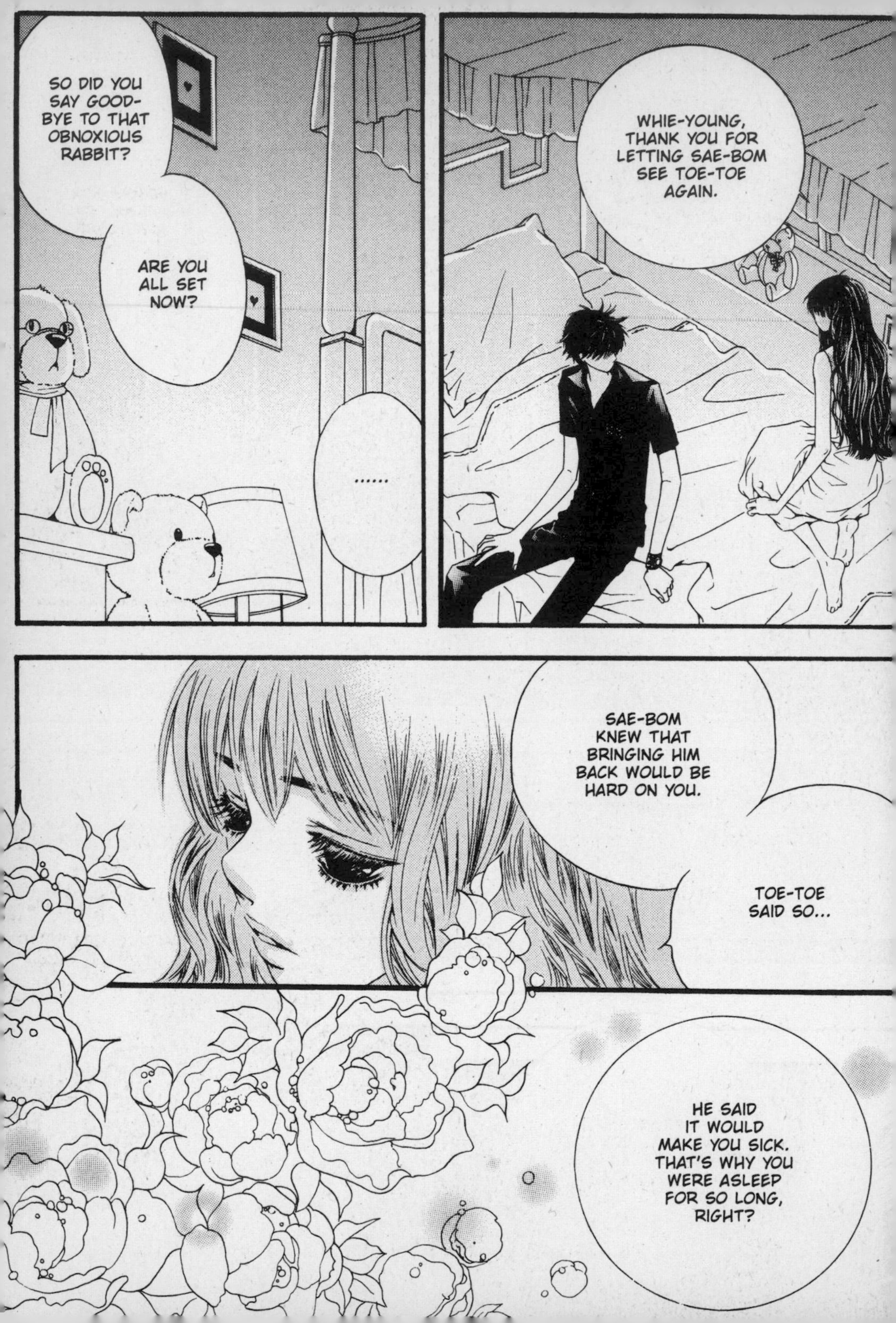
SO DID YOU SAY GOOD-BYE TO THAT OBNOXIOUS RABBIT?
ARE YOU ALL SET NOW?
......
WHIE-YOUNG, THANK YOU FOR LETTING SAE-BOM SEE TOE-TOE AGAIN.
SAE-BOM KNEW THAT BRINGING HIM BACK WOULD BE HARD ON YOU.
TOE-TOE SAID SO...
HE SAID IT WOULD MAKE YOU SICK. THAT'S WHY YOU WERE ASLEEP FOR SO LONG, RIGHT?

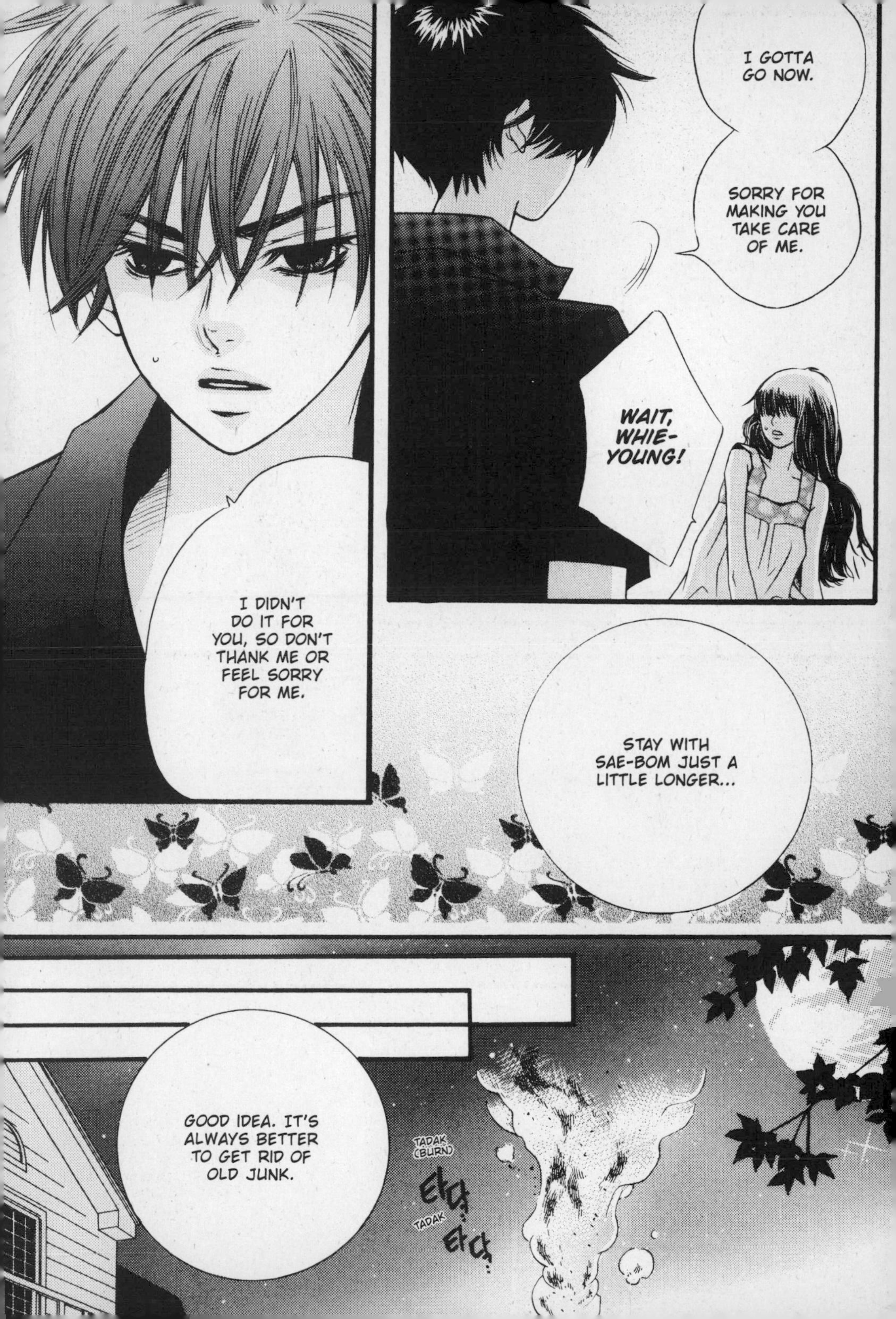
I DIDN'T DO IT FOR YOU, SO DON'T THANK ME OR FEEL SORRY FOR ME.
I GOTTA GO NOW.
SORRY FOR MAKING YOU TAKE CARE OF ME.
WAIT, WHIE-YOUNG!
STAY WITH SAE-BOM JUST A LITTLE LONGER...
GOOD IDEA. IT'S ALWAYS BETTER TO GET RID OF OLD JUNK.
TADAK (BURN)
타닥
TADAK
타닥

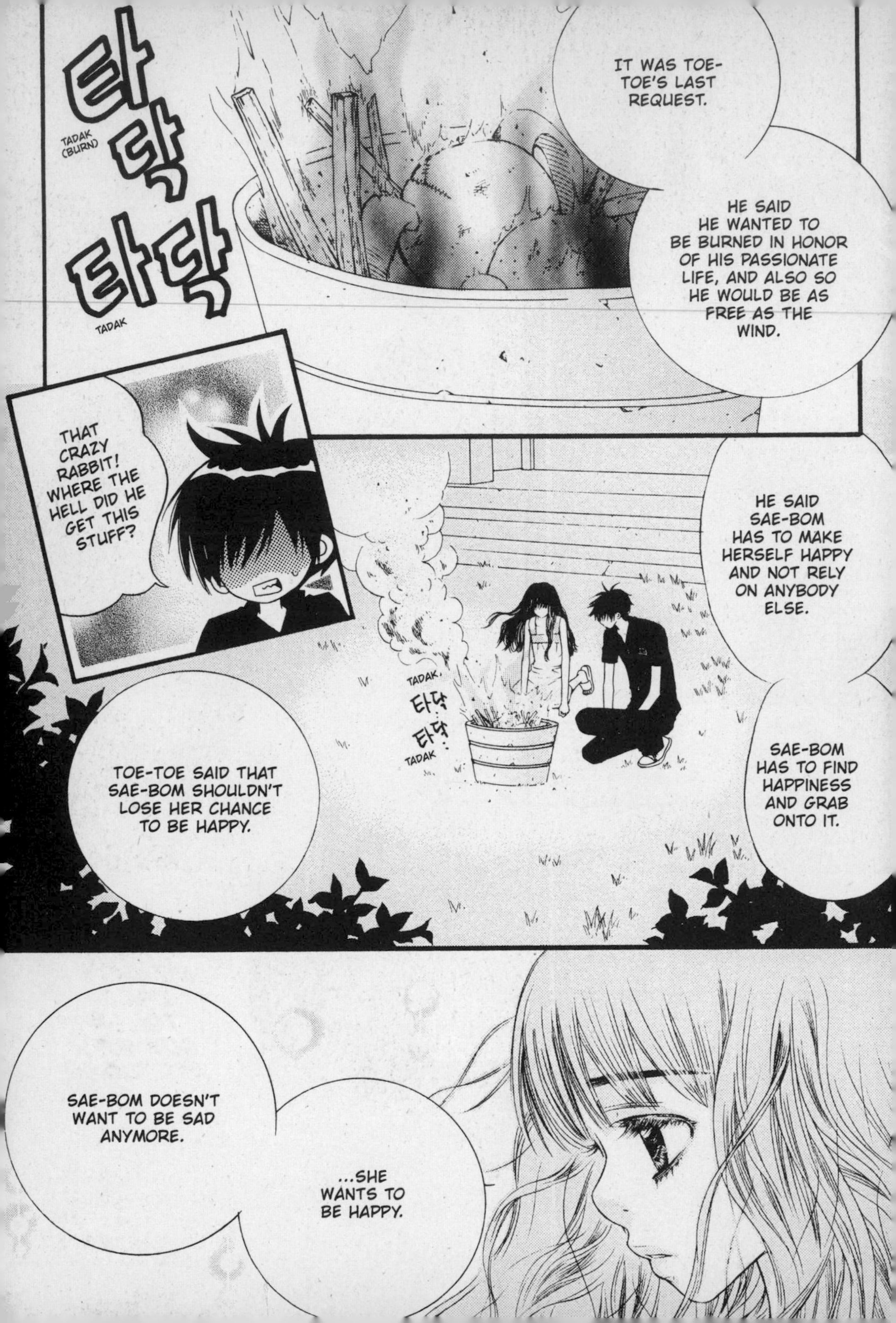

타닥
TADAK (BURN)
타닥
TADAK
IT WAS TOE-TOE'S LAST REQUEST.
HE SAID HE WANTED TO BE BURNED IN HONOR OF HIS PASSIONATE LIFE, AND ALSO SO HE WOULD BE AS FREE AS THE WIND.
THAT CRAZY RABBIT! WHERE THE HELL DID HE GET THIS STUFF?
TOE-TOE SAID THAT SAE-BOM SHOULDN'T LOSE HER CHANCE TO BE HAPPY.
TADAK
타닥
타닥
TADAK
HE SAID SAE-BOM HAS TO MAKE HERSELF HAPPY AND NOT RELY ON ANYBODY ELSE.
SAE-BOM HAS TO FIND HAPPINESS AND GRAB ONTO IT.
SAE-BOM DOESN'T WANT TO BE SAD ANYMORE.
...SHE WANTS TO BE HAPPY.

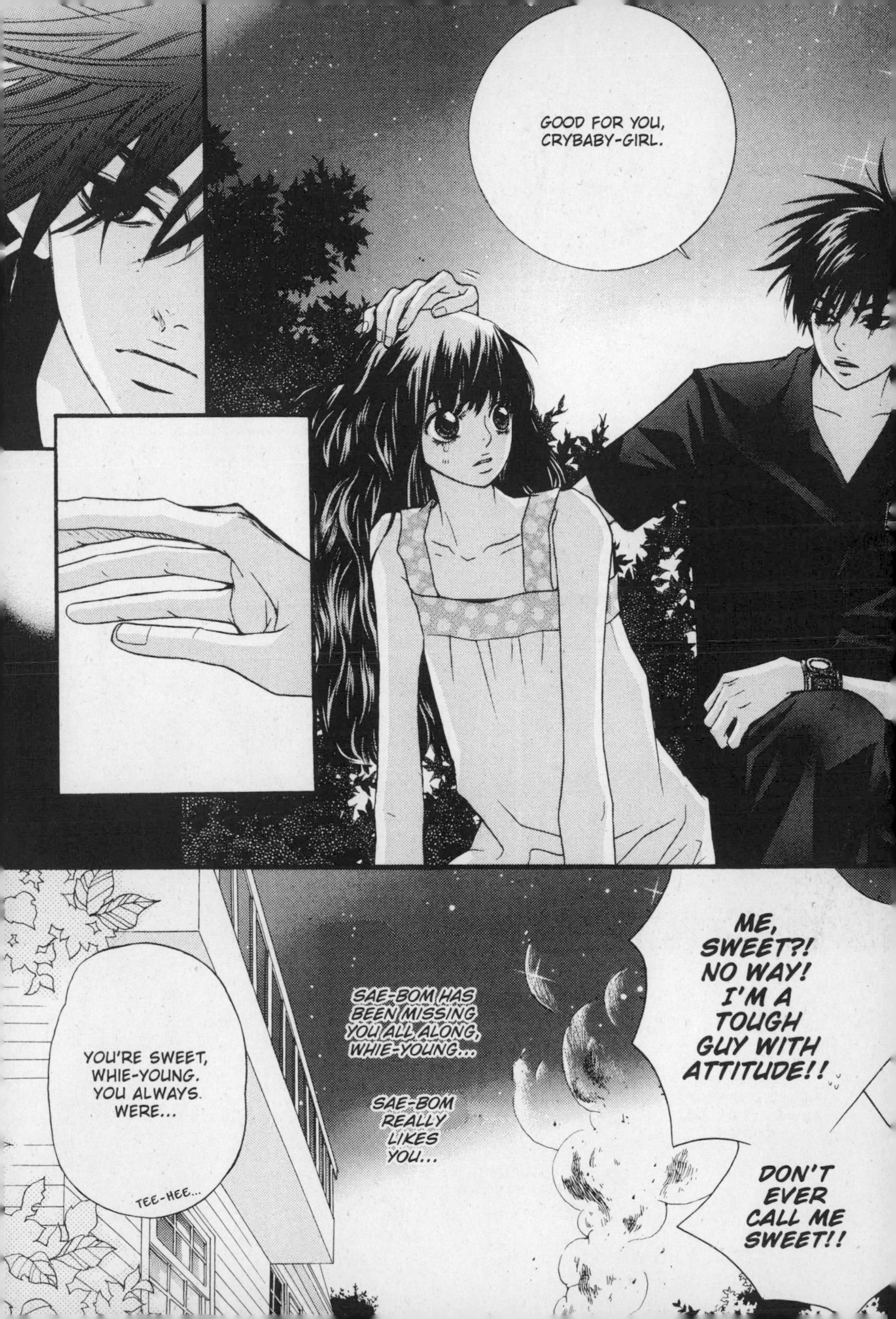
GOOD FOR YOU, CRYBABY-GIRL.
YOU'RE SWEET, WHIE-YOUNG. YOU ALWAYS WERE...
TEE-HEE...
SAE-BOM HAS BEEN MISSING YOU ALL ALONG, WHIE-YOUNG...
SAE-BOM REALLY LIKES YOU...
ME, SWEET?! NO WAY! I'M A TOUGH GUY WITH ATTITUDE!!
DON'T EVER CALL ME SWEET!!

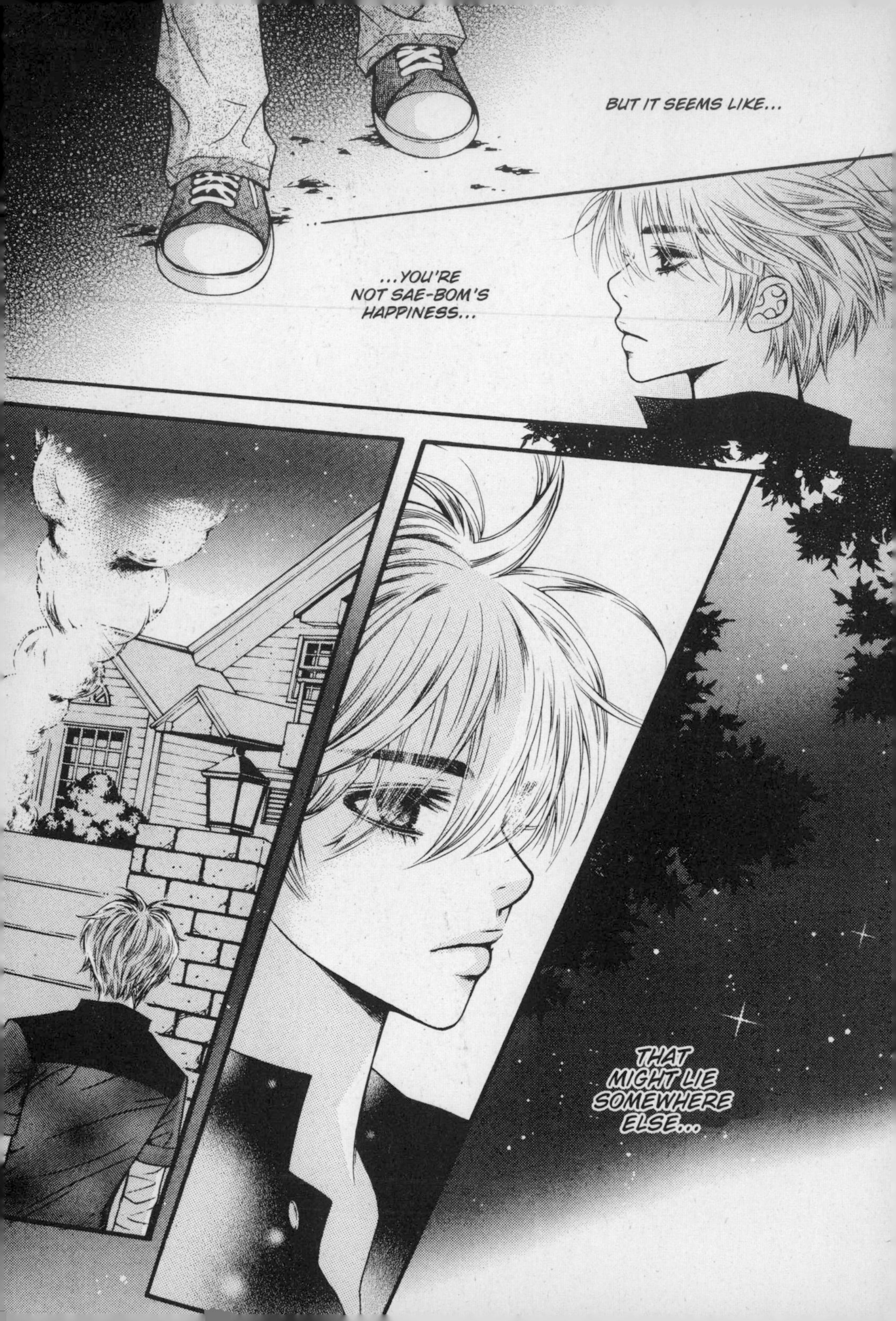
BUT IT SEEMS LIKE...
...YOU'RE NOT SAE-BOM'S HAPPINESS...
THAT MIGHT LIE SOMEWHERE ELSE...

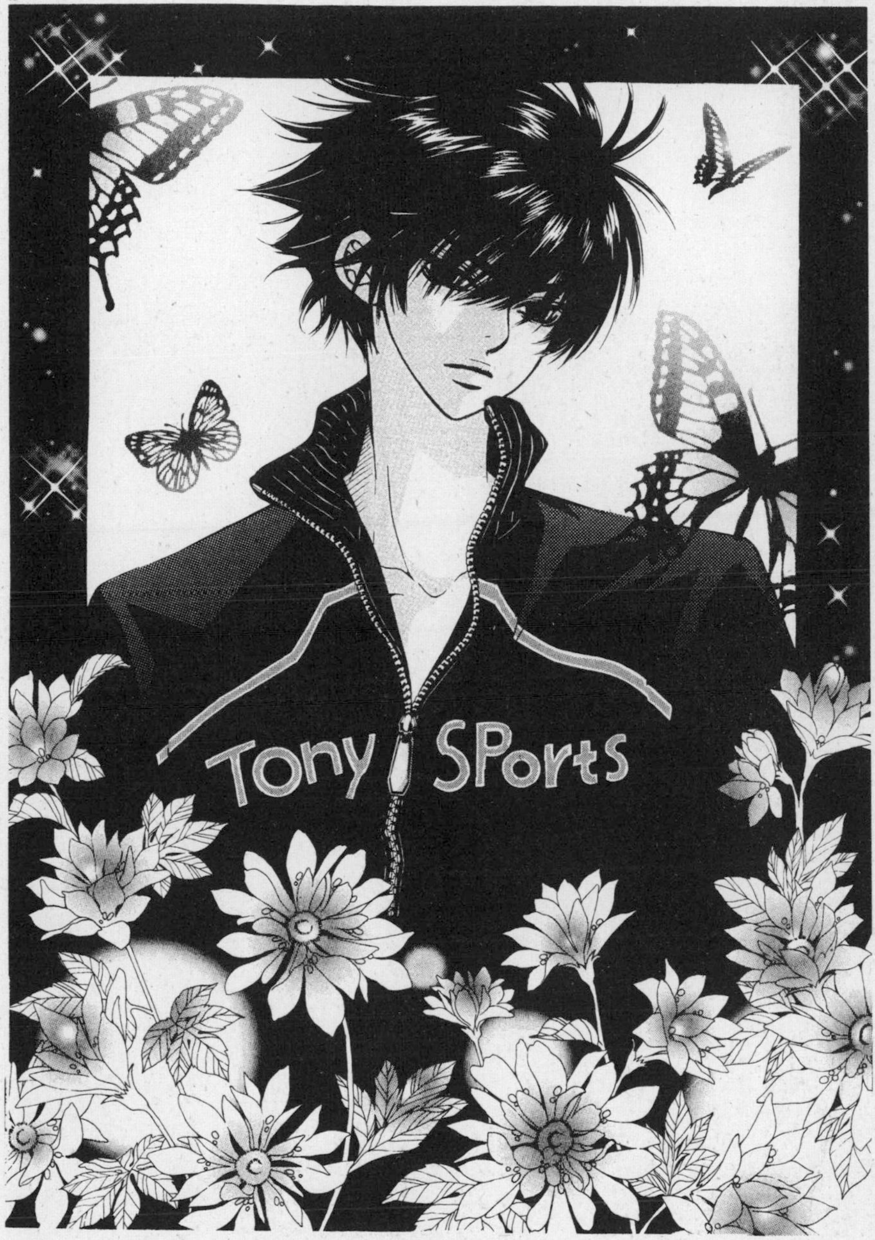
Tony SPorts

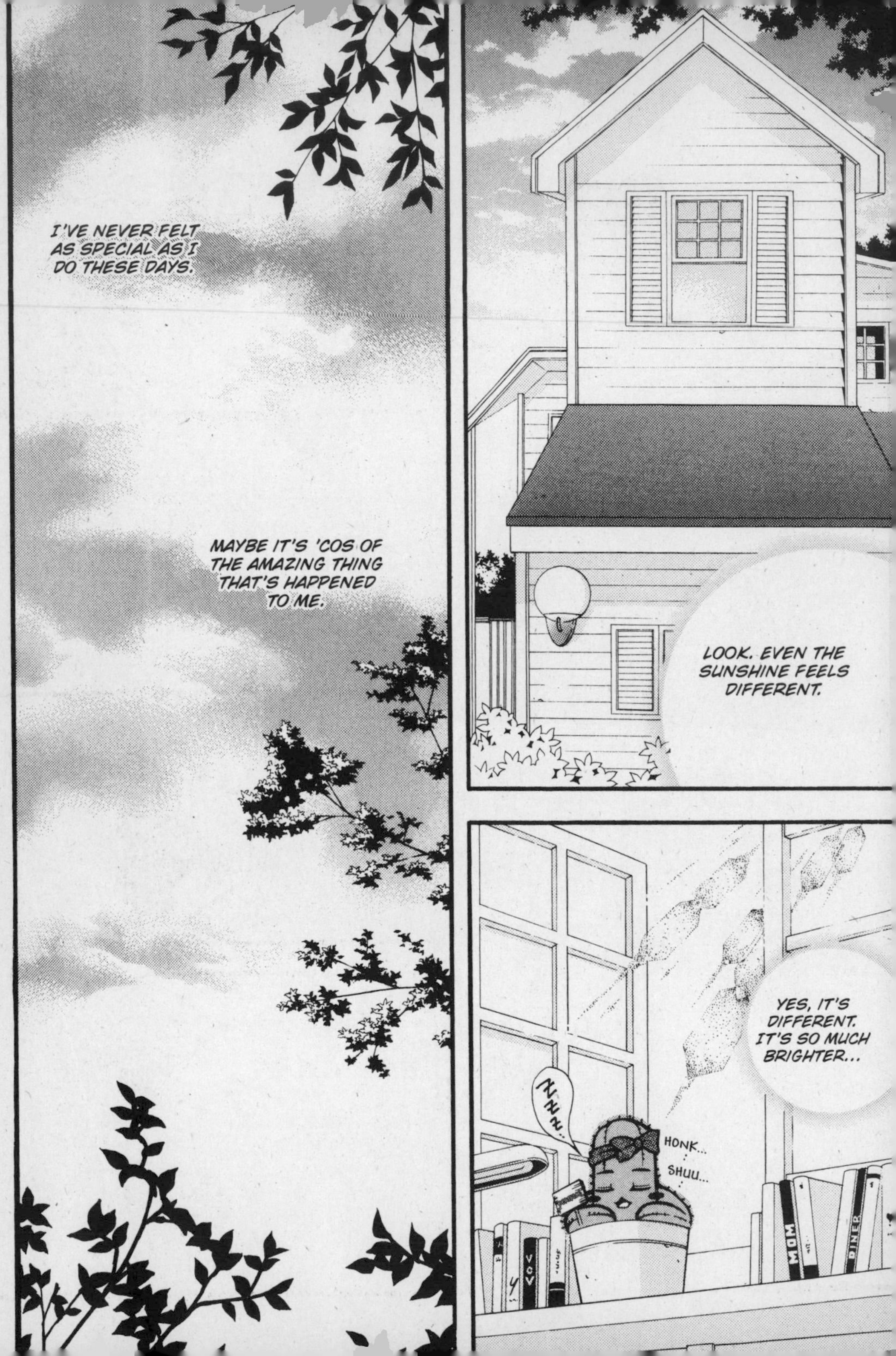
I'VE NEVER FELT AS SPECIAL AS I DO THESE DAYS.
MAYBE IT'S 'COS OF THE AMAZING THING THAT'S HAPPENED TO ME.
LOOK. EVEN THE SUNSHINE FEELS DIFFERENT.
YES, IT'S DIFFERENT. IT'S SO MUCH BRIGHTER...
HONK...
SHUU...
MOM
DINER

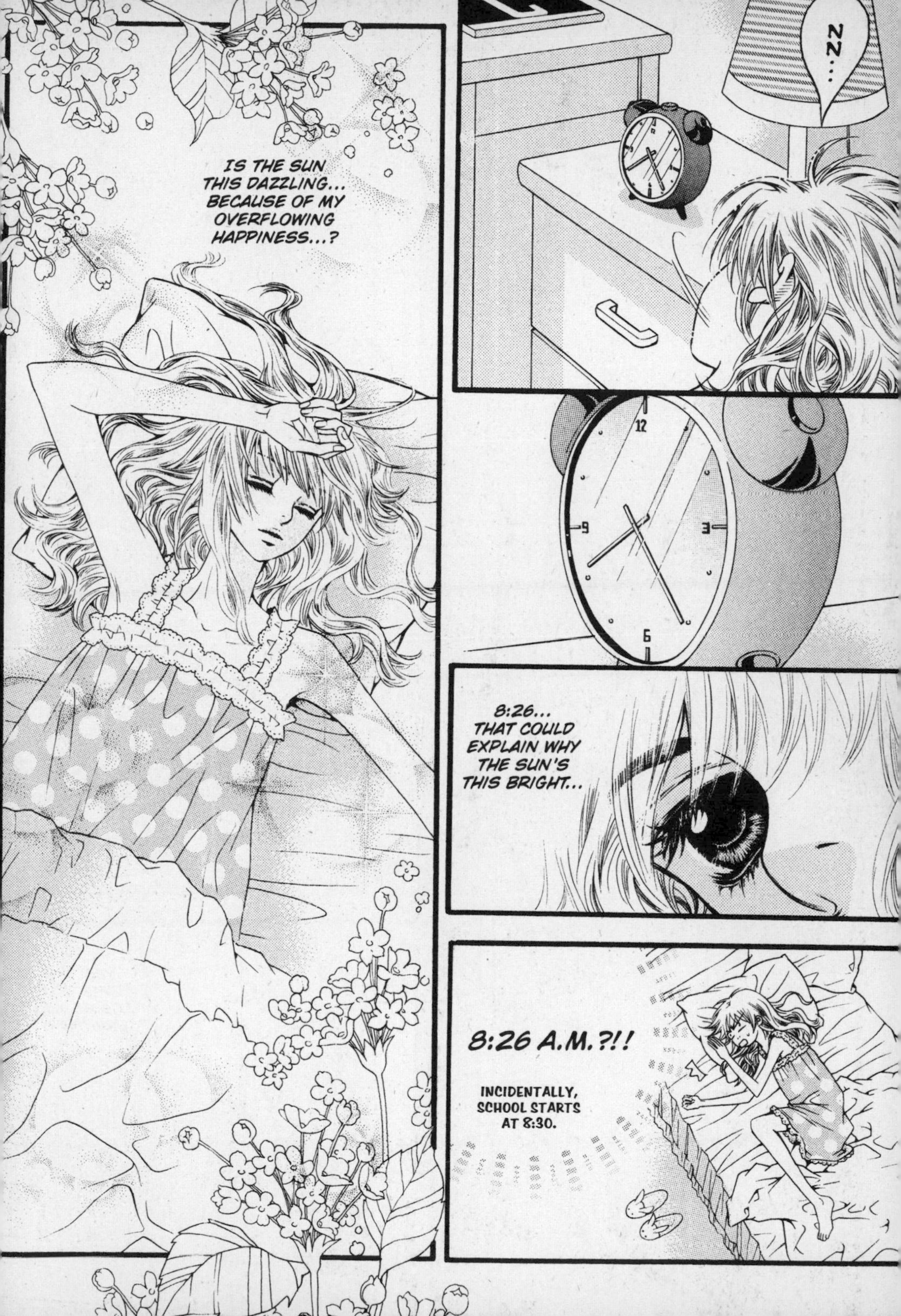
IS THE SUN THIS DAZZLING... BECAUSE OF MY OVERFLOWING HAPPINESS...?
NN...
8:26... THAT COULD EXPLAIN WHY THE SUN'S THIS BRIGHT...
8:26 A.M.?!!
INCIDENTALLY, SCHOOL STARTS AT 8:30.

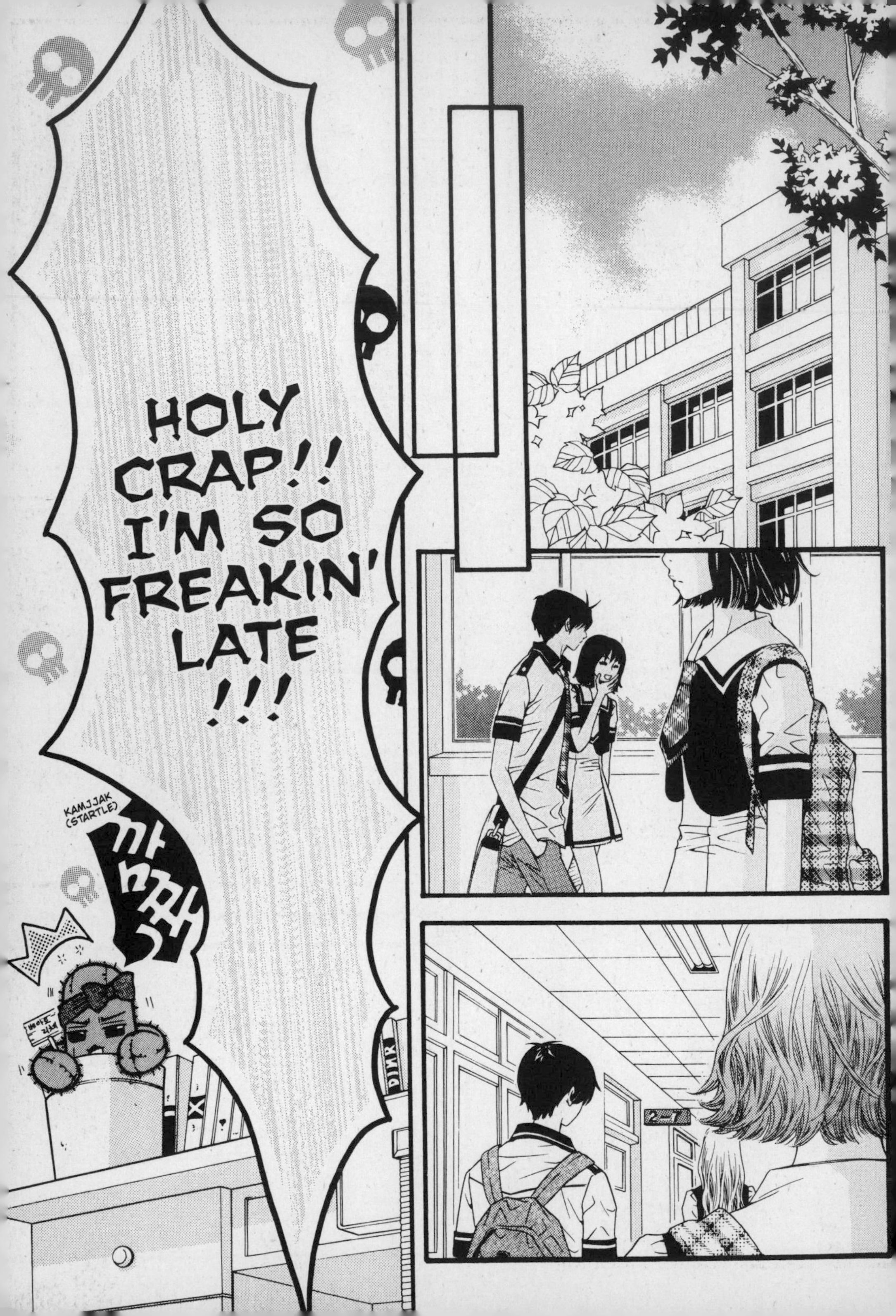
HOLY CRAP!! I'M SO FREAKIN' LATE !!!
KAMJJAK (STARTLE)
깜짝
2-7

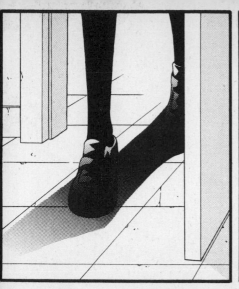

HOW COULD YOU BRING A PORN MAG LIKE THIS TO SCHOOL?! CONSIDER IT CONFISCATED UNTIL THE END OF THE DAY!

N-NAM-JOO YEO!! IT'S MY BROTHER'S! GIVE IT BACK!!

MEN SUCK!!

Hot Girl

...NAM-JOO, HOW ARE YOU?

O-OH...? YEAH, HEY—

...I WAS WORRIED ABOUT YOU SINCE YOU WERE OUT FOR A FEW DAYS. SAY, THAT'S A BIG CHANGE RIGHT THERE. WHAT BROUGHT IT ON?

TAK (TOK)

타
닥

STEP 22. THE SWEET THRILL OF CUTTING CLASS

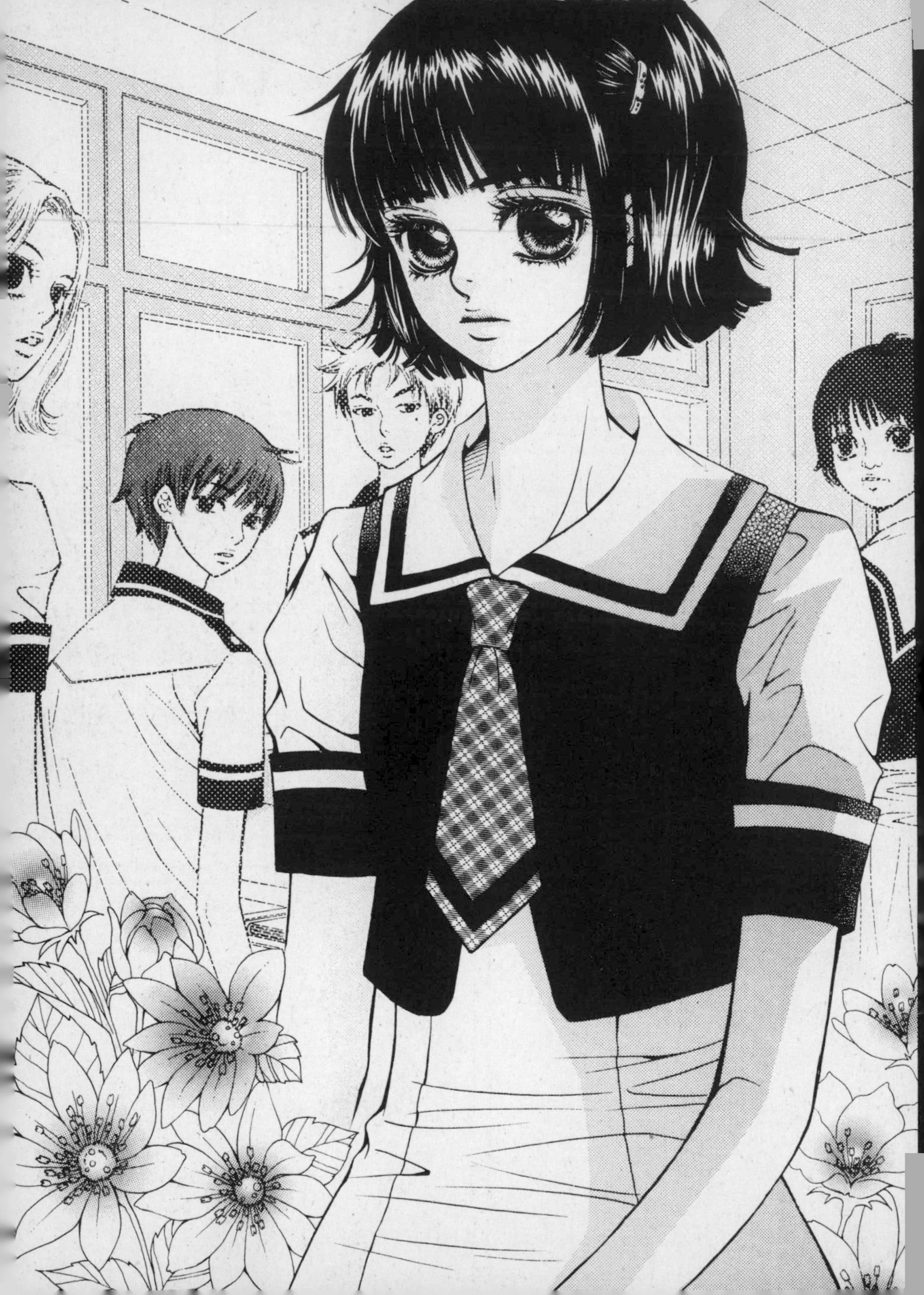

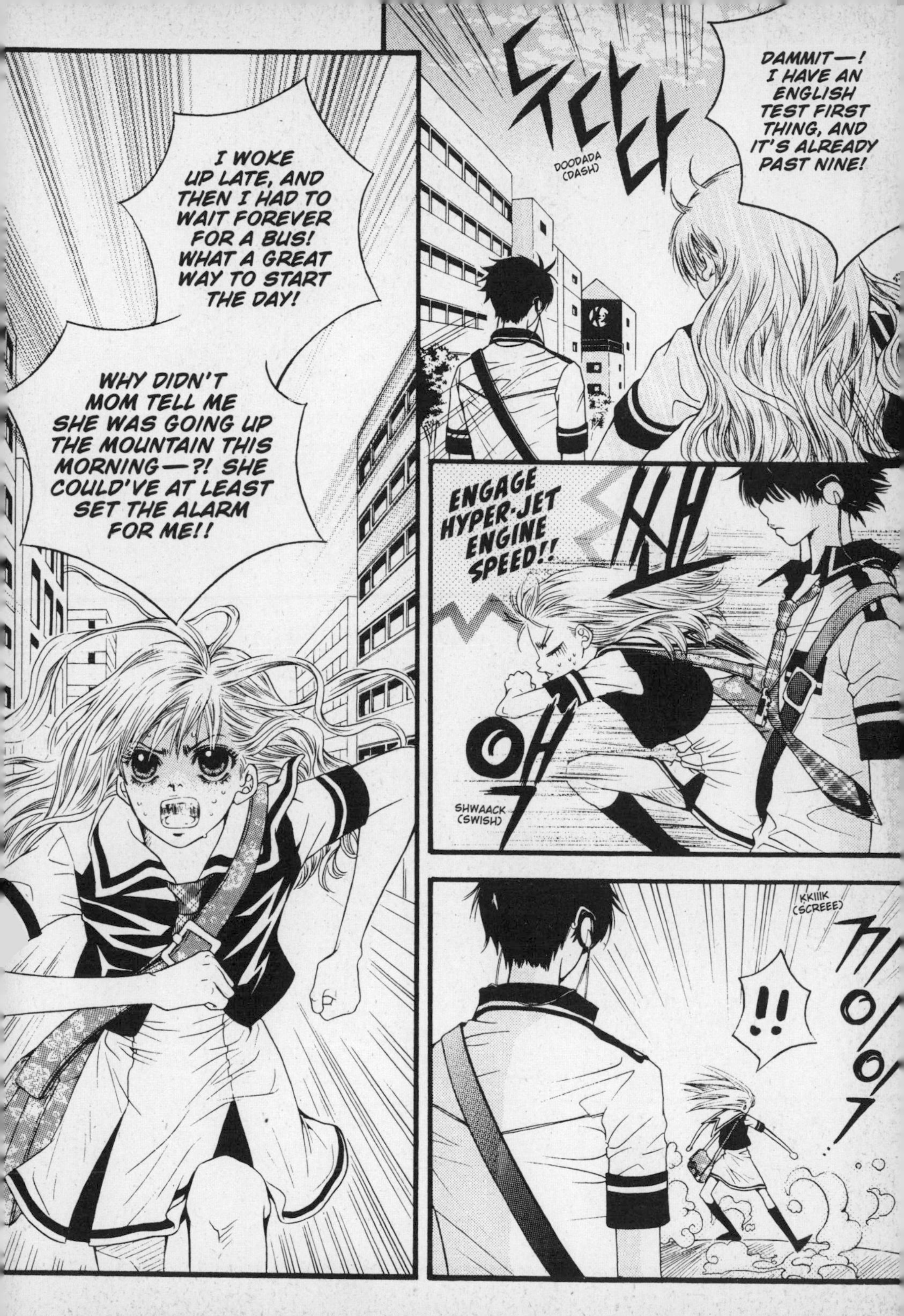
I WOKE UP LATE, AND THEN I HAD TO WAIT FOREVER FOR A BUS! WHAT A GREAT WAY TO START THE DAY!
WHY DIDN'T MOM TELL ME SHE WAS GOING UP THE MOUNTAIN THIS MORNING—?! SHE COULD'VE AT LEAST SET THE ALARM FOR ME!!
DOODADA (DASH)
DAMMIT—! I HAVE AN ENGLISH TEST FIRST THING, AND IT'S ALREADY PAST NINE!
ENGAGE HYPER-JET ENGINE SPEED!!
SHWAACK (SWISH)
KKIIIK (SCREEE)
!!

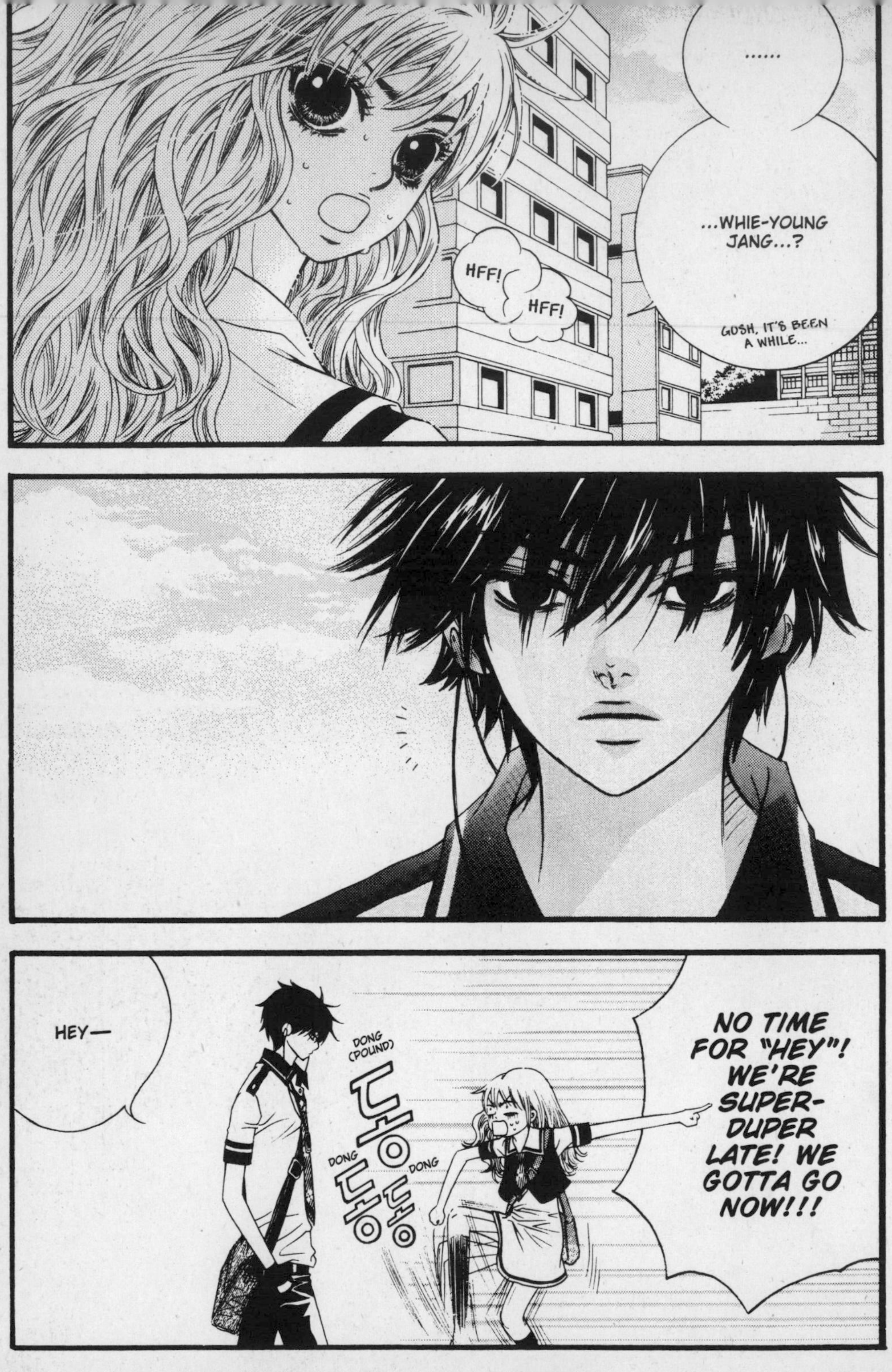
......
...WHIE-YOUNG JANG...?
HFF!
HFF!
GOSH, IT'S BEEN A WHILE...
HEY—
DONG (POUND)
DONG
DONG
NO TIME FOR "HEY"! WE'RE SUPER-DUPER LATE! WE GOTTA GO NOW!!!

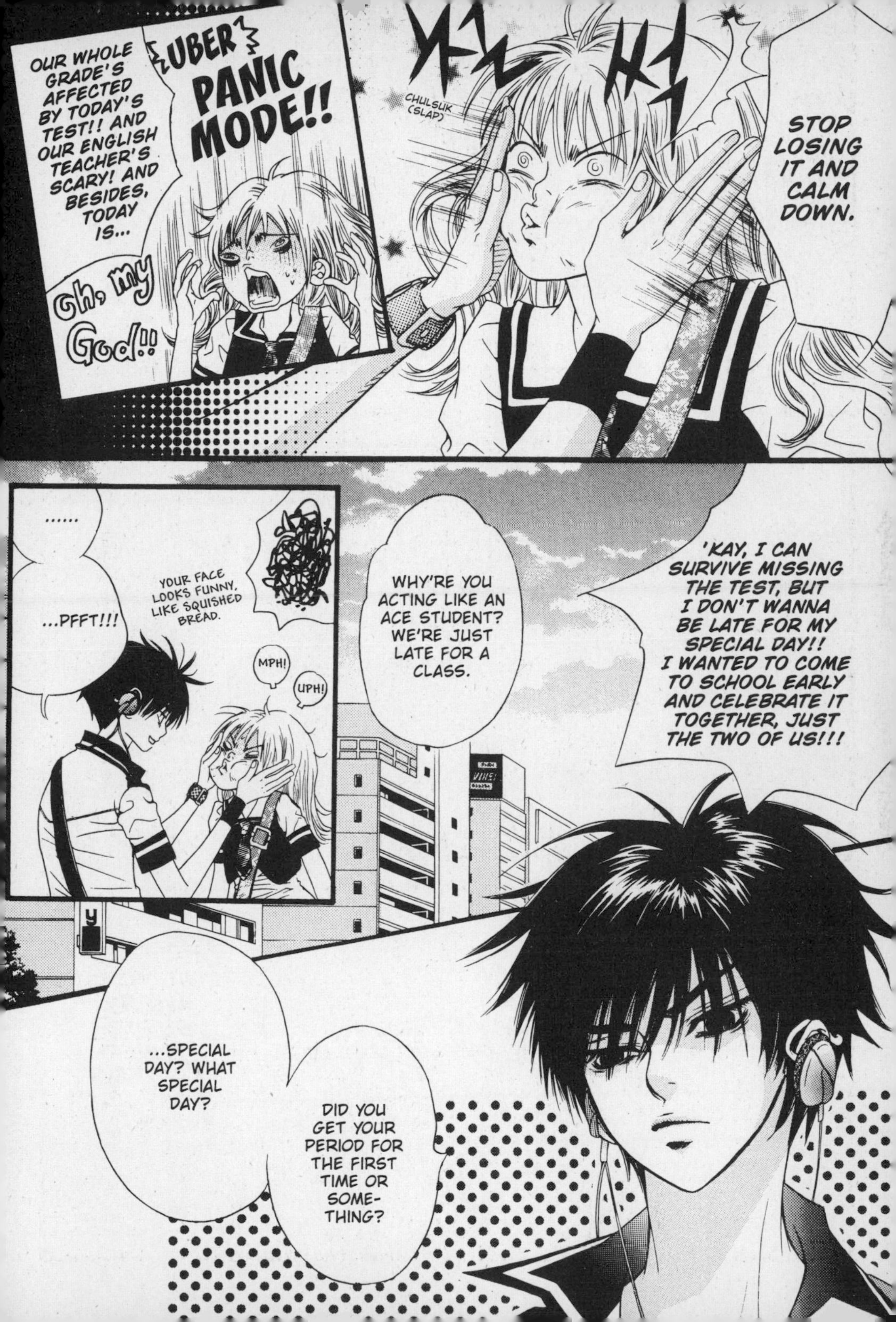
OUR WHOLE GRADE'S AFFECTED BY TODAY'S TEST!! AND OUR ENGLISH TEACHER'S SCARY! AND BESIDES, TODAY IS...
UBER PANIC MODE!!
Oh, my God!!
CHULSUK (SLAP)
STOP LOSING IT AND CALM DOWN.
......
...PFFT!!!
YOUR FACE LOOKS FUNNY, LIKE SQUISHED BREAD.
MPH!
UPH!
WHY'RE YOU ACTING LIKE AN ACE STUDENT? WE'RE JUST LATE FOR A CLASS.
'KAY, I CAN SURVIVE MISSING THE TEST, BUT I DON'T WANNA BE LATE FOR MY SPECIAL DAY!! I WANTED TO COME TO SCHOOL EARLY AND CELEBRATE IT TOGETHER, JUST THE TWO OF US!!!
...SPECIAL DAY? WHAT SPECIAL DAY?
DID YOU GET YOUR PERIOD FOR THE FIRST TIME OR SOME-THING?

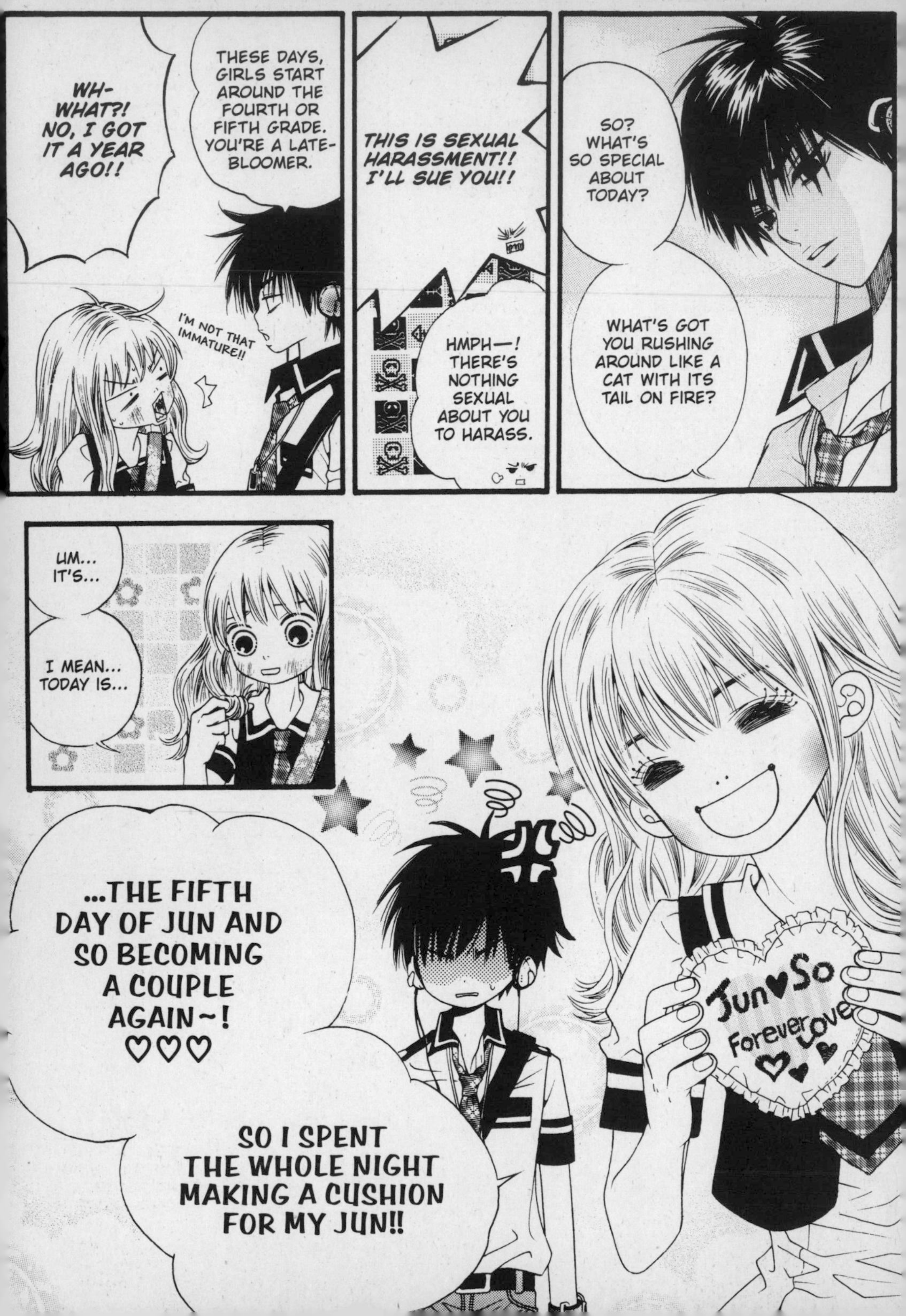
WH-WHAT?! NO, I GOT IT A YEAR AGO!!
THESE DAYS, GIRLS START AROUND THE FOURTH OR FIFTH GRADE. YOU'RE A LATE-BLOOMER.
I'M NOT THAT IMMATURE!!
THIS IS SEXUAL HARASSMENT!! I'LL SUE YOU!!
HMPH—! THERE'S NOTHING SEXUAL ABOUT YOU TO HARASS.
SO? WHAT'S SO SPECIAL ABOUT TODAY?
WHAT'S GOT YOU RUSHING AROUND LIKE A CAT WITH ITS TAIL ON FIRE?
UM... IT'S...
I MEAN... TODAY IS...
...THE FIFTH DAY OF JUN AND SO BECOMING A COUPLE AGAIN~! ♡♡♡
SO I SPENT THE WHOLE NIGHT MAKING A CUSHION FOR MY JUN!!
Jun♥So Forever Love

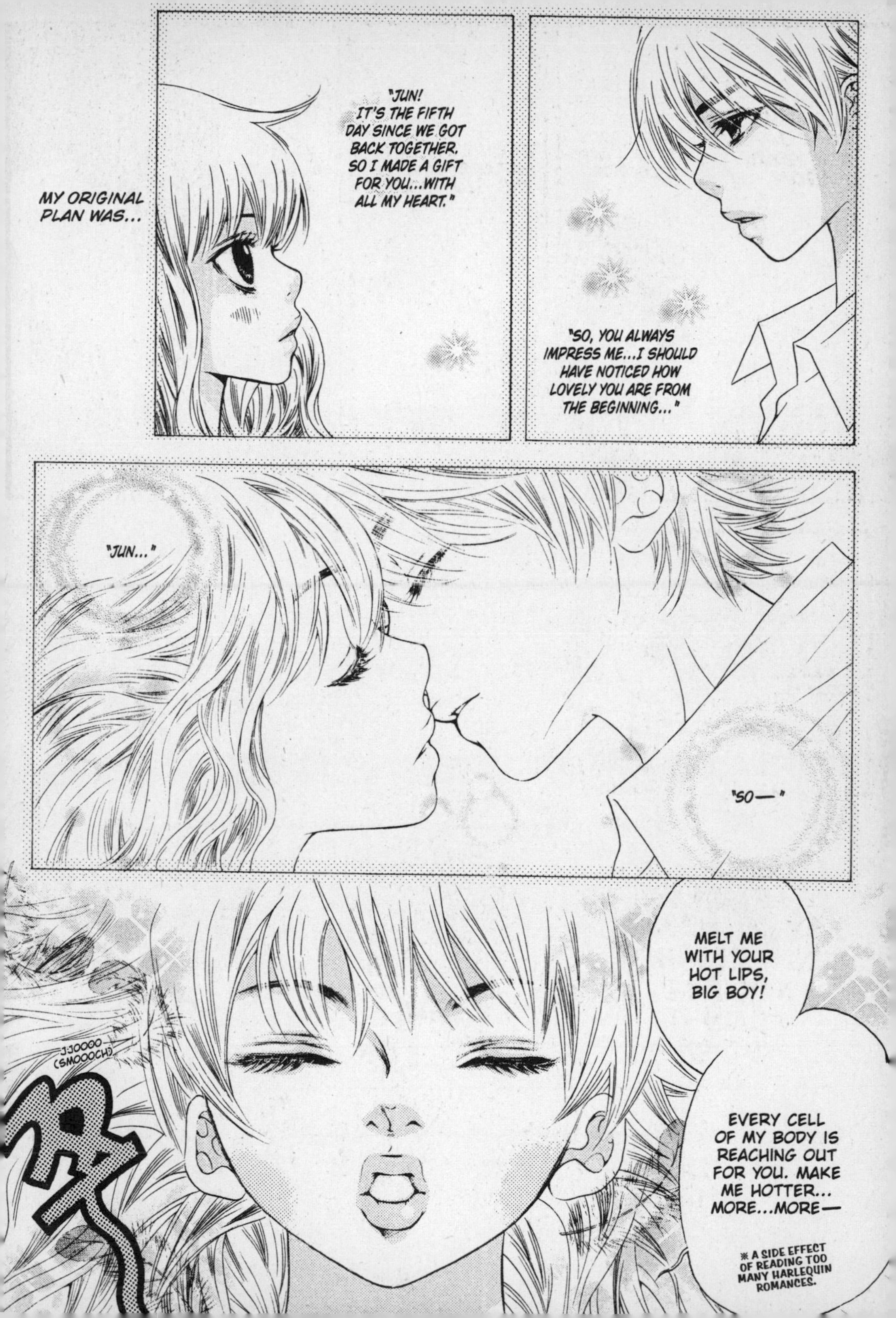
MY ORIGINAL PLAN WAS...
"JUN! IT'S THE FIFTH DAY SINCE WE GOT BACK TOGETHER. SO I MADE A GIFT FOR YOU...WITH ALL MY HEART."
"SO, YOU ALWAYS IMPRESS ME...I SHOULD HAVE NOTICED HOW LOVELY YOU ARE FROM THE BEGINNING..."
"JUN..."
"SO—"
JJOOGO (SMOOOCH)
MELT ME WITH YOUR HOT LIPS, BIG BOY!
EVERY CELL OF MY BODY IS REACHING OUT FOR YOU. MAKE ME HOTTER... MORE...MORE—
※ A SIDE EFFECT OF READING TOO MANY HARLEQUIN ROMANCES.

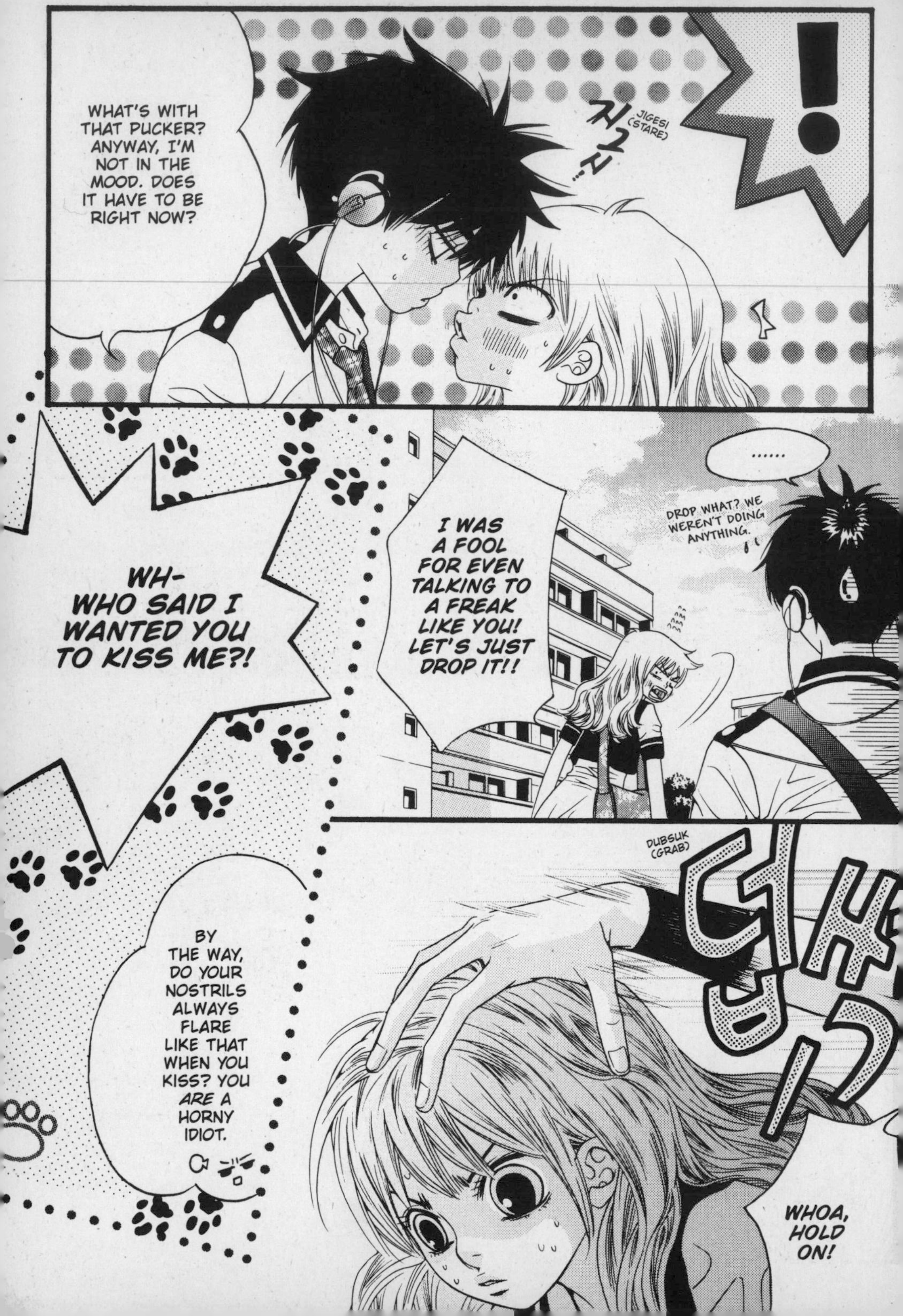
WHAT'S WITH THAT PUCKER? ANYWAY, I'M NOT IN THE MOOD. DOES IT HAVE TO BE RIGHT NOW?
JIGESI (STARE)
!
WH- WHO SAID I WANTED YOU TO KISS ME?!
I WAS A FOOL FOR EVEN TALKING TO A FREAK LIKE YOU! LET'S JUST DROP IT!!
......
DROP WHAT? WE WEREN'T DOING ANYTHING.
BY THE WAY, DO YOUR NOSTRILS ALWAYS FLARE LIKE THAT WHEN YOU KISS? YOU ARE A HORNY IDIOT.
DUBSUK (GRAB)
WHOA, HOLD ON!

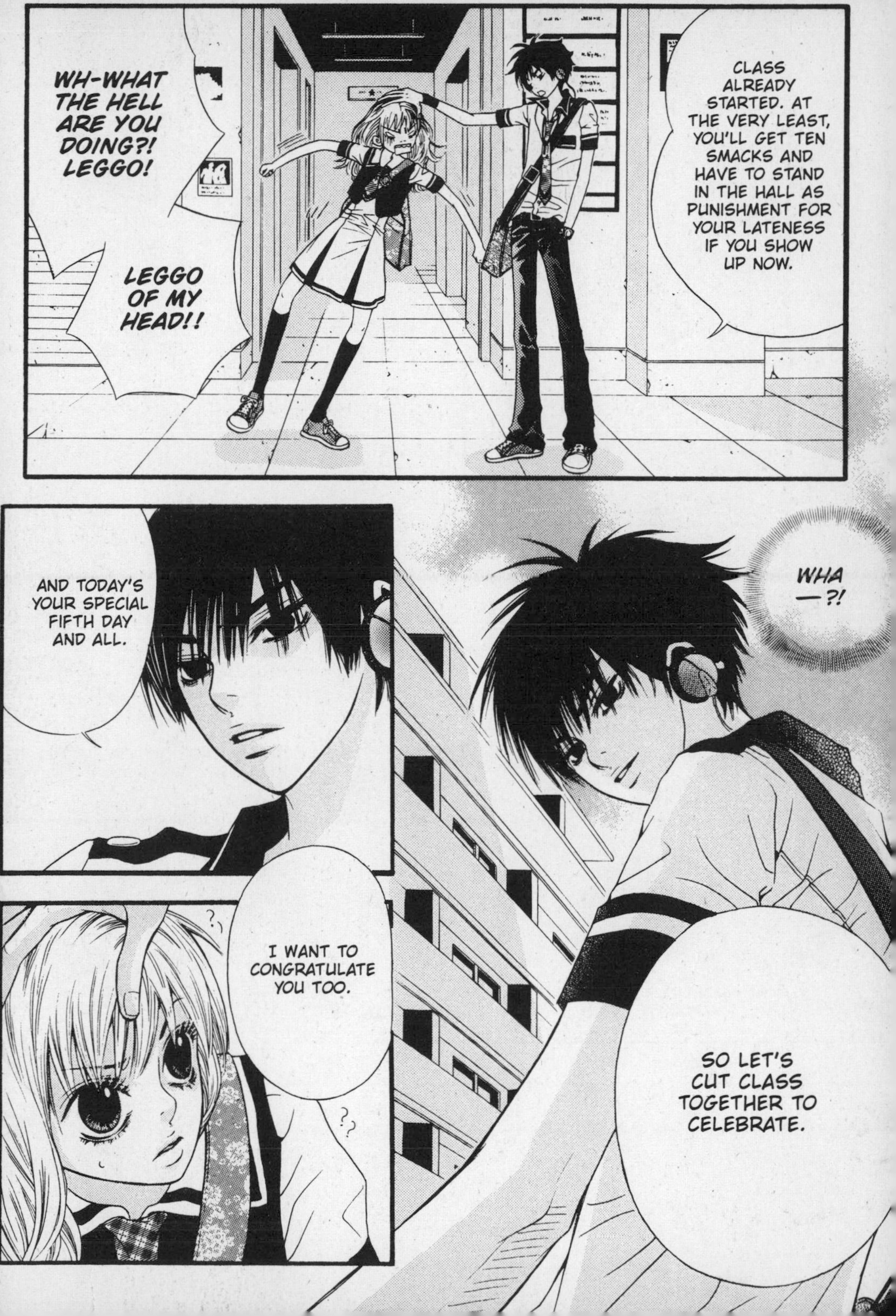
WH-WHAT THE HELL ARE YOU DOING?! LEGGO!
LEGGO OF MY HEAD!!
CLASS ALREADY STARTED. AT THE VERY LEAST, YOU'LL GET TEN SMACKS AND HAVE TO STAND IN THE HALL AS PUNISHMENT FOR YOUR LATENESS IF YOU SHOW UP NOW.
AND TODAY'S YOUR SPECIAL FIFTH DAY AND ALL.
I WANT TO CONGRATULATE YOU TOO.
WHA—?!
SO LET'S CUT CLASS TOGETHER TO CELEBRATE.

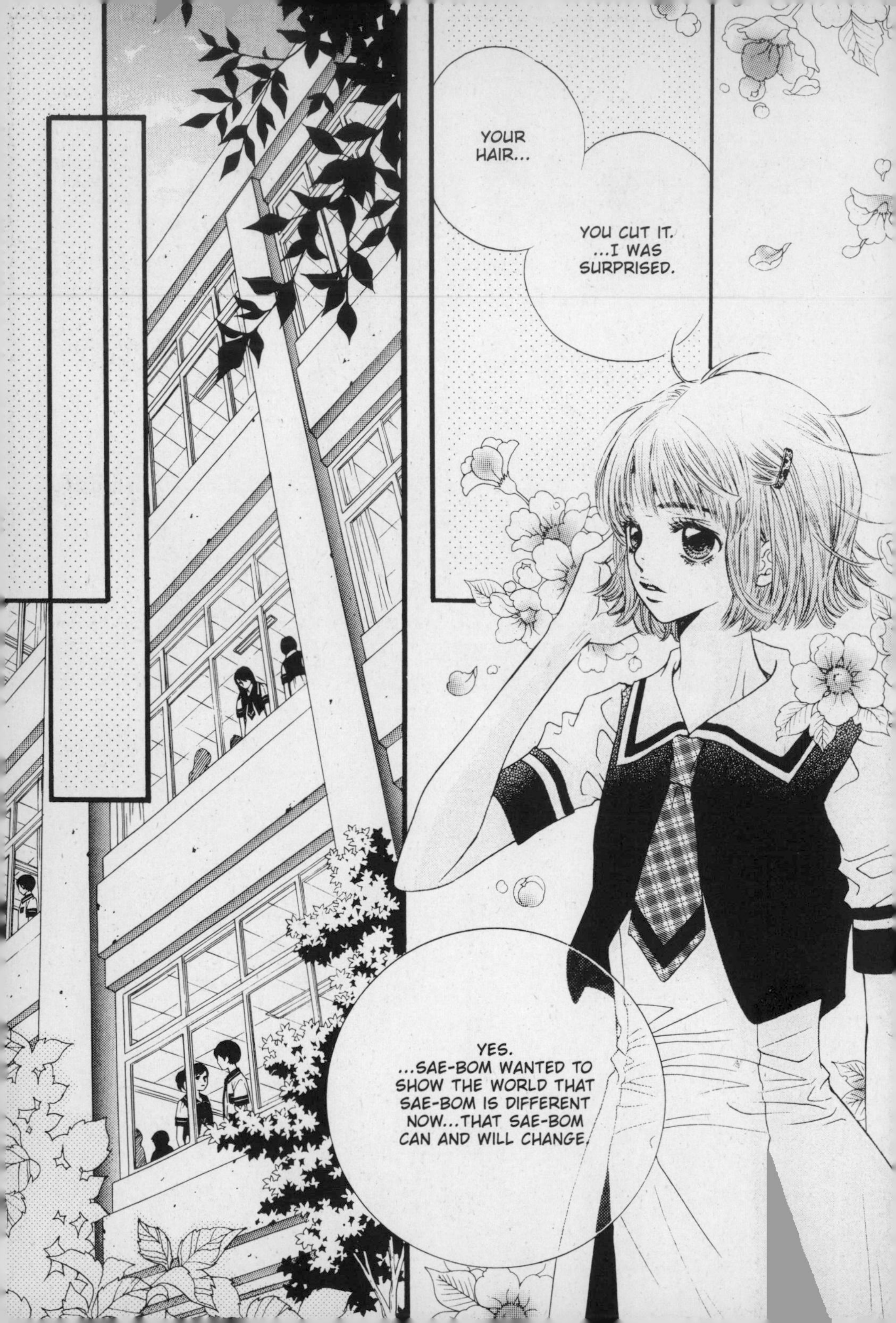
YOUR HAIR...
YOU CUT IT. ...I WAS SURPRISED.
YES. ...SAE-BOM WANTED TO SHOW THE WORLD THAT SAE-BOM IS DIFFERENT NOW...THAT SAE-BOM CAN AND WILL CHANGE.

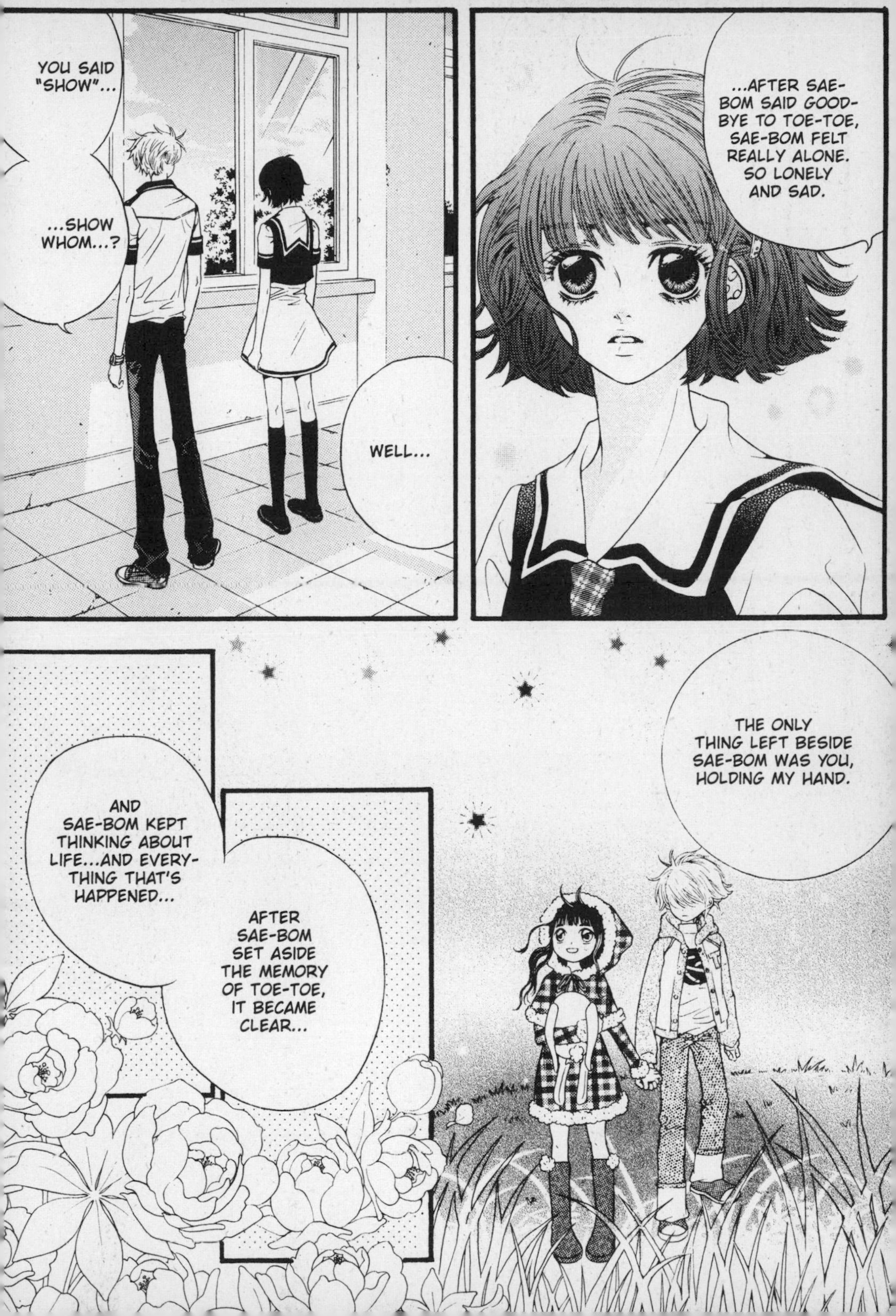
YOU SAID "SHOW"...
...SHOW WHOM...?
WELL...
...AFTER SAE-BOM SAID GOOD-BYE TO TOE-TOE, SAE-BOM FELT REALLY ALONE. SO LONELY AND SAD.
AND SAE-BOM KEPT THINKING ABOUT LIFE...AND EVERY-THING THAT'S HAPPENED...
AFTER SAE-BOM SET ASIDE THE MEMORY OF TOE-TOE, IT BECAME CLEAR...
THE ONLY THING LEFT BESIDE SAE-BOM WAS YOU, HOLDING MY HAND.

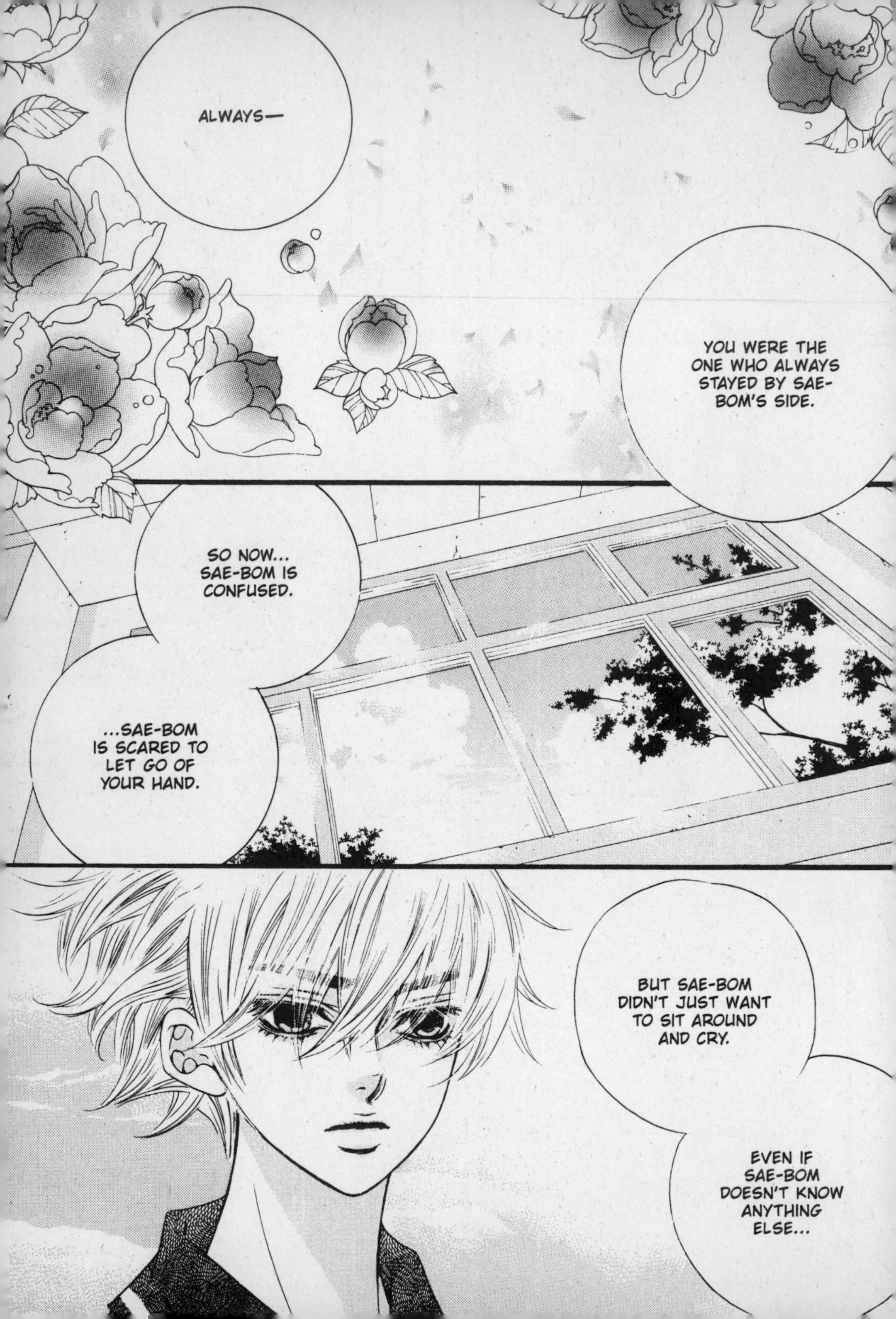
ALWAYS—
YOU WERE THE ONE WHO ALWAYS STAYED BY SAE-BOM'S SIDE.
SO NOW... SAE-BOM IS CONFUSED.
...SAE-BOM IS SCARED TO LET GO OF YOUR HAND.
BUT SAE-BOM DIDN'T JUST WANT TO SIT AROUND AND CRY.
EVEN IF SAE-BOM DOESN'T KNOW ANYTHING ELSE...

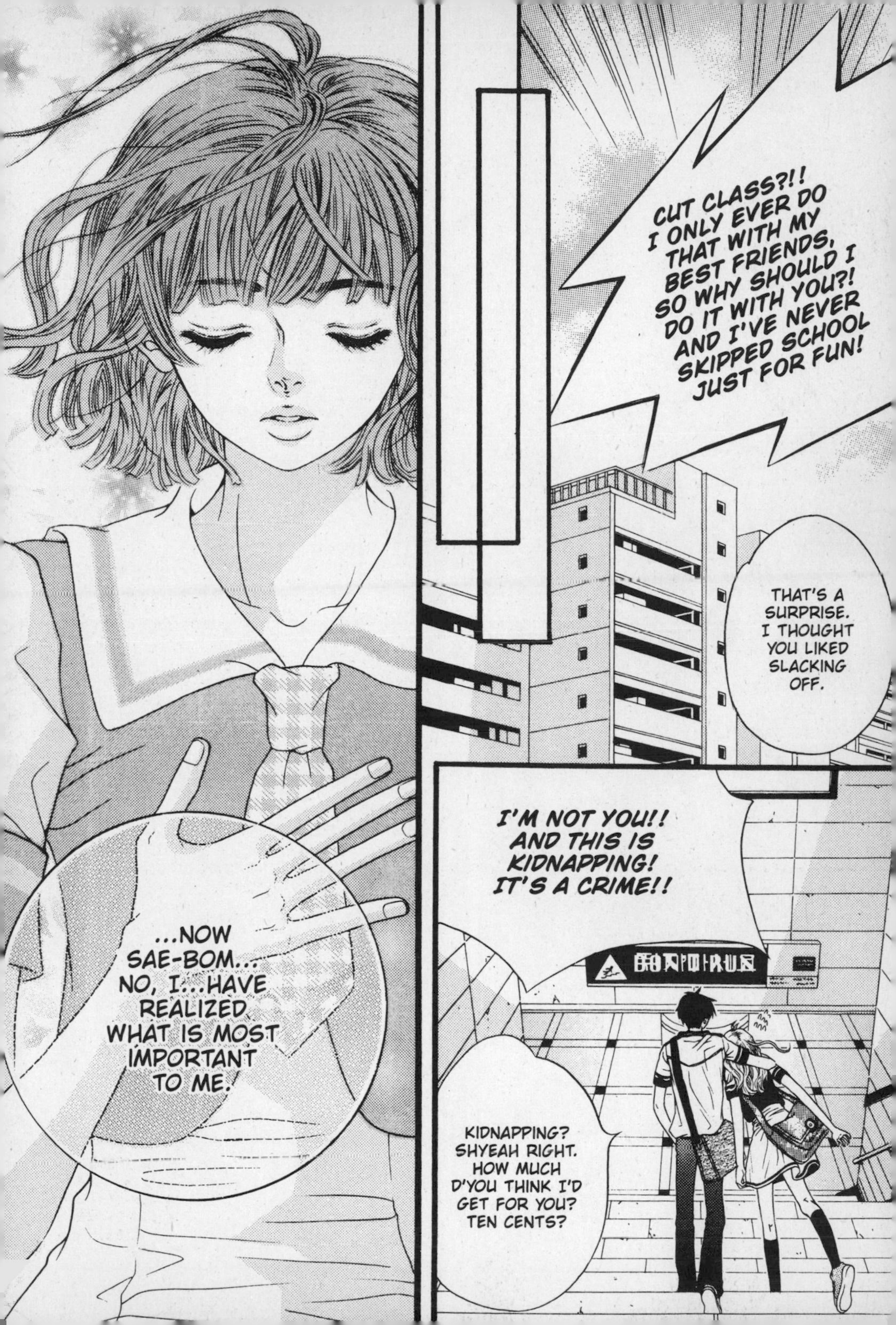
...NOW SAE-BOM... NO, I...HAVE REALIZED WHAT IS MOST IMPORTANT TO ME.
CUT CLASS?!! I ONLY EVER DO THAT WITH MY BEST FRIENDS, SO WHY SHOULD I DO IT WITH YOU?! AND I'VE NEVER SKIPPED SCHOOL JUST FOR FUN!
THAT'S A SURPRISE. I THOUGHT YOU LIKED SLACKING OFF.
I'M NOT YOU!! AND THIS IS KIDNAPPING! IT'S A CRIME!!
KIDNAPPING? SHYEAH RIGHT. HOW MUCH D'YOU THINK I'D GET FOR YOU? TEN CENTS?

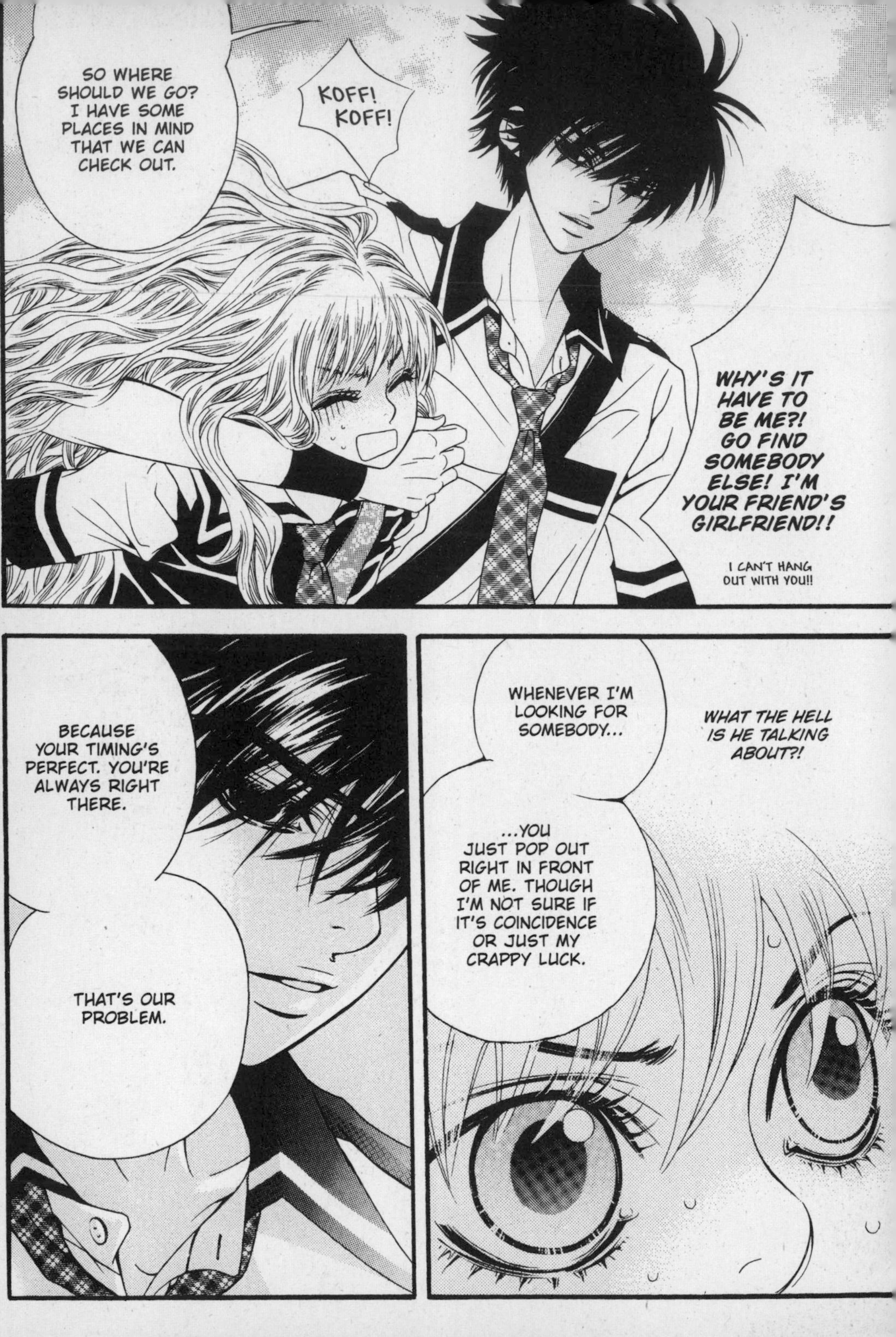
SO WHERE SHOULD WE GO? I HAVE SOME PLACES IN MIND THAT WE CAN CHECK OUT.
KOFF! KOFF!
WHY'S IT HAVE TO BE ME?! GO FIND SOMEBODY ELSE! I'M YOUR FRIEND'S GIRLFRIEND!!
I CAN'T HANG OUT WITH YOU!!
BECAUSE YOUR TIMING'S PERFECT. YOU'RE ALWAYS RIGHT THERE.
THAT'S OUR PROBLEM.
WHENEVER I'M LOOKING FOR SOMEBODY...
WHAT THE HELL IS HE TALKING ABOUT?!
...YOU JUST POP OUT RIGHT IN FRONT OF ME. THOUGH I'M NOT SURE IF IT'S COINCIDENCE OR JUST MY CRAPPY LUCK.

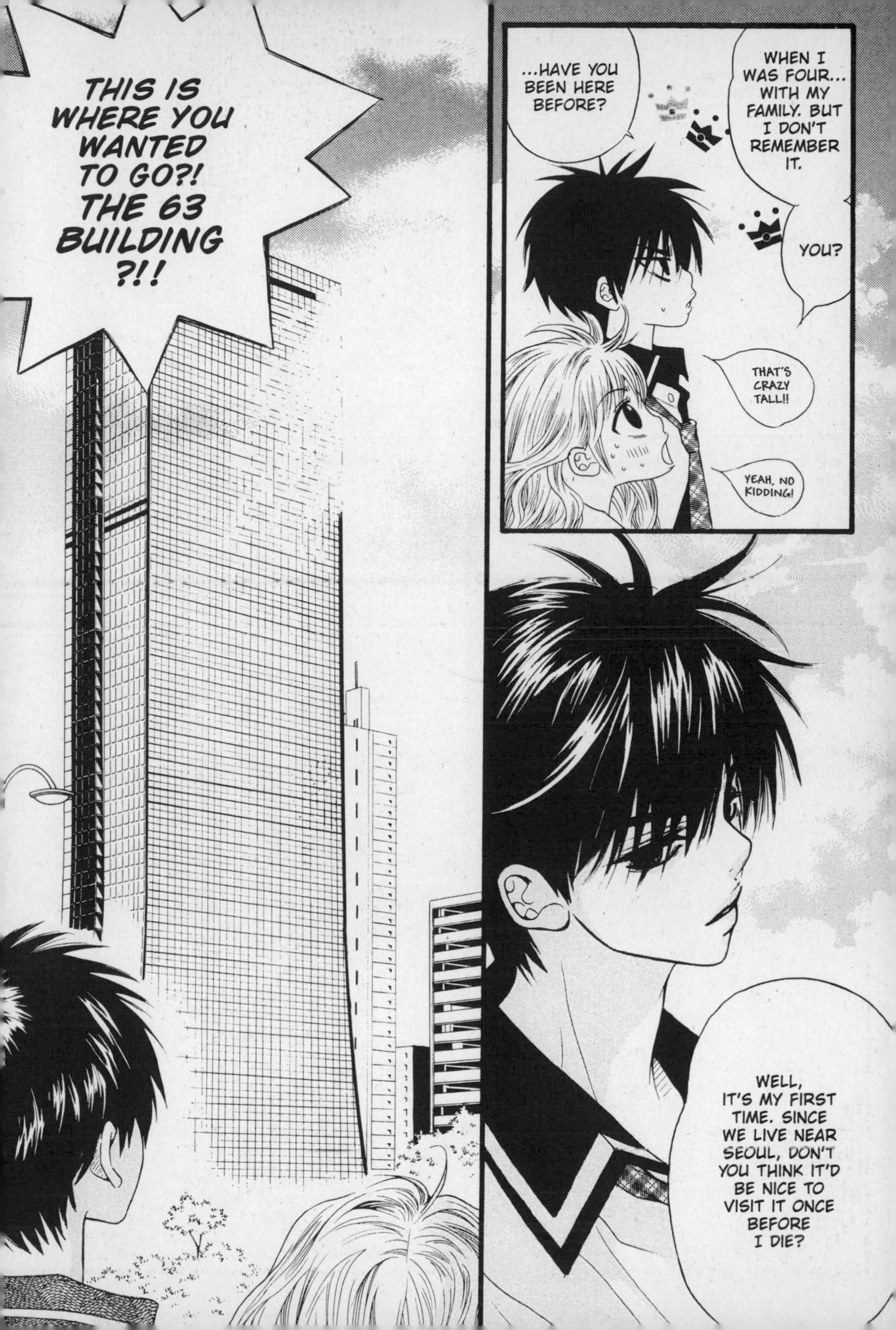
THIS IS WHERE YOU WANTED TO GO?! THE 63 BUILDING ?!!
...HAVE YOU BEEN HERE BEFORE?
WHEN I WAS FOUR... WITH MY FAMILY. BUT I DON'T REMEMBER IT.
YOU?
THAT'S CRAZY TALL!!
YEAH, NO KIDDING!
WELL, IT'S MY FIRST TIME. SINCE WE LIVE NEAR SEOUL, DON'T YOU THINK IT'D BE NICE TO VISIT IT ONCE BEFORE I DIE?

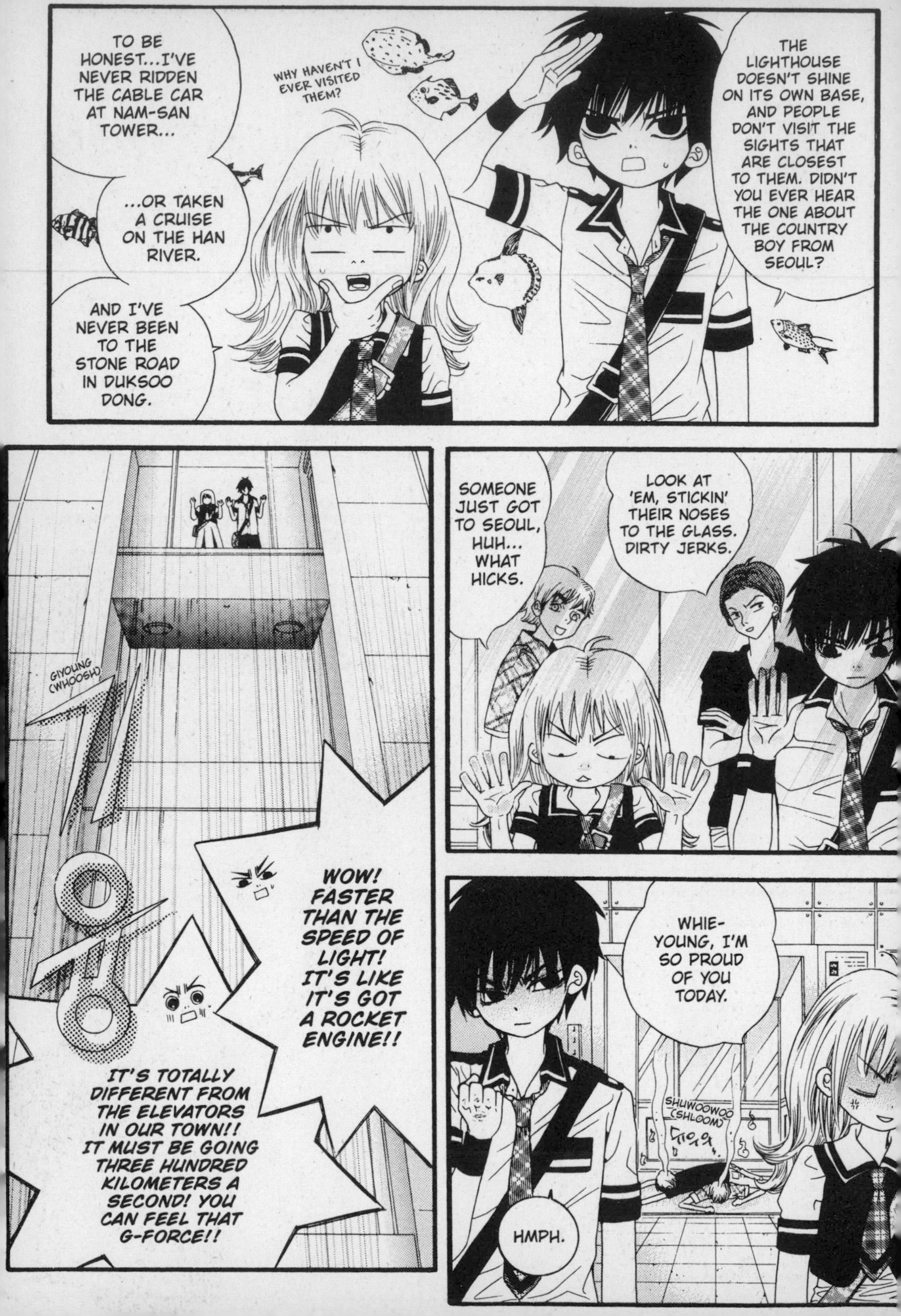
TO BE HONEST...I'VE NEVER RIDDEN THE CABLE CAR AT NAM-SAN TOWER...
WHY HAVEN'T I EVER VISITED THEM?
...OR TAKEN A CRUISE ON THE HAN RIVER.
AND I'VE NEVER BEEN TO THE STONE ROAD IN DUKSOO DONG.
THE LIGHTHOUSE DOESN'T SHINE ON ITS OWN BASE, AND PEOPLE DON'T VISIT THE SIGHTS THAT ARE CLOSEST TO THEM. DIDN'T YOU EVER HEAR THE ONE ABOUT THE COUNTRY BOY FROM SEOUL?
GIYOUNG (WHOOSH)
WOW! FASTER THAN THE SPEED OF LIGHT! IT'S LIKE IT'S GOT A ROCKET ENGINE!!
IT'S TOTALLY DIFFERENT FROM THE ELEVATORS IN OUR TOWN!! IT MUST BE GOING THREE HUNDRED KILOMETERS A SECOND! YOU CAN FEEL THAT G-FORCE!!
SOMEONE JUST GOT TO SEOUL, HUH... WHAT HICKS.
LOOK AT 'EM, STICKIN' THEIR NOSES TO THE GLASS. DIRTY JERKS.
WHIE-YOUNG, I'M SO PROUD OF YOU TODAY.
SHUWOOWOO (SHLOOM)
HMPH.

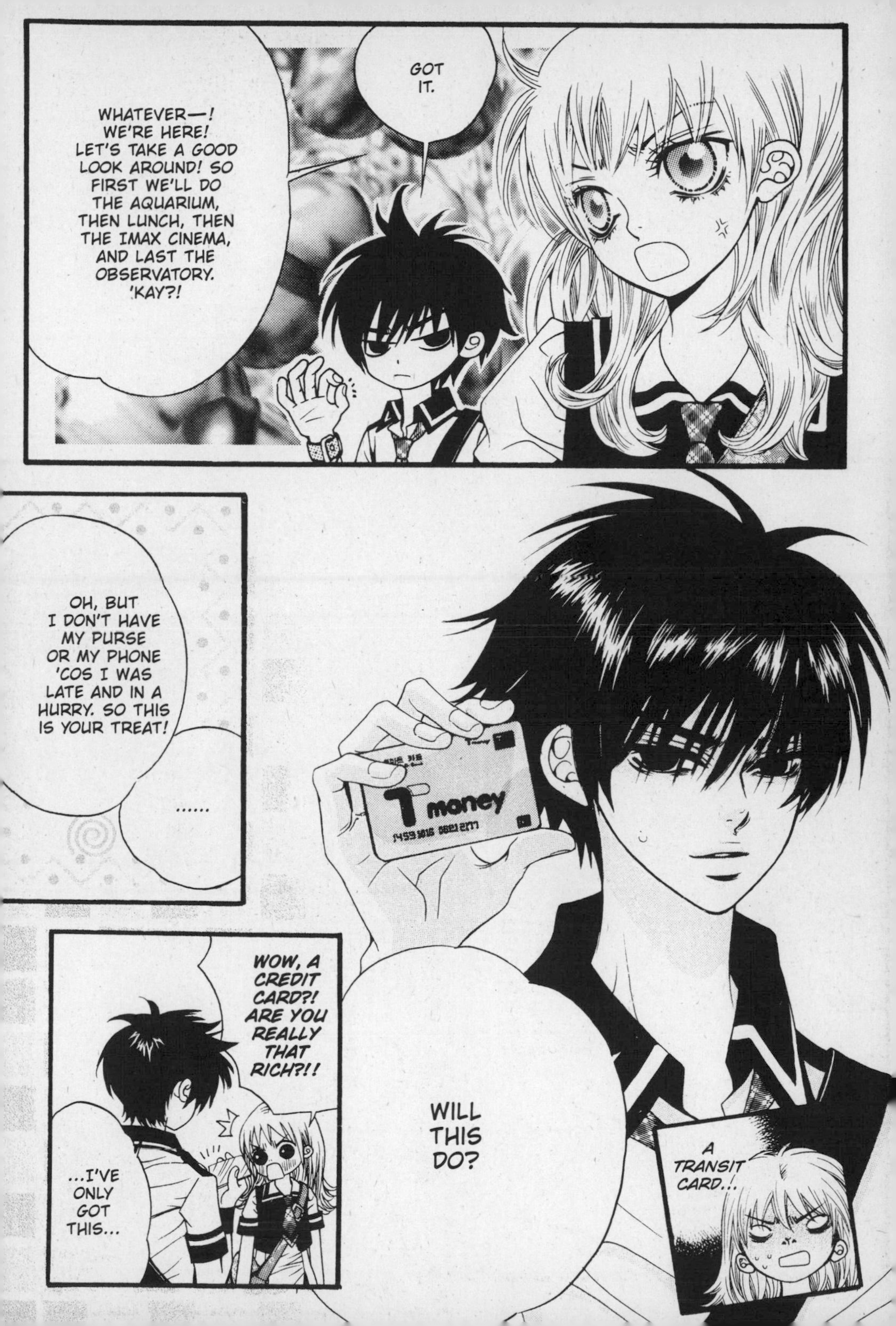
WHATEVER—! WE'RE HERE! LET'S TAKE A GOOD LOOK AROUND! SO FIRST WE'LL DO THE AQUARIUM, THEN LUNCH, THEN THE IMAX CINEMA, AND LAST THE OBSERVATORY. 'KAY?!
GOT IT.
OH, BUT I DON'T HAVE MY PURSE OR MY PHONE 'COS I WAS LATE AND IN A HURRY. SO THIS IS YOUR TREAT!
......
WOW, A CREDIT CARD?! ARE YOU REALLY THAT RICH?!!
...I'VE ONLY GOT THIS...
T money
WILL THIS DO?
A TRANSIT CARD..

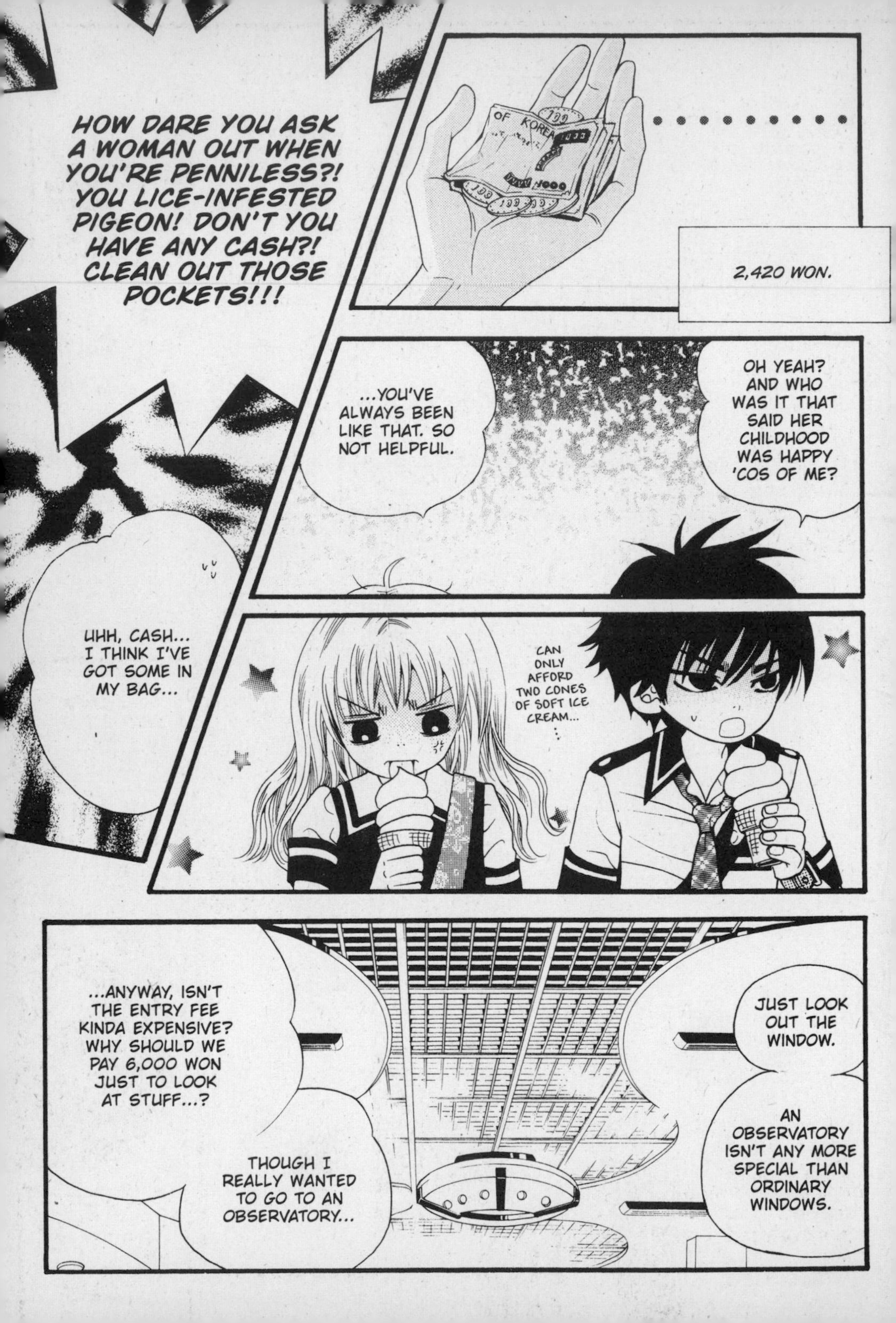
HOW DARE YOU ASK A WOMAN OUT WHEN YOU'RE PENNILESS?! YOU LICE-INFESTED PIGEON! DON'T YOU HAVE ANY CASH?! CLEAN OUT THOSE POCKETS!!!
UHH, CASH... I THINK I'VE GOT SOME IN MY BAG...
OF KOREA
2,420 WON.
...YOU'VE ALWAYS BEEN LIKE THAT. SO NOT HELPFUL.
OH YEAH? AND WHO WAS IT THAT SAID HER CHILDHOOD WAS HAPPY 'COS OF ME?
CAN ONLY AFFORD TWO CONES OF SOFT ICE CREAM...
...ANYWAY, ISN'T THE ENTRY FEE KINDA EXPENSIVE? WHY SHOULD WE PAY 6,000 WON JUST TO LOOK AT STUFF...?
THOUGH I REALLY WANTED TO GO TO AN OBSERVATORY...
JUST LOOK OUT THE WINDOW.
AN OBSERVATORY ISN'T ANY MORE SPECIAL THAN ORDINARY WINDOWS.

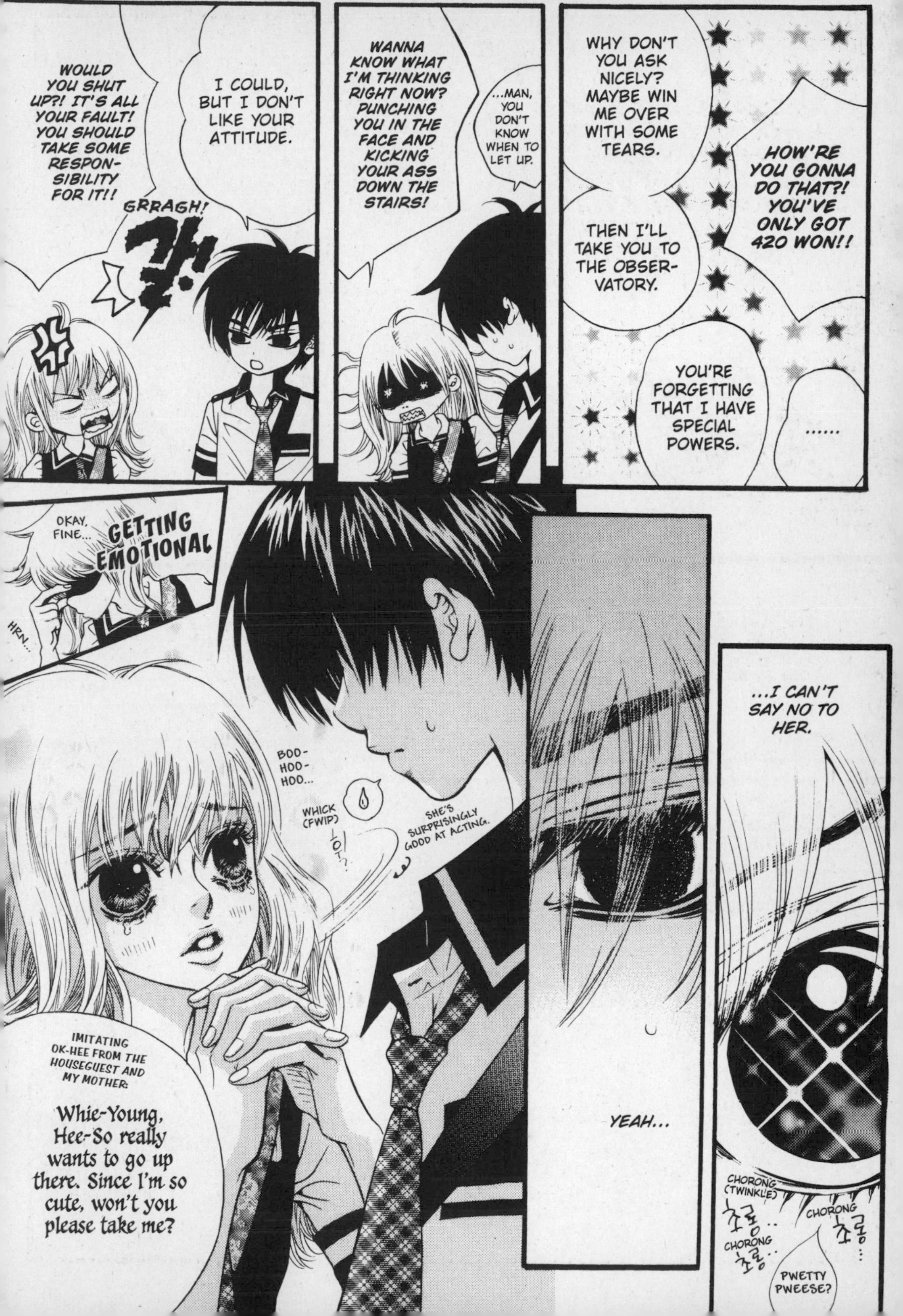
WOULD YOU SHUT UP?! IT'S ALL YOUR FAULT! YOU SHOULD TAKE SOME RESPON-SIBILITY FOR IT!!
I COULD, BUT I DON'T LIKE YOUR ATTITUDE.
GRRAGH!
WANNA KNOW WHAT I'M THINKING RIGHT NOW? PUNCHING YOU IN THE FACE AND KICKING YOUR ASS DOWN THE STAIRS!
...MAN, YOU DON'T KNOW WHEN TO LET UP.
WHY DON'T YOU ASK NICELY? MAYBE WIN ME OVER WITH SOME TEARS.
HOW'RE YOU GONNA DO THAT?! YOU'VE ONLY GOT 420 WON!!
THEN I'LL TAKE YOU TO THE OBSER-VATORY.
YOU'RE FORGETTING THAT I HAVE SPECIAL POWERS.
......
OKAY, FINE...
GETTING EMOTIONAL
HRN...
BOO-HOO-HOO...
WHICK (FWIP)
SHE'S SURPRISINGLY GOOD AT ACTING.
IMITATING OK-HEE FROM THE HOUSEGUEST AND MY MOTHER:
Whie-Young, Hee-So really wants to go up there. Since I'm so cute, won't you please take me?
YEAH...
...I CAN'T SAY NO TO HER.
CHORONG (TWINKLE)
CHORONG
CHORONG
PWETTY PWEESE?

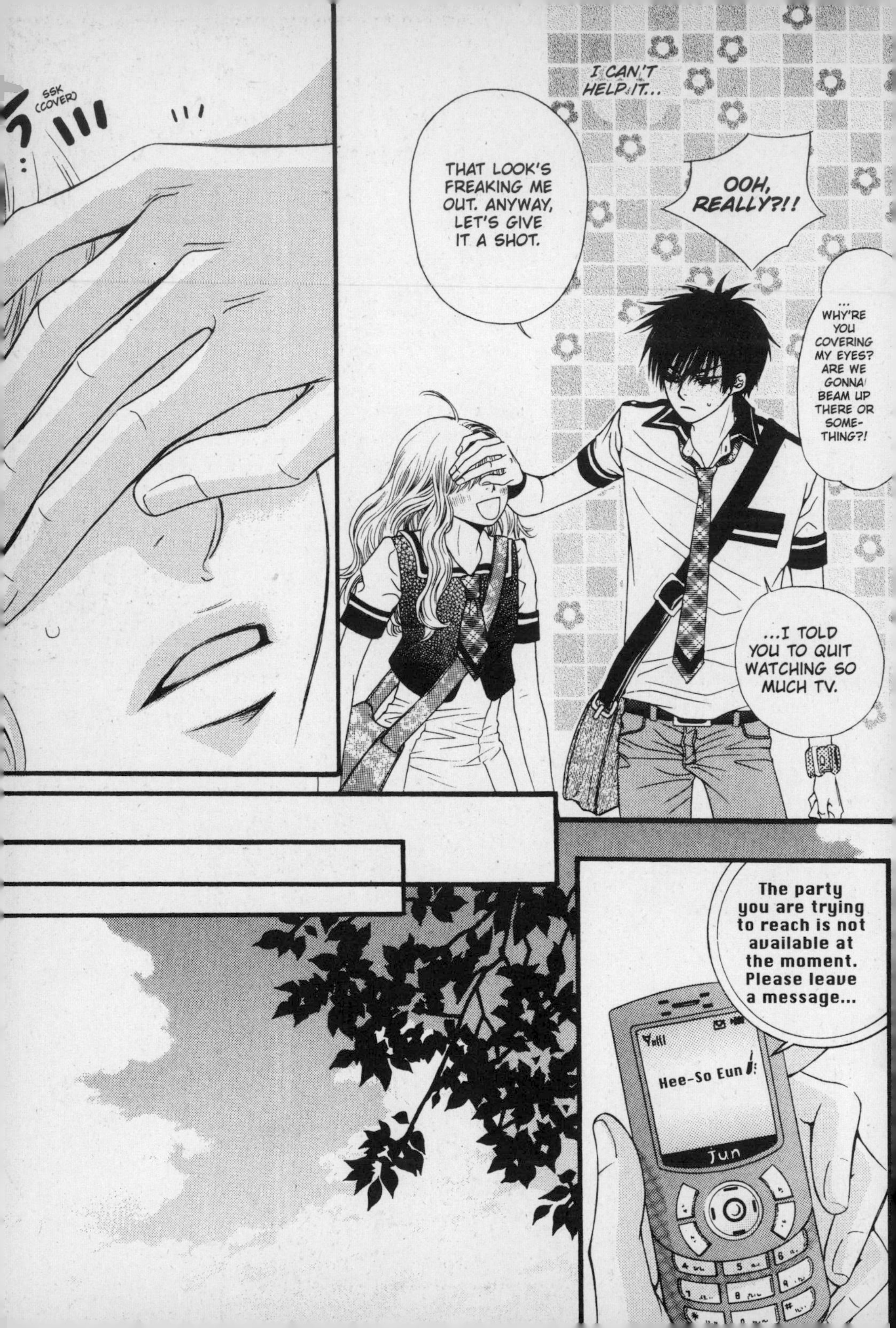
SSK (COVER)
I CAN'T HELP IT...
THAT LOOK'S FREAKING ME OUT. ANYWAY, LET'S GIVE IT A SHOT.
OOH, REALLY?!!
... WHY'RE YOU COVERING MY EYES? ARE WE GONNA BEAM UP THERE OR SOME-THING?!
...I TOLD YOU TO QUIT WATCHING SO MUCH TV.
The party you are trying to reach is not available at the moment. Please leave a message...
Hee-So Eun
jun

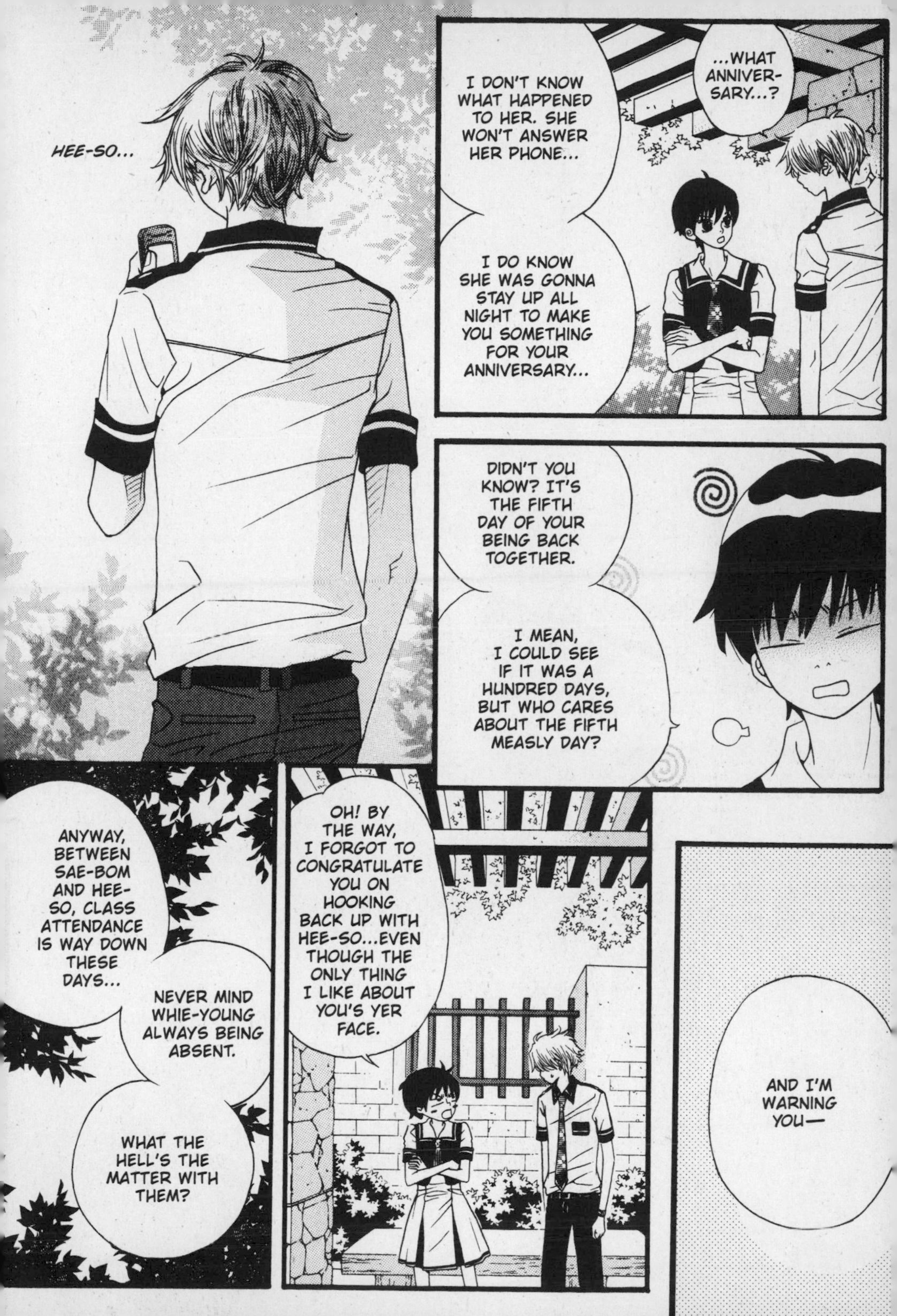
HEE-SO...
I DON'T KNOW WHAT HAPPENED TO HER. SHE WON'T ANSWER HER PHONE...
I DO KNOW SHE WAS GONNA STAY UP ALL NIGHT TO MAKE YOU SOMETHING FOR YOUR ANNIVERSARY...
...WHAT ANNIVER-SARY...?
DIDN'T YOU KNOW? IT'S THE FIFTH DAY OF YOUR BEING BACK TOGETHER.
I MEAN, I COULD SEE IF IT WAS A HUNDRED DAYS, BUT WHO CARES ABOUT THE FIFTH MEASLY DAY?
ANYWAY, BETWEEN SAE-BOM AND HEE-SO, CLASS ATTENDANCE IS WAY DOWN THESE DAYS...
NEVER MIND WHIE-YOUNG ALWAYS BEING ABSENT.
WHAT THE HELL'S THE MATTER WITH THEM?
OH! BY THE WAY, I FORGOT TO CONGRATULATE YOU ON HOOKING BACK UP WITH HEE-SO...EVEN THOUGH THE ONLY THING I LIKE ABOUT YOU'S YER FACE.
AND I'M WARNING YOU—

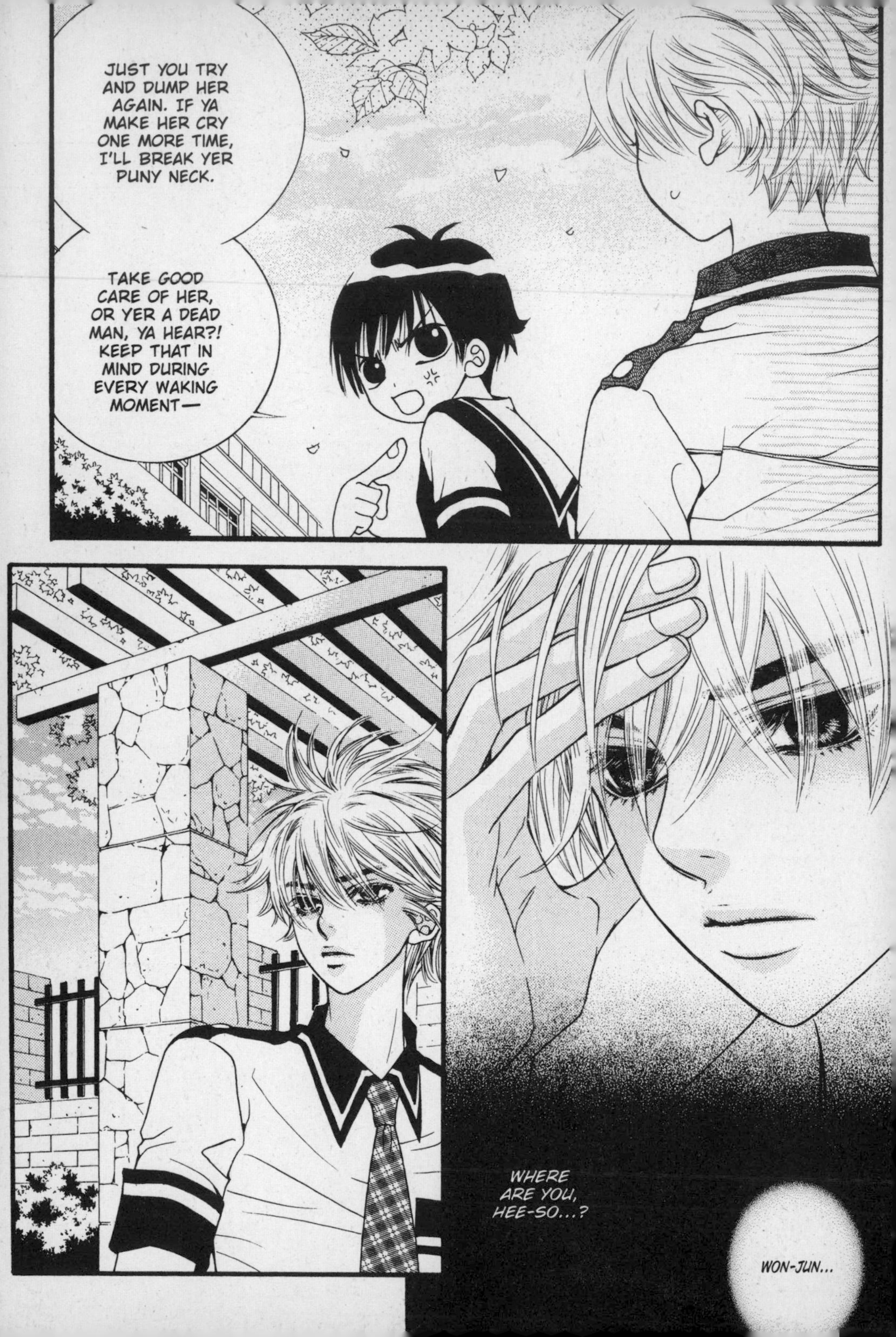
JUST YOU TRY AND DUMP HER AGAIN. IF YA MAKE HER CRY ONE MORE TIME, I'LL BREAK YER PUNY NECK.
TAKE GOOD CARE OF HER, OR YER A DEAD MAN, YA HEAR?! KEEP THAT IN MIND DURING EVERY WAKING MOMENT—
WHERE ARE YOU, HEE-SO...?
WON-JUN...

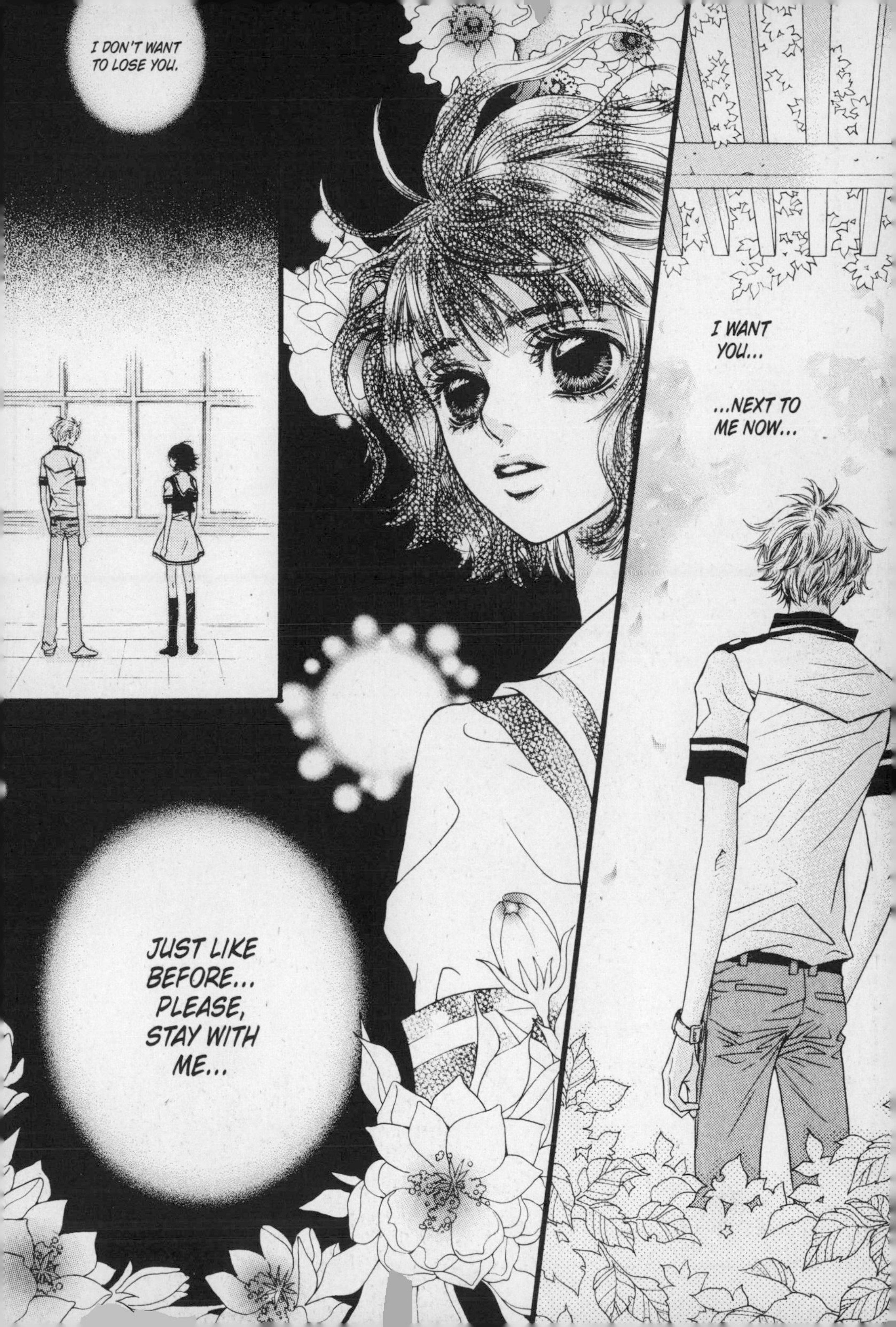
I DON'T WANT TO LOSE YOU.
JUST LIKE BEFORE... PLEASE, STAY WITH ME...
I WANT YOU...
...NEXT TO ME NOW...

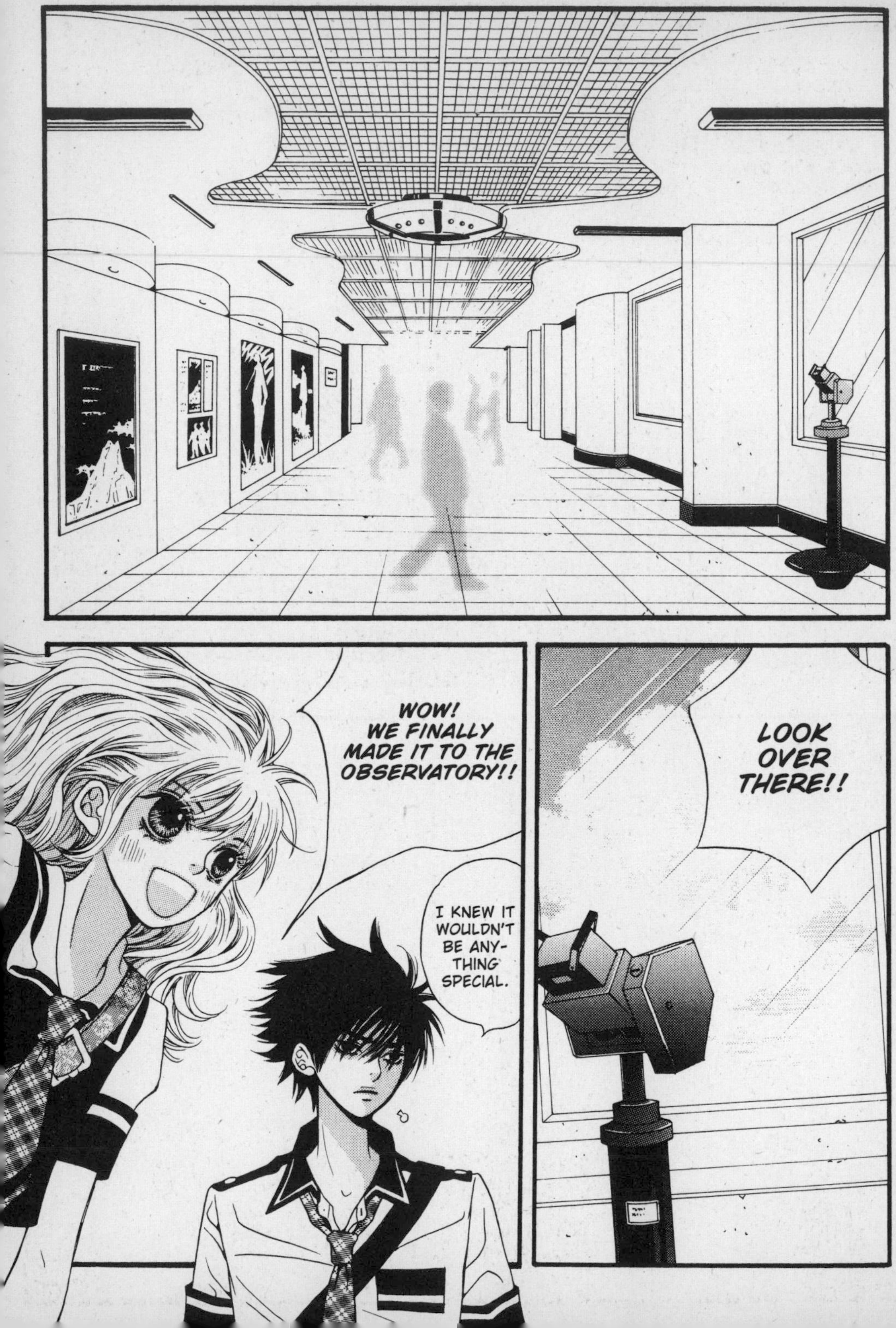
WOW! WE FINALLY MADE IT TO THE OBSERVATORY!!
I KNEW IT WOULDN'T BE ANY-THING SPECIAL.
LOOK OVER THERE!!

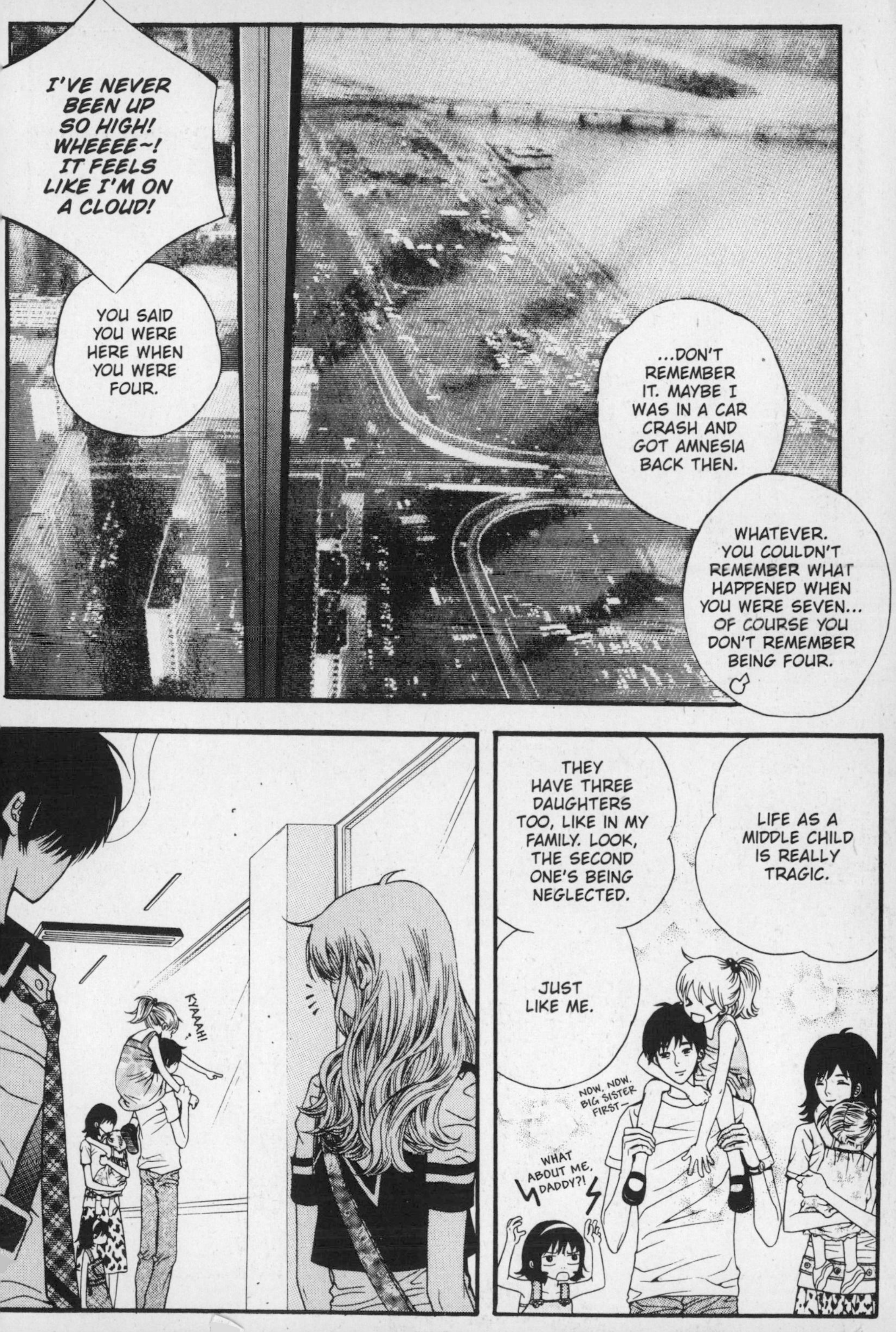

I'VE NEVER BEEN UP SO HIGH! WHEEEE~! IT FEELS LIKE I'M ON A CLOUD!
YOU SAID YOU WERE HERE WHEN YOU WERE FOUR.
...DON'T REMEMBER IT. MAYBE I WAS IN A CAR CRASH AND GOT AMNESIA BACK THEN.
WHATEVER. YOU COULDN'T REMEMBER WHAT HAPPENED WHEN YOU WERE SEVEN... OF COURSE YOU DON'T REMEMBER BEING FOUR.
KYAAAH!
THEY HAVE THREE DAUGHTERS TOO, LIKE IN MY FAMILY. LOOK, THE SECOND ONE'S BEING NEGLECTED.
LIFE AS A MIDDLE CHILD IS REALLY TRAGIC.
JUST LIKE ME.
NOW, NOW. BIG SISTER FIRST—
WHAT ABOUT ME, DADDY?!

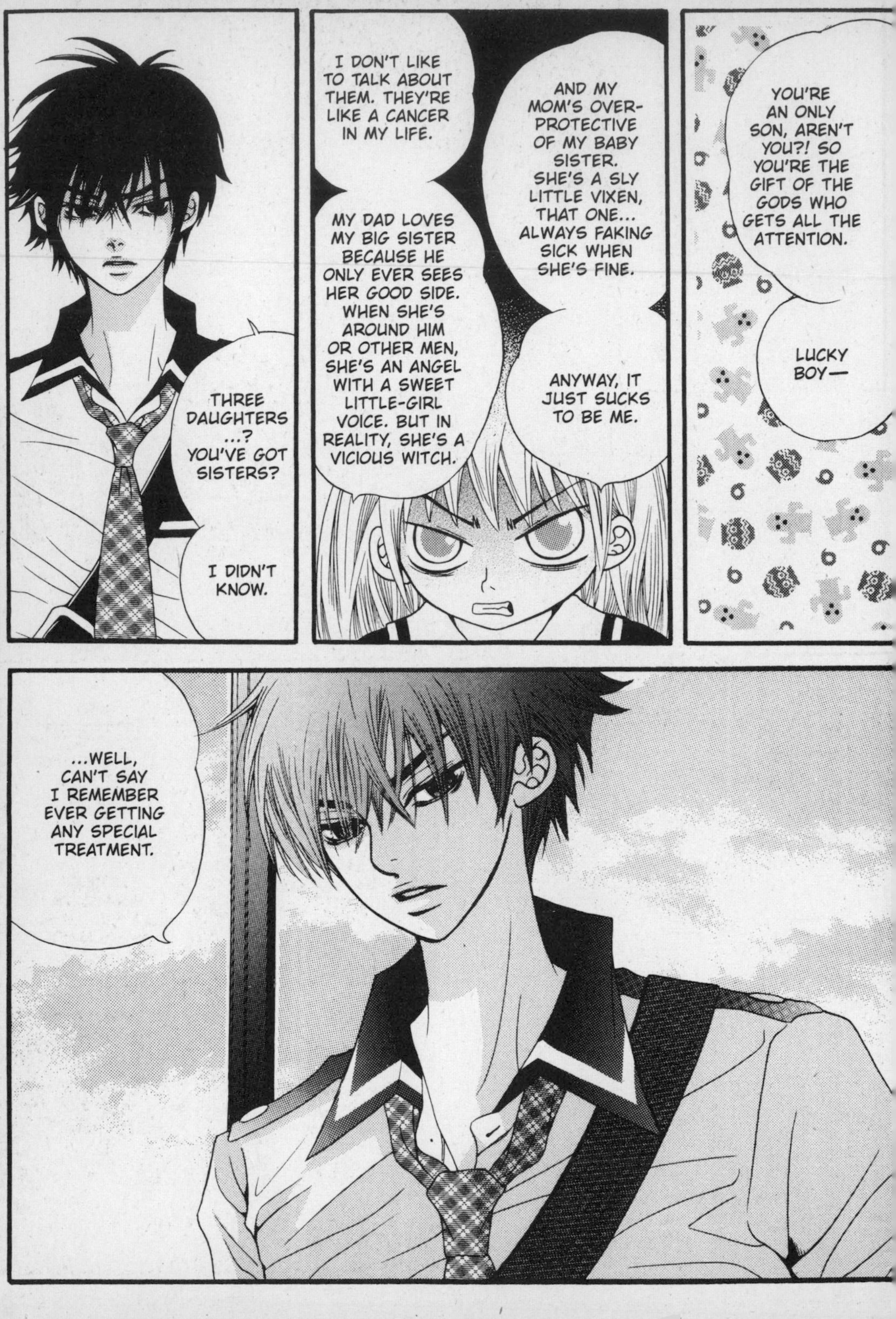
THREE DAUGHTERS ...? YOU'VE GOT SISTERS?
I DIDN'T KNOW.
I DON'T LIKE TO TALK ABOUT THEM. THEY'RE LIKE A CANCER IN MY LIFE.
MY DAD LOVES MY BIG SISTER BECAUSE HE ONLY EVER SEES HER GOOD SIDE. WHEN SHE'S AROUND HIM OR OTHER MEN, SHE'S AN ANGEL WITH A SWEET LITTLE-GIRL VOICE. BUT IN REALITY, SHE'S A VICIOUS WITCH.
AND MY MOM'S OVER-PROTECTIVE OF MY BABY SISTER. SHE'S A SLY LITTLE VIXEN, THAT ONE... ALWAYS FAKING SICK WHEN SHE'S FINE.
ANYWAY, IT JUST SUCKS TO BE ME.
YOU'RE AN ONLY SON, AREN'T YOU?! SO YOU'RE THE GIFT OF THE GODS WHO GETS ALL THE ATTENTION.
LUCKY BOY—
...WELL, CAN'T SAY I REMEMBER EVER GETTING ANY SPECIAL TREATMENT.

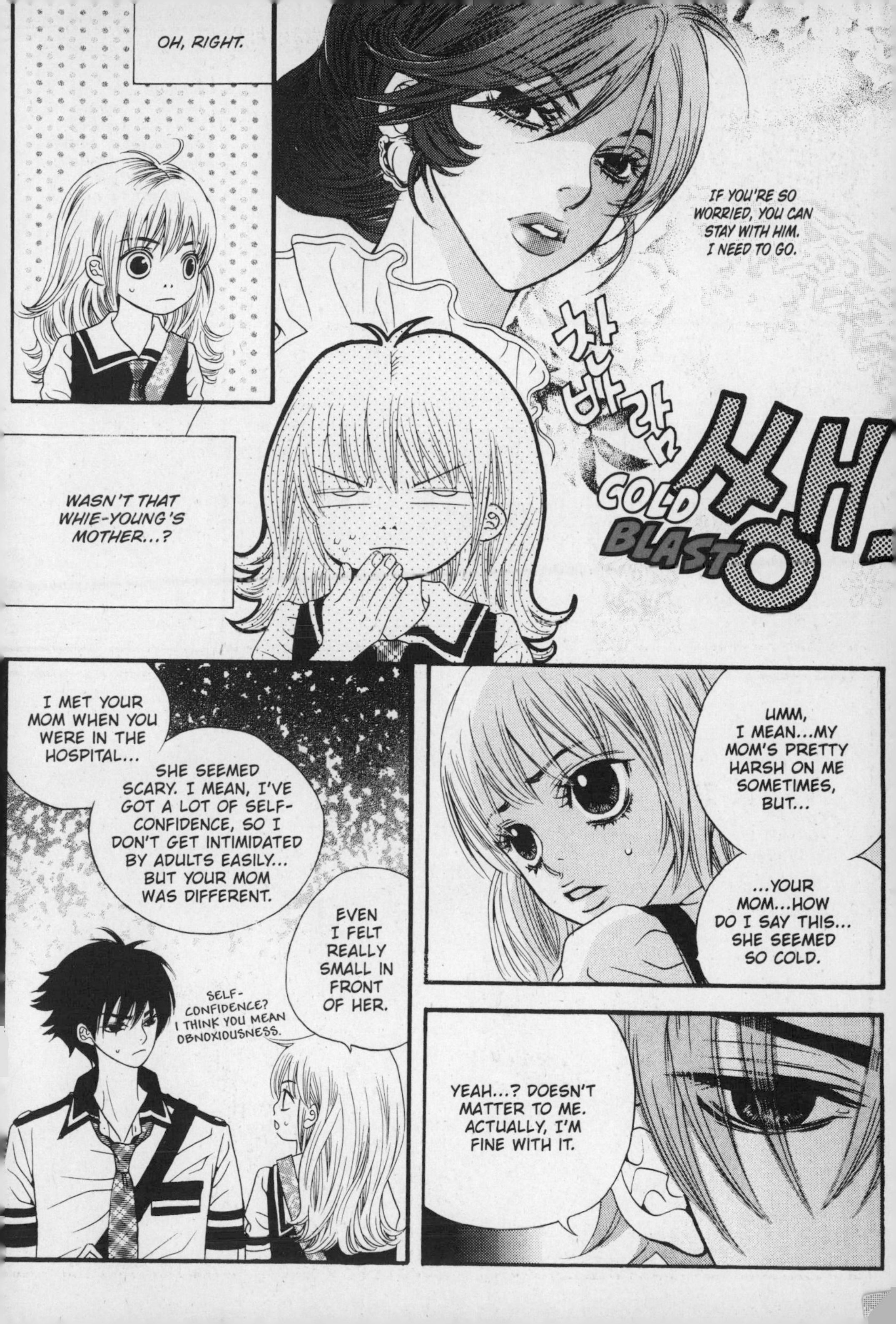
OH, RIGHT.
IF YOU'RE SO WORRIED, YOU CAN STAY WITH HIM. I NEED TO GO.
찬바람
쌩
COLD BLAST
WASN'T THAT WHIE-YOUNG'S MOTHER...?
I MET YOUR MOM WHEN YOU WERE IN THE HOSPITAL...
SHE SEEMED SCARY. I MEAN, I'VE GOT A LOT OF SELF-CONFIDENCE, SO I DON'T GET INTIMIDATED BY ADULTS EASILY... BUT YOUR MOM WAS DIFFERENT.
EVEN I FELT REALLY SMALL IN FRONT OF HER.
SELF-CONFIDENCE? I THINK YOU MEAN OBNOXIOUSNESS.
UMM, I MEAN...MY MOM'S PRETTY HARSH ON ME SOMETIMES, BUT...
...YOUR MOM...HOW DO I SAY THIS... SHE SEEMED SO COLD.
YEAH...? DOESN'T MATTER TO ME. ACTUALLY, I'M FINE WITH IT.

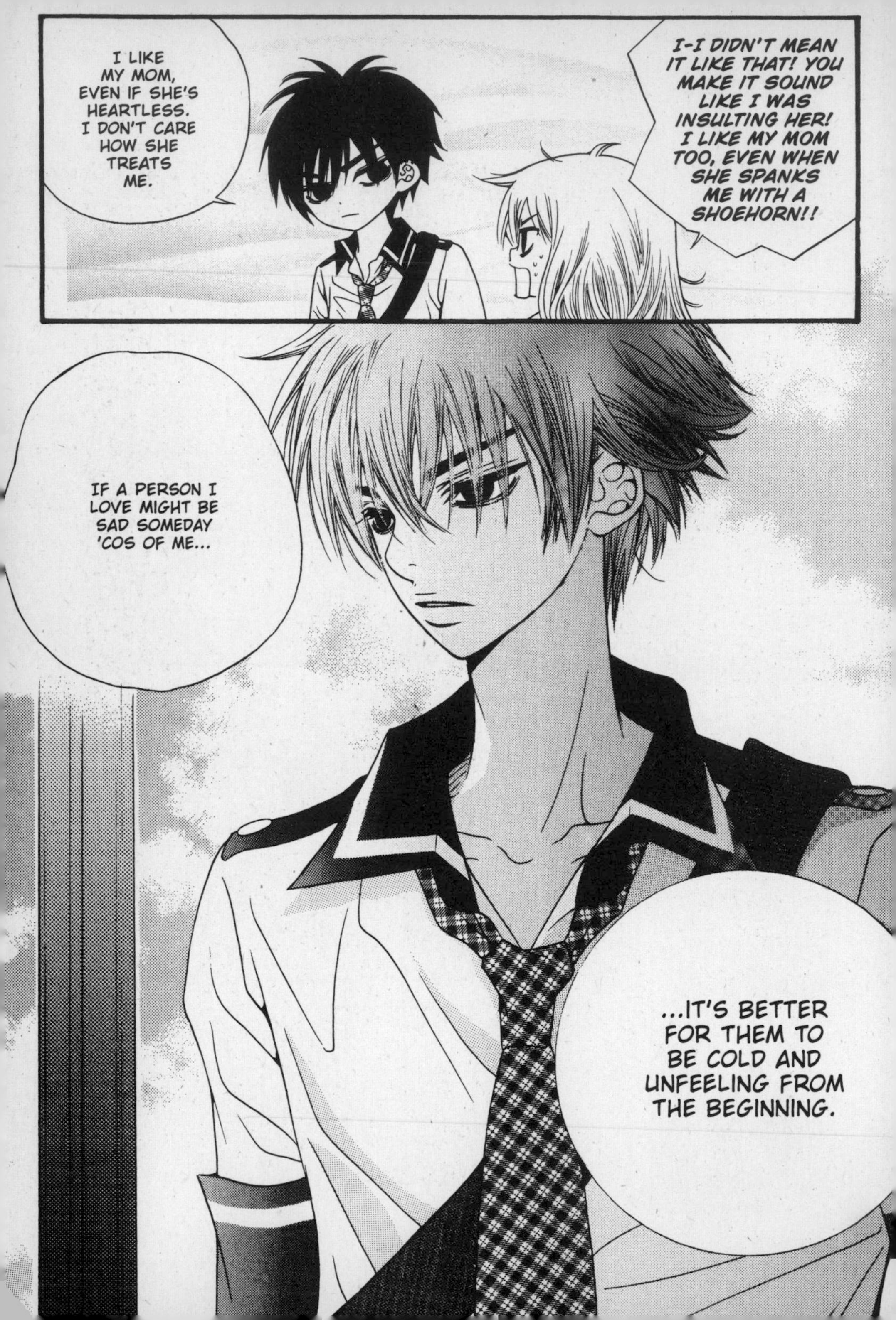
I LIKE MY MOM, EVEN IF SHE'S HEARTLESS. I DON'T CARE HOW SHE TREATS ME.
I-I DIDN'T MEAN IT LIKE THAT! YOU MAKE IT SOUND LIKE I WAS INSULTING HER! I LIKE MY MOM TOO, EVEN WHEN SHE SPANKS ME WITH A SHOEHORN!!
IF A PERSON I LOVE MIGHT BE SAD SOMEDAY 'COS OF ME...
...IT'S BETTER FOR THEM TO BE COLD AND UNFEELING FROM THE BEGINNING.

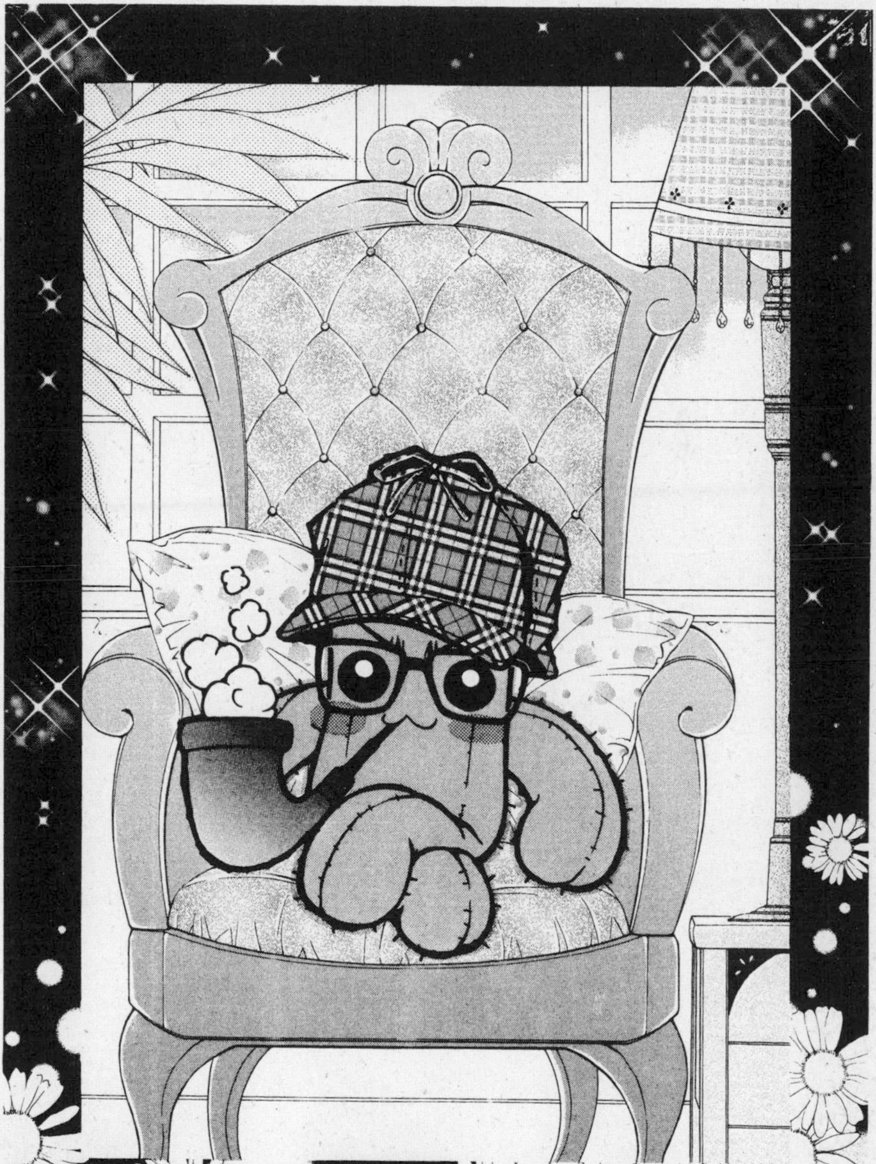

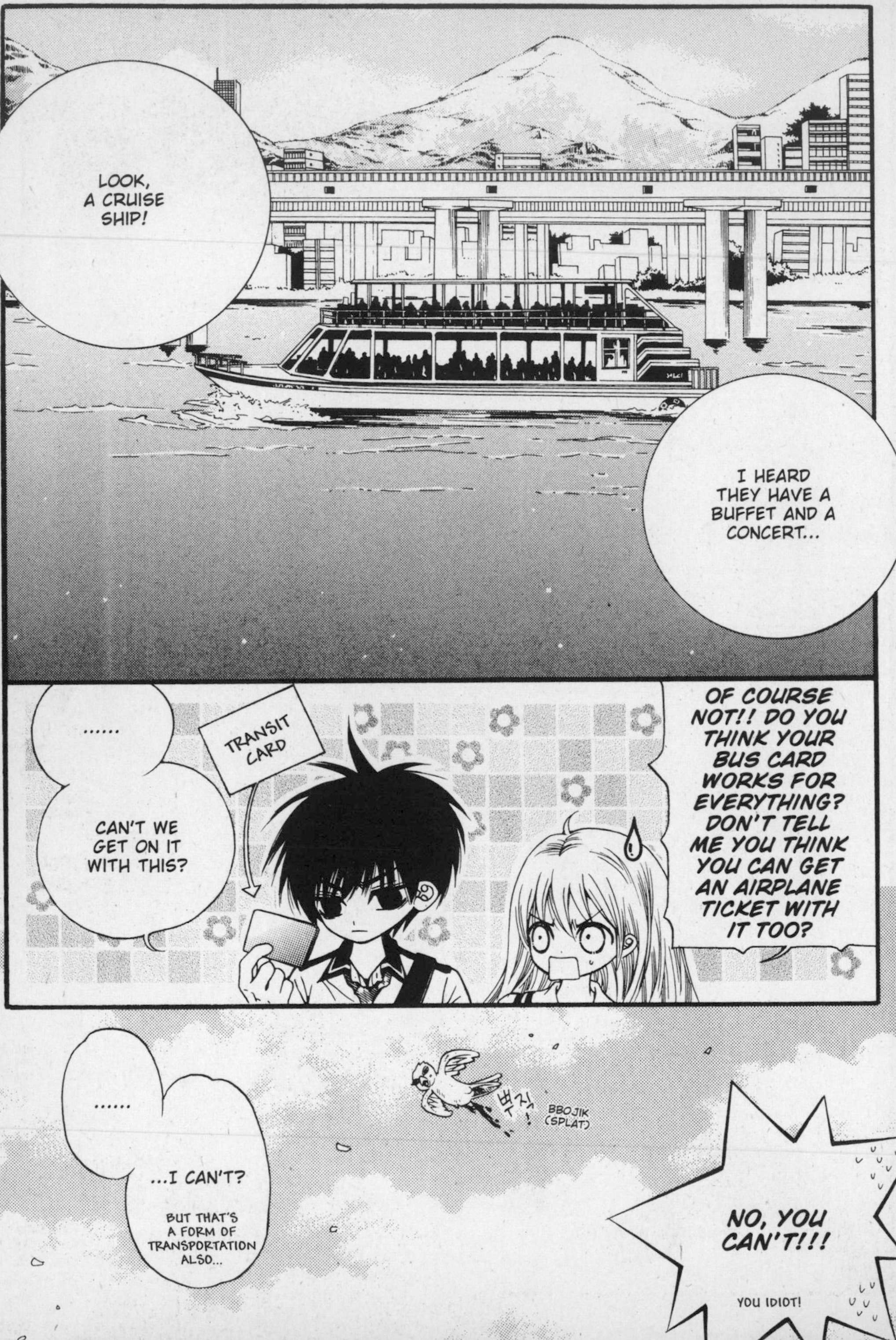
LOOK, A CRUISE SHIP!
I HEARD THEY HAVE A BUFFET AND A CONCERT...
......
CAN'T WE GET ON IT WITH THIS?
TRANSIT CARD
OF COURSE NOT!! DO YOU THINK YOUR BUS CARD WORKS FOR EVERYTHING? DON'T TELL ME YOU THINK YOU CAN GET AN AIRPLANE TICKET WITH IT TOO?
......
...I CAN'T?
BUT THAT'S A FORM OF TRANSPORTATION ALSO...
뽀직!
BBOJIK (SPLAT)
NO, YOU CAN'T!!!
YOU IDIOT!

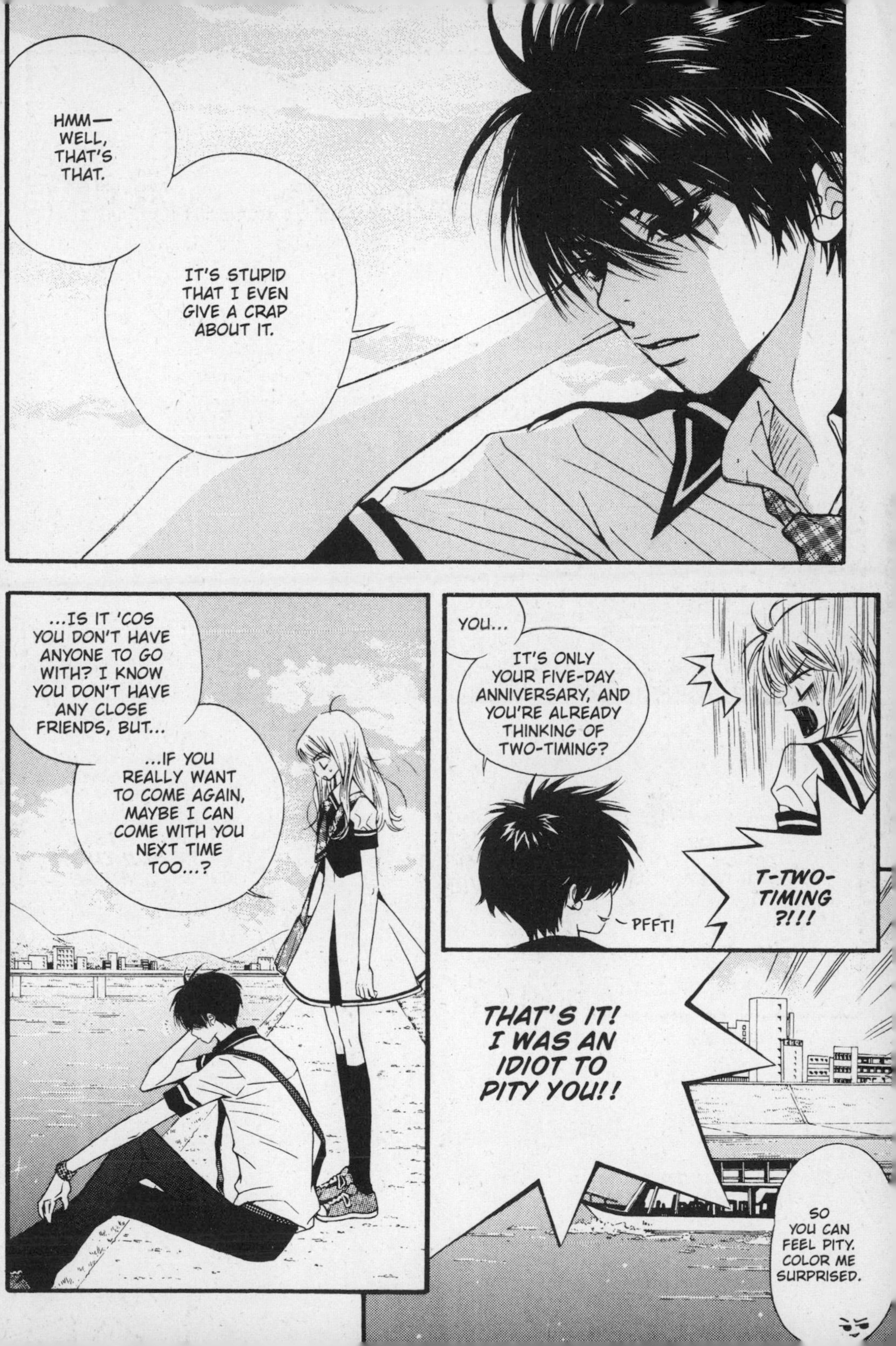
HMM— WELL, THAT'S THAT.
IT'S STUPID THAT I EVEN GIVE A CRAP ABOUT IT.
...IS IT 'COS YOU DON'T HAVE ANYONE TO GO WITH? I KNOW YOU DON'T HAVE ANY CLOSE FRIENDS, BUT...
...IF YOU REALLY WANT TO COME AGAIN, MAYBE I CAN COME WITH YOU NEXT TIME TOO...?
YOU...
IT'S ONLY YOUR FIVE-DAY ANNIVERSARY, AND YOU'RE ALREADY THINKING OF TWO-TIMING?
PFFT!
T-TWO-TIMING ?!!!
THAT'S IT! I WAS AN IDIOT TO PITY YOU!!
SO YOU CAN FEEL PITY. COLOR ME SURPRISED.

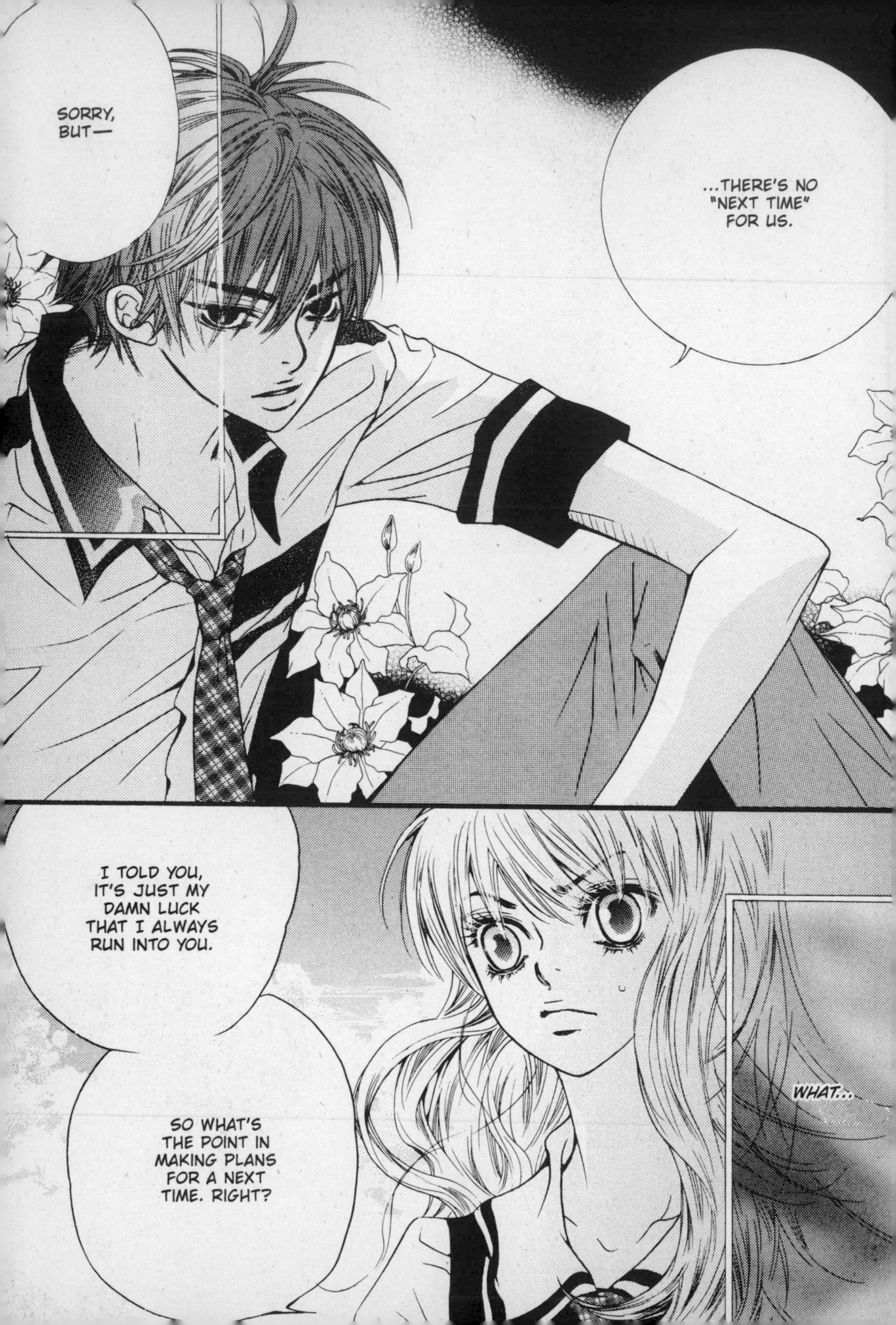
SORRY, BUT—
...THERE'S NO "NEXT TIME" FOR US.
I TOLD YOU, IT'S JUST MY DAMN LUCK THAT I ALWAYS RUN INTO YOU.
SO WHAT'S THE POINT IN MAKING PLANS FOR A NEXT TIME. RIGHT?
WHAT...

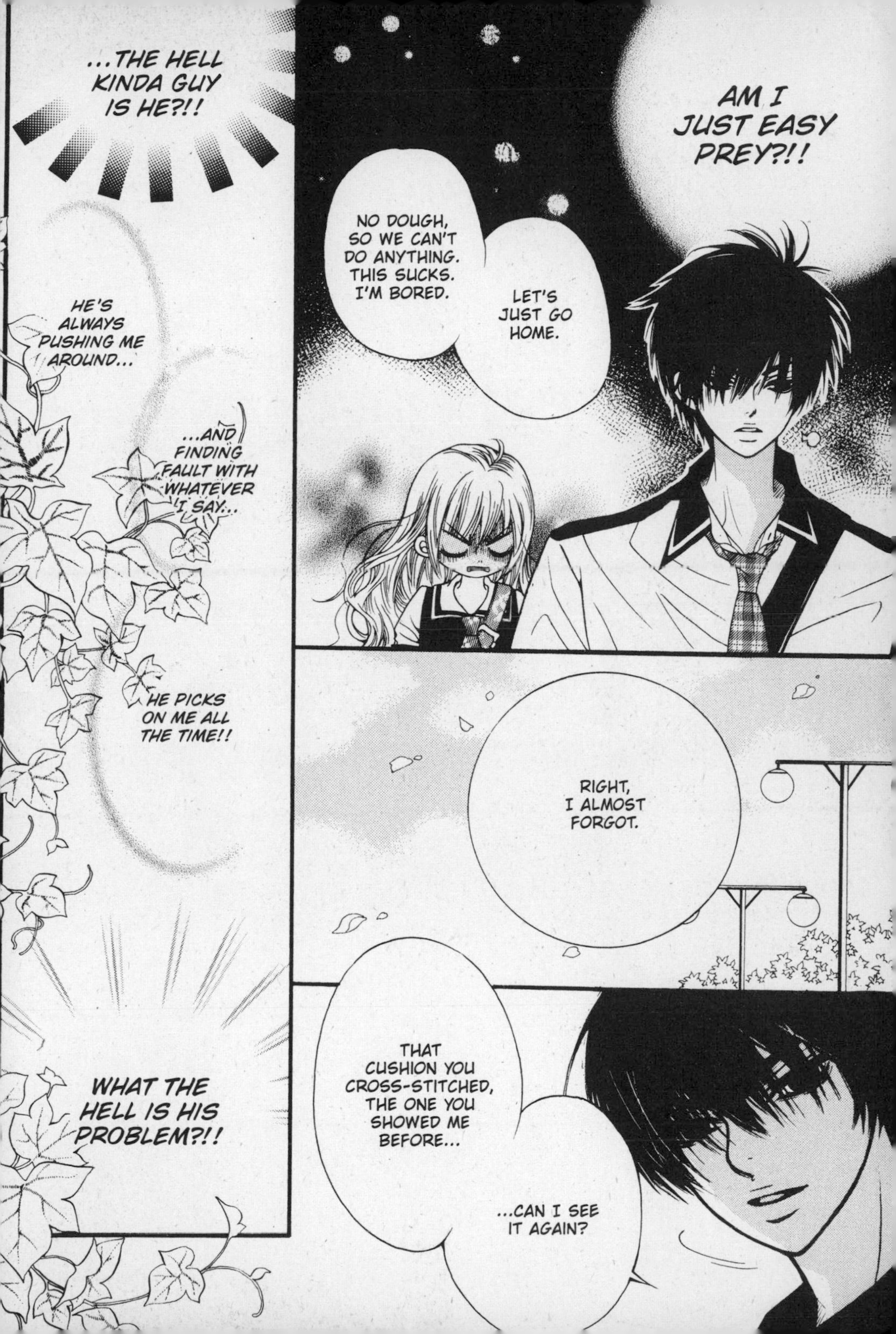
...THE HELL KINDA GUY IS HE?!!
HE'S ALWAYS PUSHING ME AROUND...
...AND FINDING FAULT WITH WHATEVER I SAY...
HE PICKS ON ME ALL THE TIME!!
WHAT THE HELL IS HIS PROBLEM?!!
NO DOUGH, SO WE CAN'T DO ANYTHING. THIS SUCKS. I'M BORED.
LET'S JUST GO HOME.
AM I JUST EASY PREY?!!
RIGHT, I ALMOST FORGOT.
THAT CUSHION YOU CROSS-STITCHED, THE ONE YOU SHOWED ME BEFORE...
...CAN I SEE IT AGAIN?

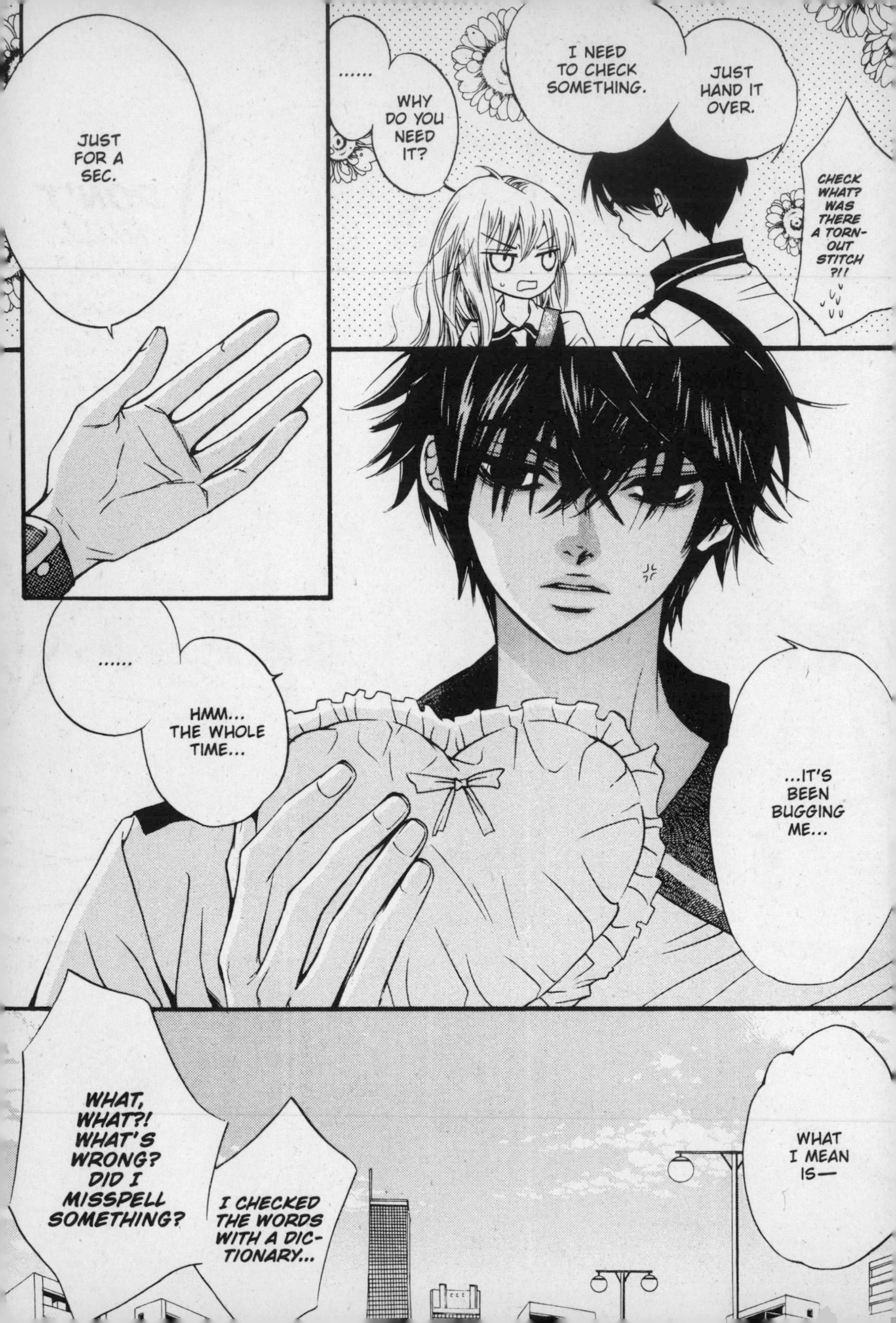
JUST FOR A SEC.
......
WHY DO YOU NEED IT?
I NEED TO CHECK SOMETHING.
JUST HAND IT OVER.
CHECK WHAT? WAS THERE A TORN-OUT STITCH ?!!
......
HMM... THE WHOLE TIME...
...IT'S BEEN BUGGING ME...
WHAT, WHAT?! WHAT'S WRONG? DID I MISSPELL SOMETHING?
I CHECKED THE WORDS WITH A DIC-TIONARY...
WHAT I MEAN IS—

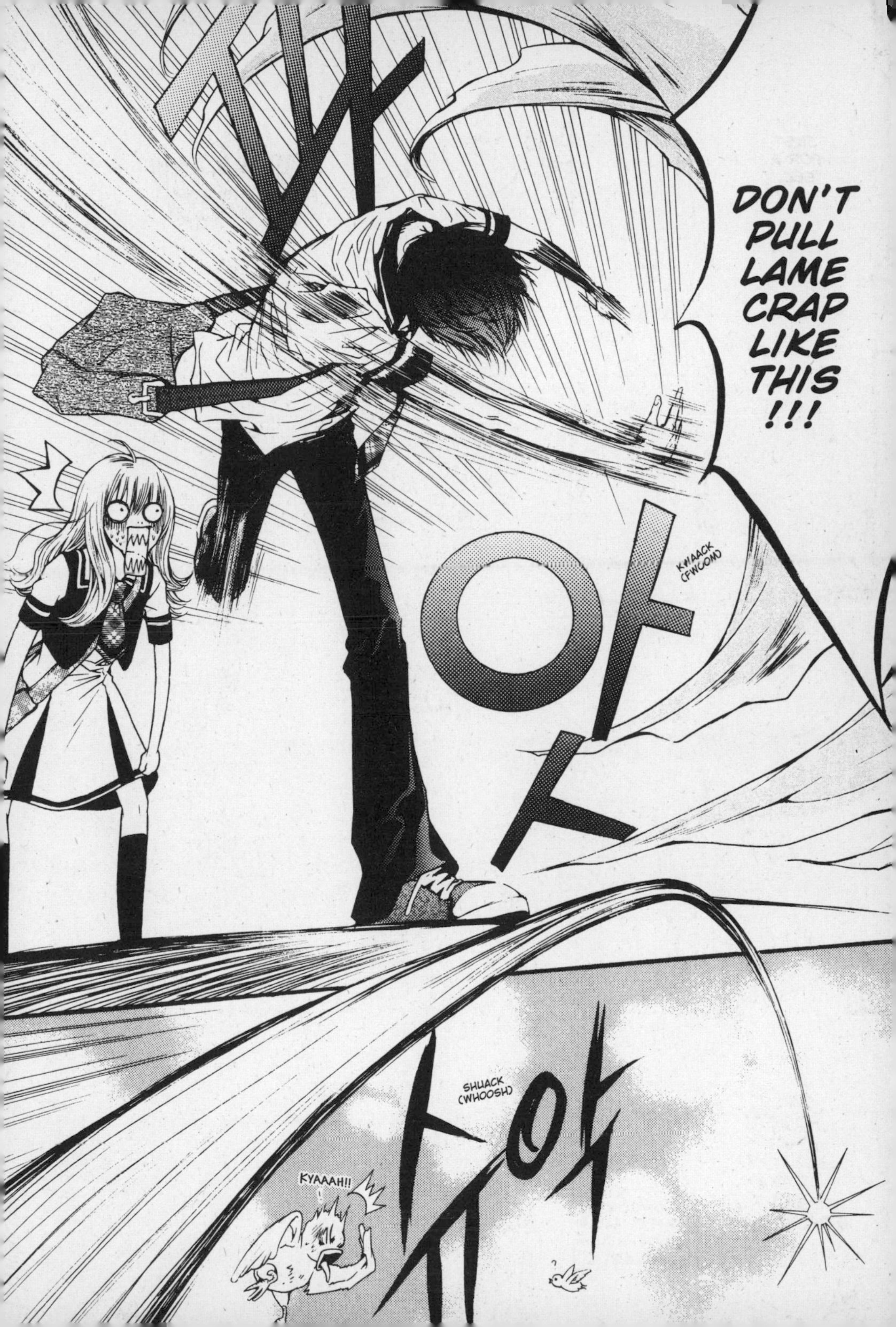
DON'T PULL LAME CRAP LIKE THIS!!!
KWAACK (FWOOM)
SHUACK (WHOOSH)
KYAAAH!!

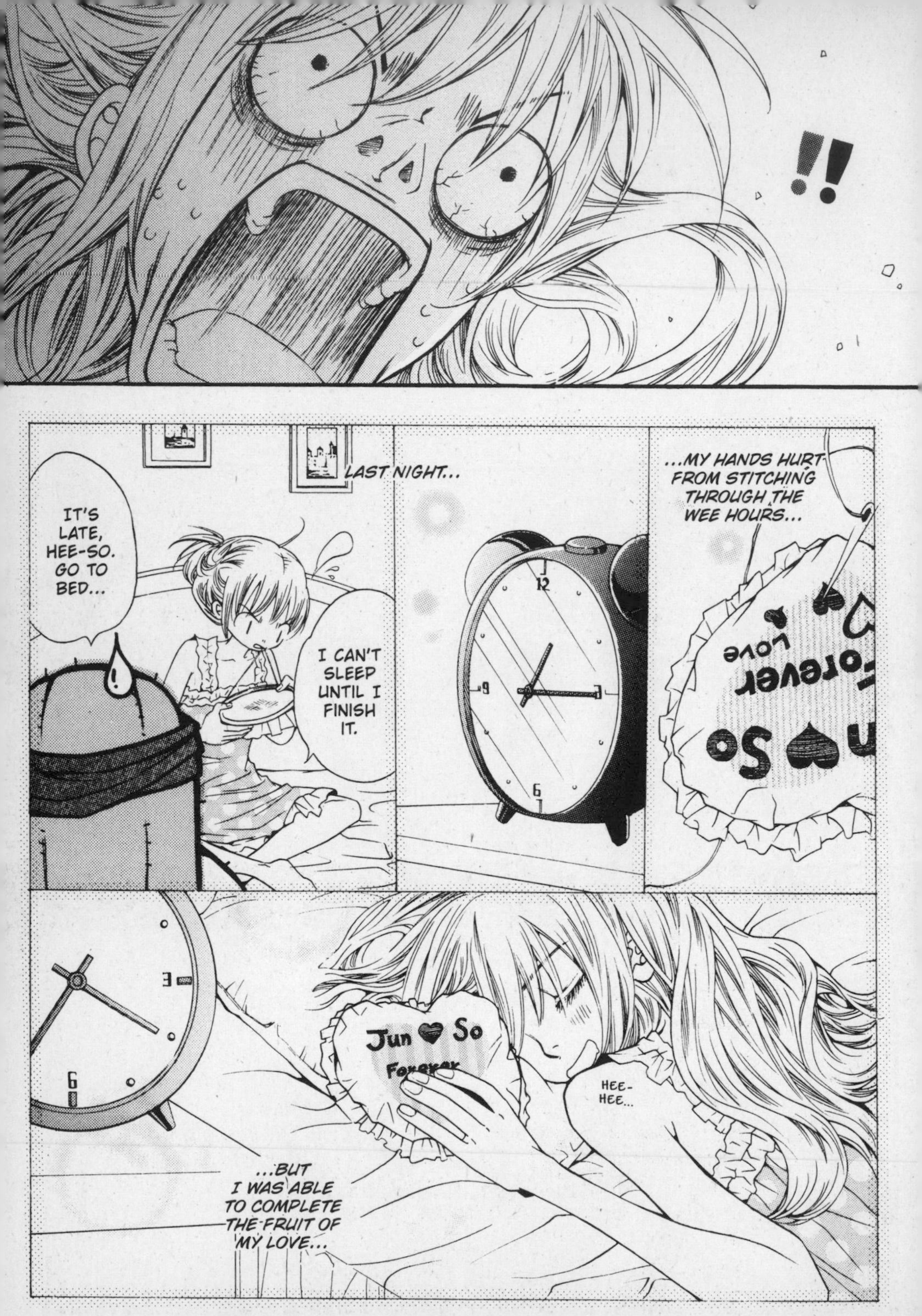
!!
LAST NIGHT...
IT'S LATE, HEE-SO. GO TO BED...
I CAN'T SLEEP UNTIL I FINISH IT.
...MY HANDS HURT FROM STITCHING THROUGH THE WEE HOURS...
Jun ♥ So
HEE-HEE...
...BUT I WAS ABLE TO COMPLETE THE FRUIT OF MY LOVE...

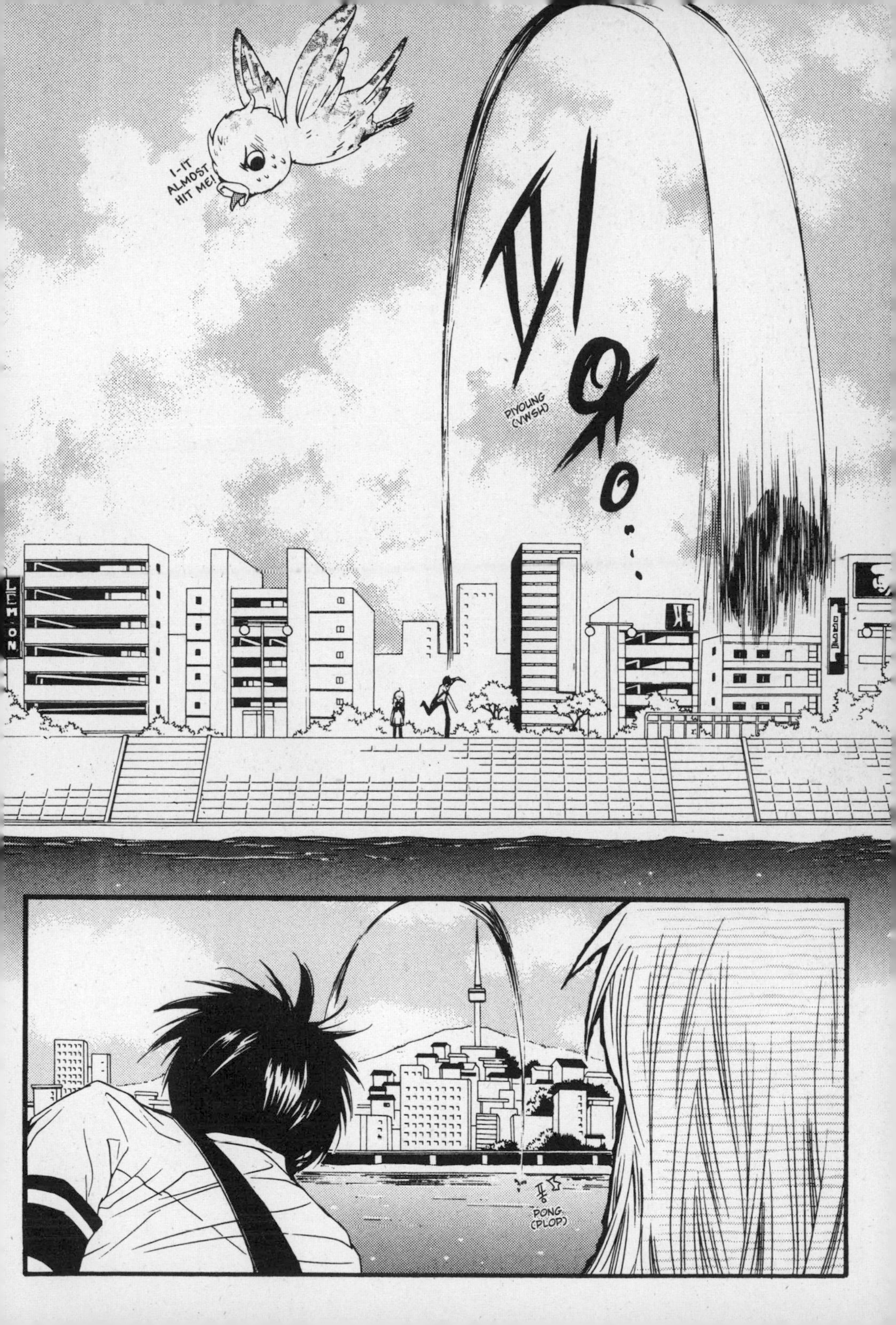
I-IT ALMOST HIT ME!
피용
PIYOUNG (VWSH)
LEMON
퐁
PONG (PLOP)

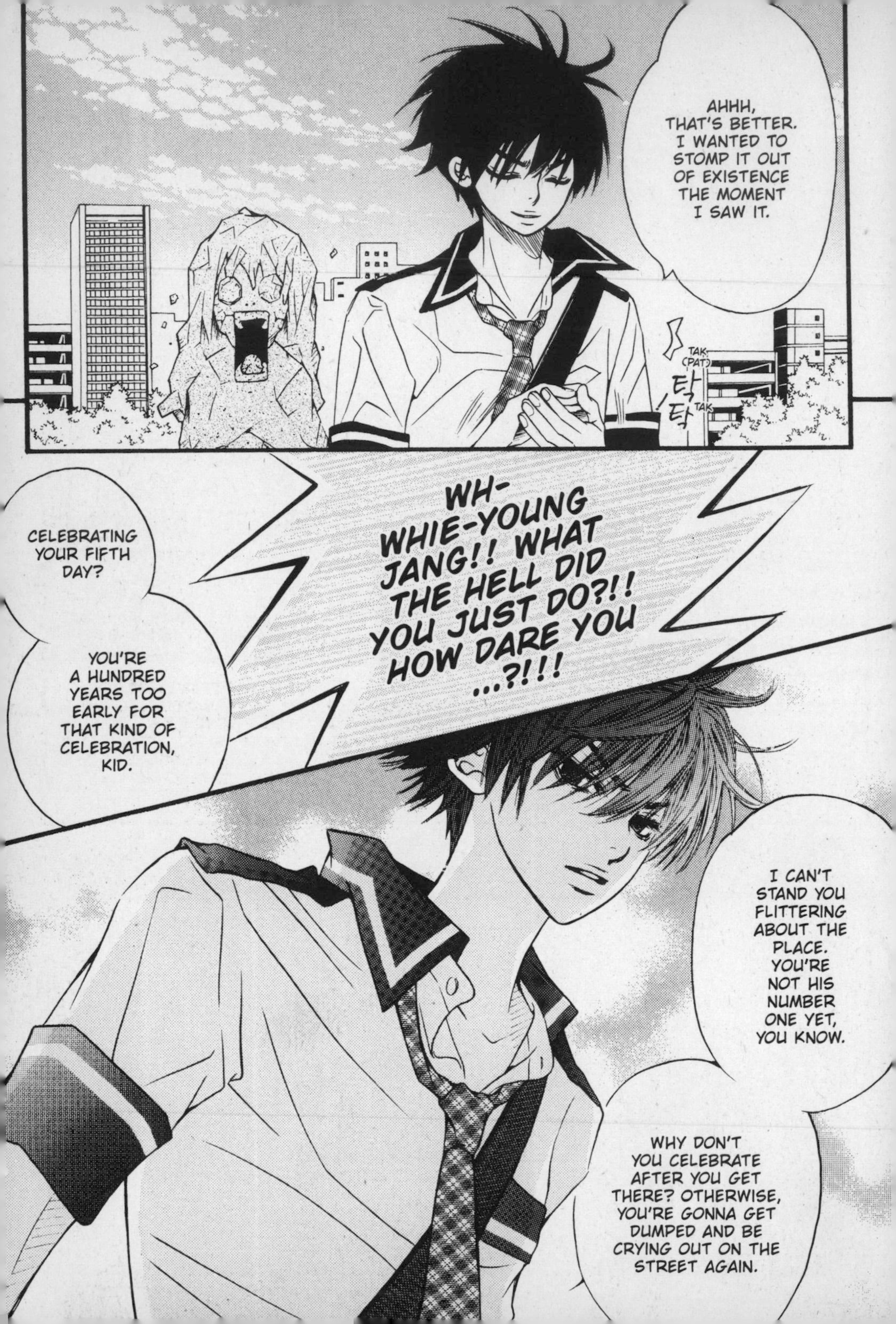
AHHH, THAT'S BETTER. I WANTED TO STOMP IT OUT OF EXISTENCE THE MOMENT I SAW IT.
TAK (PAT) 탁 탁 TAK
WH- WHIE-YOUNG JANG!! WHAT THE HELL DID YOU JUST DO?!! HOW DARE YOU ...?!!!
CELEBRATING YOUR FIFTH DAY?
YOU'RE A HUNDRED YEARS TOO EARLY FOR THAT KIND OF CELEBRATION, KID.
I CAN'T STAND YOU FLITTERING ABOUT THE PLACE. YOU'RE NOT HIS NUMBER ONE YET, YOU KNOW.
WHY DON'T YOU CELEBRATE AFTER YOU GET THERE? OTHERWISE, YOU'RE GONNA GET DUMPED AND BE CRYING OUT ON THE STREET AGAIN.

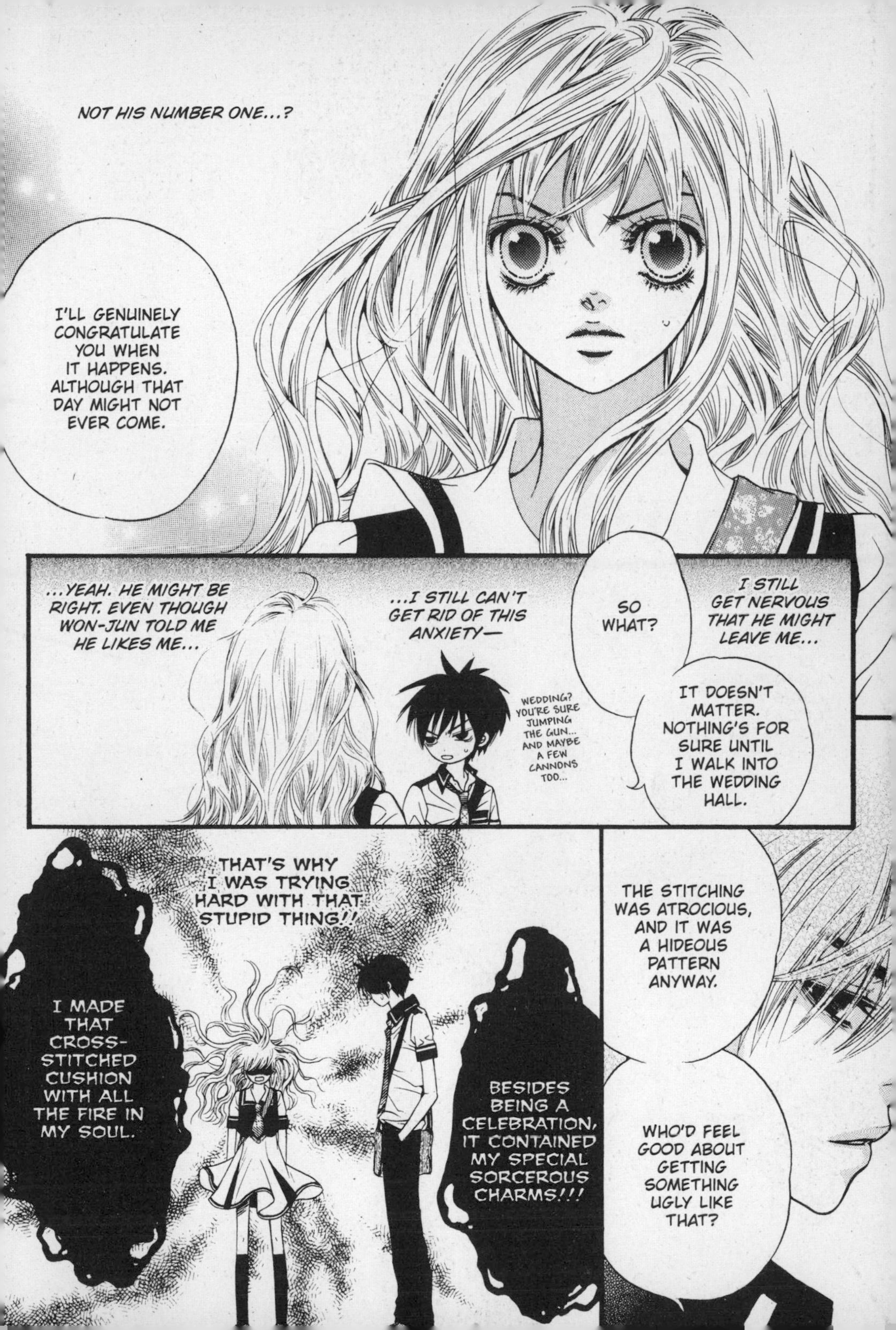
NOT HIS NUMBER ONE...?
I'LL GENUINELY CONGRATULATE YOU WHEN IT HAPPENS. ALTHOUGH THAT DAY MIGHT NOT EVER COME.
...YEAH. HE MIGHT BE RIGHT. EVEN THOUGH WON-JUN TOLD ME HE LIKES ME...
...I STILL CAN'T GET RID OF THIS ANXIETY—
WEDDING? YOU'RE SURE JUMPING THE GUN... AND MAYBE A FEW CANNONS TOO...
SO WHAT?
I STILL GET NERVOUS THAT HE MIGHT LEAVE ME...
IT DOESN'T MATTER. NOTHING'S FOR SURE UNTIL I WALK INTO THE WEDDING HALL.
THAT'S WHY I WAS TRYING HARD WITH THAT STUPID THING!!
I MADE THAT CROSS-STITCHED CUSHION WITH ALL THE FIRE IN MY SOUL.
BESIDES BEING A CELEBRATION, IT CONTAINED MY SPECIAL SORCEROUS CHARMS!!!
THE STITCHING WAS ATROCIOUS, AND IT WAS A HIDEOUS PATTERN ANYWAY.
WHO'D FEEL GOOD ABOUT GETTING SOMETHING UGLY LIKE THAT?

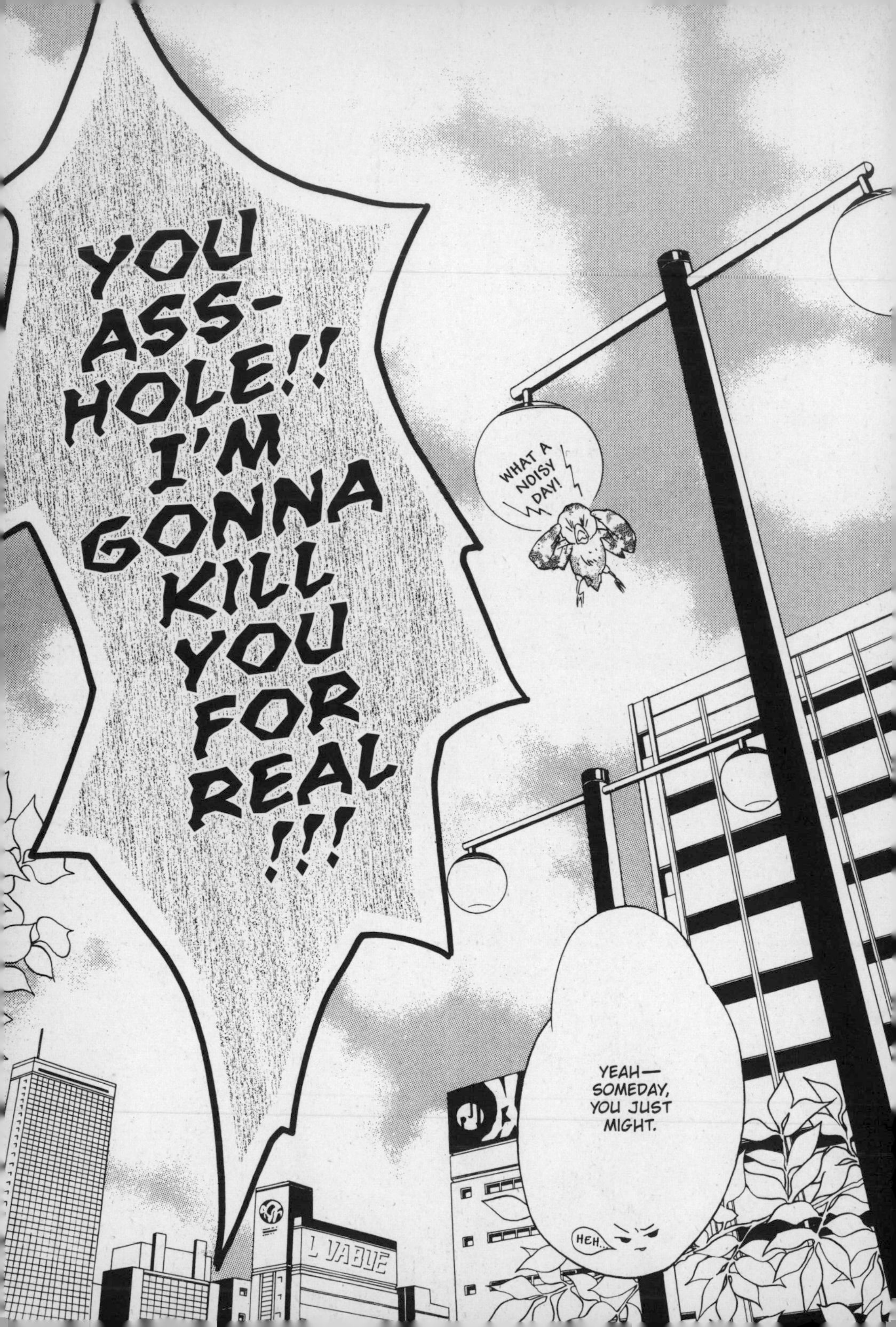

YOU ASS-HOLE!! I'M GONNA KILL YOU FOR REAL!!!
WHAT A NOISY DAY!
YEAH— SOMEDAY, YOU JUST MIGHT.
HEH...
L VABUE

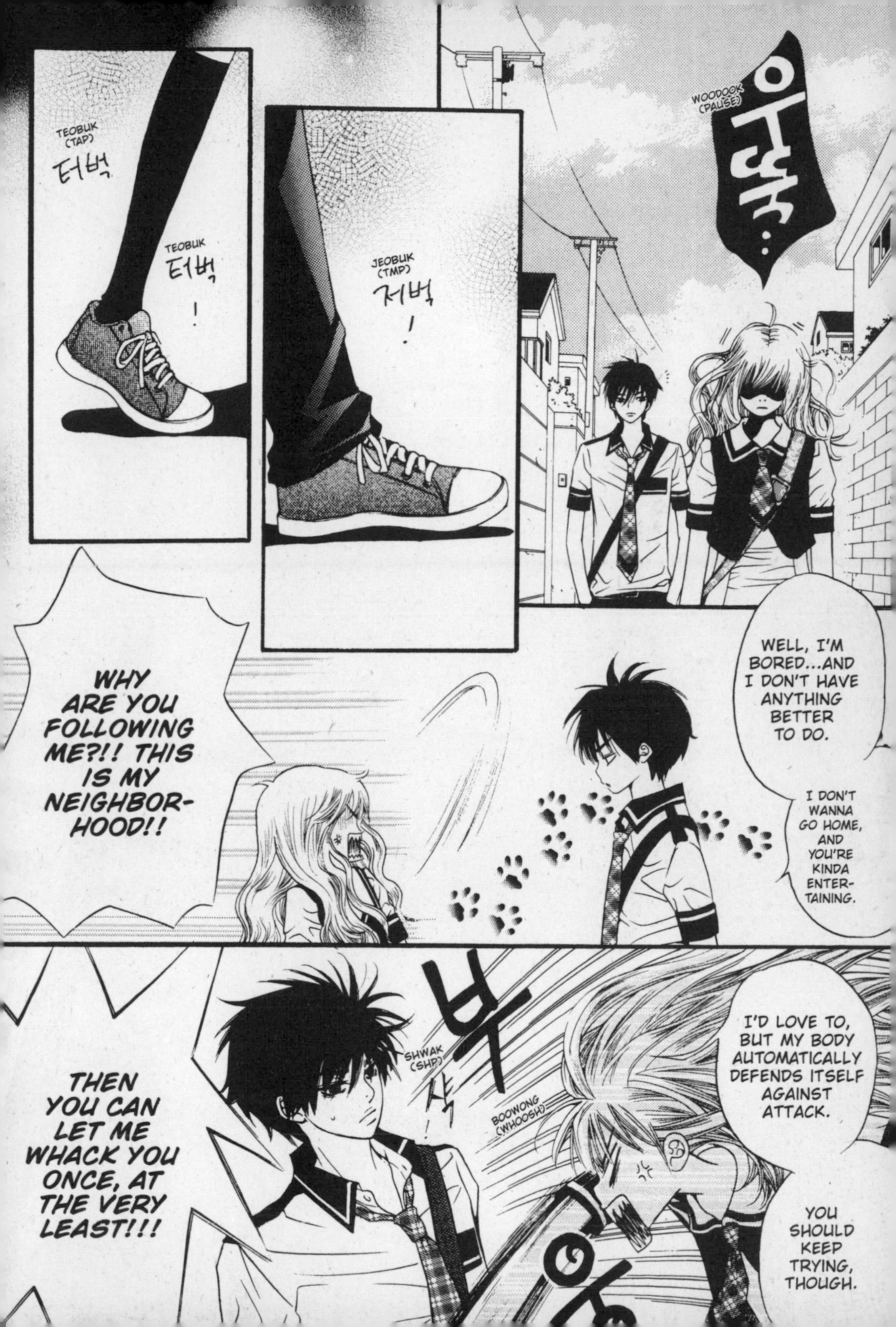

TEOBUK (TAP)
터벅
TEOBUK
터벅!
JEOBUK (TMP)
저벅!
WOODOOK (PAUSE)
우뚝...
WHY ARE YOU FOLLOWING ME?!! THIS IS MY NEIGHBOR-HOOD!!
WELL, I'M BORED...AND I DON'T HAVE ANYTHING BETTER TO DO.
I DON'T WANNA GO HOME, AND YOU'RE KINDA ENTER-TAINING.
THEN YOU CAN LET ME WHACK YOU ONCE, AT THE VERY LEAST!!!
SHWAK (SHP)
샥!
BOOWONG (WHOOSH)
I'D LOVE TO, BUT MY BODY AUTOMATICALLY DEFENDS ITSELF AGAINST ATTACK.
YOU SHOULD KEEP TRYING, THOUGH.

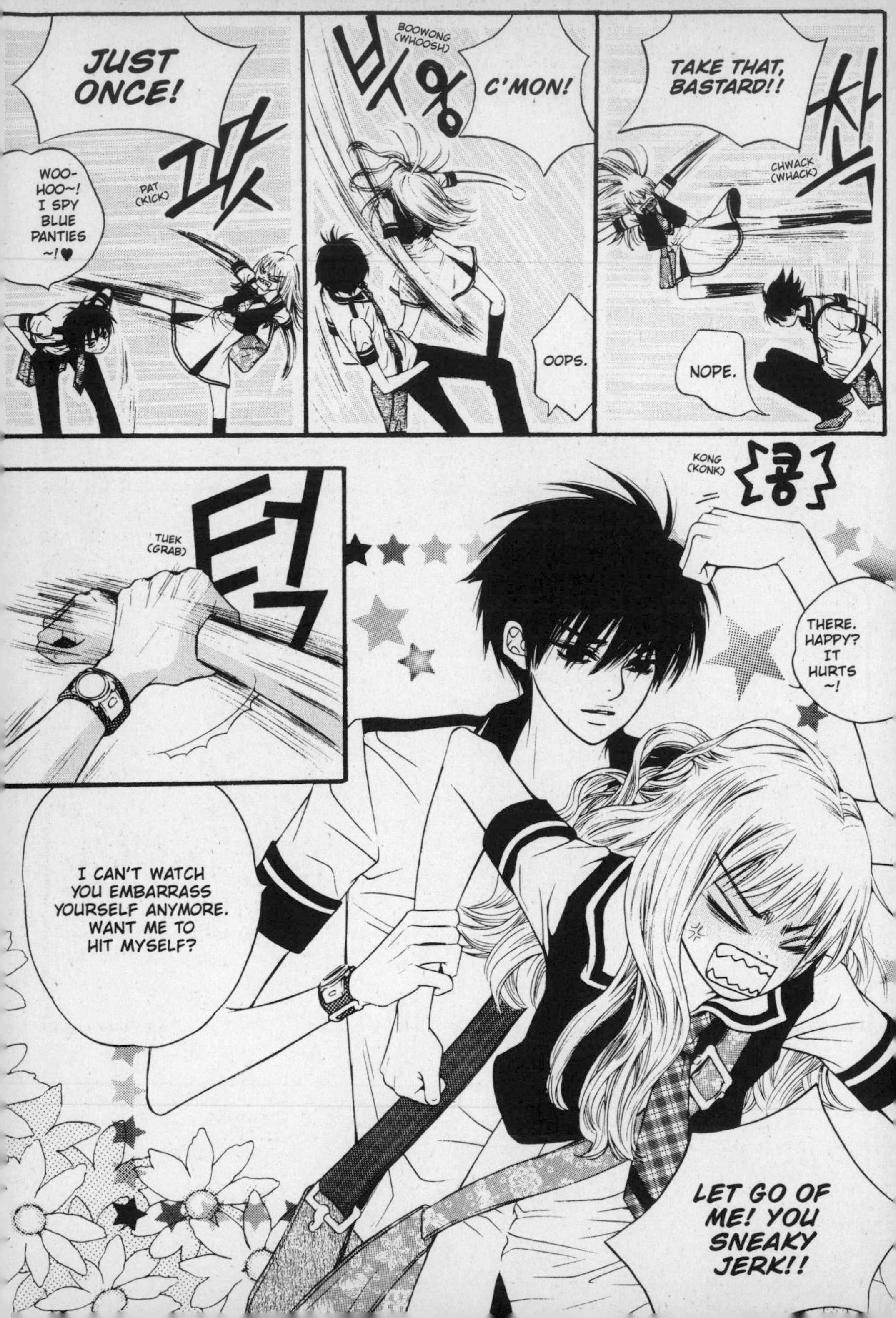
JUST ONCE!
WOO-HOO~! I SPY BLUE PANTIES ~!♥
PAT (KICK)
BOOWONG (WHOOSH)
C'MON!
OOPS.
TAKE THAT, BASTARD!!
CHWACK (WHACK)
NOPE.
TUEK (GRAB)
KONG (KONK)
콩
THERE. HAPPY? IT HURTS ~!
I CAN'T WATCH YOU EMBARRASS YOURSELF ANYMORE. WANT ME TO HIT MYSELF?
LET GO OF ME! YOU SNEAKY JERK!!

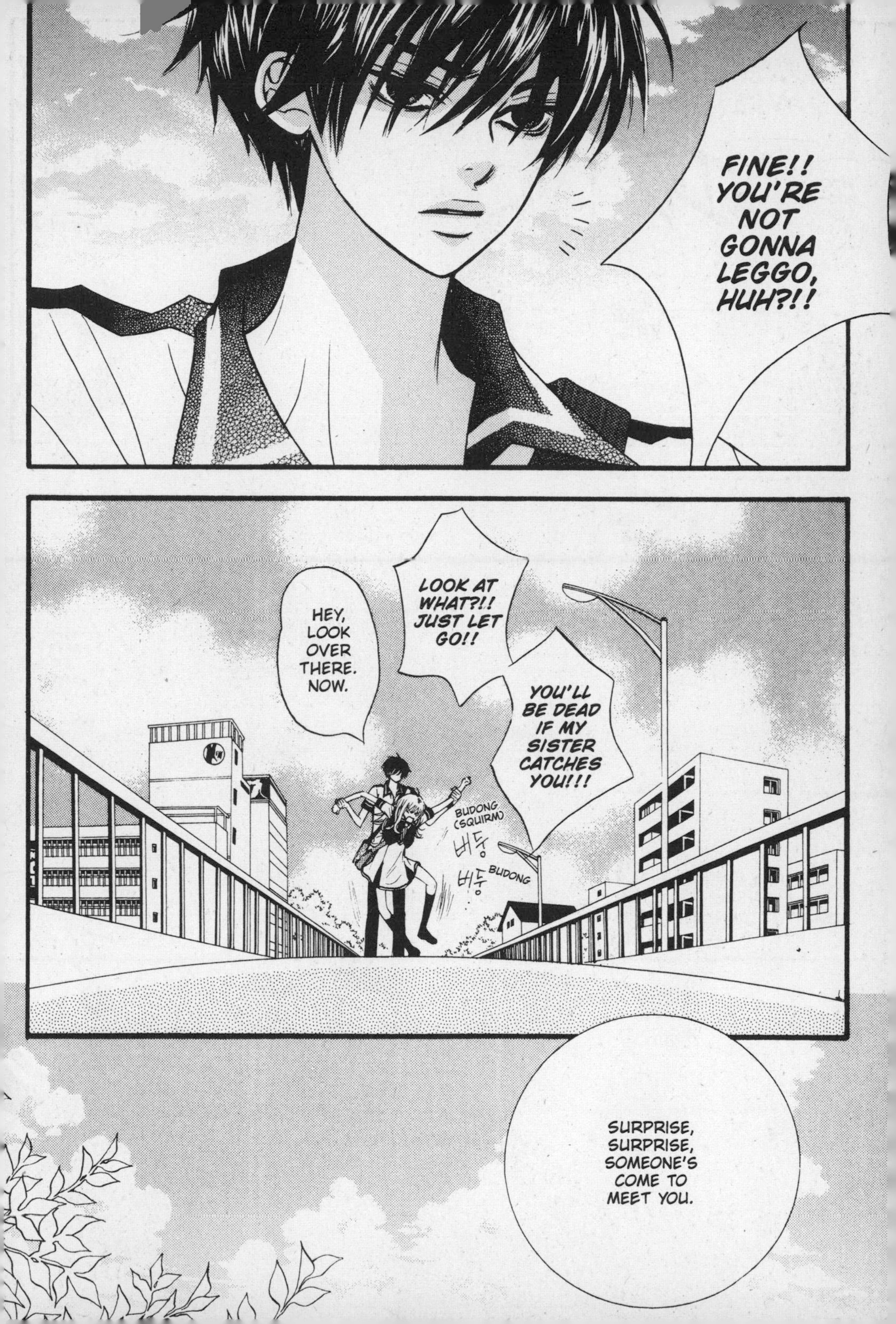
FINE!! YOU'RE NOT GONNA LEGGO, HUH?!!
HEY, LOOK OVER THERE. NOW.
LOOK AT WHAT?!! JUST LET GO!!
YOU'LL BE DEAD IF MY SISTER CATCHES YOU!!!
BUDONG (SQUIRM)
버둥
버둥
BUDONG
SURPRISE, SURPRISE, SOMEONE'S COME TO MEET YOU.

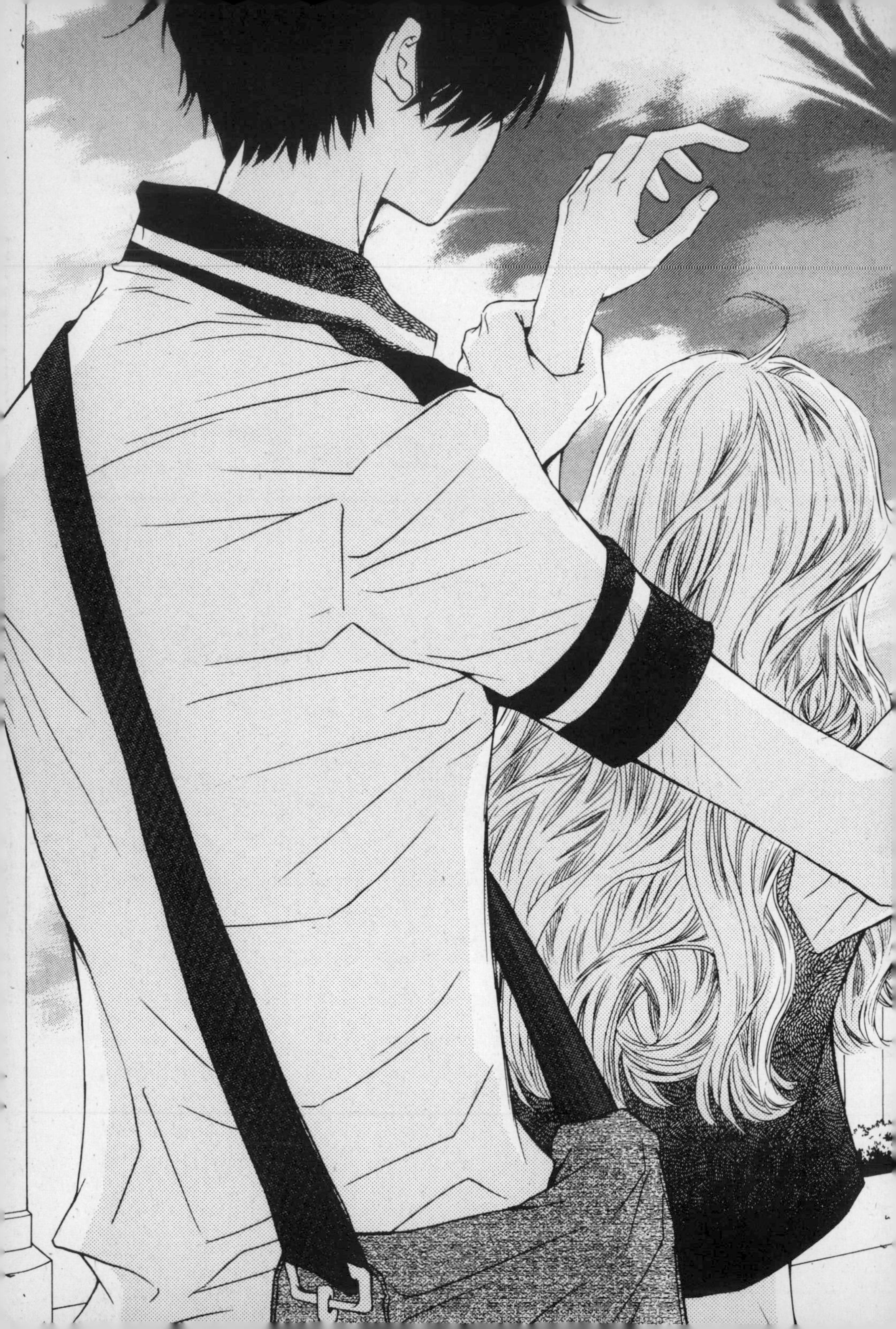

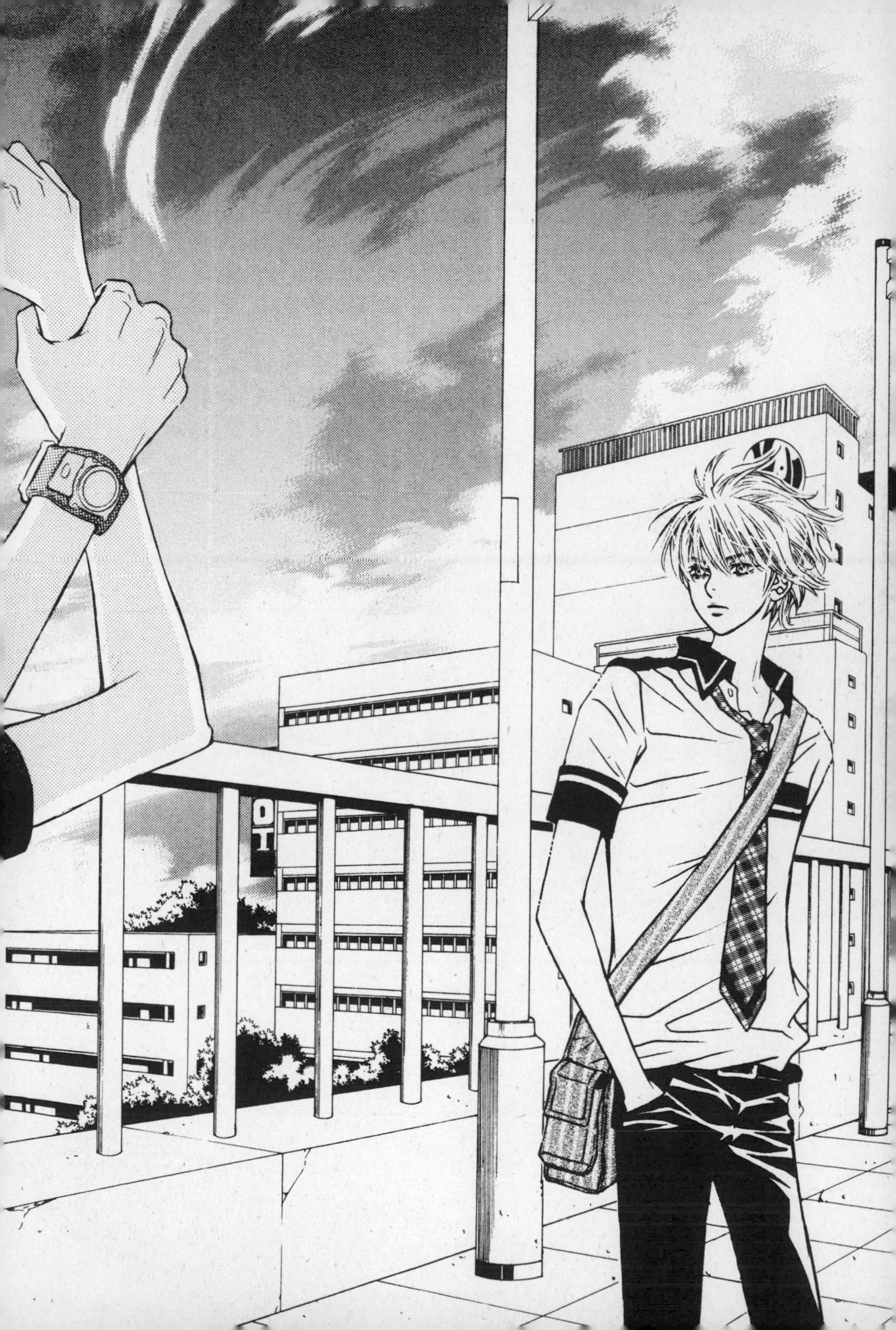

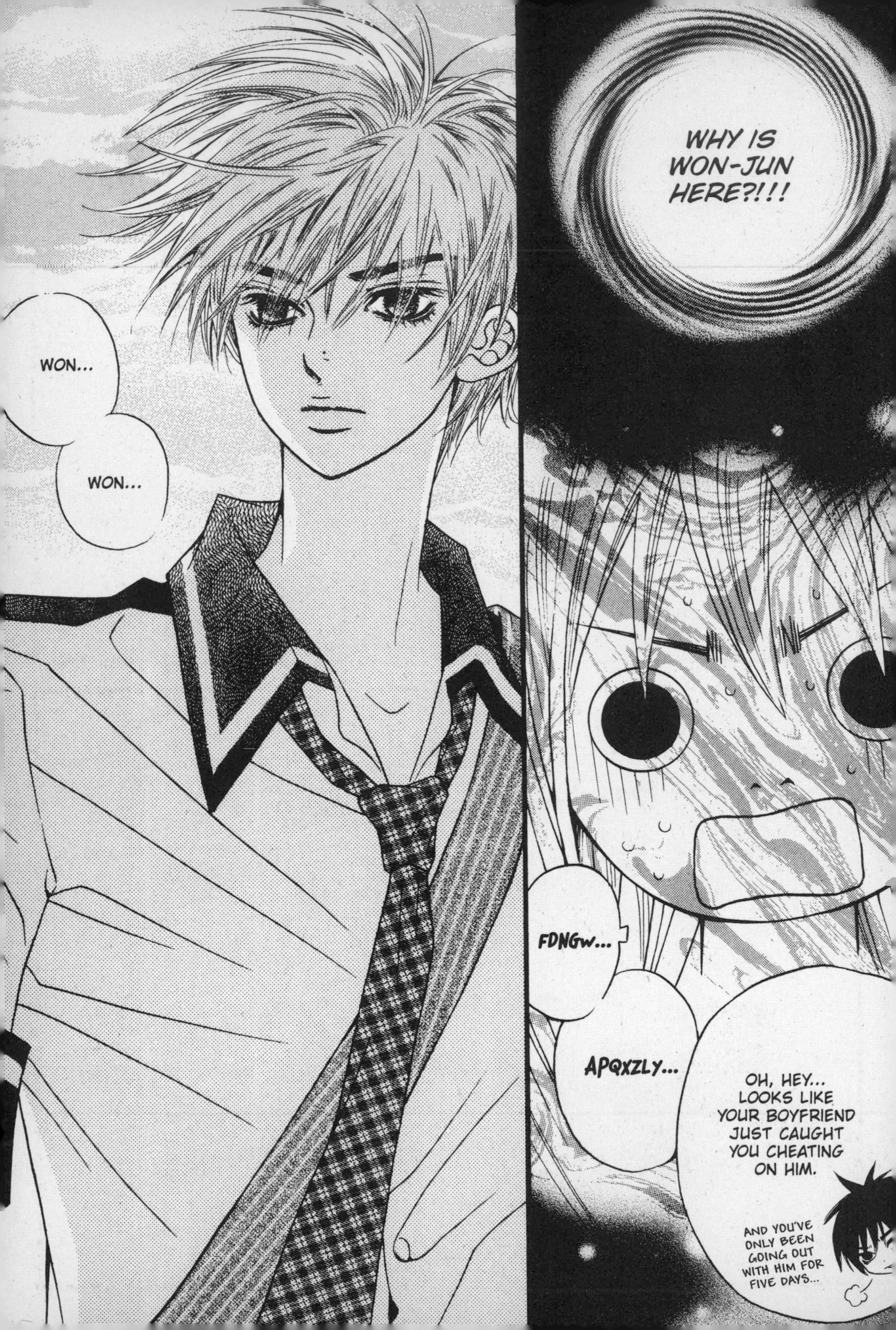
WON...
WON...
WHY IS WON-JUN HERE?!!!
FDNGW...
APQXZLY...
OH, HEY... LOOKS LIKE YOUR BOYFRIEND JUST CAUGHT YOU CHEATING ON HIM.
AND YOU'VE ONLY BEEN GOING OUT WITH HIM FOR FIVE DAYS...

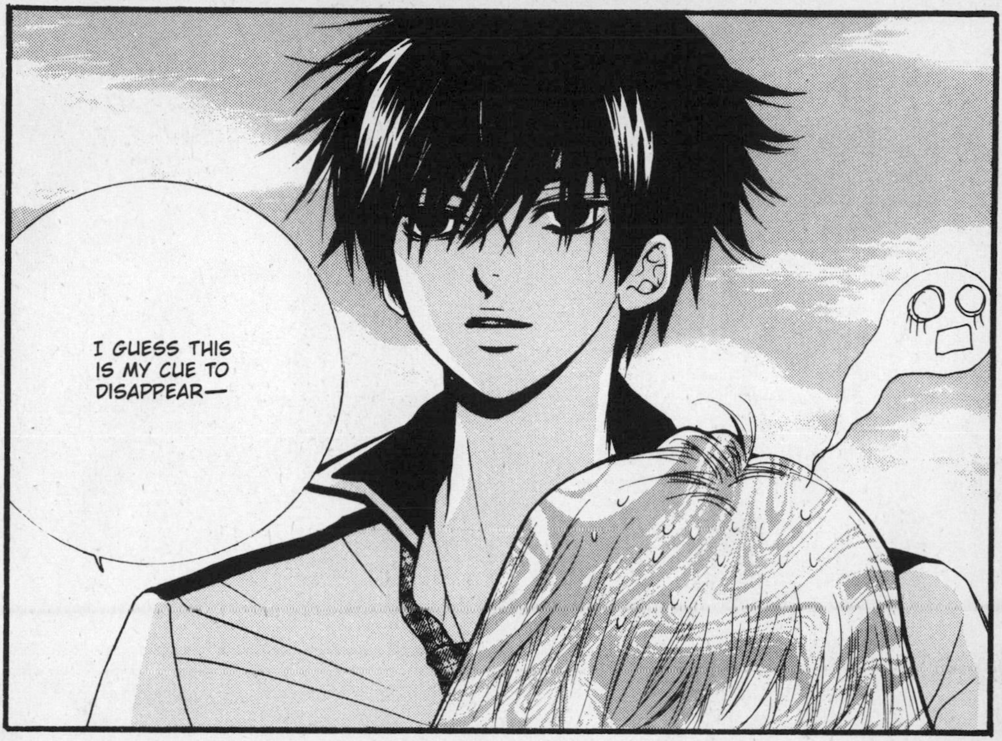
I GUESS THIS IS MY CUE TO DISAPPEAR—
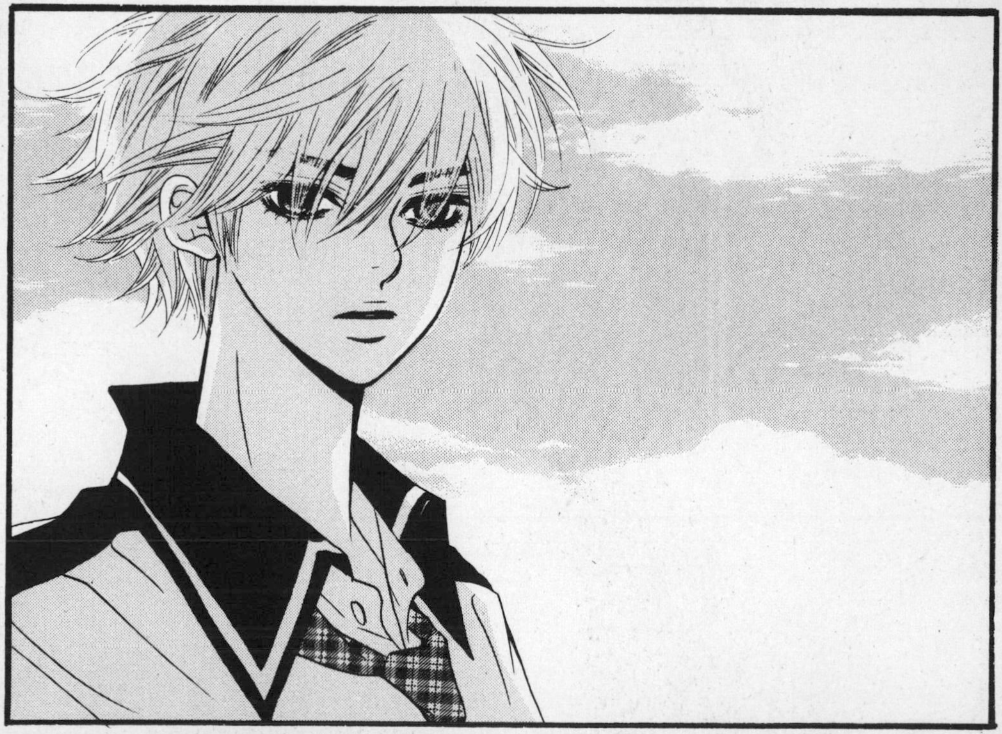

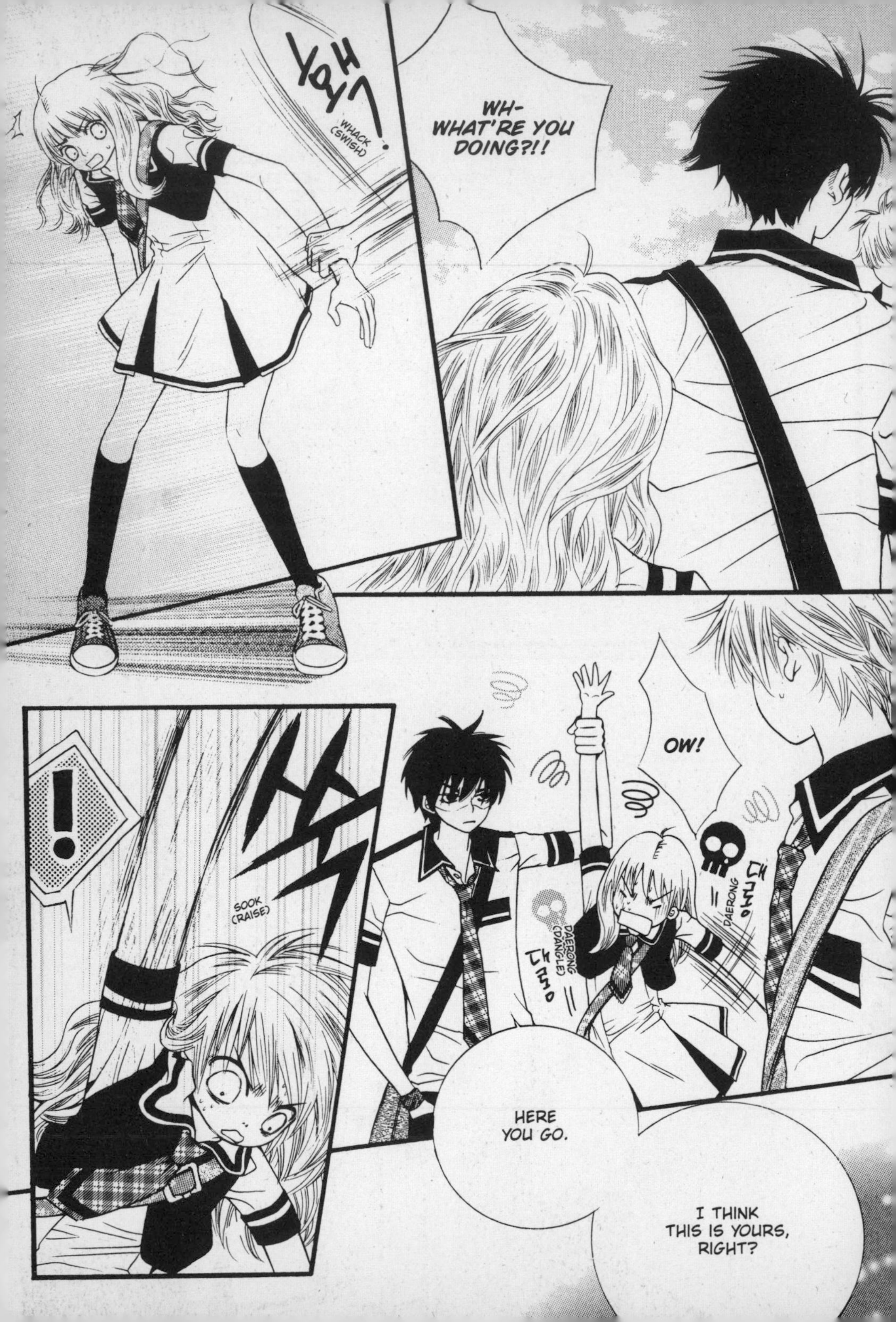
WHACK (SWISH)
WH- WHAT'RE YOU DOING?!!
SOOK (RAISE)
DAERONG (DANGLE)
대롱
OW!
대롱
DAERONG
HERE YOU GO.
I THINK THIS IS YOURS, RIGHT?

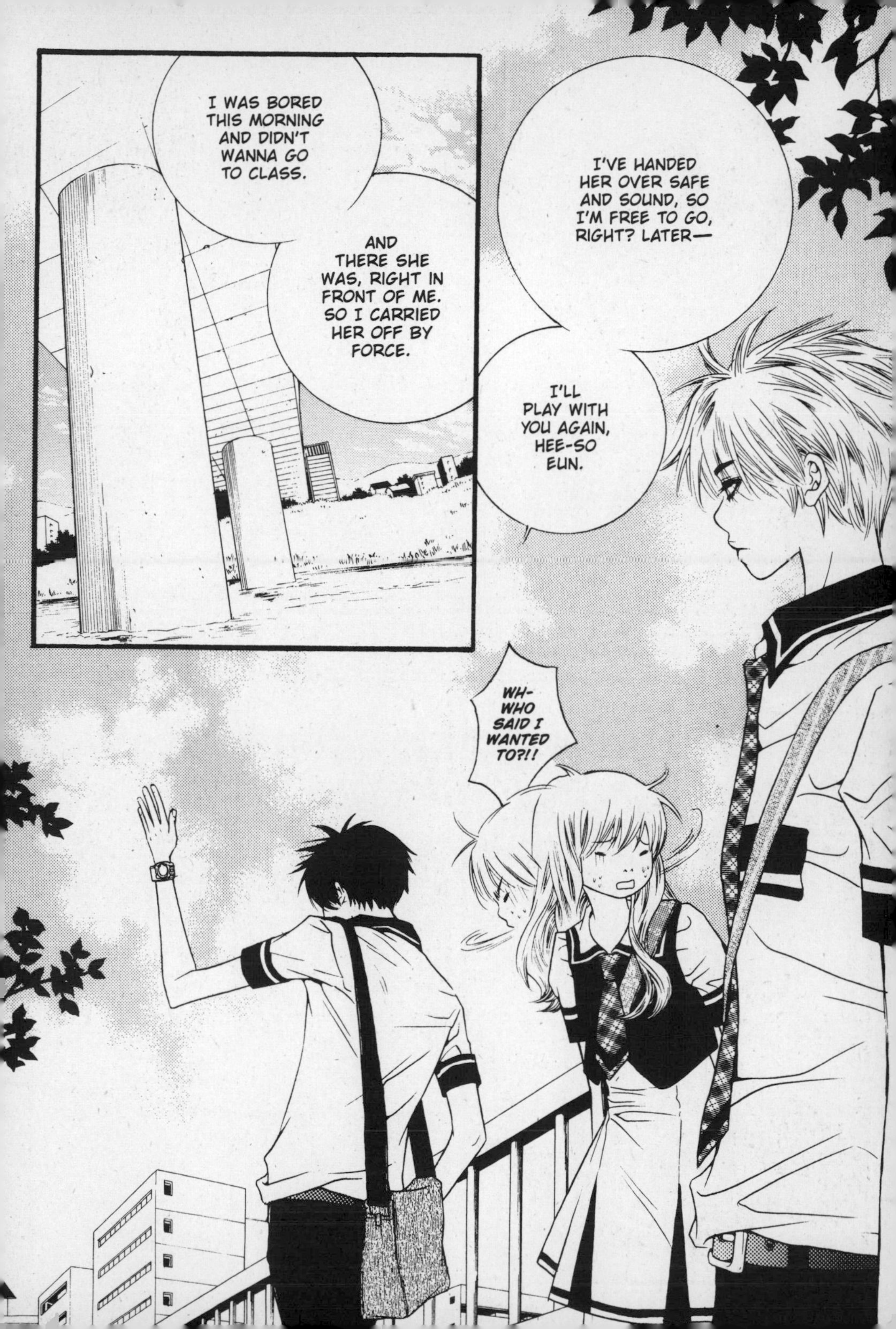
I WAS BORED THIS MORNING AND DIDN'T WANNA GO TO CLASS.
AND THERE SHE WAS, RIGHT IN FRONT OF ME. SO I CARRIED HER OFF BY FORCE.
I'VE HANDED HER OVER SAFE AND SOUND, SO I'M FREE TO GO, RIGHT? LATER—
I'LL PLAY WITH YOU AGAIN, HEE-SO EUN.
WH-WHO SAID I WANTED TO?!!

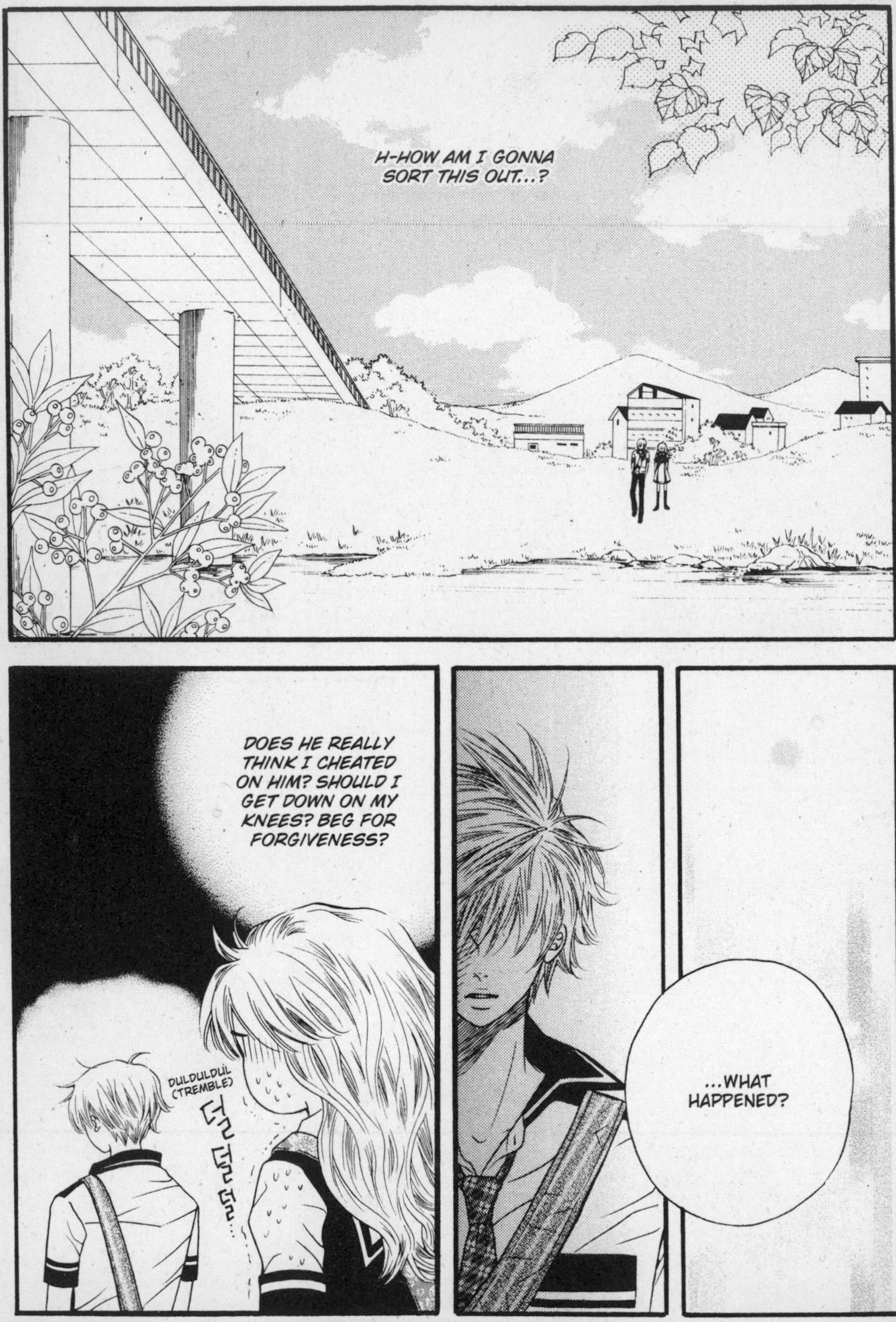
H-HOW AM I GONNA SORT THIS OUT...?
DOES HE REALLY THINK I CHEATED ON HIM? SHOULD I GET DOWN ON MY KNEES? BEG FOR FORGIVENESS?
DULDULDUL (TREMBLE)
덜덜덜...
...WHAT HAPPENED?

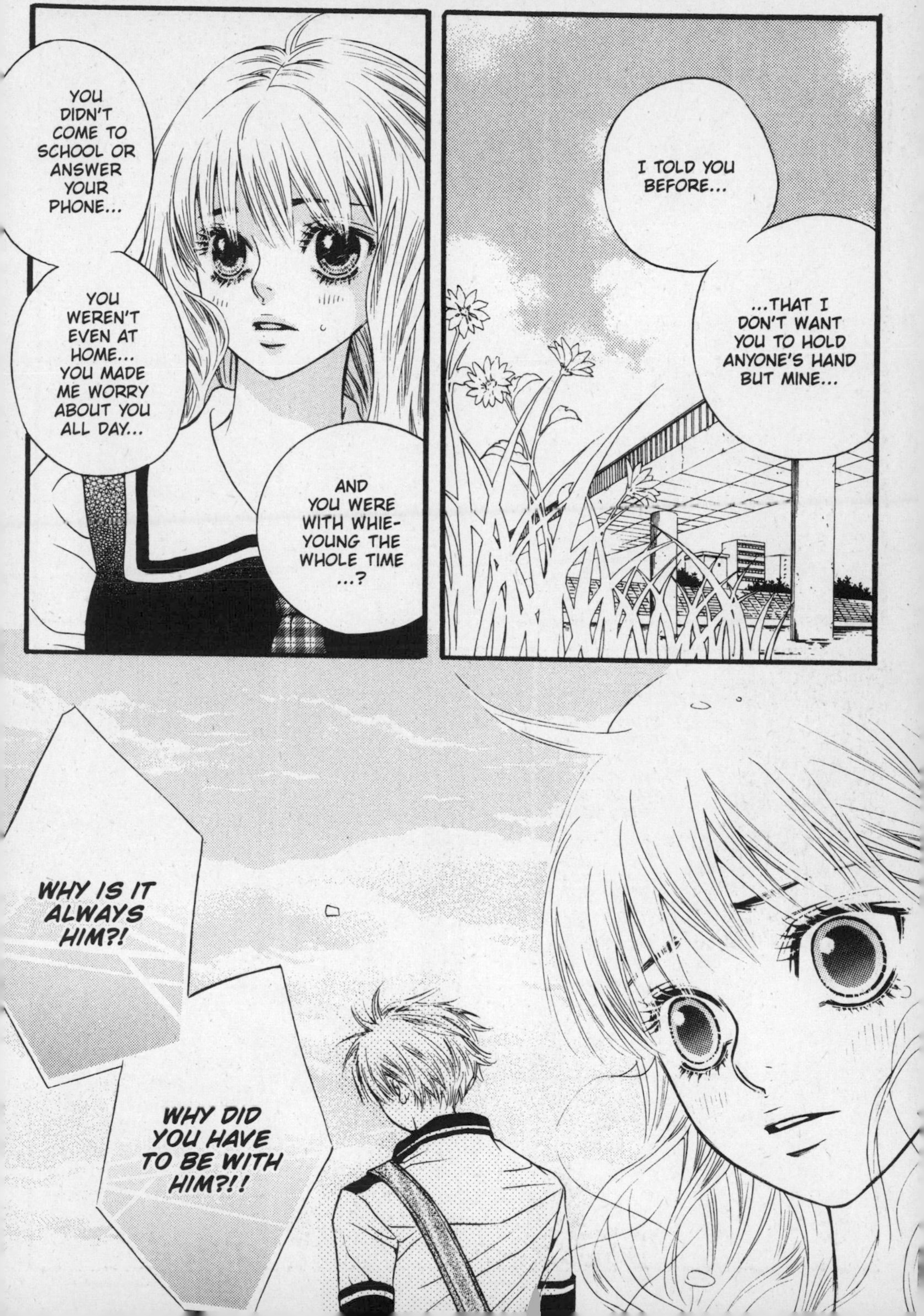
YOU DIDN'T COME TO SCHOOL OR ANSWER YOUR PHONE...
YOU WEREN'T EVEN AT HOME... YOU MADE ME WORRY ABOUT YOU ALL DAY...
AND YOU WERE WITH WHIE-YOUNG THE WHOLE TIME ...?
I TOLD YOU BEFORE...
...THAT I DON'T WANT YOU TO HOLD ANYONE'S HAND BUT MINE...
WHY IS IT ALWAYS HIM?!
WHY DID YOU HAVE TO BE WITH HIM?!!

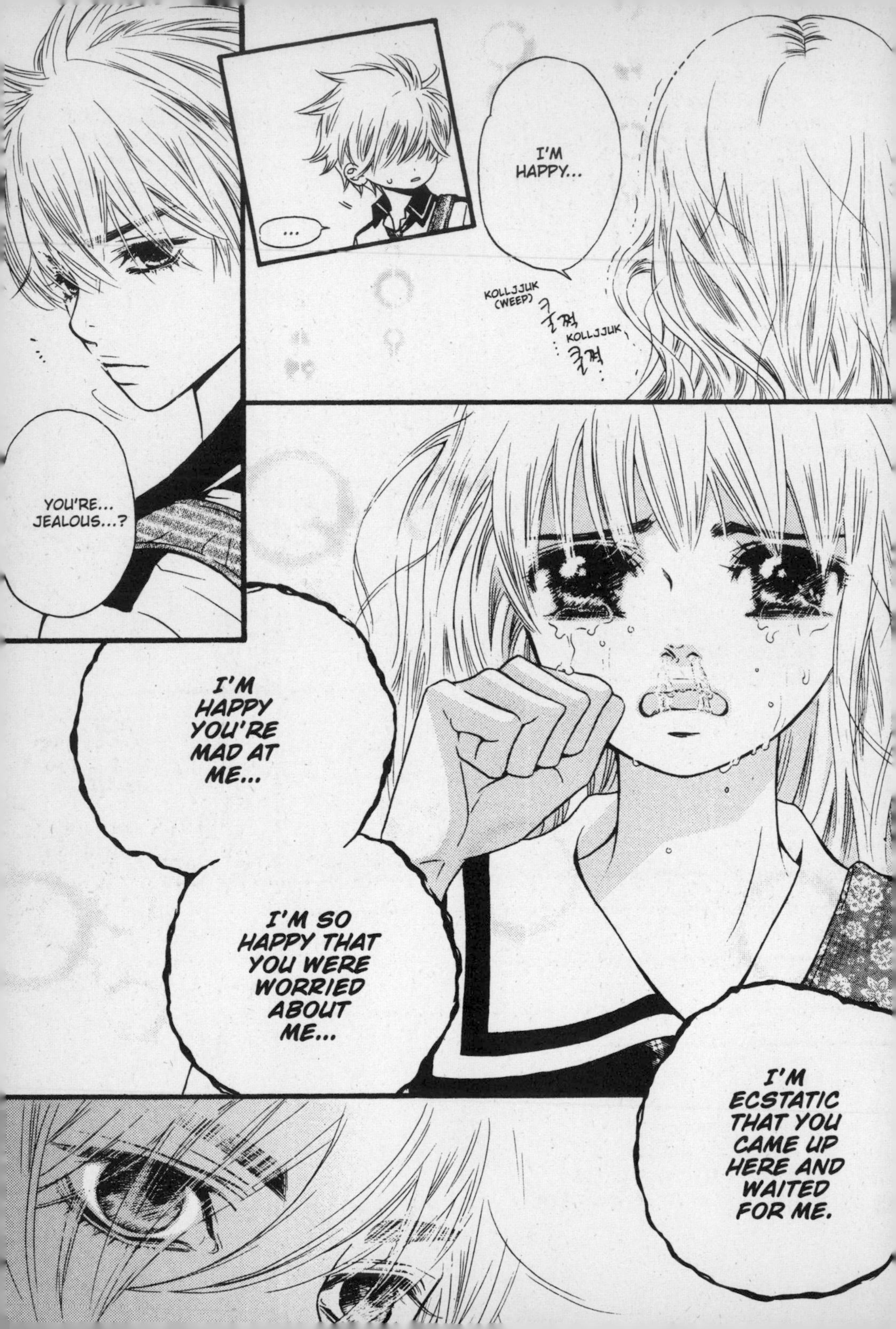
YOU'RE... JEALOUS...?
...
I'M HAPPY...
KOLLJJUK (WEEP)
쿨쩍
KOLLJJUK
쿨쩍
I'M HAPPY YOU'RE MAD AT ME...
I'M SO HAPPY THAT YOU WERE WORRIED ABOUT ME...
I'M ECSTATIC THAT YOU CAME UP HERE AND WAITED FOR ME.

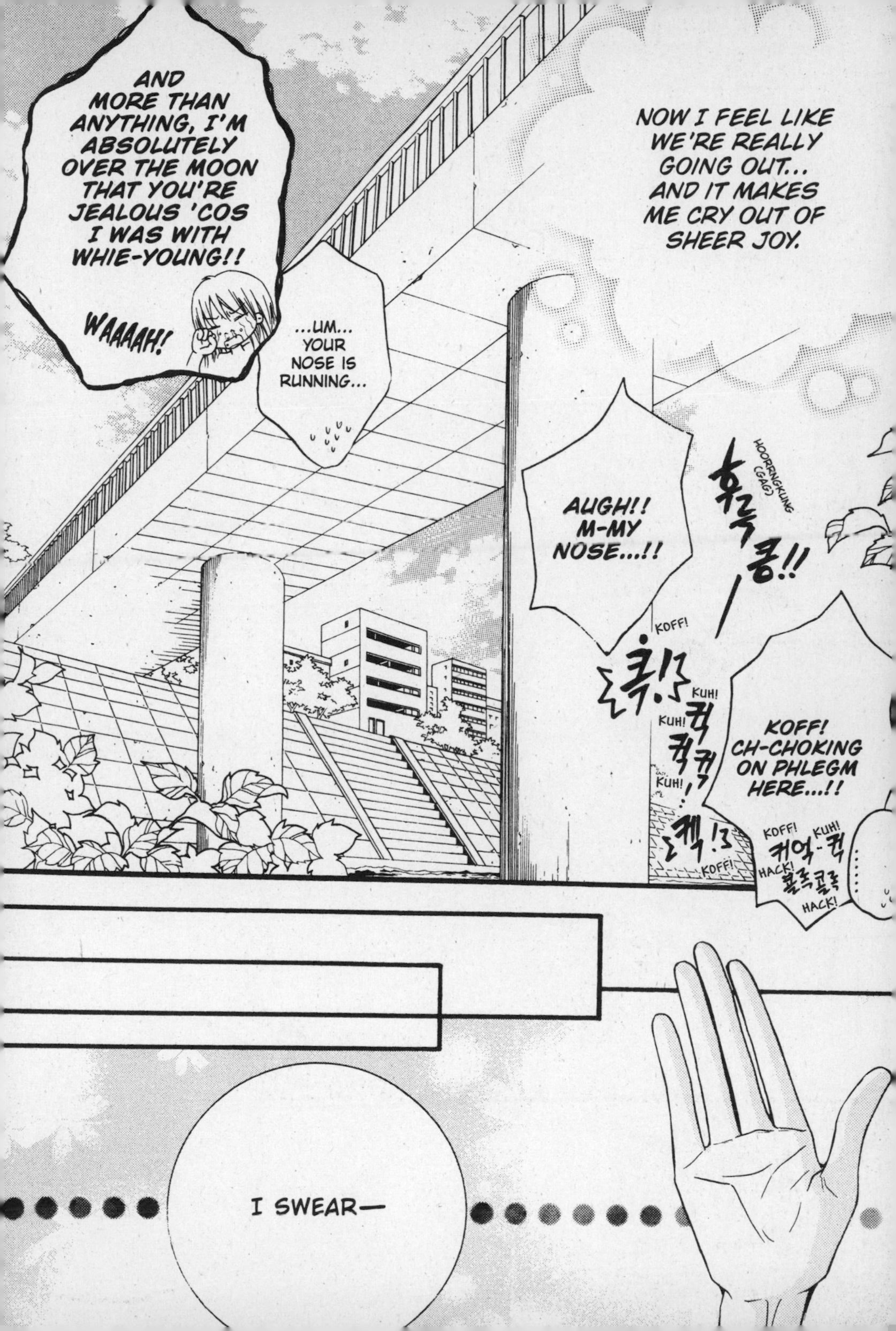
AND MORE THAN ANYTHING, I'M ABSOLUTELY OVER THE MOON THAT YOU'RE JEALOUS 'COS I WAS WITH WHIE-YOUNG!!
WAAAAH!
...UM... YOUR NOSE IS RUNNING...
NOW I FEEL LIKE WE'RE REALLY GOING OUT... AND IT MAKES ME CRY OUT OF SHEER JOY.
AUGH!! M-MY NOSE...!!
HOORRNGKUNG (GAG)
후룩 콩!!
KOFF!
KUH!
KUH!
KUH!
KOFF!
KOFF! CH-CHOKING ON PHLEGM HERE...!!
KOFF! KUH!
HACK!
HACK!
I SWEAR—

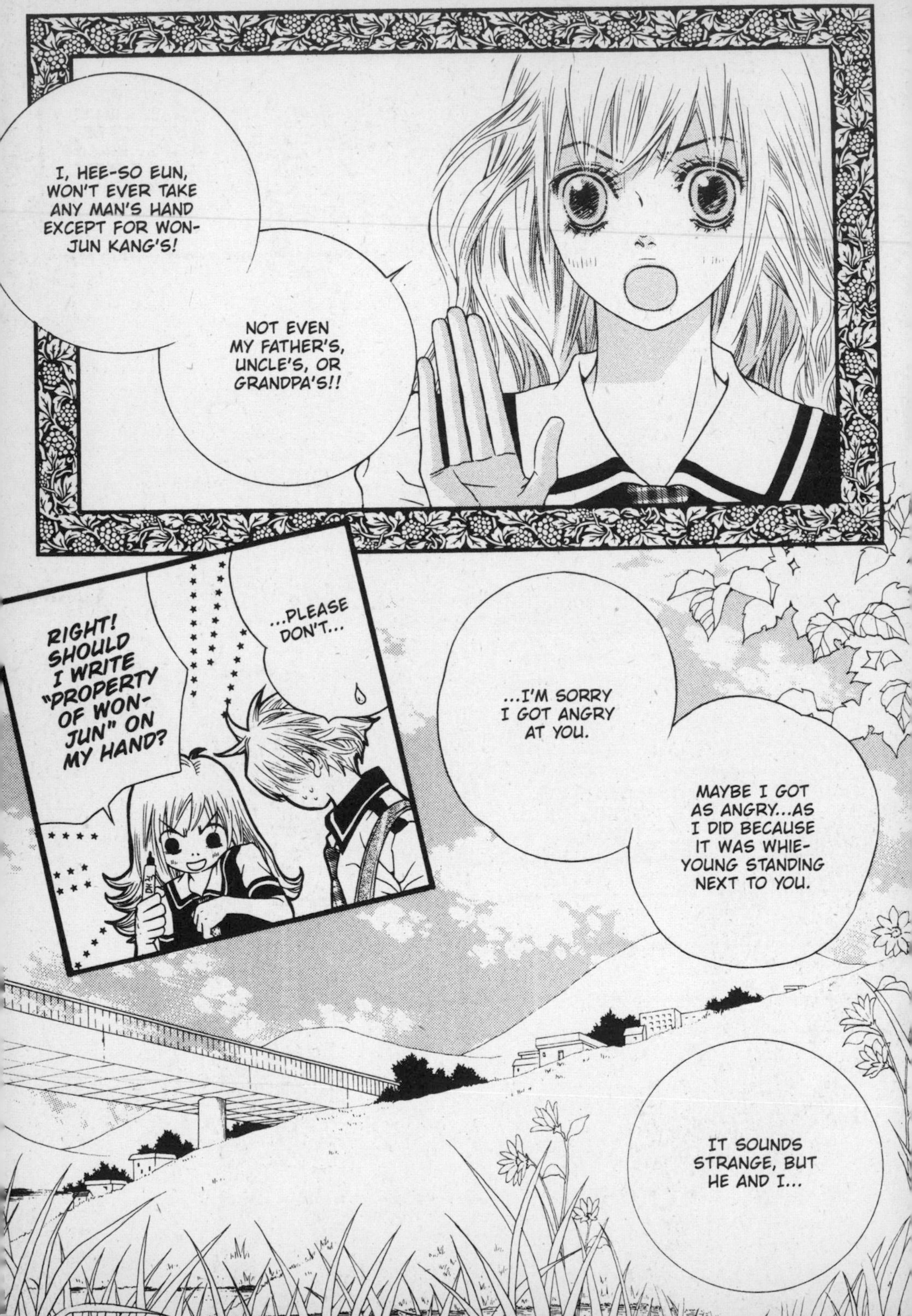
I, HEE-SO EUN, WON'T EVER TAKE ANY MAN'S HAND EXCEPT FOR WON-JUN KANG'S!
NOT EVEN MY FATHER'S, UNCLE'S, OR GRANDPA'S!!
RIGHT! SHOULD I WRITE "PROPERTY OF WON-JUN" ON MY HAND?
...PLEASE DON'T...
...I'M SORRY I GOT ANGRY AT YOU.
MAYBE I GOT AS ANGRY...AS I DID BECAUSE IT WAS WHIE-YOUNG STANDING NEXT TO YOU.
IT SOUNDS STRANGE, BUT HE AND I...

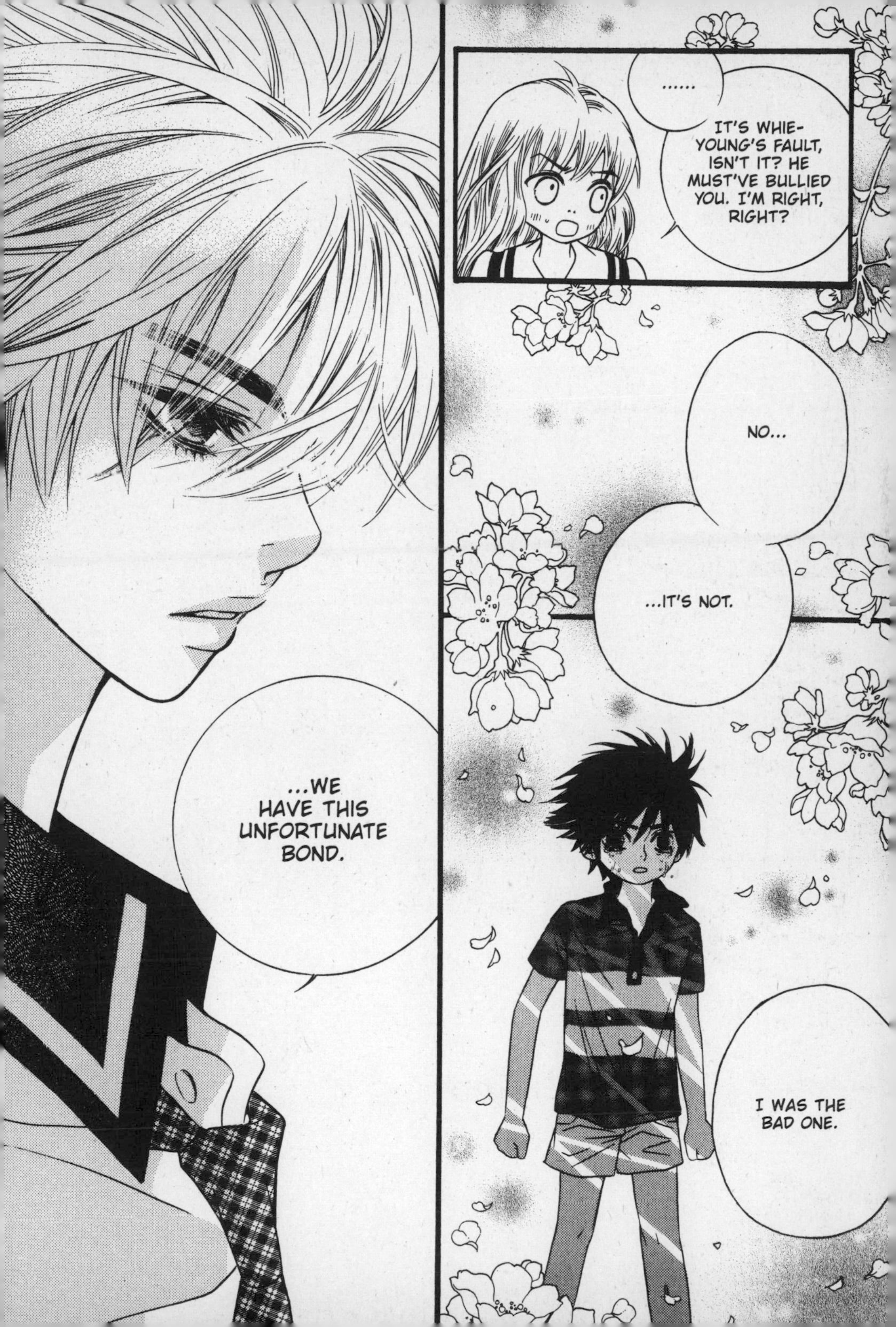
...WE HAVE THIS UNFORTUNATE BOND.
......
IT'S WHIE-YOUNG'S FAULT, ISN'T IT? HE MUST'VE BULLIED YOU. I'M RIGHT, RIGHT?
NO...
...IT'S NOT.
I WAS THE BAD ONE.

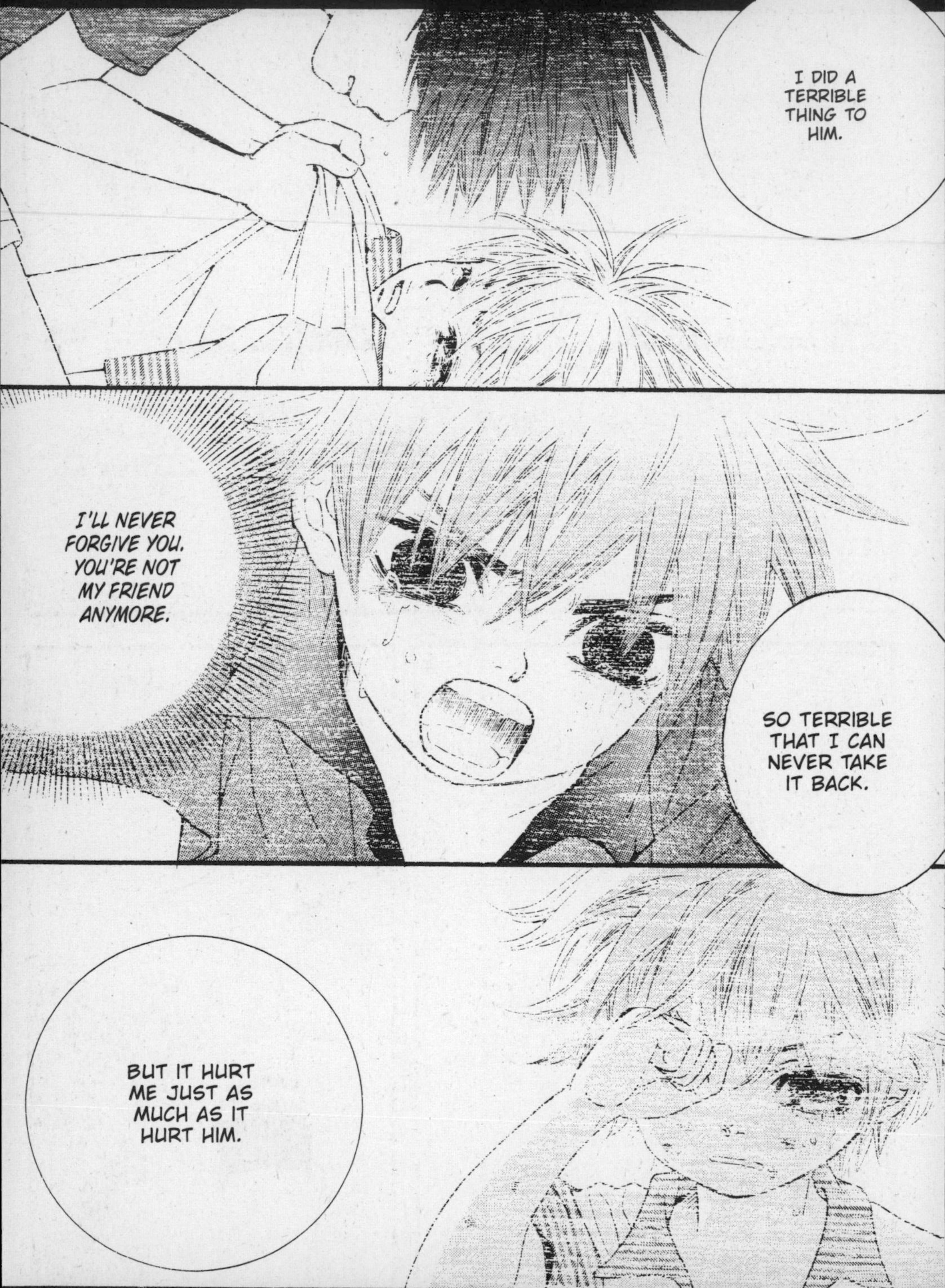
I DID A TERRIBLE THING TO HIM.
I'LL NEVER FORGIVE YOU. YOU'RE NOT MY FRIEND ANYMORE.
SO TERRIBLE THAT I CAN NEVER TAKE IT BACK.
BUT IT HURT ME JUST AS MUCH AS IT HURT HIM.

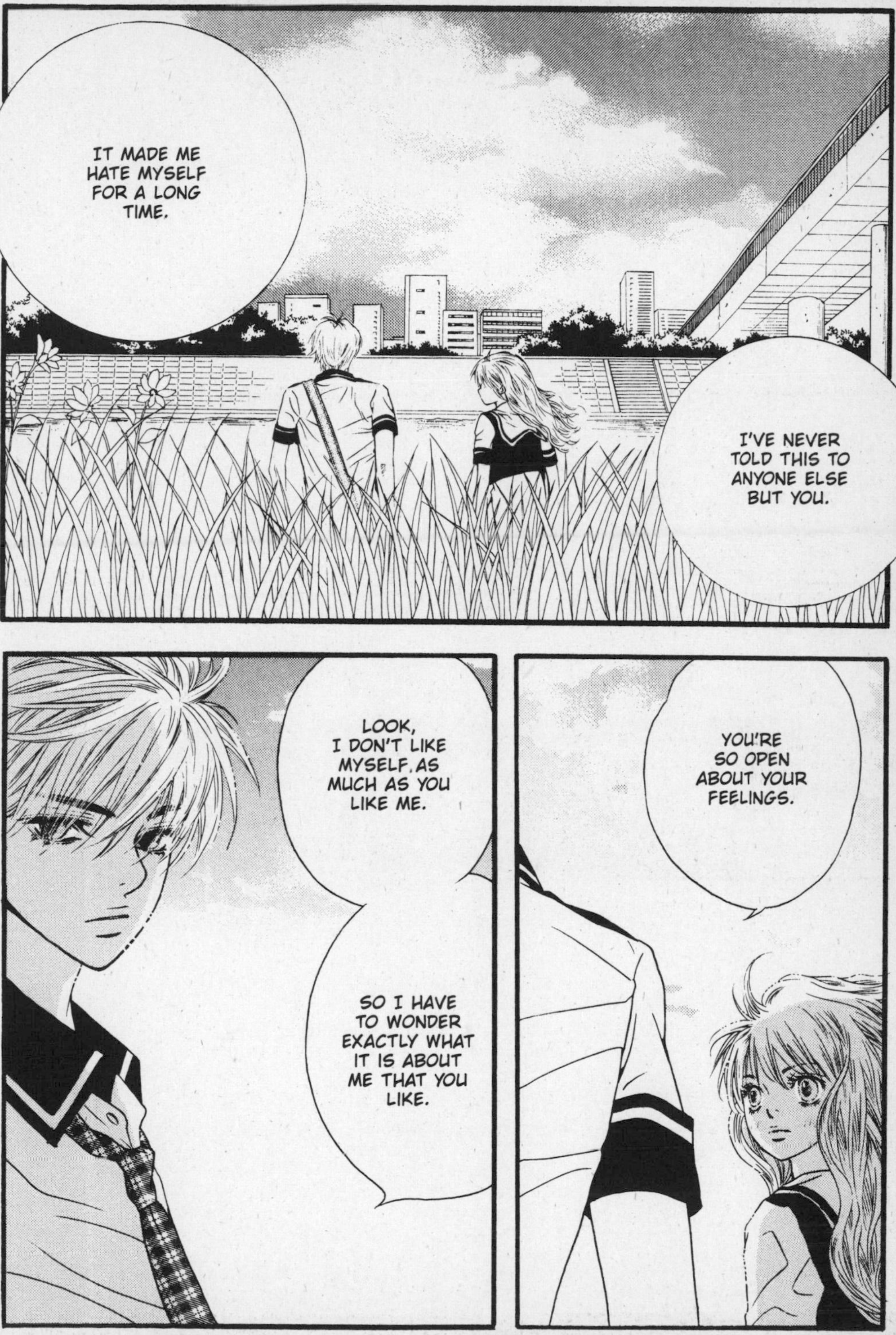
IT MADE ME HATE MYSELF FOR A LONG TIME.
I'VE NEVER TOLD THIS TO ANYONE ELSE BUT YOU.
LOOK, I DON'T LIKE MYSELF AS MUCH AS YOU LIKE ME.
SO I HAVE TO WONDER EXACTLY WHAT IT IS ABOUT ME THAT YOU LIKE.
YOU'RE SO OPEN ABOUT YOUR FEELINGS.

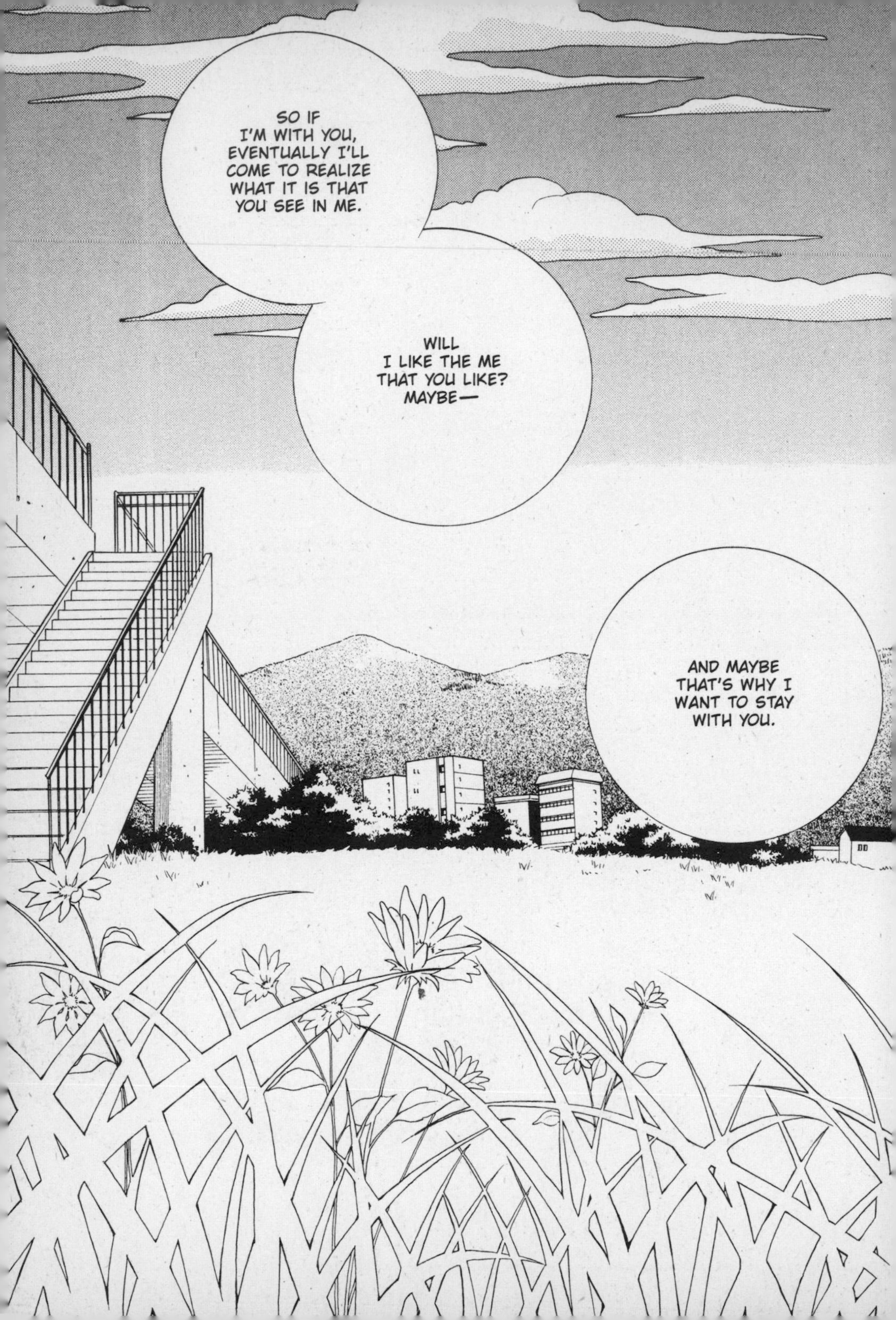
SO IF I'M WITH YOU, EVENTUALLY I'LL COME TO REALIZE WHAT IT IS THAT YOU SEE IN ME.
WILL I LIKE THE ME THAT YOU LIKE? MAYBE—
AND MAYBE THAT'S WHY I WANT TO STAY WITH YOU.

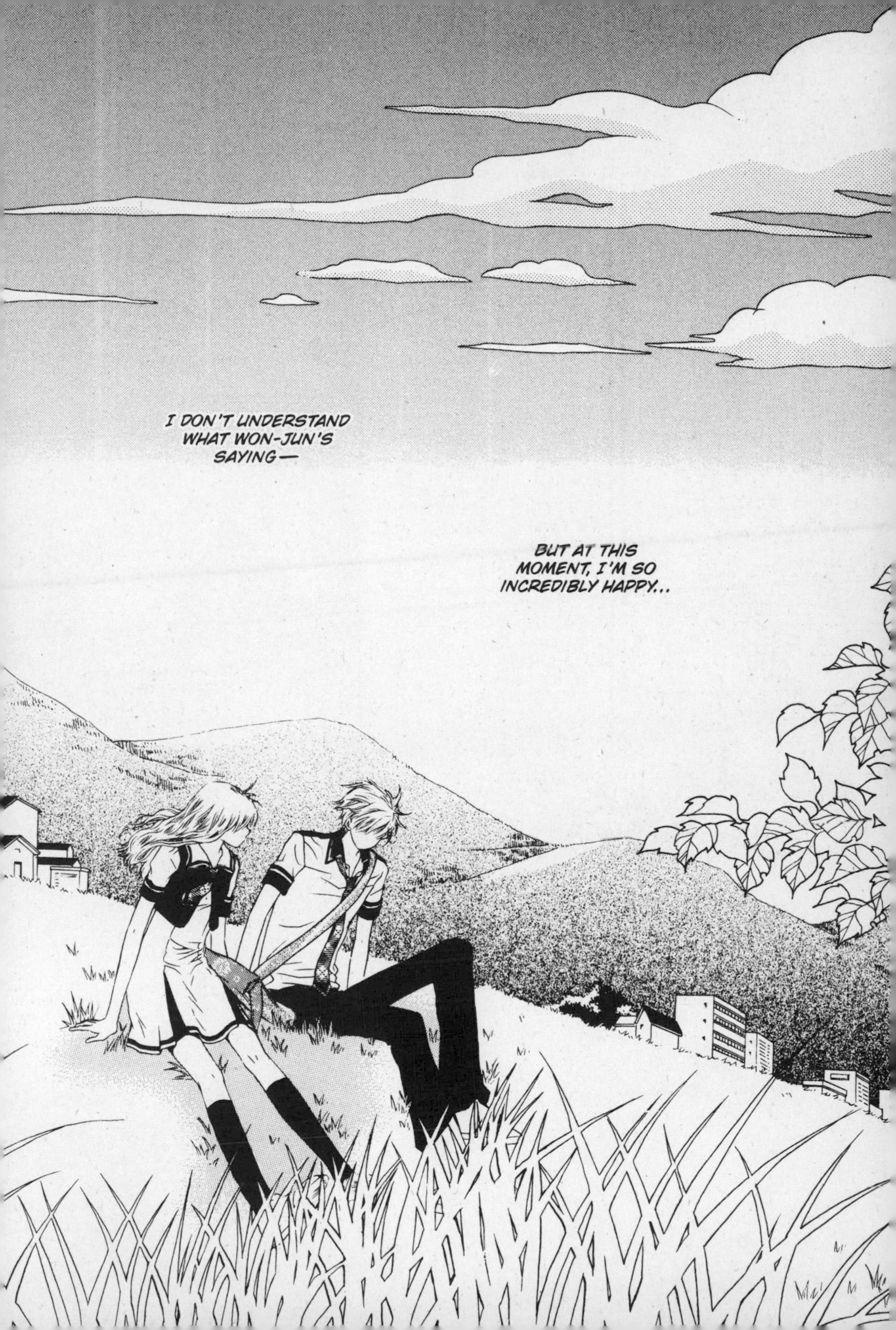
I DON'T UNDERSTAND WHAT WON-JUN'S SAYING—
BUT AT THIS MOMENT, I'M SO INCREDIBLY HAPPY...

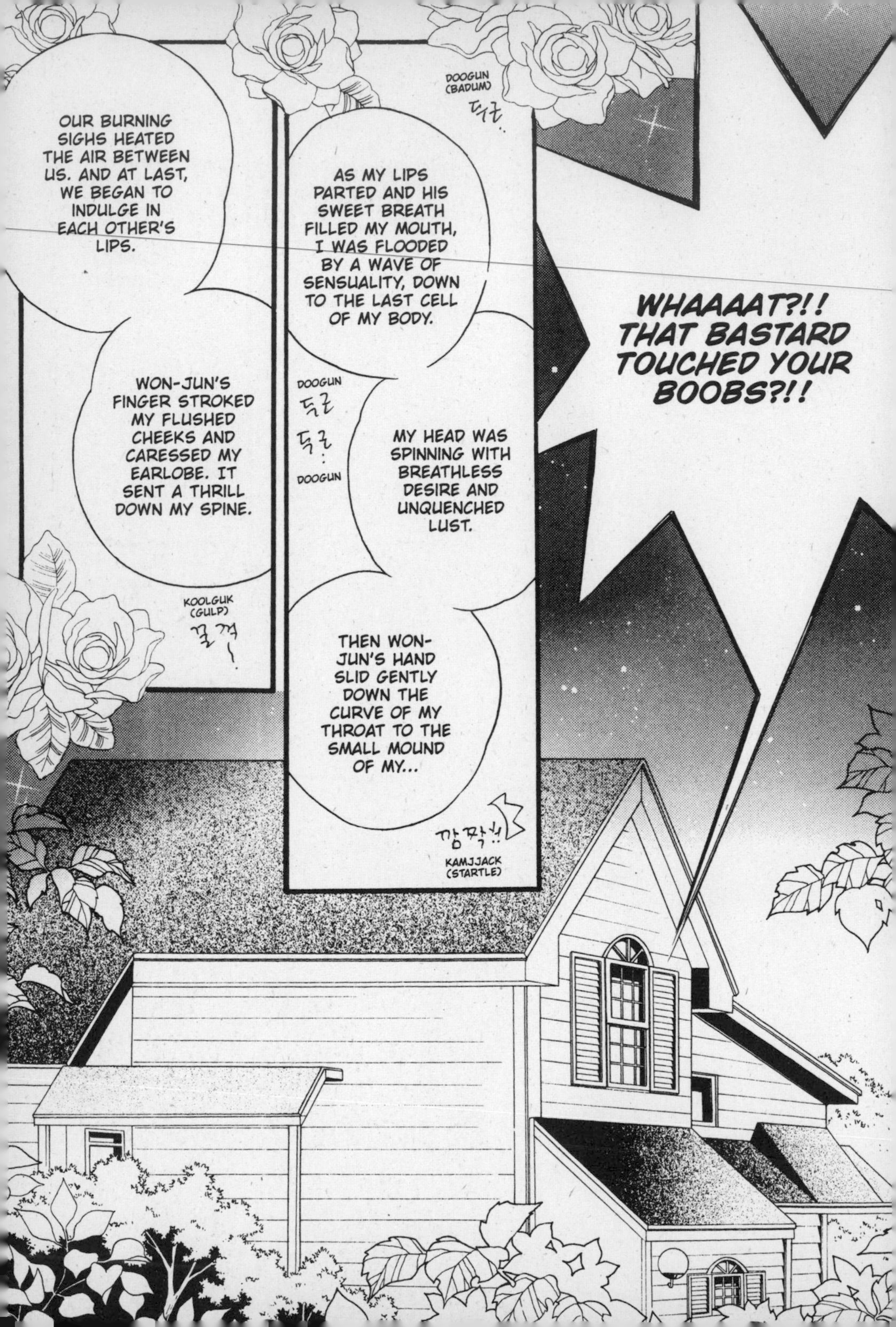

OUR BURNING SIGHS HEATED THE AIR BETWEEN US. AND AT LAST, WE BEGAN TO INDULGE IN EACH OTHER'S LIPS.
WON-JUN'S FINGER STROKED MY FLUSHED CHEEKS AND CARESSED MY EARLOBE. IT SENT A THRILL DOWN MY SPINE.
KOOLGUK (GULP)
꿀꺽
DOOGUN (BADUM)
두근..
AS MY LIPS PARTED AND HIS SWEET BREATH FILLED MY MOUTH, I WAS FLOODED BY A WAVE OF SENSUALITY, DOWN TO THE LAST CELL OF MY BODY.
DOOGUN
두근
두근
DOOGUN
MY HEAD WAS SPINNING WITH BREATHLESS DESIRE AND UNQUENCHED LUST.
THEN WON-JUN'S HAND SLID GENTLY DOWN THE CURVE OF MY THROAT TO THE SMALL MOUND OF MY...
깜짝!!
KAMJJACK (STARTLE)
WHAAAAT?!! THAT BASTARD TOUCHED YOUR BOOBS?!!

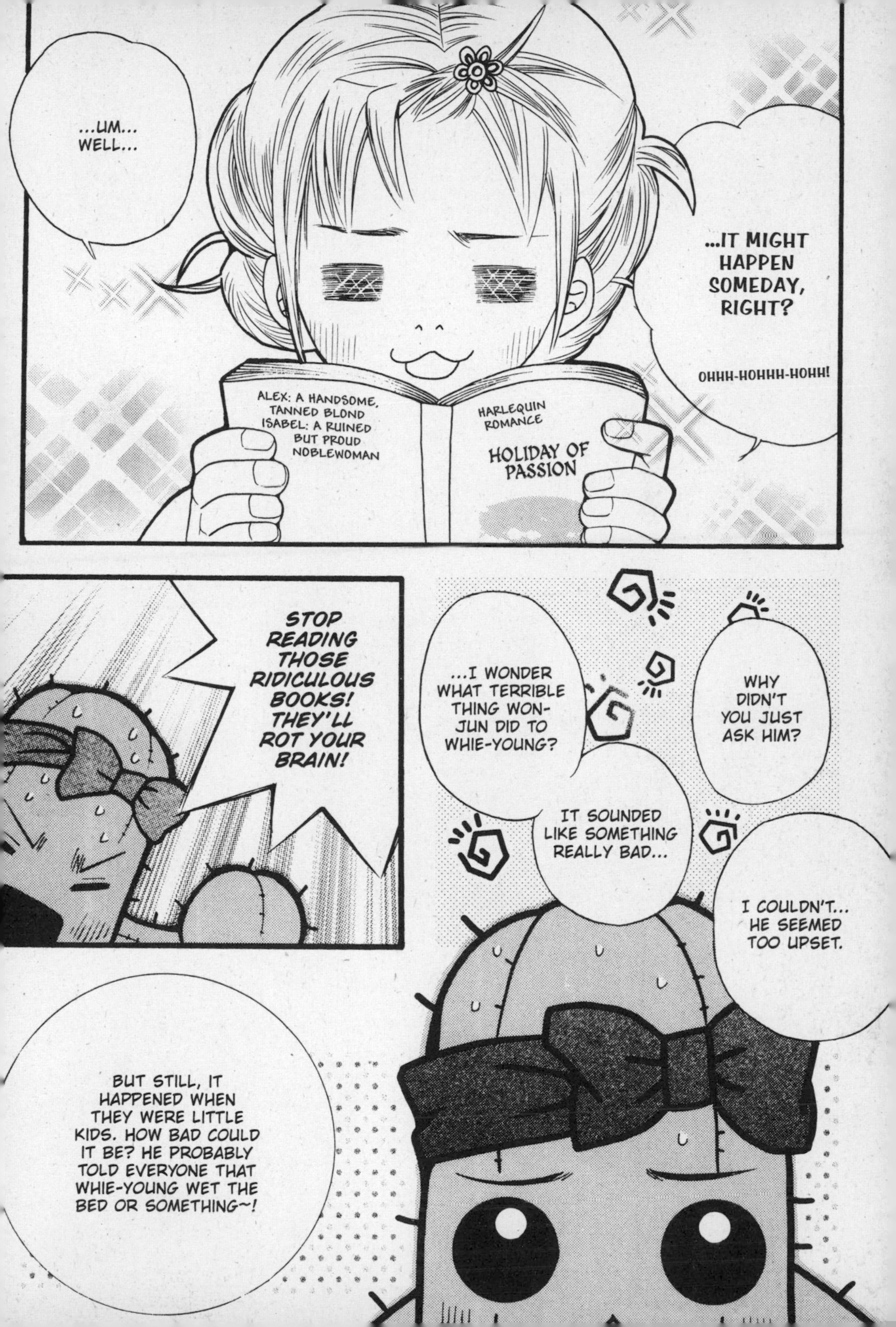
...UM... WELL...
ALEX: A HANDSOME, TANNED BLOND
ISABEL: A RUINED BUT PROUD NOBLEWOMAN
HARLEQUIN ROMANCE
HOLIDAY OF PASSION
...IT MIGHT HAPPEN SOMEDAY, RIGHT?
OHHH-HOHHH-HOHH!
STOP READING THOSE RIDICULOUS BOOKS! THEY'LL ROT YOUR BRAIN!
...I WONDER WHAT TERRIBLE THING WON-JUN DID TO WHIE-YOUNG?
WHY DIDN'T YOU JUST ASK HIM?
IT SOUNDED LIKE SOMETHING REALLY BAD...
I COULDN'T... HE SEEMED TOO UPSET.
BUT STILL, IT HAPPENED WHEN THEY WERE LITTLE KIDS. HOW BAD COULD IT BE? HE PROBABLY TOLD EVERYONE THAT WHIE-YOUNG WET THE BED OR SOMETHING~!

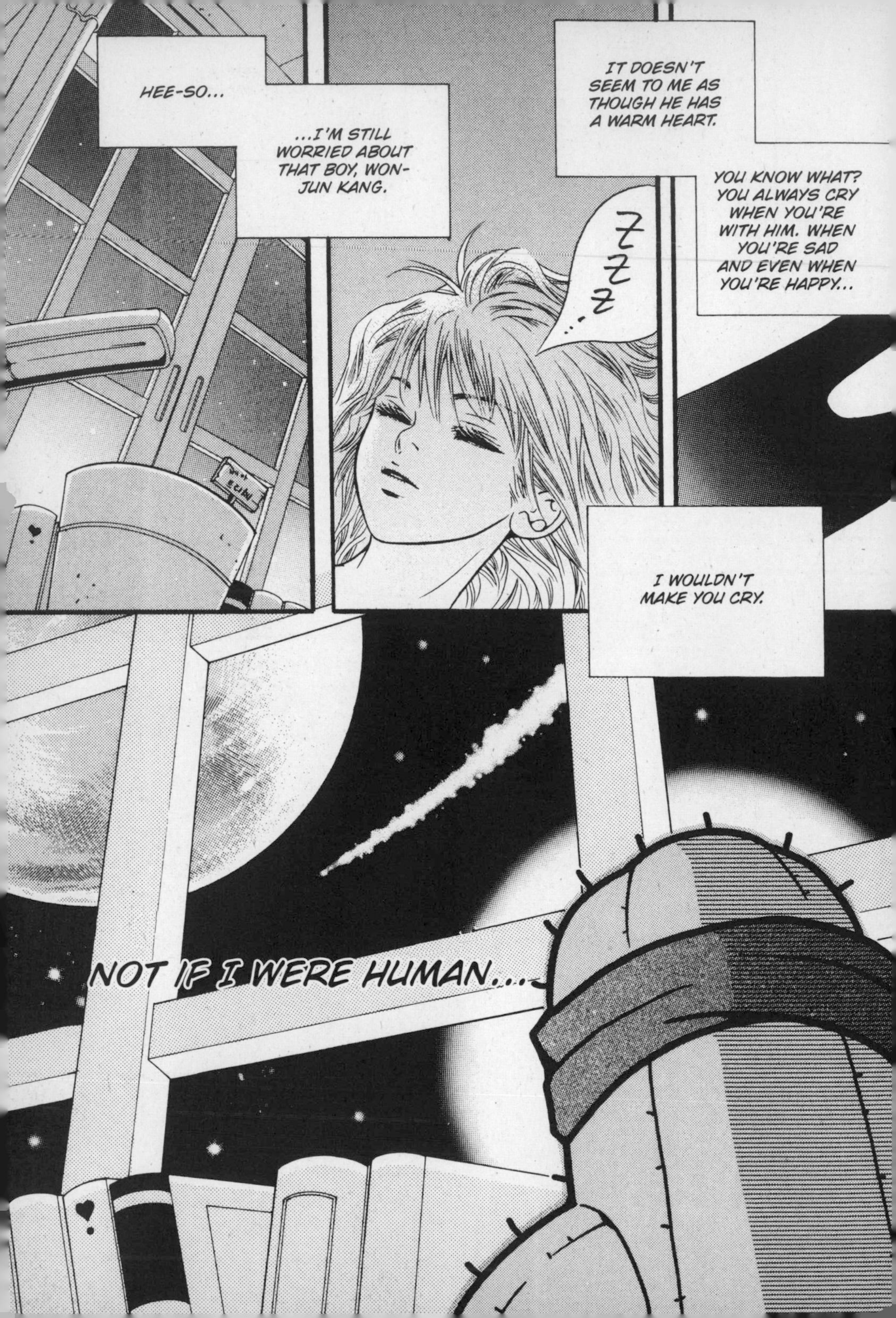

HEE-SO...
...I'M STILL WORRIED ABOUT THAT BOY, WON-JUN KANG.
ZZZ...
IT DOESN'T SEEM TO ME AS THOUGH HE HAS A WARM HEART.
YOU KNOW WHAT? YOU ALWAYS CRY WHEN YOU'RE WITH HIM. WHEN YOU'RE SAD AND EVEN WHEN YOU'RE HAPPY...
I WOULDN'T MAKE YOU CRY.
NOT IF I WERE HUMAN...

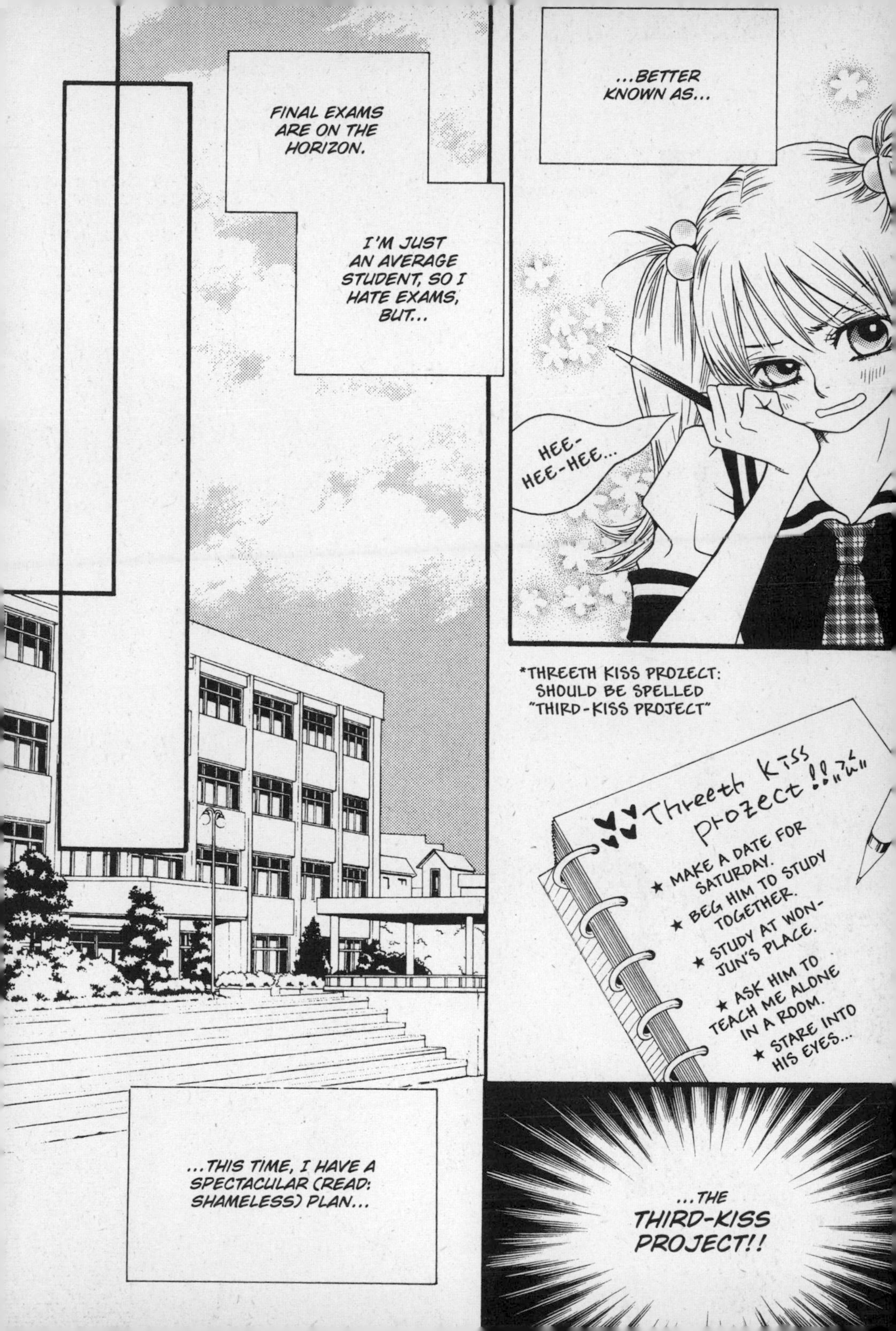
FINAL EXAMS ARE ON THE HORIZON.
I'M JUST AN AVERAGE STUDENT, SO I HATE EXAMS, BUT...
...THIS TIME, I HAVE A SPECTACULAR (READ: SHAMELESS) PLAN...
...BETTER KNOWN AS...
HEE-HEE-HEE...
*THREETH KISS PROZECT: SHOULD BE SPELLED "THIRD-KISS PROJECT"
Threeth Kiss prozect!!
★ MAKE A DATE FOR SATURDAY.
★ BEG HIM TO STUDY TOGETHER.
★ STUDY AT WON-JUN'S PLACE.
★ ASK HIM TO TEACH ME ALONE IN A ROOM.
★ STARE INTO HIS EYES...
...THE THIRD-KISS PROJECT!!

STEP 23. GO IN FOR THE THIRD KISS!

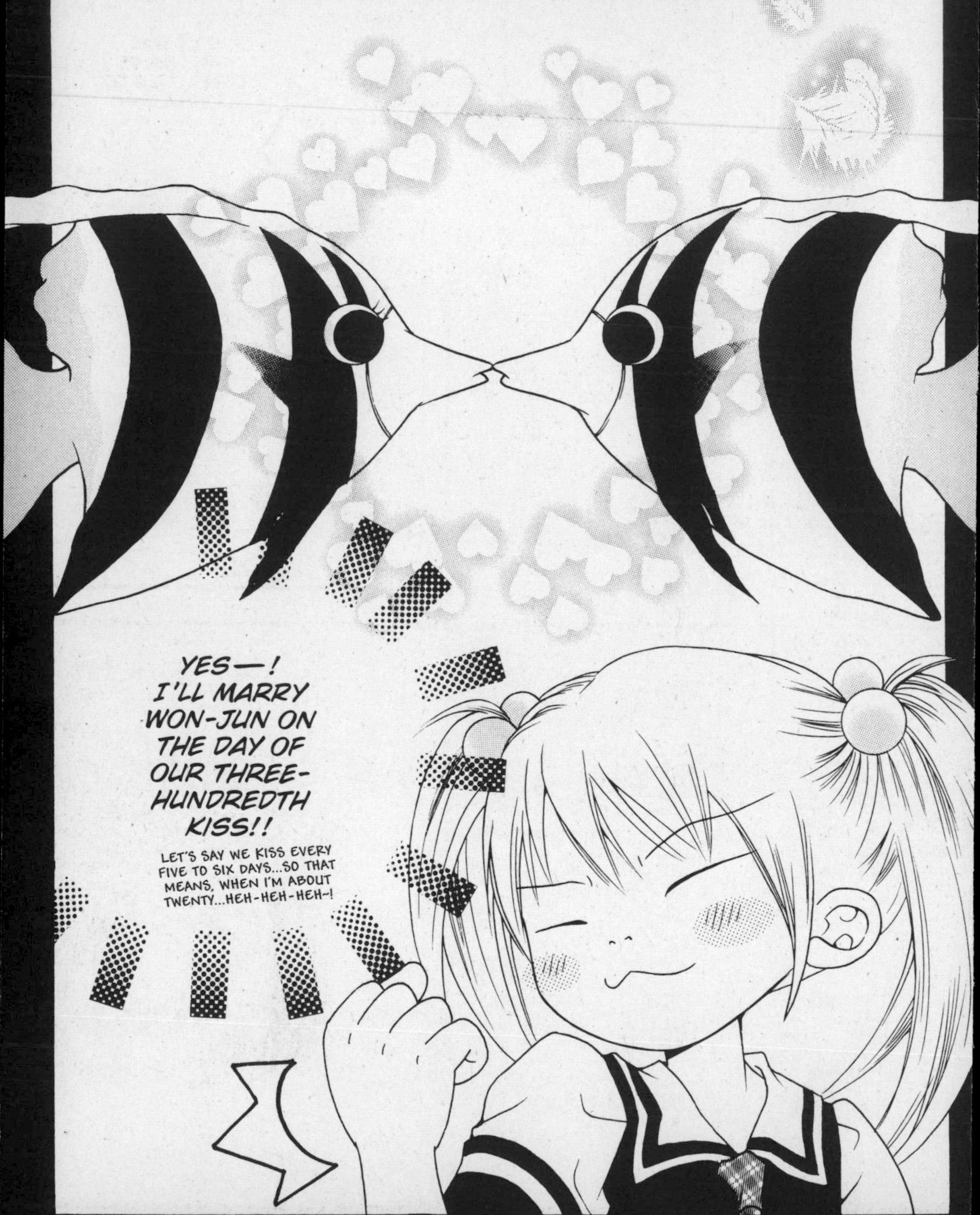
YES—! I'LL MARRY WON-JUN ON THE DAY OF OUR THREE-HUNDREDTH KISS!!
LET'S SAY WE KISS EVERY FIVE TO SIX DAYS...SO THAT MEANS, WHEN I'M ABOUT TWENTY...HEH-HEH-HEH~!

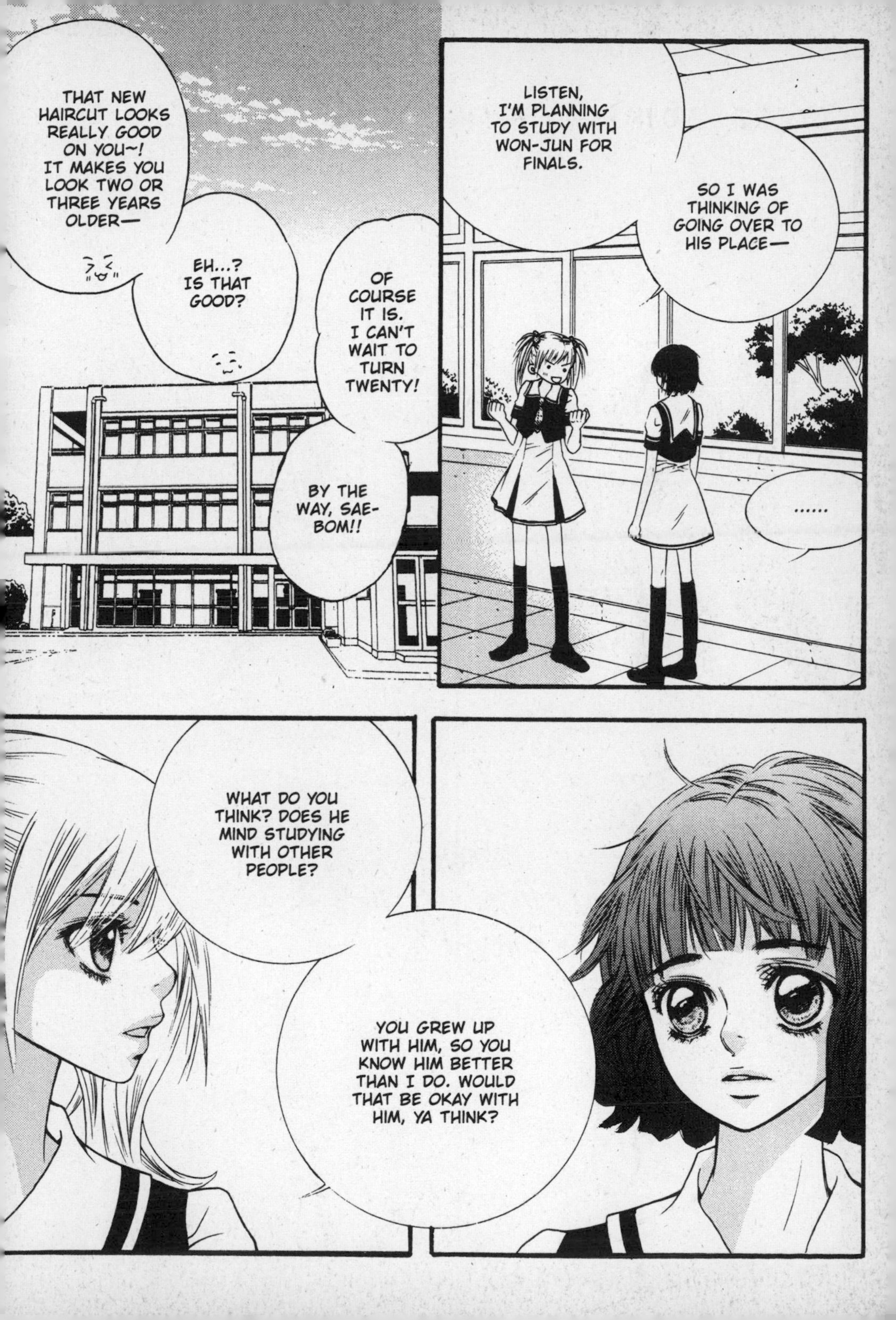
THAT NEW HAIRCUT LOOKS REALLY GOOD ON YOU~! IT MAKES YOU LOOK TWO OR THREE YEARS OLDER—
EH...? IS THAT GOOD?
OF COURSE IT IS. I CAN'T WAIT TO TURN TWENTY!
BY THE WAY, SAE-BOM!!
LISTEN, I'M PLANNING TO STUDY WITH WON-JUN FOR FINALS.
SO I WAS THINKING OF GOING OVER TO HIS PLACE—
......
WHAT DO YOU THINK? DOES HE MIND STUDYING WITH OTHER PEOPLE?
YOU GREW UP WITH HIM, SO YOU KNOW HIM BETTER THAN I DO. WOULD THAT BE OKAY WITH HIM, YA THINK?

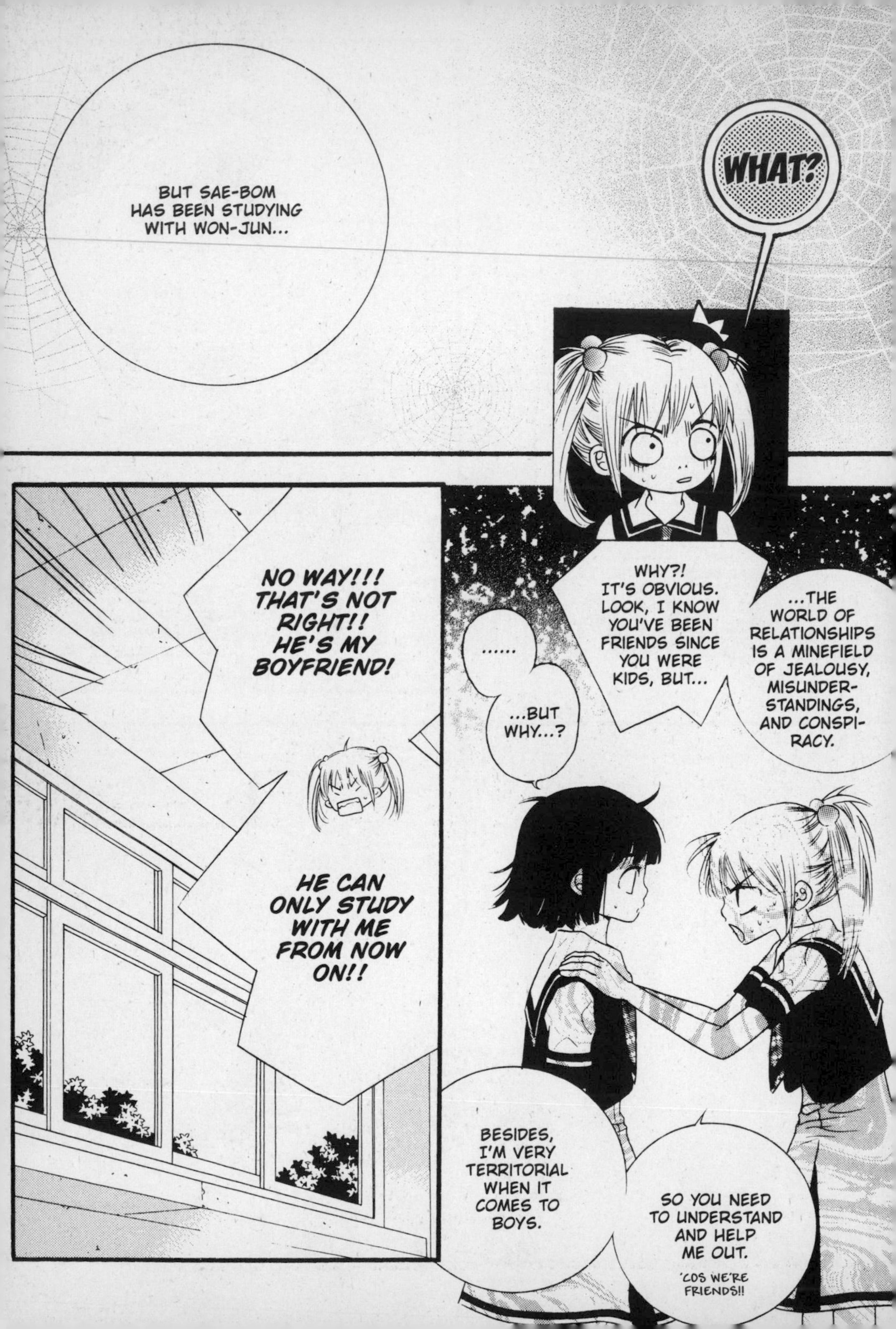

BUT SAE-BOM HAS BEEN STUDYING WITH WON-JUN...
WHAT?
NO WAY!!! THAT'S NOT RIGHT!! HE'S MY BOYFRIEND!
HE CAN ONLY STUDY WITH ME FROM NOW ON!!
......
...BUT WHY...?
WHY?! IT'S OBVIOUS. LOOK, I KNOW YOU'VE BEEN FRIENDS SINCE YOU WERE KIDS, BUT...
...THE WORLD OF RELATIONSHIPS IS A MINEFIELD OF JEALOUSY, MISUNDER-STANDINGS, AND CONSPI-RACY.
BESIDES, I'M VERY TERRITORIAL WHEN IT COMES TO BOYS.
SO YOU NEED TO UNDERSTAND AND HELP ME OUT.
'COS WE'RE FRIENDS!!

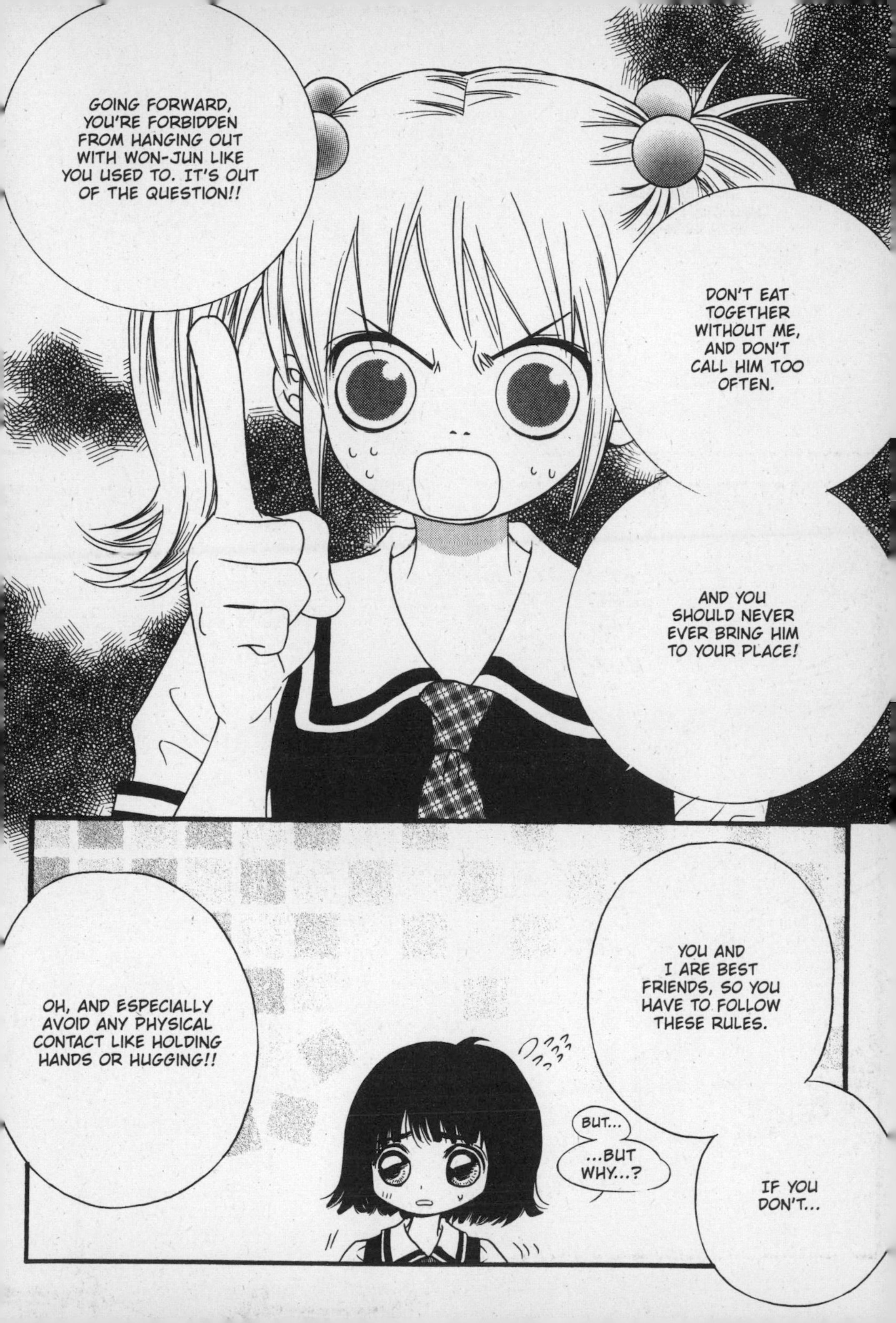
GOING FORWARD, YOU'RE FORBIDDEN FROM HANGING OUT WITH WON-JUN LIKE YOU USED TO. IT'S OUT OF THE QUESTION!!
DON'T EAT TOGETHER WITHOUT ME, AND DON'T CALL HIM TOO OFTEN.
AND YOU SHOULD NEVER EVER BRING HIM TO YOUR PLACE!
OH, AND ESPECIALLY AVOID ANY PHYSICAL CONTACT LIKE HOLDING HANDS OR HUGGING!!
YOU AND I ARE BEST FRIENDS, SO YOU HAVE TO FOLLOW THESE RULES.
BUT...
...BUT WHY...?
IF YOU DON'T...

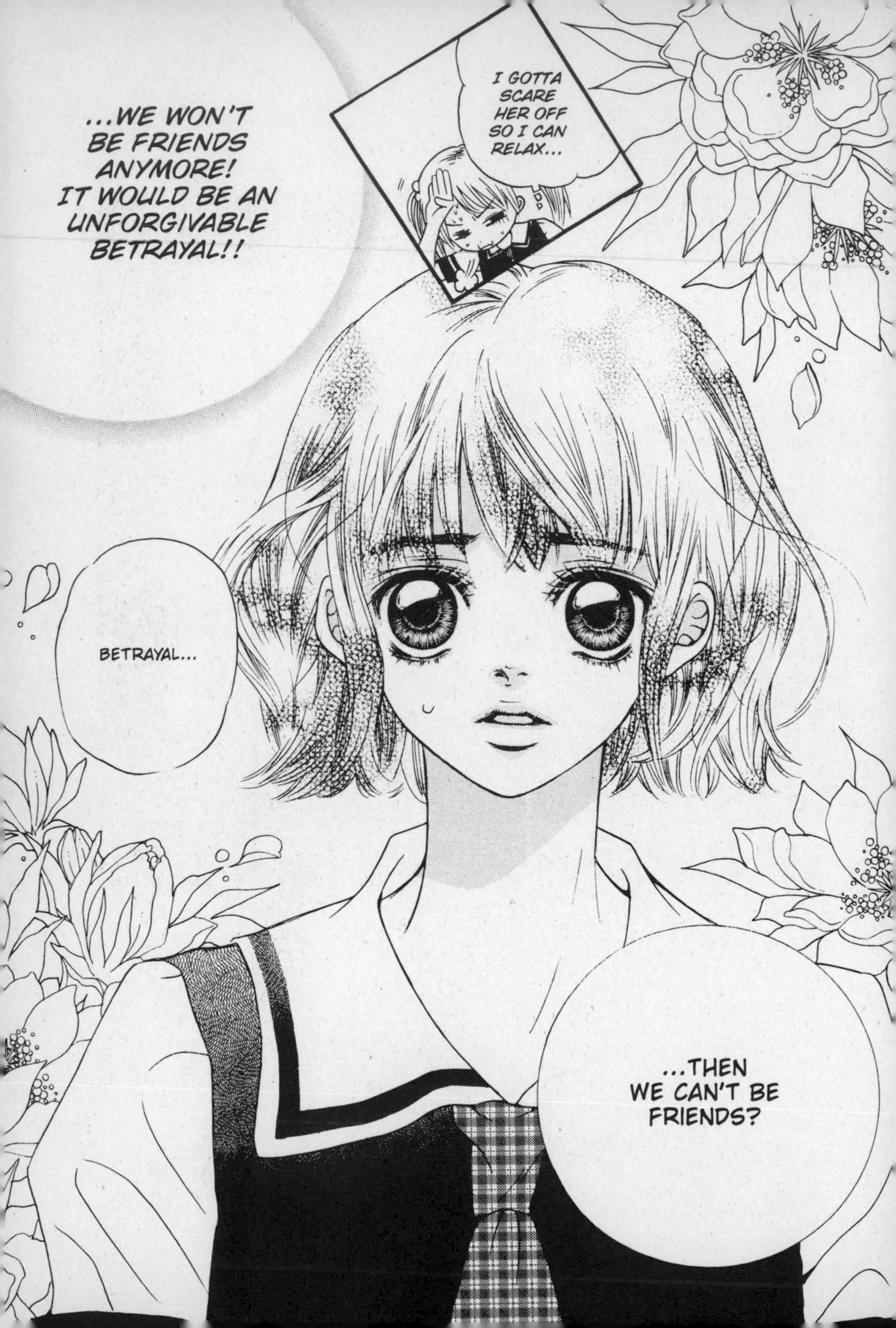
I GOTTA SCARE HER OFF SO I CAN RELAX...
...WE WON'T BE FRIENDS ANYMORE! IT WOULD BE AN UNFORGIVABLE BETRAYAL!!
BETRAYAL...
...THEN WE CAN'T BE FRIENDS?

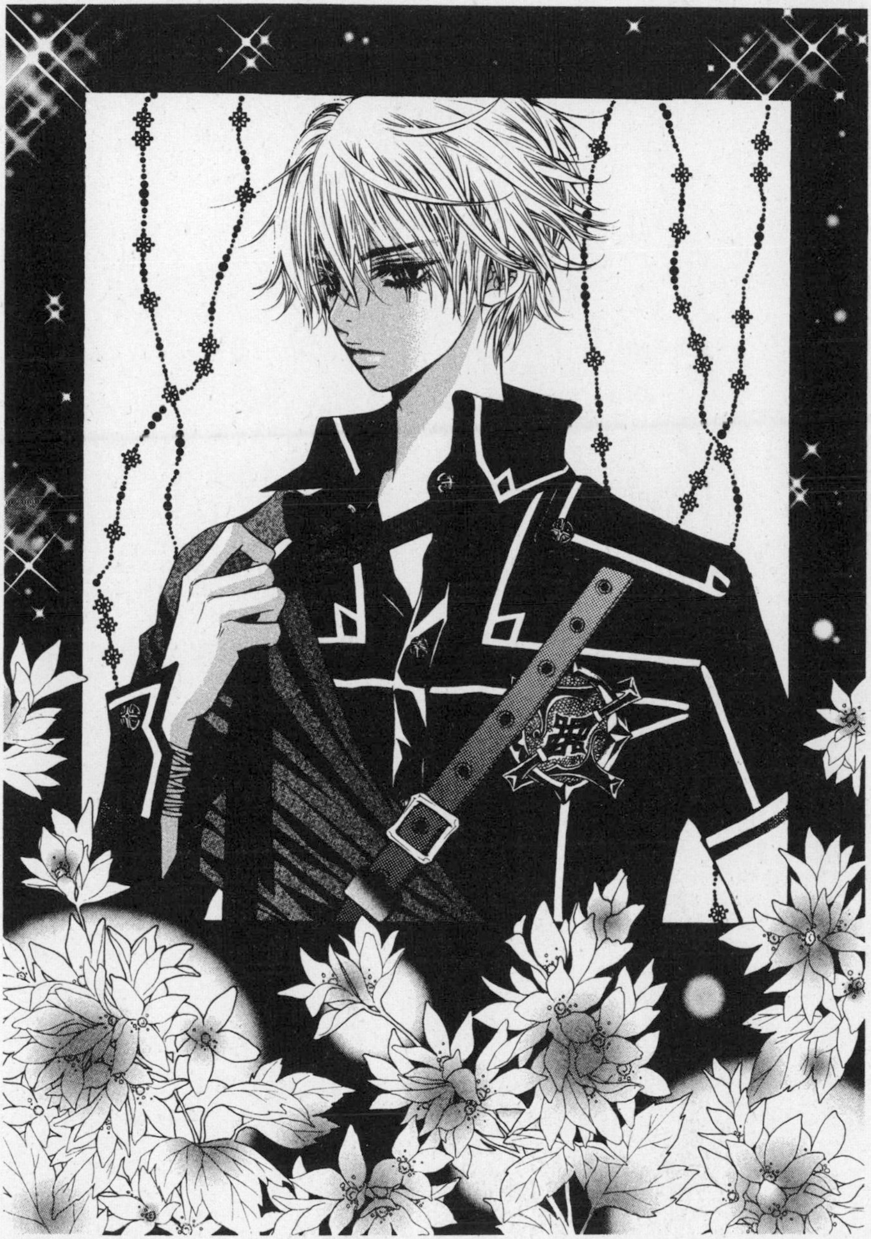

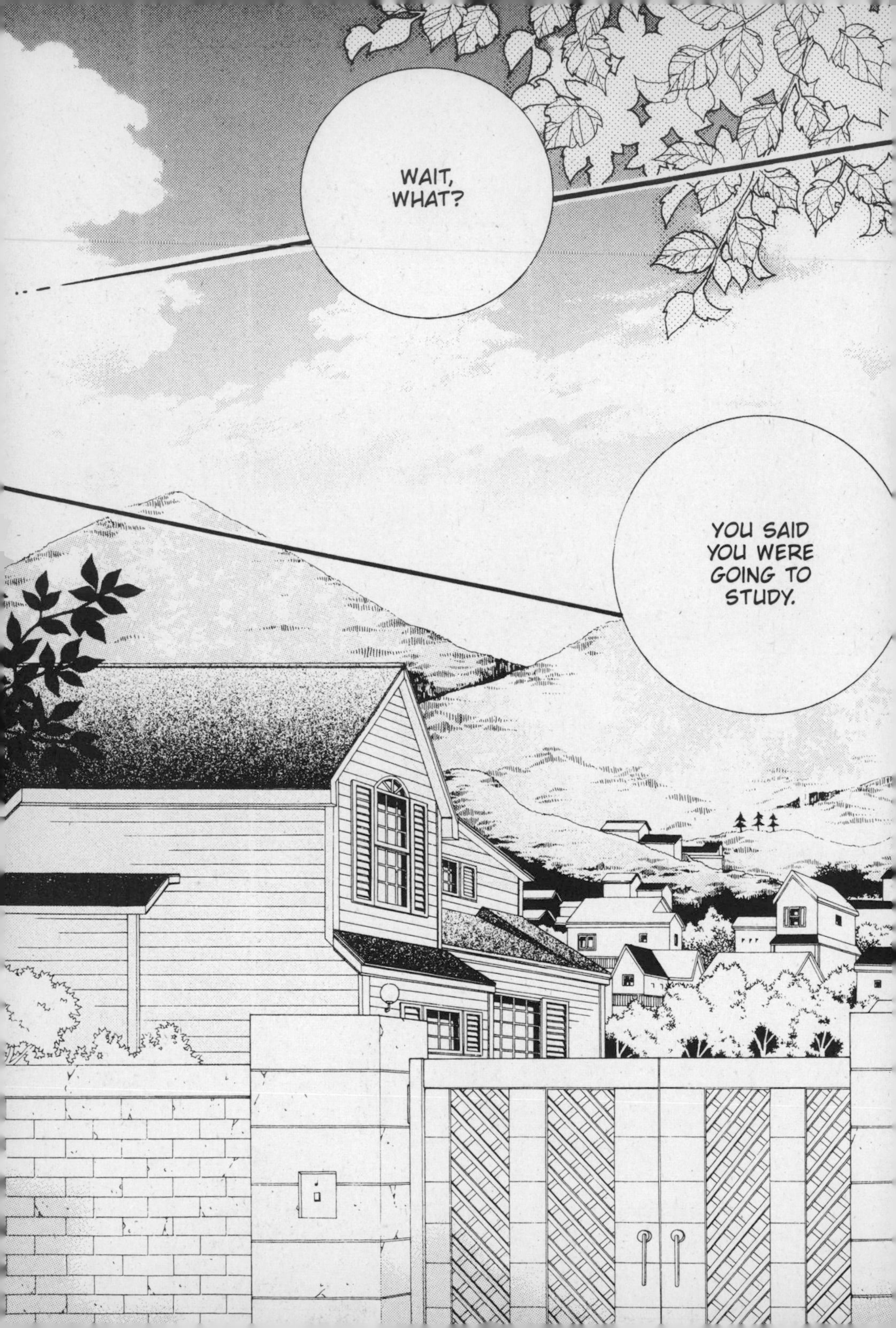
WAIT, WHAT?
YOU SAID YOU WERE GOING TO STUDY.

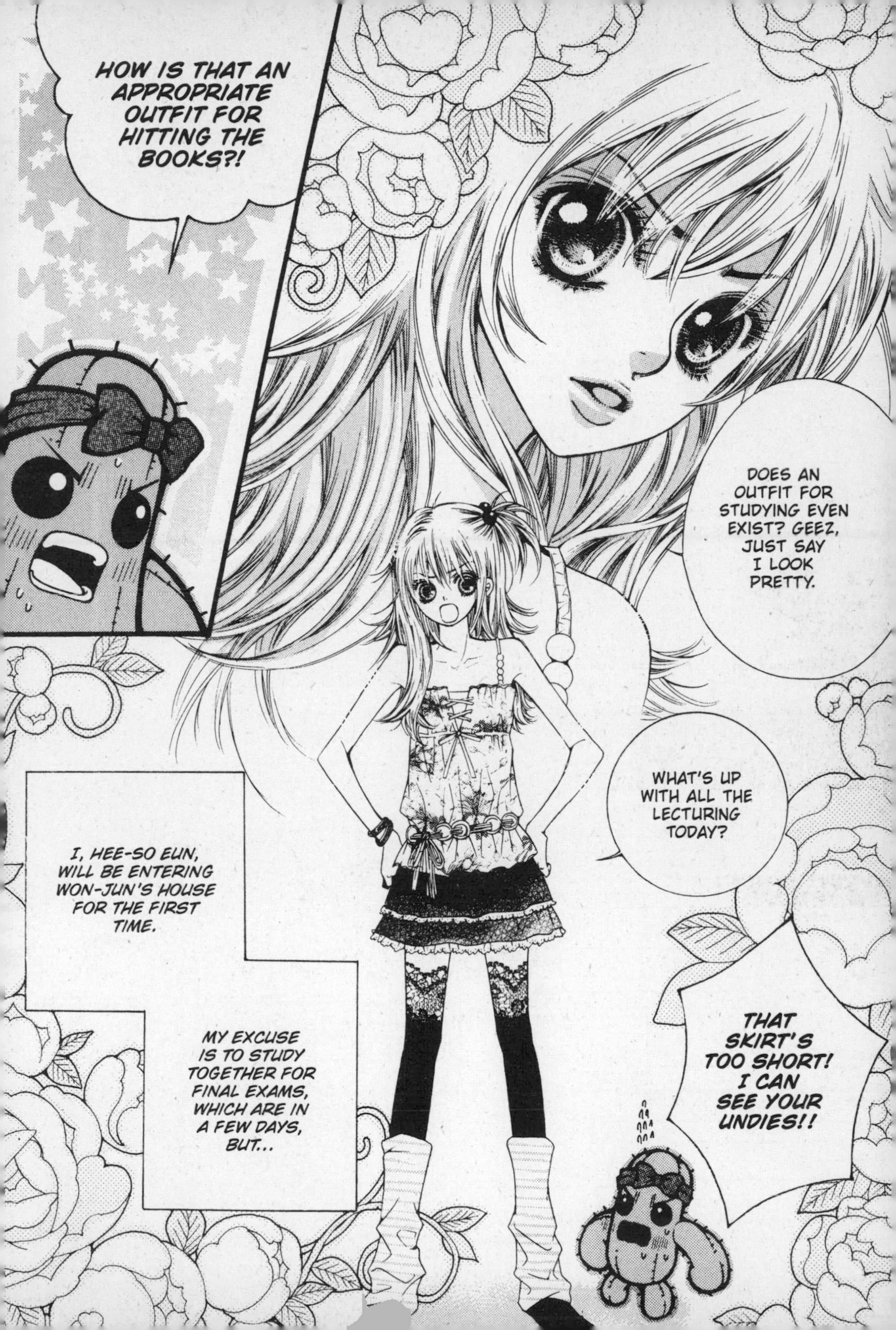
HOW IS THAT AN APPROPRIATE OUTFIT FOR HITTING THE BOOKS?!
DOES AN OUTFIT FOR STUDYING EVEN EXIST? GEEZ, JUST SAY I LOOK PRETTY.
WHAT'S UP WITH ALL THE LECTURING TODAY?
I, HEE-SO EUN, WILL BE ENTERING WON-JUN'S HOUSE FOR THE FIRST TIME.
MY EXCUSE IS TO STUDY TOGETHER FOR FINAL EXAMS, WHICH ARE IN A FEW DAYS, BUT...
THAT SKIRT'S TOO SHORT! I CAN SEE YOUR UNDIES!!

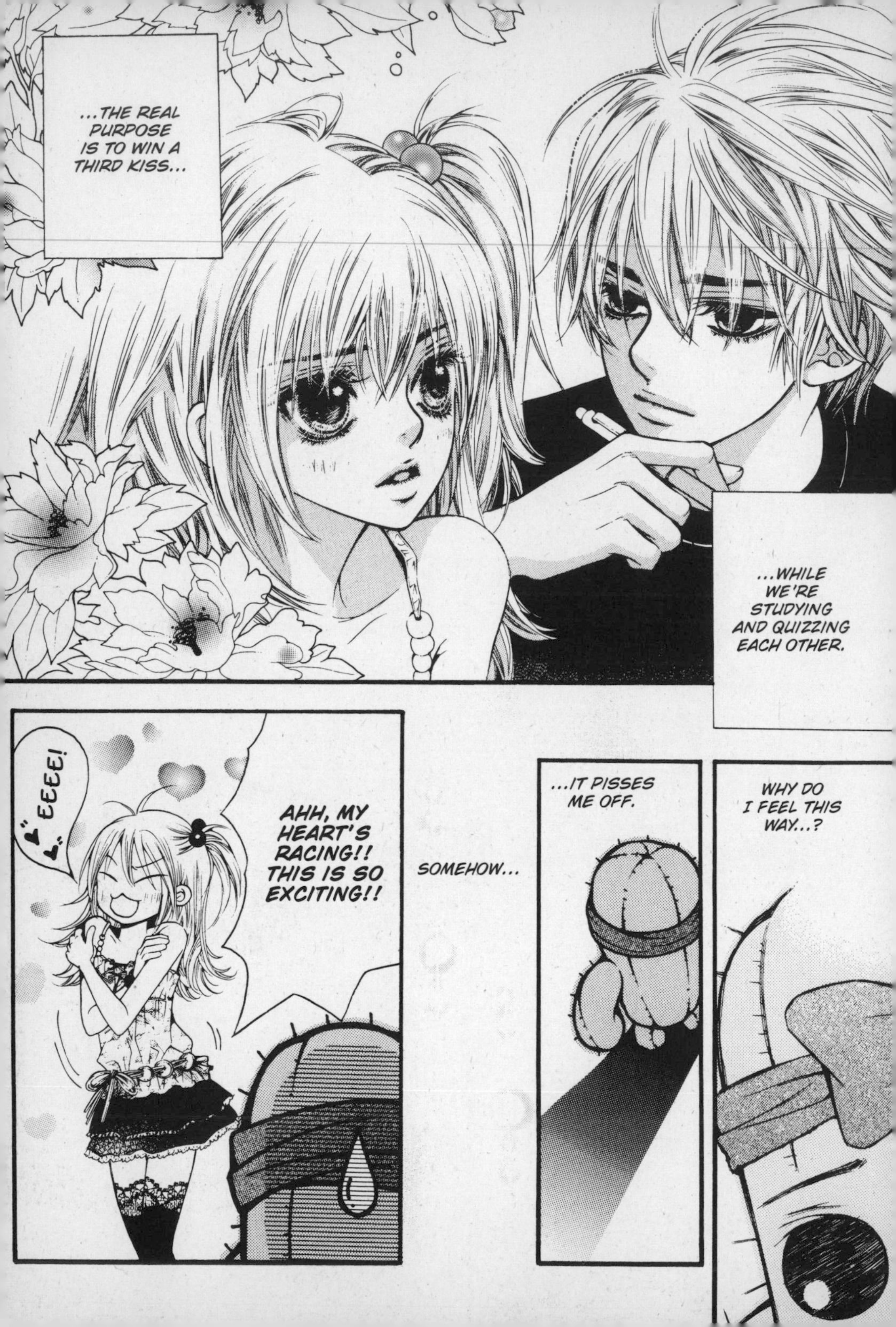
...THE REAL PURPOSE IS TO WIN A THIRD KISS...
...WHILE WE'RE STUDYING AND QUIZZING EACH OTHER.
EEEE!
AHH, MY HEART'S RACING!! THIS IS SO EXCITING!!
SOMEHOW...
...IT PISSES ME OFF.
WHY DO I FEEL THIS WAY...?

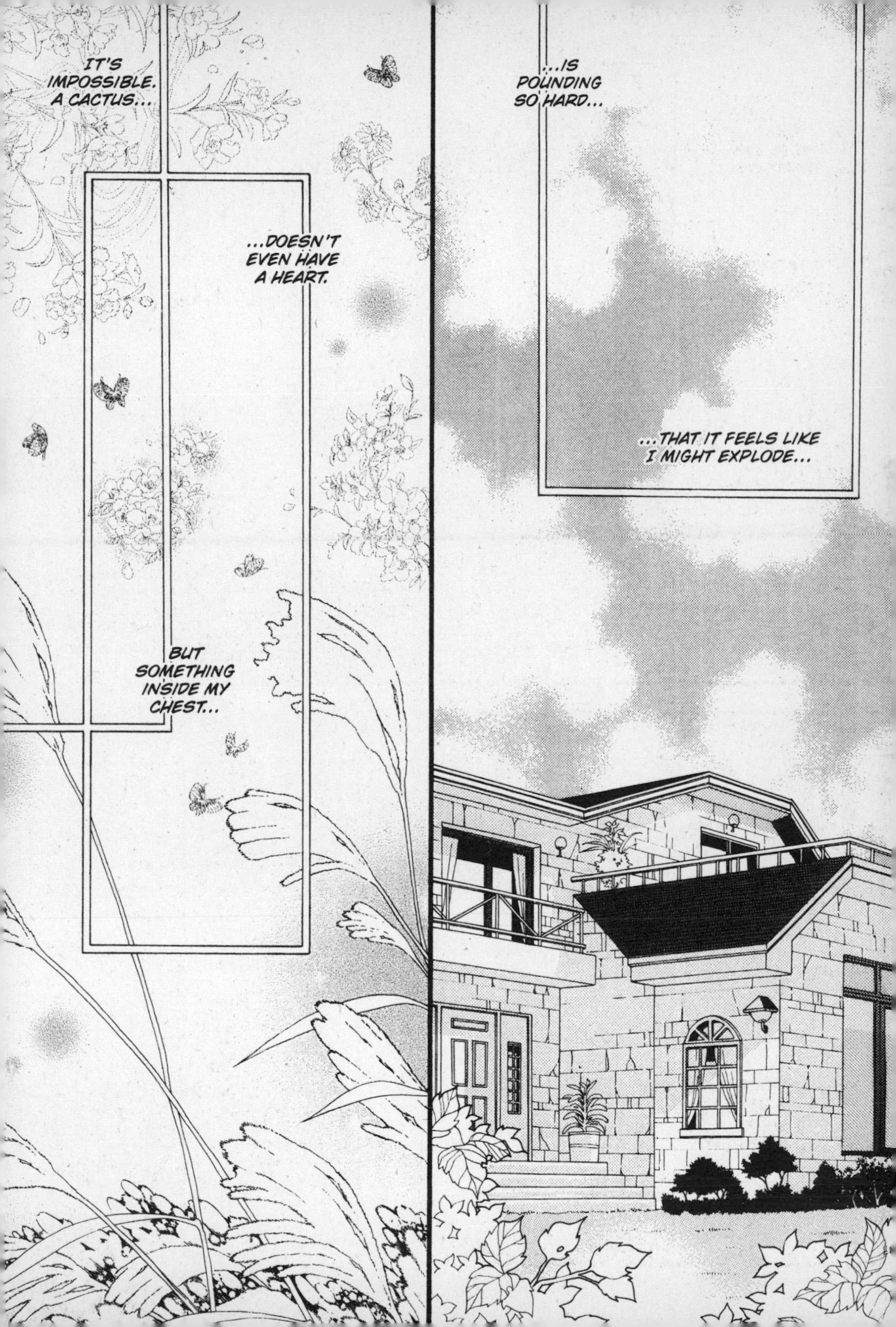
IT'S IMPOSSIBLE. A CACTUS...
...DOESN'T EVEN HAVE A HEART.
BUT SOMETHING INSIDE MY CHEST...
...IS POUNDING SO HARD...
...THAT IT FEELS LIKE I MIGHT EXPLODE...

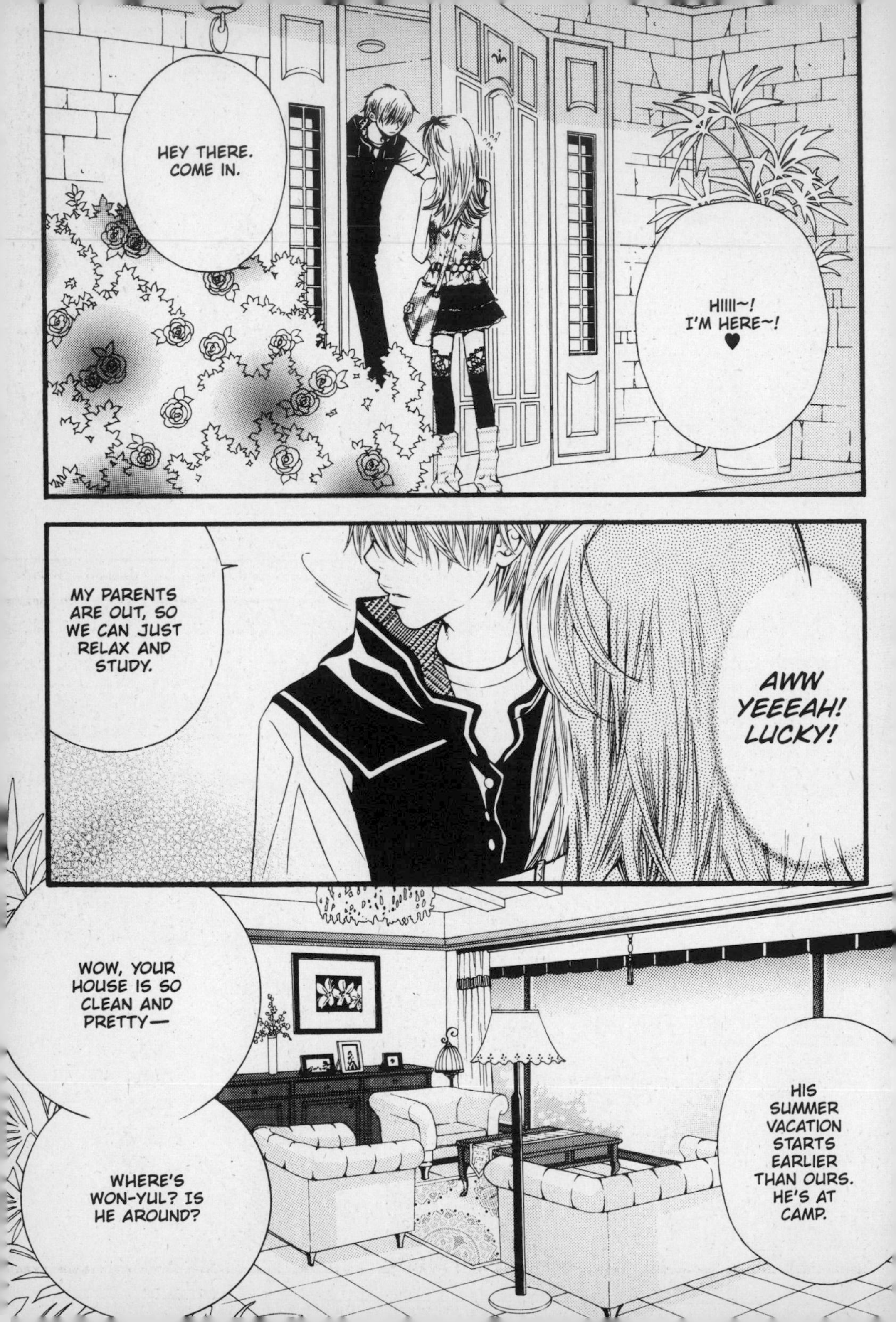
HEY THERE. COME IN.
HIIII~! I'M HERE~! ♥
MY PARENTS ARE OUT, SO WE CAN JUST RELAX AND STUDY.
AWW YEEEAH! LUCKY!
WOW, YOUR HOUSE IS SO CLEAN AND PRETTY—
WHERE'S WON-YUL? IS HE AROUND?
HIS SUMMER VACATION STARTS EARLIER THAN OURS. HE'S AT CAMP.

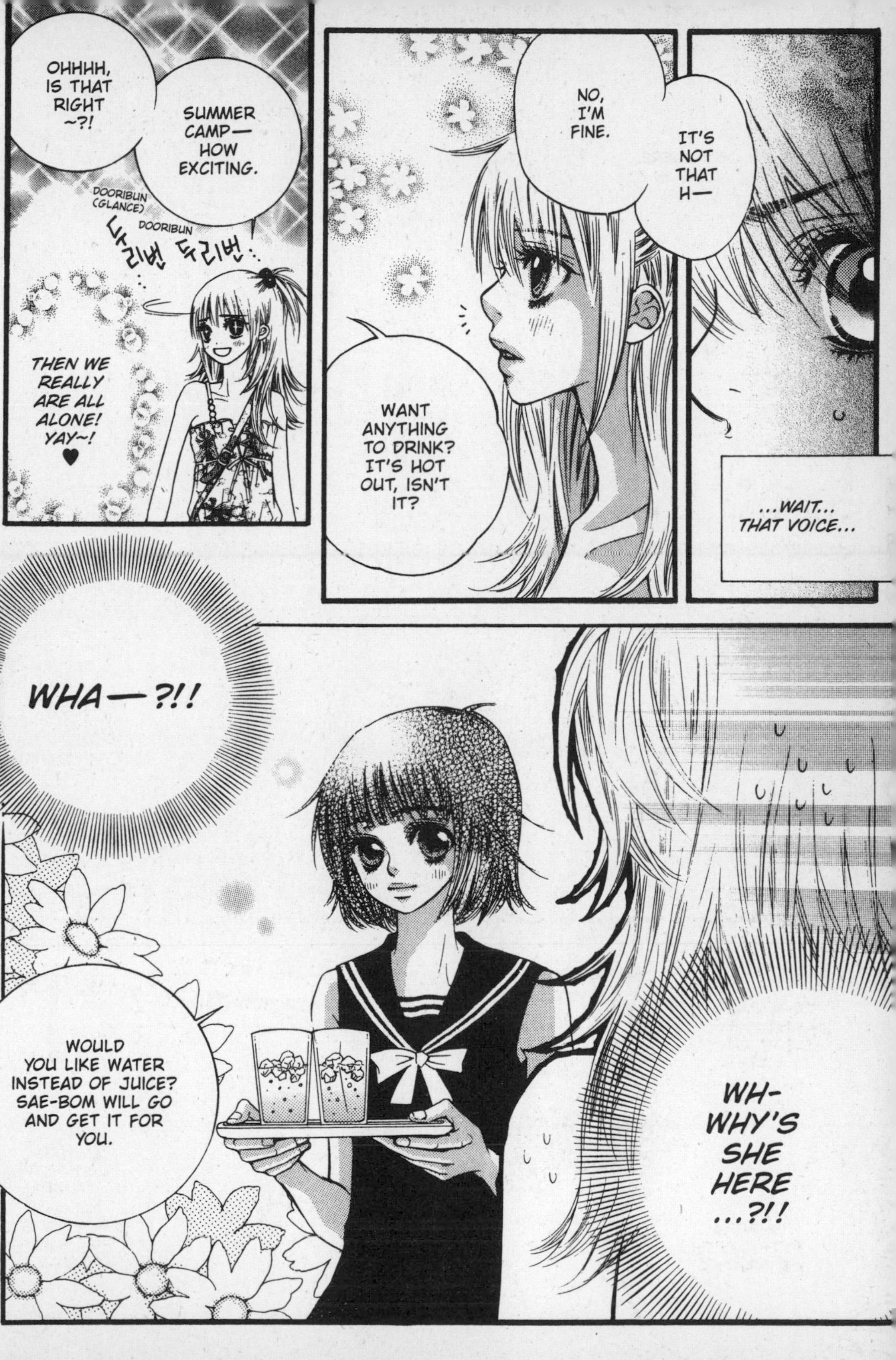
OHHHH, IS THAT RIGHT ~?!
SUMMER CAMP— HOW EXCITING.
DOORIBUN (GLANCE)
DOORIBUN
두리번 두리번
THEN WE REALLY ARE ALL ALONE! YAY~! ♥
NO, I'M FINE.
IT'S NOT THAT H—
WANT ANYTHING TO DRINK? IT'S HOT OUT, ISN'T IT?
...WAIT... THAT VOICE...
WHA—?!!
WOULD YOU LIKE WATER INSTEAD OF JUICE? SAE-BOM WILL GO AND GET IT FOR YOU.
WH- WHY'S SHE HERE ...?!!

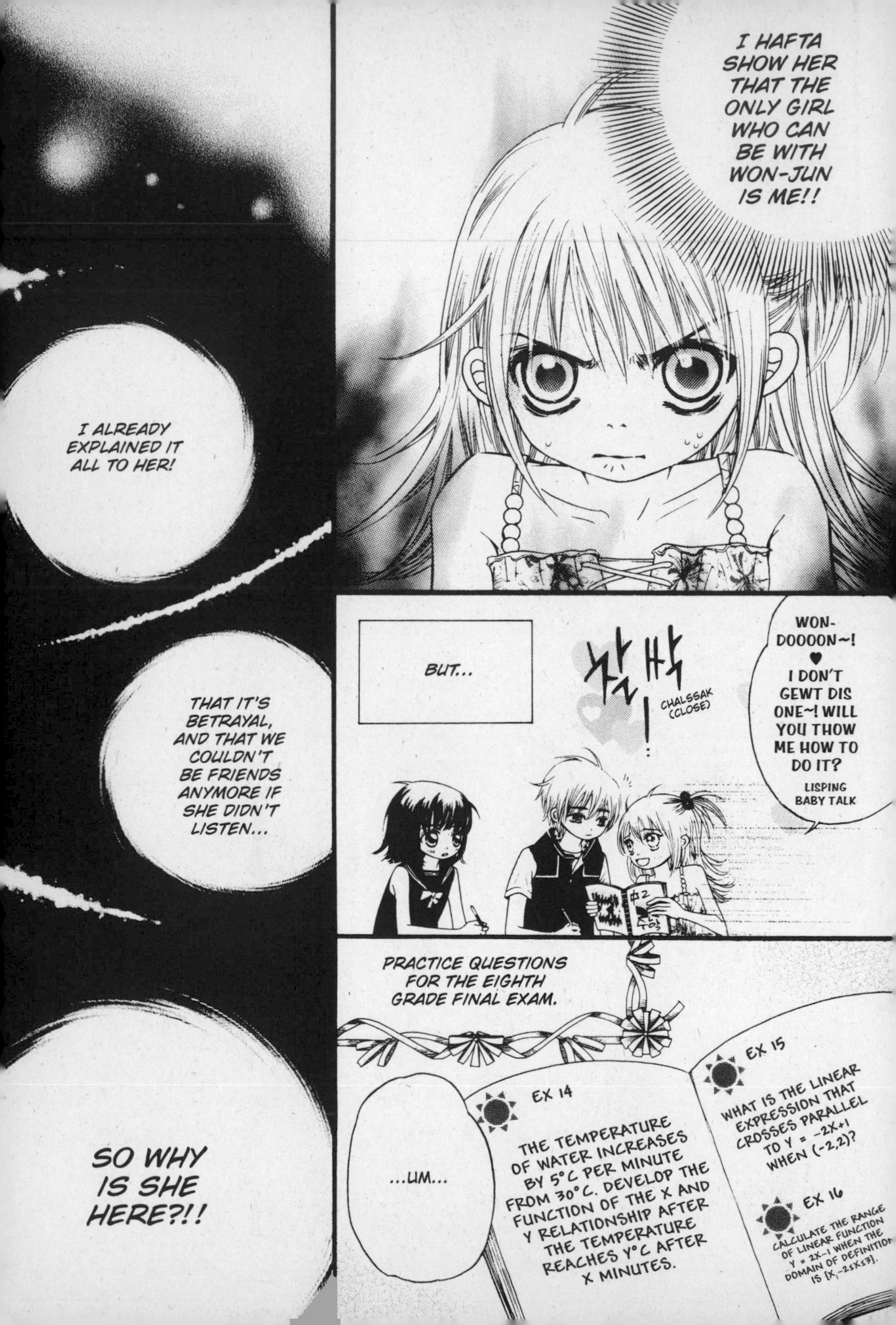
I ALREADY EXPLAINED IT ALL TO HER!
THAT IT'S BETRAYAL, AND THAT WE COULDN'T BE FRIENDS ANYMORE IF SHE DIDN'T LISTEN...
SO WHY IS SHE HERE?!!
I HAFTA SHOW HER THAT THE ONLY GIRL WHO CAN BE WITH WON-JUN IS ME!!
BUT...
찰싹!
CHALSSAK (CLOSE)
WON-DOOOON~! ♥ I DON'T GEWT DIS ONE~! WILL YOU THOW ME HOW TO DO IT?
LISPING BABY TALK
PRACTICE QUESTIONS FOR THE EIGHTH GRADE FINAL EXAM.
...UM...
EX 14
THE TEMPERATURE OF WATER INCREASES BY 5°C PER MINUTE FROM 30°C. DEVELOP THE FUNCTION OF THE X AND Y RELATIONSHIP AFTER THE TEMPERATURE REACHES Y°C AFTER X MINUTES.
EX 15
WHAT IS THE LINEAR EXPRESSION THAT CROSSES PARALLEL TO Y = −2X+1 WHEN (−2,2)?
EX 16
CALCULATE THE RANGE OF LINEAR FUNCTION Y = 2X−1 WHEN THE DOMAIN OF DEFINITION IS {X, −2≤X≤3}.

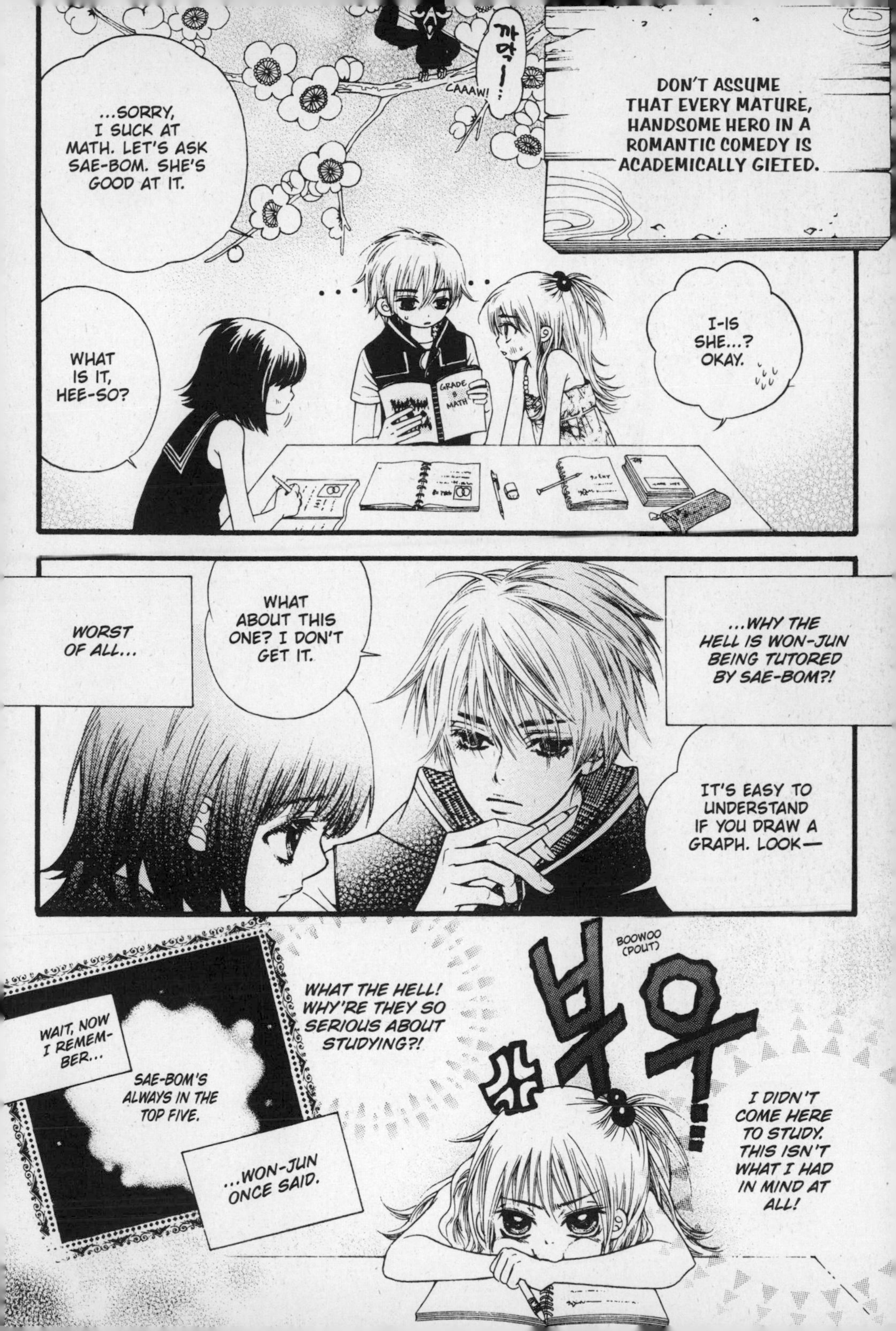
...SORRY, I SUCK AT MATH. LET'S ASK SAE-BOM. SHE'S GOOD AT IT.
까악—!!
CAAAW!
DON'T ASSUME THAT EVERY MATURE, HANDSOME HERO IN A ROMANTIC COMEDY IS ACADEMICALLY GIFTED.
WHAT IS IT, HEE-SO?
...
GRADE 8 MATH
I-IS SHE...? OKAY.
WORST OF ALL...
WHAT ABOUT THIS ONE? I DON'T GET IT.
...WHY THE HELL IS WON-JUN BEING TUTORED BY SAE-BOM?!
IT'S EASY TO UNDERSTAND IF YOU DRAW A GRAPH. LOOK—
WAIT, NOW I REMEMBER...
SAE-BOM'S ALWAYS IN THE TOP FIVE.
...WON-JUN ONCE SAID.
WHAT THE HELL! WHY'RE THEY SO SERIOUS ABOUT STUDYING?!
부우
BOOWOO (POUT)
I DIDN'T COME HERE TO STUDY. THIS ISN'T WHAT I HAD IN MIND AT ALL!

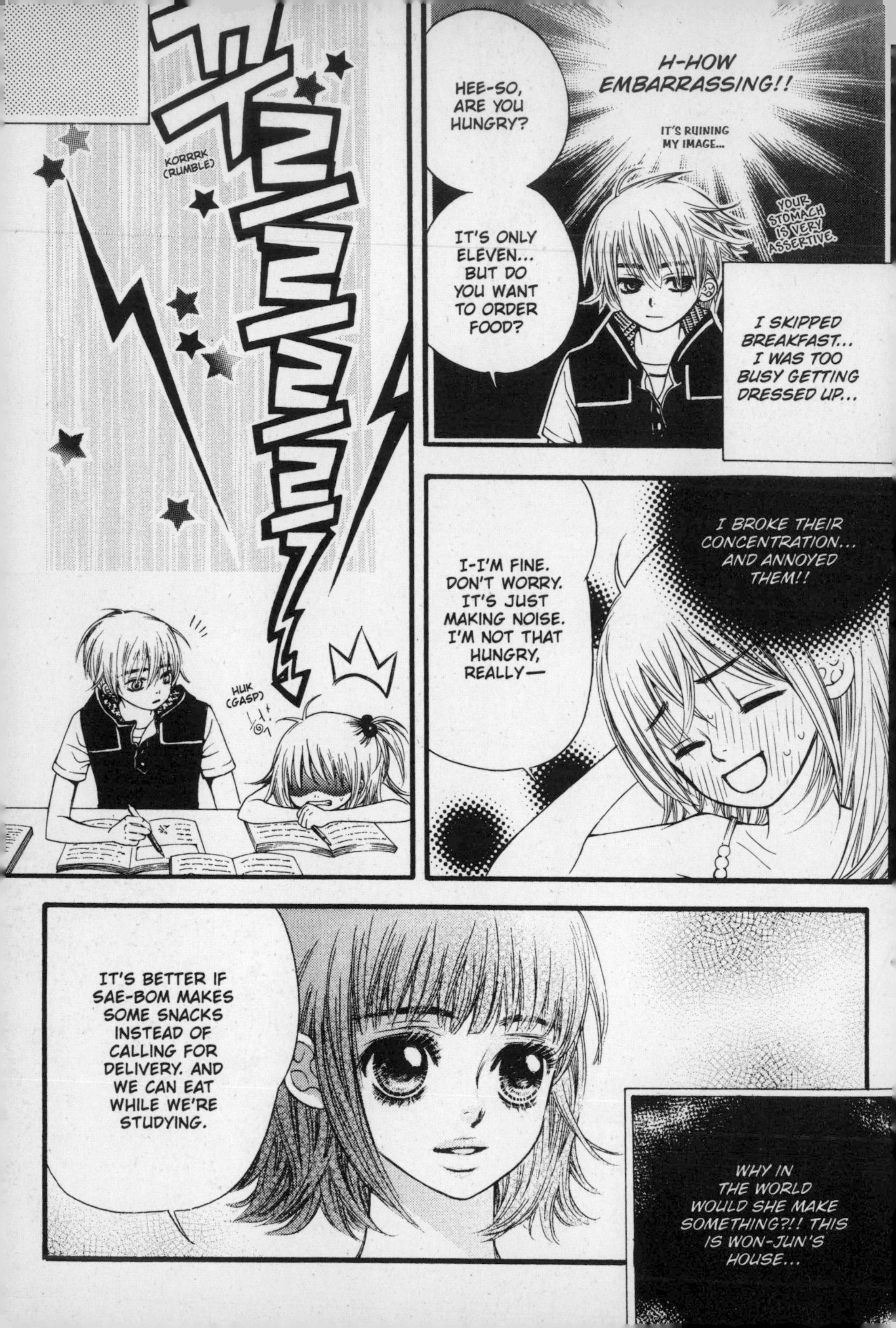
KORRRK (RUMBLE)
HUK (GASP)
HEE-SO, ARE YOU HUNGRY?
IT'S ONLY ELEVEN... BUT DO YOU WANT TO ORDER FOOD?
H-HOW EMBARRASSING!!
IT'S RUINING MY IMAGE...
YOUR STOMACH IS VERY ASSERTIVE.
I SKIPPED BREAKFAST... I WAS TOO BUSY GETTING DRESSED UP...
I-I'M FINE. DON'T WORRY. IT'S JUST MAKING NOISE. I'M NOT THAT HUNGRY, REALLY—
I BROKE THEIR CONCENTRATION... AND ANNOYED THEM!!
IT'S BETTER IF SAE-BOM MAKES SOME SNACKS INSTEAD OF CALLING FOR DELIVERY. AND WE CAN EAT WHILE WE'RE STUDYING.
WHY IN THE WORLD WOULD SHE MAKE SOMETHING?!! THIS IS WON-JUN'S HOUSE...

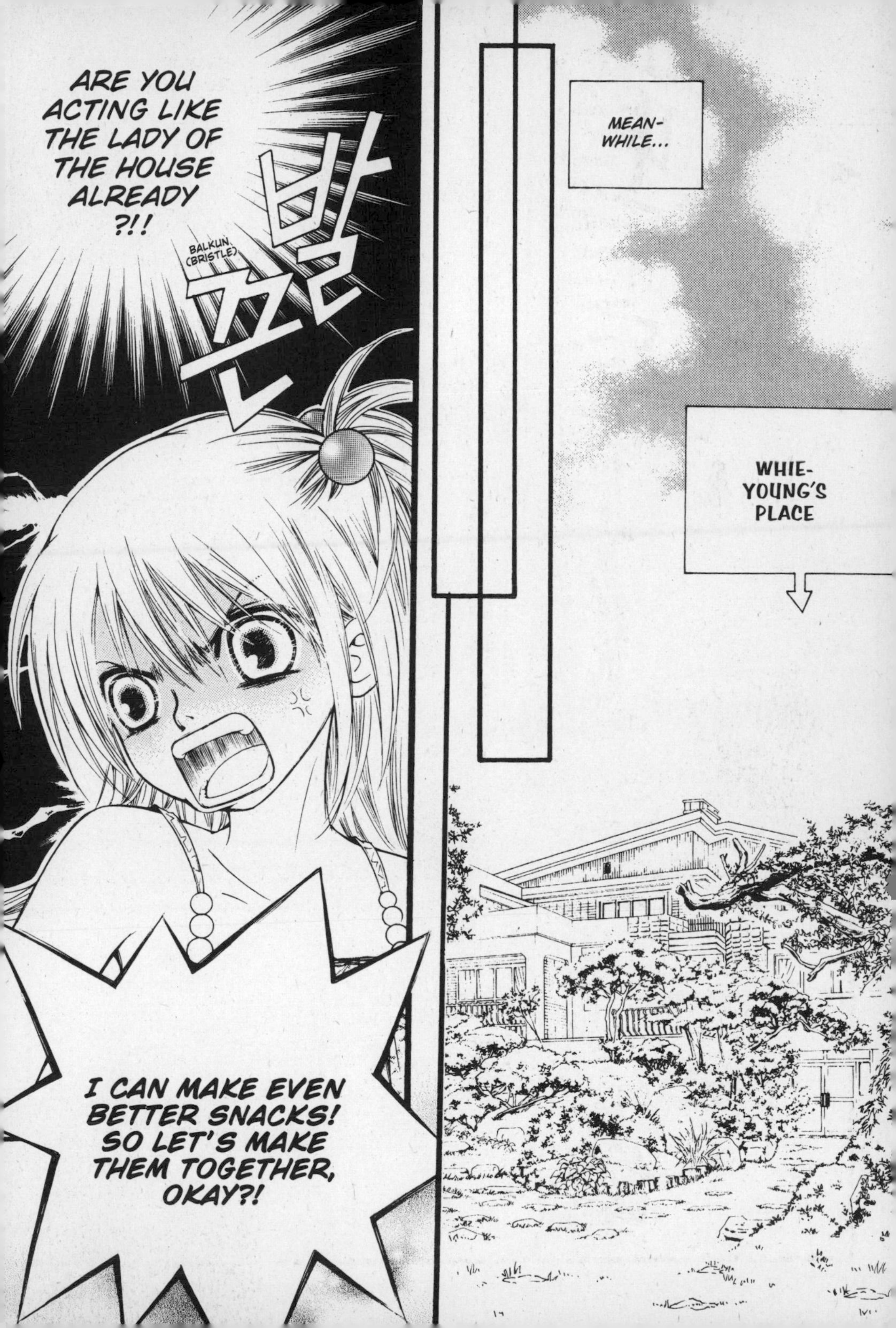

ARE YOU ACTING LIKE THE LADY OF THE HOUSE ALREADY ?!!
발끈
BALKUN (BRISTLE)
I CAN MAKE EVEN BETTER SNACKS! SO LET'S MAKE THEM TOGETHER, OKAY?!
MEAN-WHILE...
WHIE-YOUNG'S PLACE

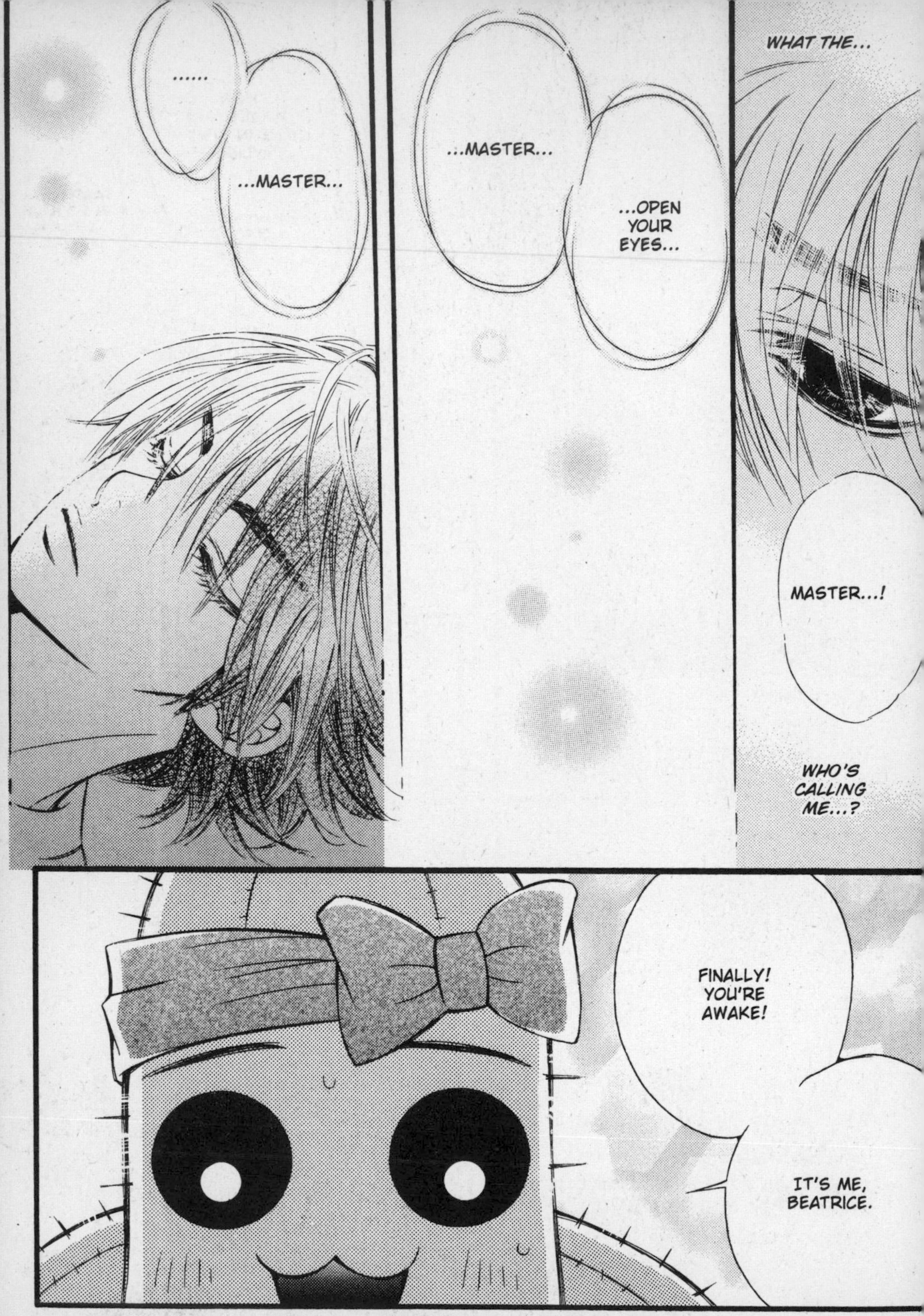
......
...MASTER...
...MASTER...
...OPEN YOUR EYES...
WHAT THE...
MASTER...!
WHO'S CALLING ME...?
FINALLY! YOU'RE AWAKE!
IT'S ME, BEATRICE.

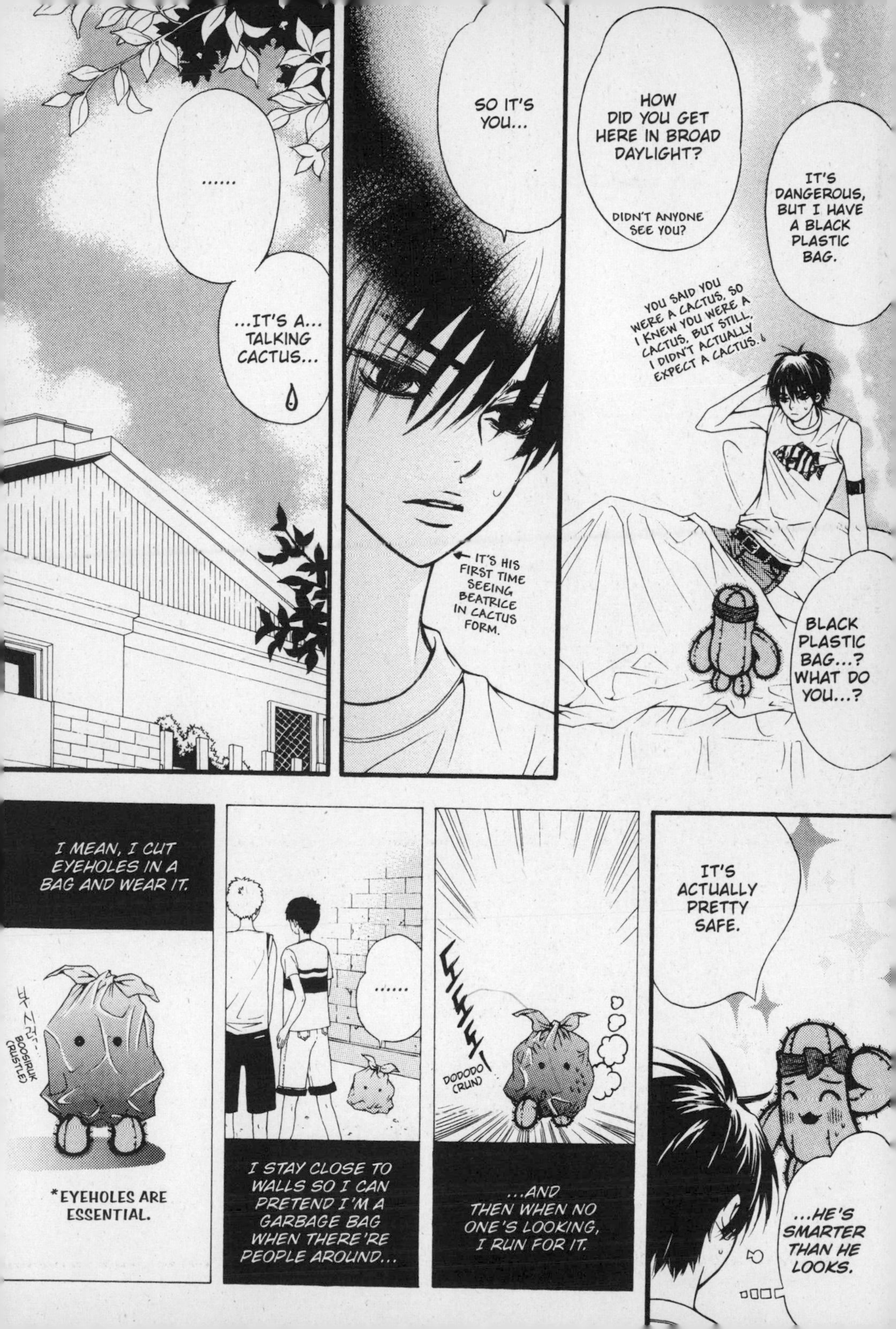
......
...IT'S A... TALKING CACTUS...
SO IT'S YOU...
IT'S HIS FIRST TIME SEEING BEATRICE IN CACTUS FORM.
HOW DID YOU GET HERE IN BROAD DAYLIGHT?
DIDN'T ANYONE SEE YOU?
IT'S DANGEROUS, BUT I HAVE A BLACK PLASTIC BAG.
YOU SAID YOU WERE A CACTUS, SO I KNEW YOU WERE A CACTUS, BUT STILL, I DIDN'T ACTUALLY EXPECT A CACTUS.
BLACK PLASTIC BAG...? WHAT DO YOU...?
I MEAN, I CUT EYEHOLES IN A BAG AND WEAR IT.
BOOSIRUK (RUSTLE)
*EYEHOLES ARE ESSENTIAL.
......
I STAY CLOSE TO WALLS SO I CAN PRETEND I'M A GARBAGE BAG WHEN THERE'RE PEOPLE AROUND...
DODODO (RUN)
...AND THEN WHEN NO ONE'S LOOKING, I RUN FOR IT.
IT'S ACTUALLY PRETTY SAFE.
...HE'S SMARTER THAN HE LOOKS.

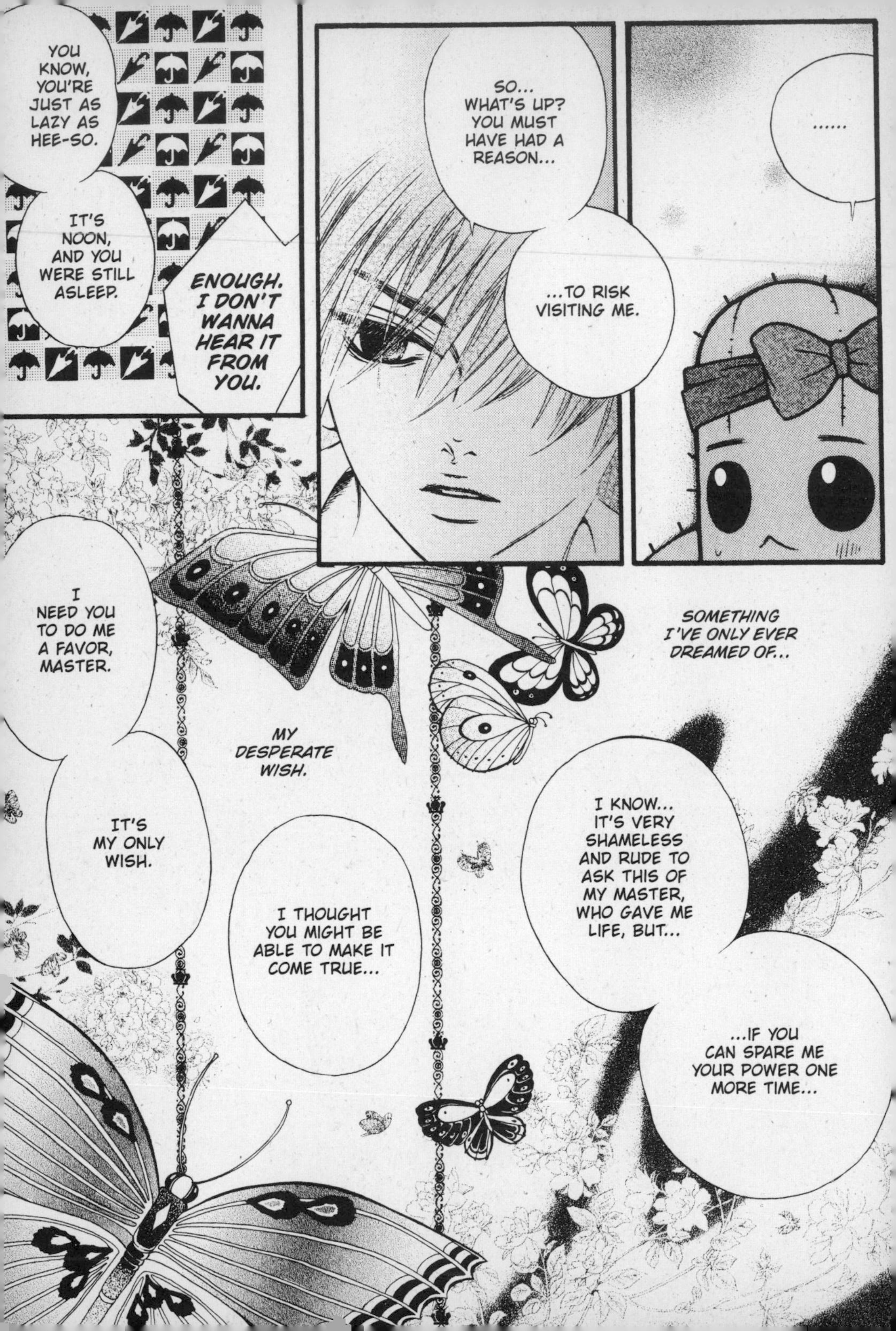
YOU KNOW, YOU'RE JUST AS LAZY AS HEE-SO.
IT'S NOON, AND YOU WERE STILL ASLEEP.
ENOUGH. I DON'T WANNA HEAR IT FROM YOU.
SO... WHAT'S UP? YOU MUST HAVE HAD A REASON...
...TO RISK VISITING ME.
......
I NEED YOU TO DO ME A FAVOR, MASTER.
IT'S MY ONLY WISH.
MY DESPERATE WISH.
I THOUGHT YOU MIGHT BE ABLE TO MAKE IT COME TRUE...
SOMETHING I'VE ONLY EVER DREAMED OF...
I KNOW... IT'S VERY SHAMELESS AND RUDE TO ASK THIS OF MY MASTER, WHO GAVE ME LIFE, BUT...
...IF YOU CAN SPARE ME YOUR POWER ONE MORE TIME...

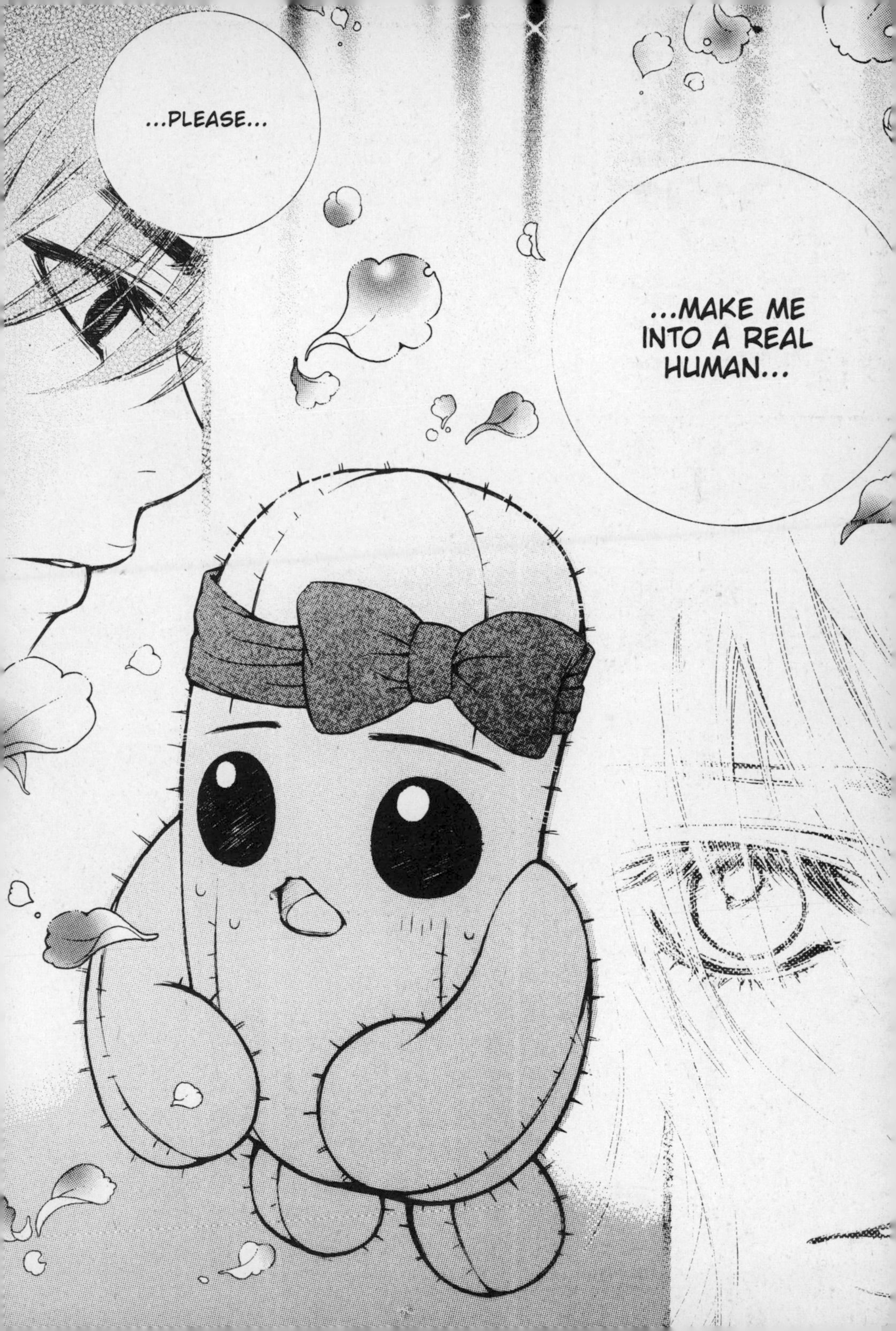
...PLEASE...
...MAKE ME INTO A REAL HUMAN...

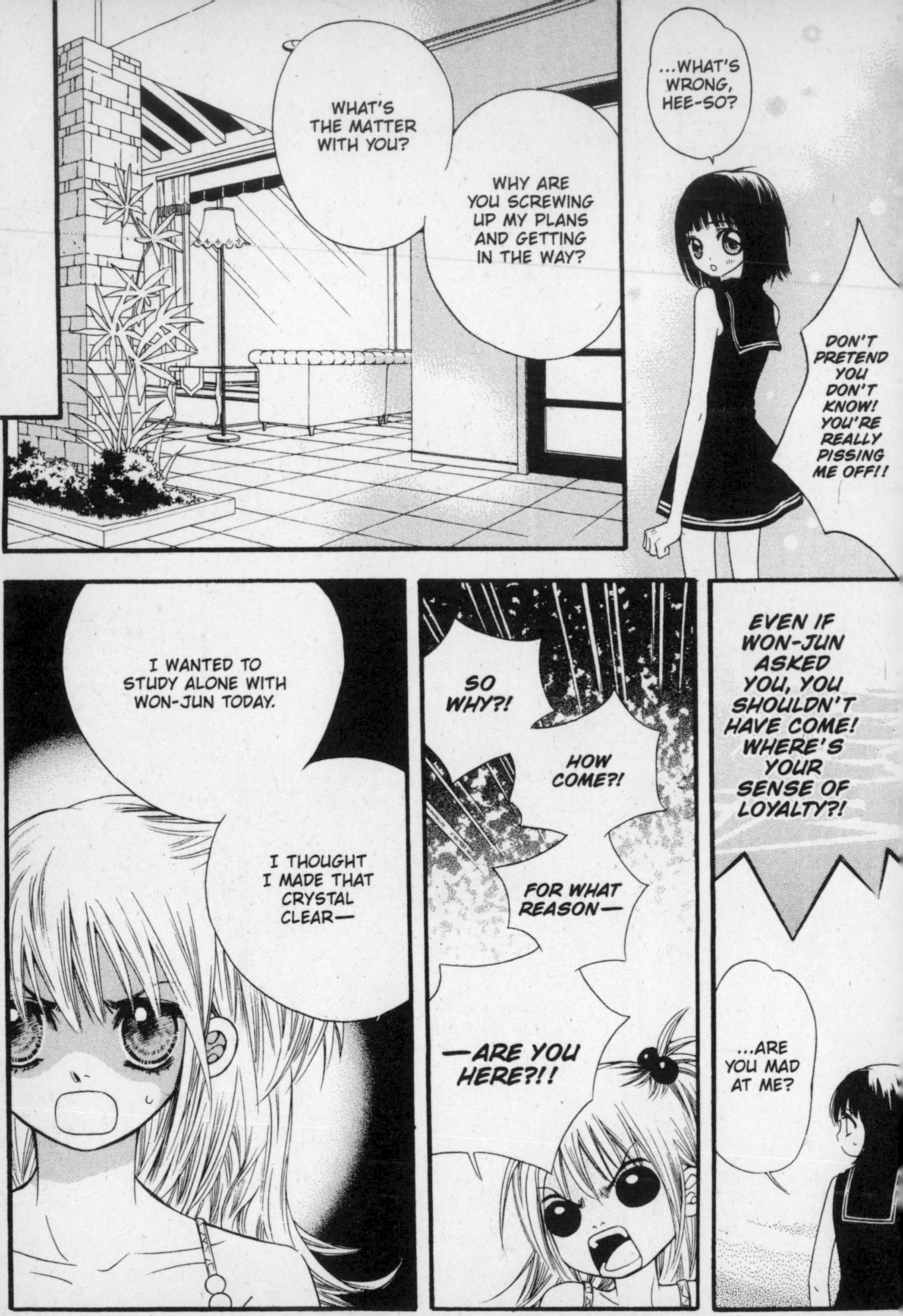
WHAT'S THE MATTER WITH YOU?
WHY ARE YOU SCREWING UP MY PLANS AND GETTING IN THE WAY?
...WHAT'S WRONG, HEE-SO?
DON'T PRETEND YOU DON'T KNOW! YOU'RE REALLY PISSING ME OFF!!
I WANTED TO STUDY ALONE WITH WON-JUN TODAY.
I THOUGHT I MADE THAT CRYSTAL CLEAR—
SO WHY?!
HOW COME?!
FOR WHAT REASON—
—ARE YOU HERE?!!
EVEN IF WON-JUN ASKED YOU, YOU SHOULDN'T HAVE COME! WHERE'S YOUR SENSE OF LOYALTY?!
...ARE YOU MAD AT ME?

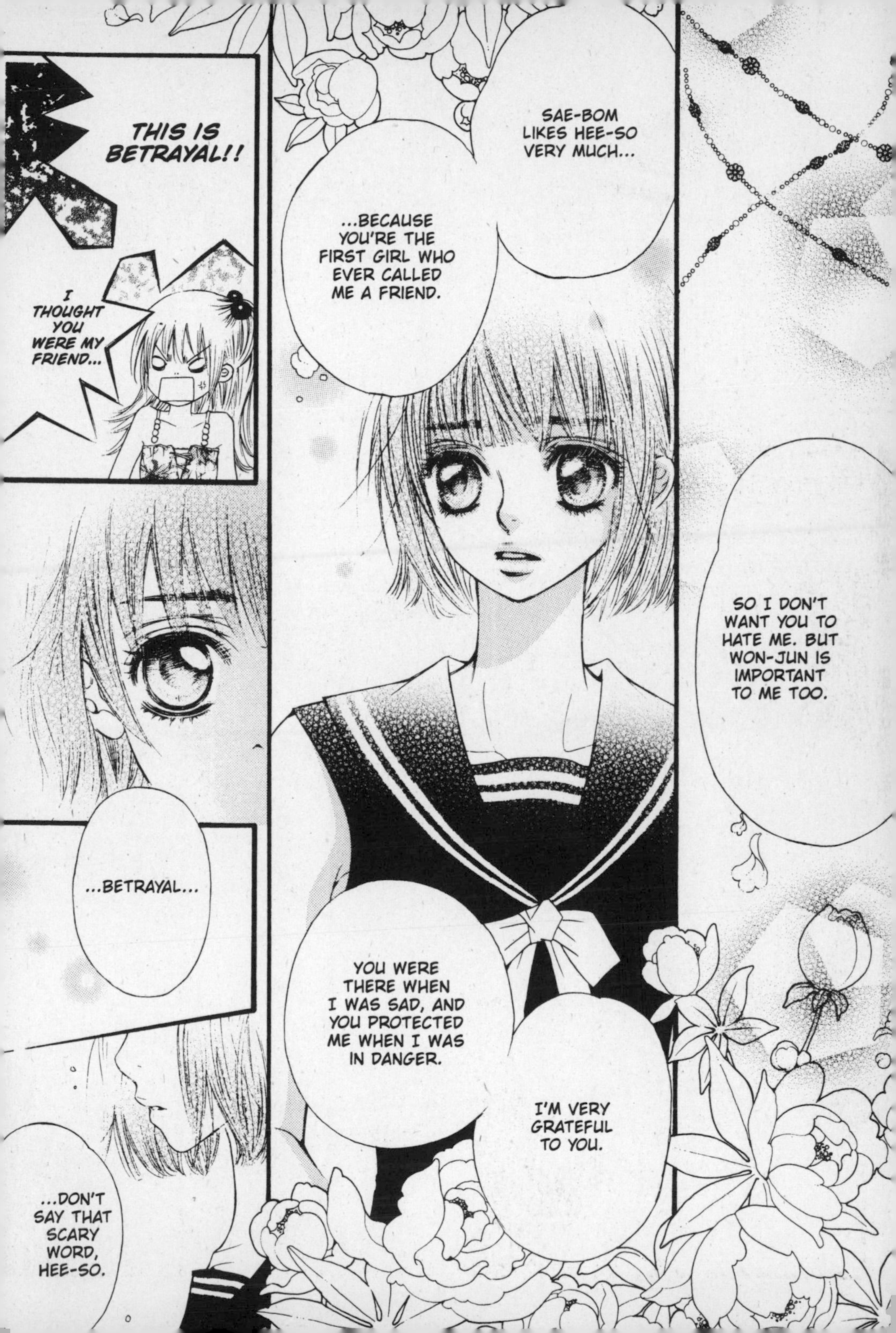

THIS IS BETRAYAL!!
I THOUGHT YOU WERE MY FRIEND...
...BETRAYAL...
...DON'T SAY THAT SCARY WORD, HEE-SO.
SAE-BOM LIKES HEE-SO VERY MUCH...
...BECAUSE YOU'RE THE FIRST GIRL WHO EVER CALLED ME A FRIEND.
YOU WERE THERE WHEN I WAS SAD, AND YOU PROTECTED ME WHEN I WAS IN DANGER.
I'M VERY GRATEFUL TO YOU.
SO I DON'T WANT YOU TO HATE ME. BUT WON-JUN IS IMPORTANT TO ME TOO.

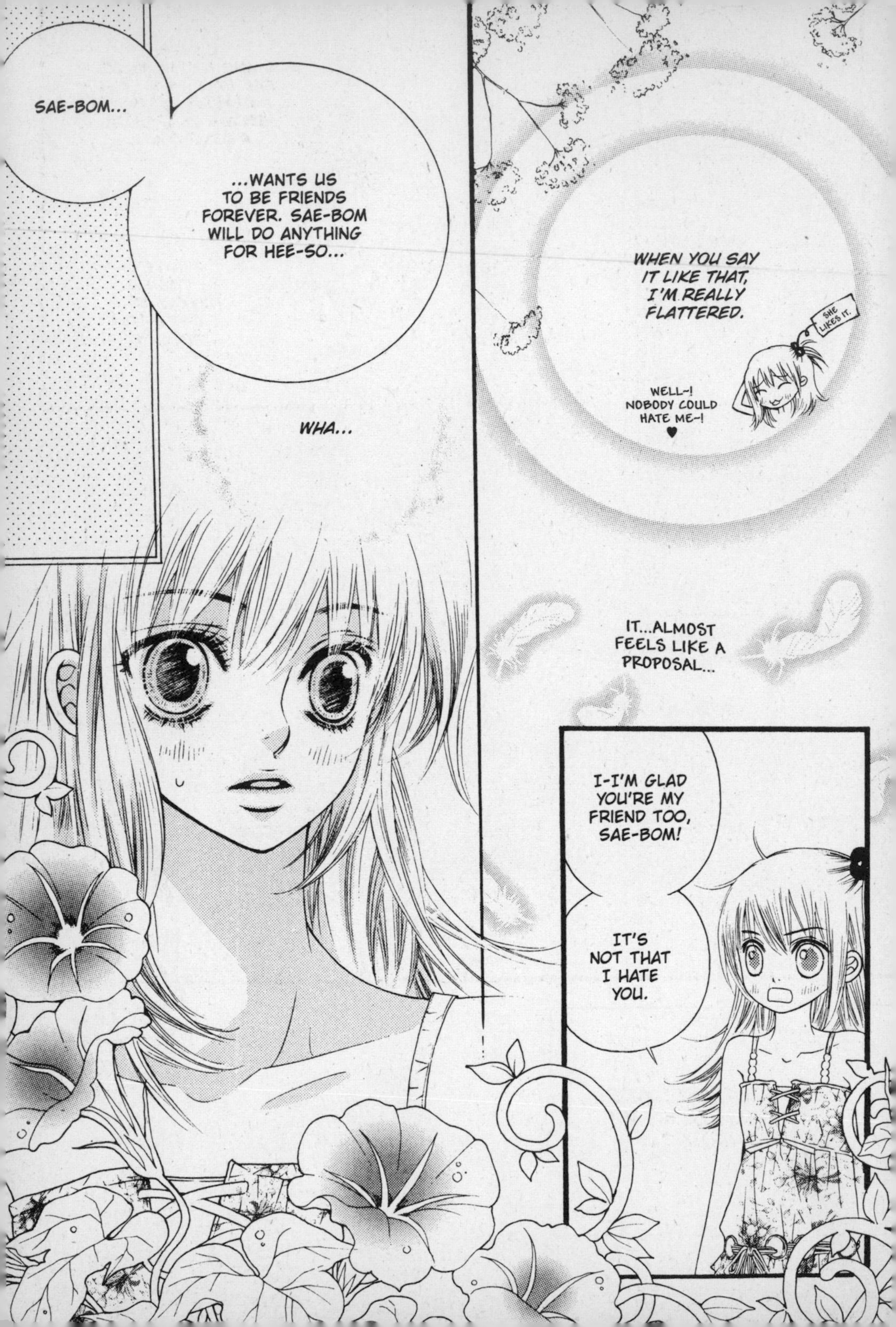
SAE-BOM...
...WANTS US TO BE FRIENDS FOREVER. SAE-BOM WILL DO ANYTHING FOR HEE-SO...
WHA...
WHEN YOU SAY IT LIKE THAT, I'M REALLY FLATTERED.
SHE LIKES IT.
WELL~! NOBODY COULD HATE ME~! ♥
IT...ALMOST FEELS LIKE A PROPOSAL...
I-I'M GLAD YOU'RE MY FRIEND TOO, SAE-BOM!
IT'S NOT THAT I HATE YOU.

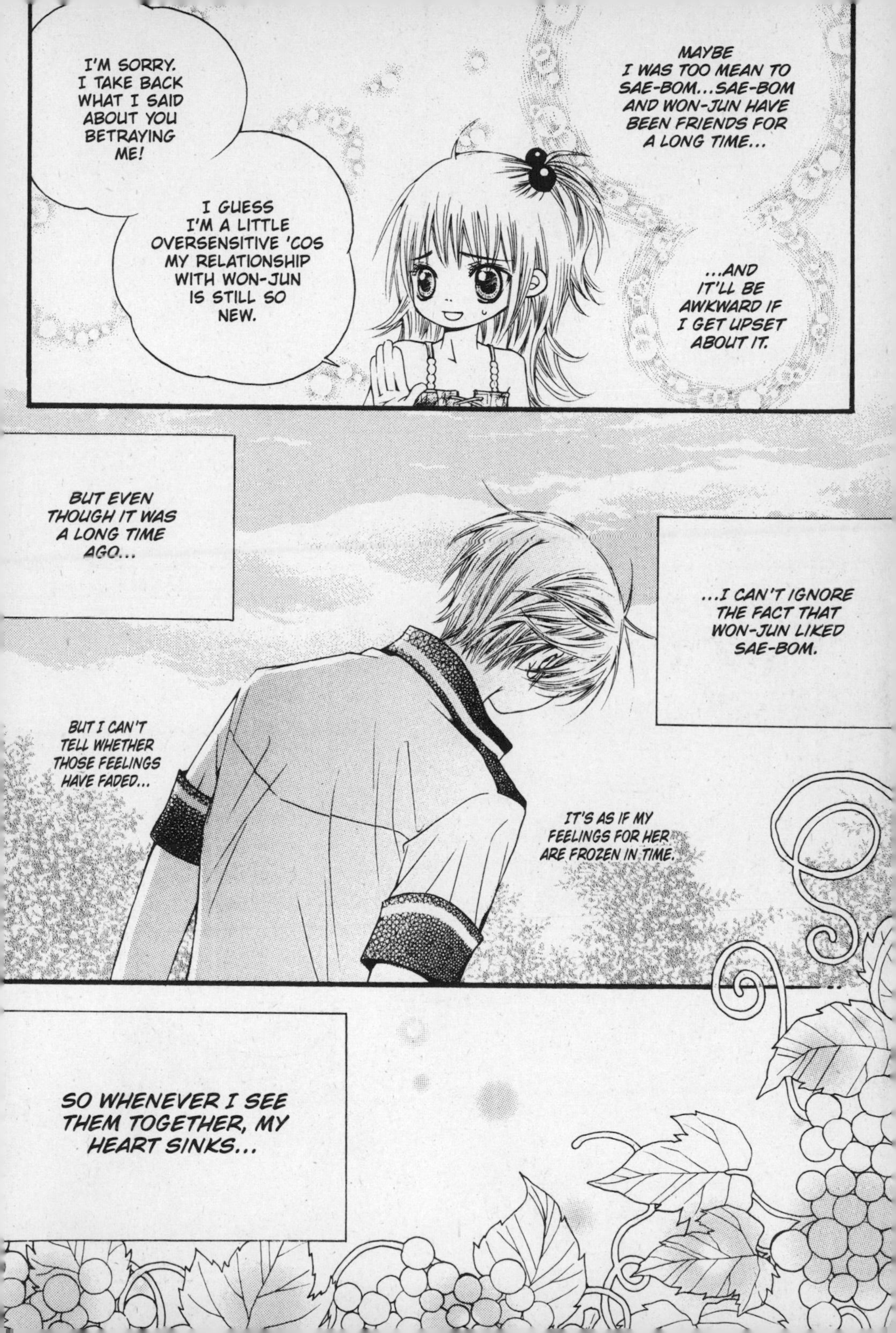
I'M SORRY. I TAKE BACK WHAT I SAID ABOUT YOU BETRAYING ME!
I GUESS I'M A LITTLE OVERSENSITIVE 'COS MY RELATIONSHIP WITH WON-JUN IS STILL SO NEW.
MAYBE I WAS TOO MEAN TO SAE-BOM...SAE-BOM AND WON-JUN HAVE BEEN FRIENDS FOR A LONG TIME...
...AND IT'LL BE AWKWARD IF I GET UPSET ABOUT IT.
BUT EVEN THOUGH IT WAS A LONG TIME AGO...
...I CAN'T IGNORE THE FACT THAT WON-JUN LIKED SAE-BOM.
BUT I CAN'T TELL WHETHER THOSE FEELINGS HAVE FADED...
IT'S AS IF MY FEELINGS FOR HER ARE FROZEN IN TIME.
SO WHENEVER I SEE THEM TOGETHER, MY HEART SINKS...

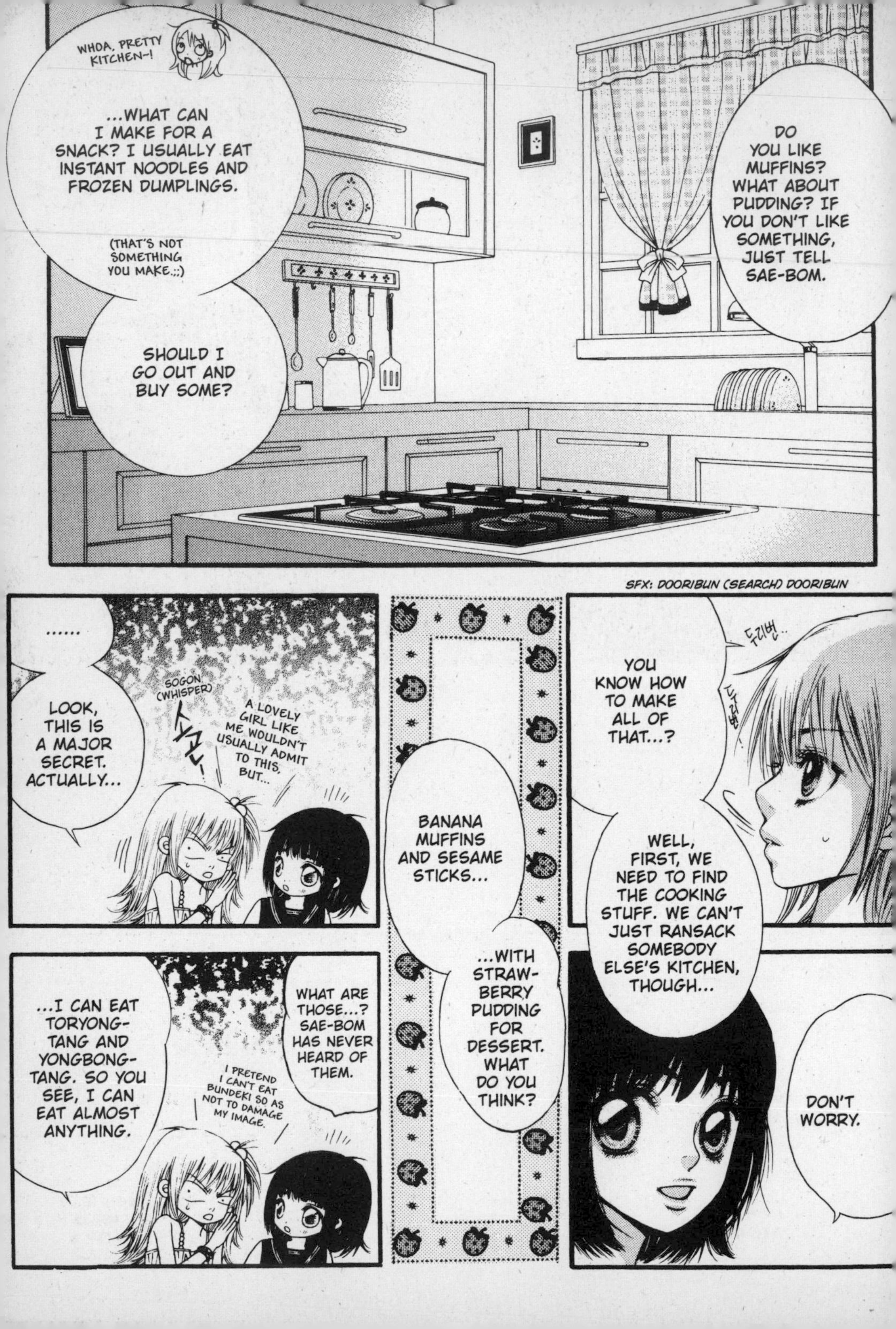
WHOA, PRETTY KITCHEN~!
...WHAT CAN I MAKE FOR A SNACK? I USUALLY EAT INSTANT NOODLES AND FROZEN DUMPLINGS.
(THAT'S NOT SOMETHING YOU MAKE.;;)
SHOULD I GO OUT AND BUY SOME?
DO YOU LIKE MUFFINS? WHAT ABOUT PUDDING? IF YOU DON'T LIKE SOMETHING, JUST TELL SAE-BOM.
SFX: DOORIBUN (SEARCH) DOORIBUN
......
LOOK, THIS IS A MAJOR SECRET. ACTUALLY...
SOGON (WHISPER)
A LOVELY GIRL LIKE ME WOULDN'T USUALLY ADMIT TO THIS, BUT...
...I CAN EAT TORYONG-TANG AND YONGBONG-TANG. SO YOU SEE, I CAN EAT ALMOST ANYTHING.
I PRETEND I CAN'T EAT BUNDEKI SO AS NOT TO DAMAGE MY IMAGE.
WHAT ARE THOSE...? SAE-BOM HAS NEVER HEARD OF THEM.
BANANA MUFFINS AND SESAME STICKS...
...WITH STRAWBERRY PUDDING FOR DESSERT. WHAT DO YOU THINK?
두리번..
YOU KNOW HOW TO MAKE ALL OF THAT...?
WELL, FIRST, WE NEED TO FIND THE COOKING STUFF. WE CAN'T JUST RANSACK SOMEBODY ELSE'S KITCHEN, THOUGH...
DON'T WORRY.

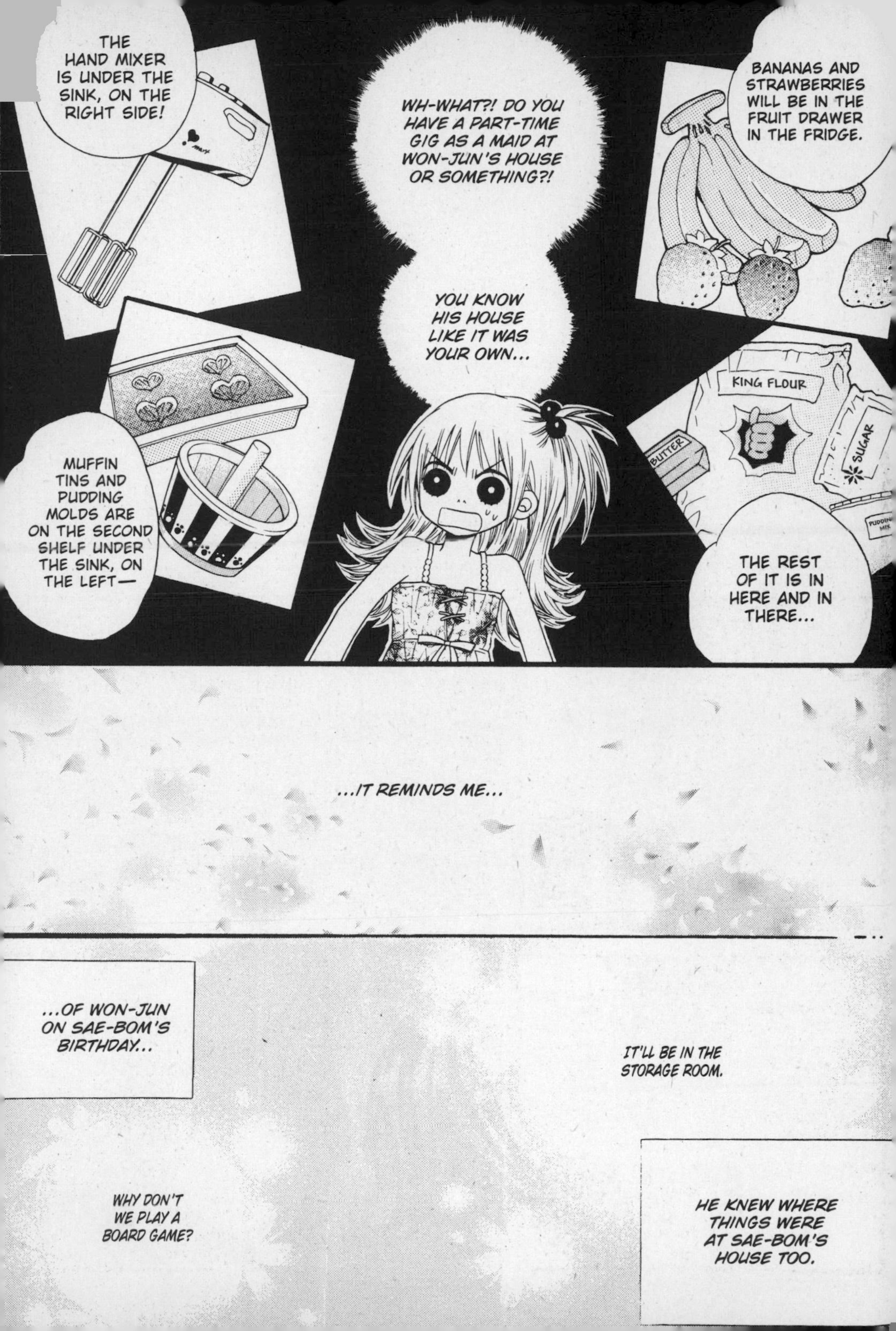
THE HAND MIXER IS UNDER THE SINK, ON THE RIGHT SIDE!
WH-WHAT?! DO YOU HAVE A PART-TIME GIG AS A MAID AT WON-JUN'S HOUSE OR SOMETHING?!
BANANAS AND STRAWBERRIES WILL BE IN THE FRUIT DRAWER IN THE FRIDGE.
YOU KNOW HIS HOUSE LIKE IT WAS YOUR OWN...
KING FLOUR
MUFFIN TINS AND PUDDING MOLDS ARE ON THE SECOND SHELF UNDER THE SINK, ON THE LEFT—
BUTTER
SUGAR
THE REST OF IT IS IN HERE AND IN THERE...
...IT REMINDS ME...
...OF WON-JUN ON SAE-BOM'S BIRTHDAY...
IT'LL BE IN THE STORAGE ROOM.
WHY DON'T WE PLAY A BOARD GAME?
HE KNEW WHERE THINGS WERE AT SAE-BOM'S HOUSE TOO.

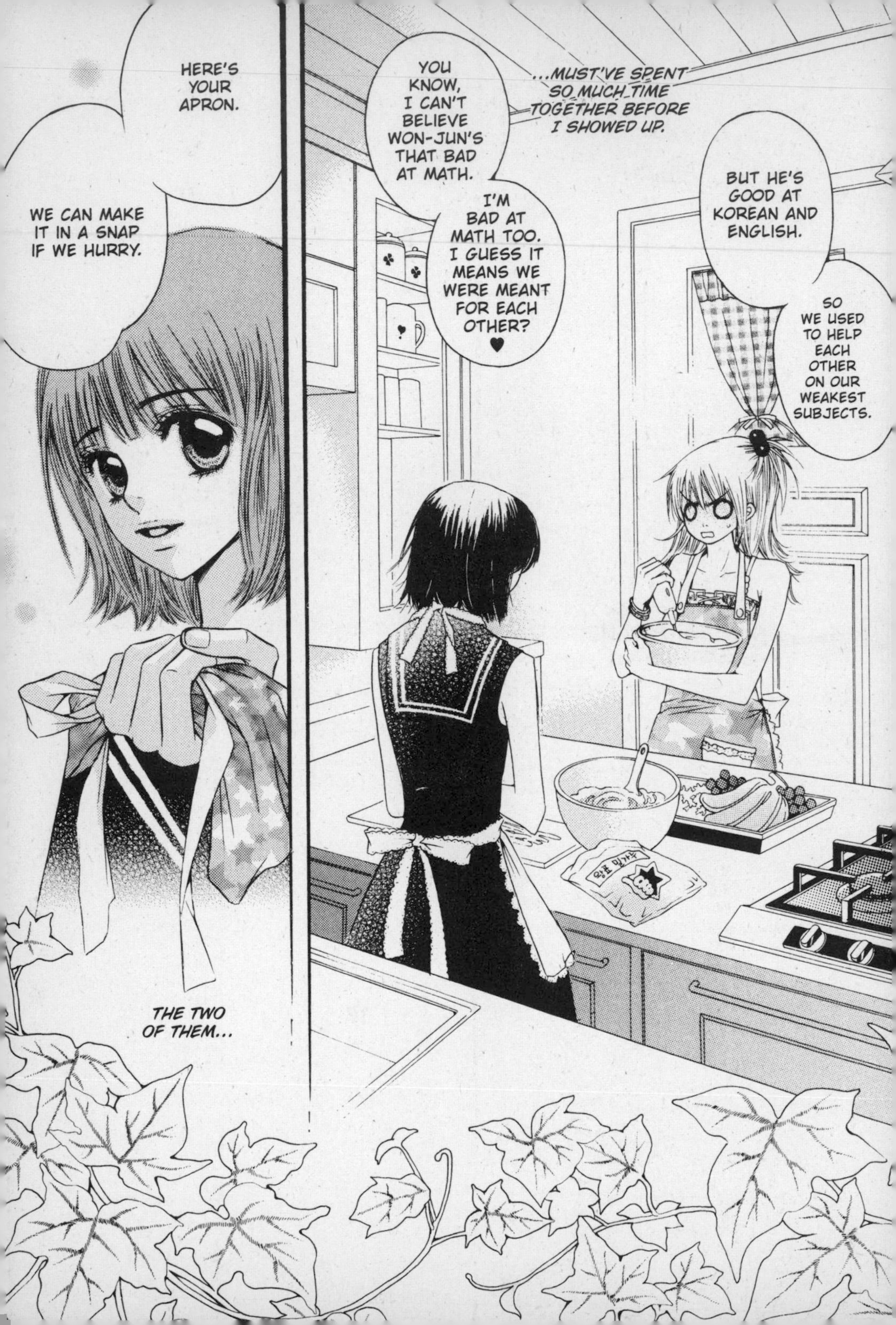
HERE'S YOUR APRON.
WE CAN MAKE IT IN A SNAP IF WE HURRY.
THE TWO OF THEM...
YOU KNOW, I CAN'T BELIEVE WON-JUN'S THAT BAD AT MATH.
...MUST'VE SPENT SO MUCH TIME TOGETHER BEFORE I SHOWED UP.
I'M BAD AT MATH TOO. I GUESS IT MEANS WE WERE MEANT FOR EACH OTHER? ♥
BUT HE'S GOOD AT KOREAN AND ENGLISH.
SO WE USED TO HELP EACH OTHER ON OUR WEAKEST SUBJECTS.

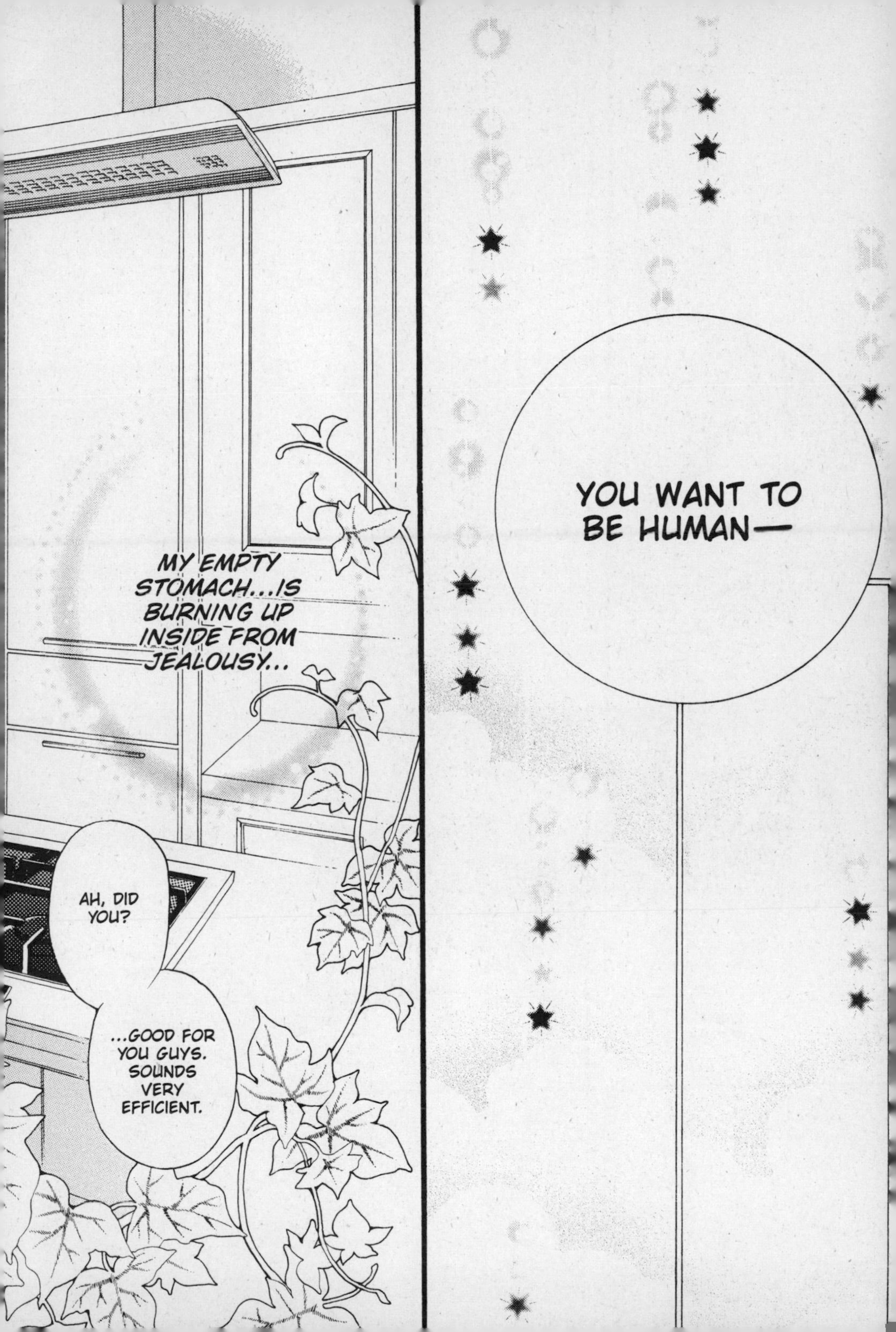
MY EMPTY STOMACH...IS BURNING UP INSIDE FROM JEALOUSY...
AH, DID YOU?
...GOOD FOR YOU GUYS. SOUNDS VERY EFFICIENT.
YOU WANT TO BE HUMAN—

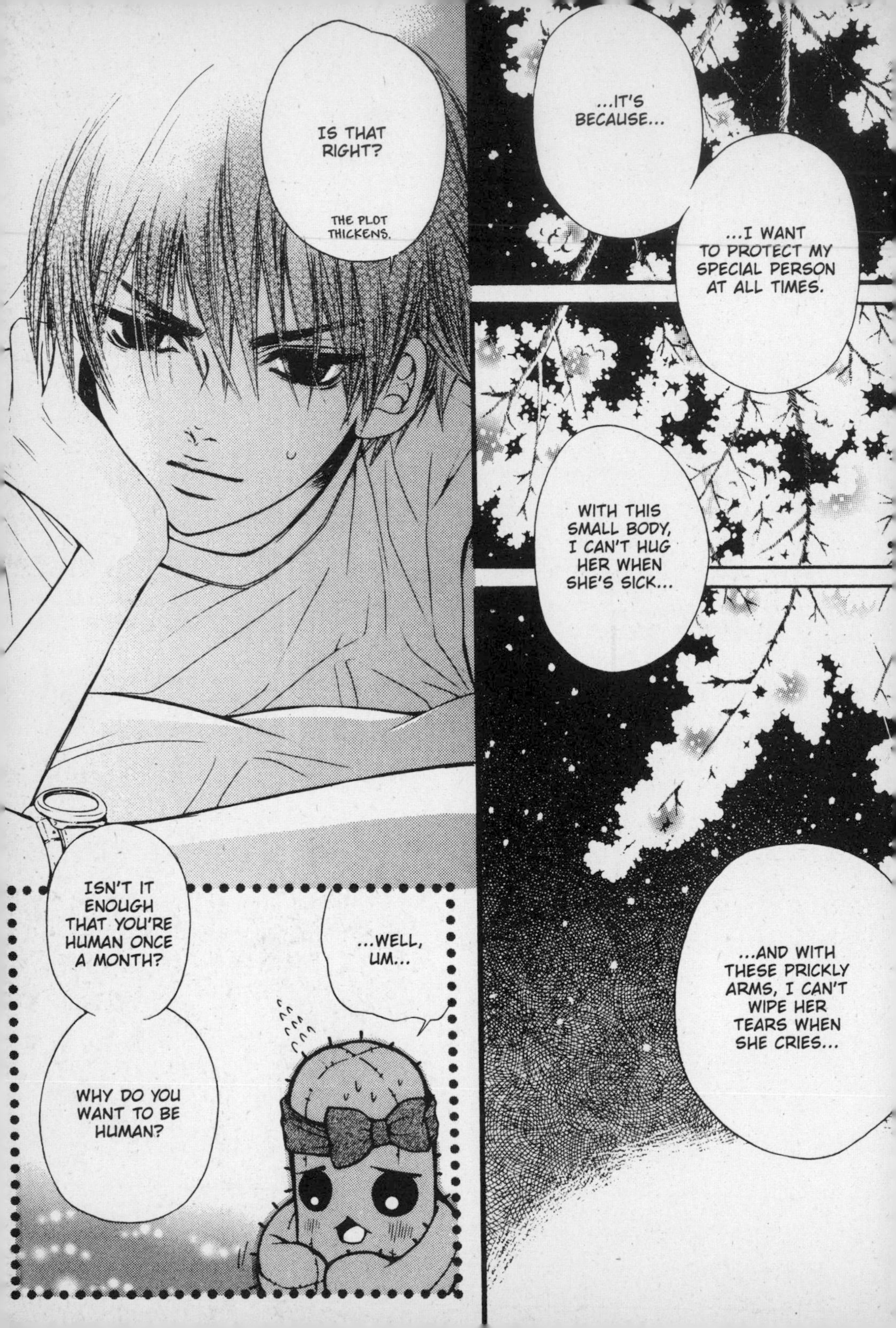
IS THAT RIGHT?
THE PLOT THICKENS.
ISN'T IT ENOUGH THAT YOU'RE HUMAN ONCE A MONTH?
WHY DO YOU WANT TO BE HUMAN?
...WELL, UM...
...IT'S BECAUSE...
...I WANT TO PROTECT MY SPECIAL PERSON AT ALL TIMES.
WITH THIS SMALL BODY, I CAN'T HUG HER WHEN SHE'S SICK...
...AND WITH THESE PRICKLY ARMS, I CAN'T WIPE HER TEARS WHEN SHE CRIES...

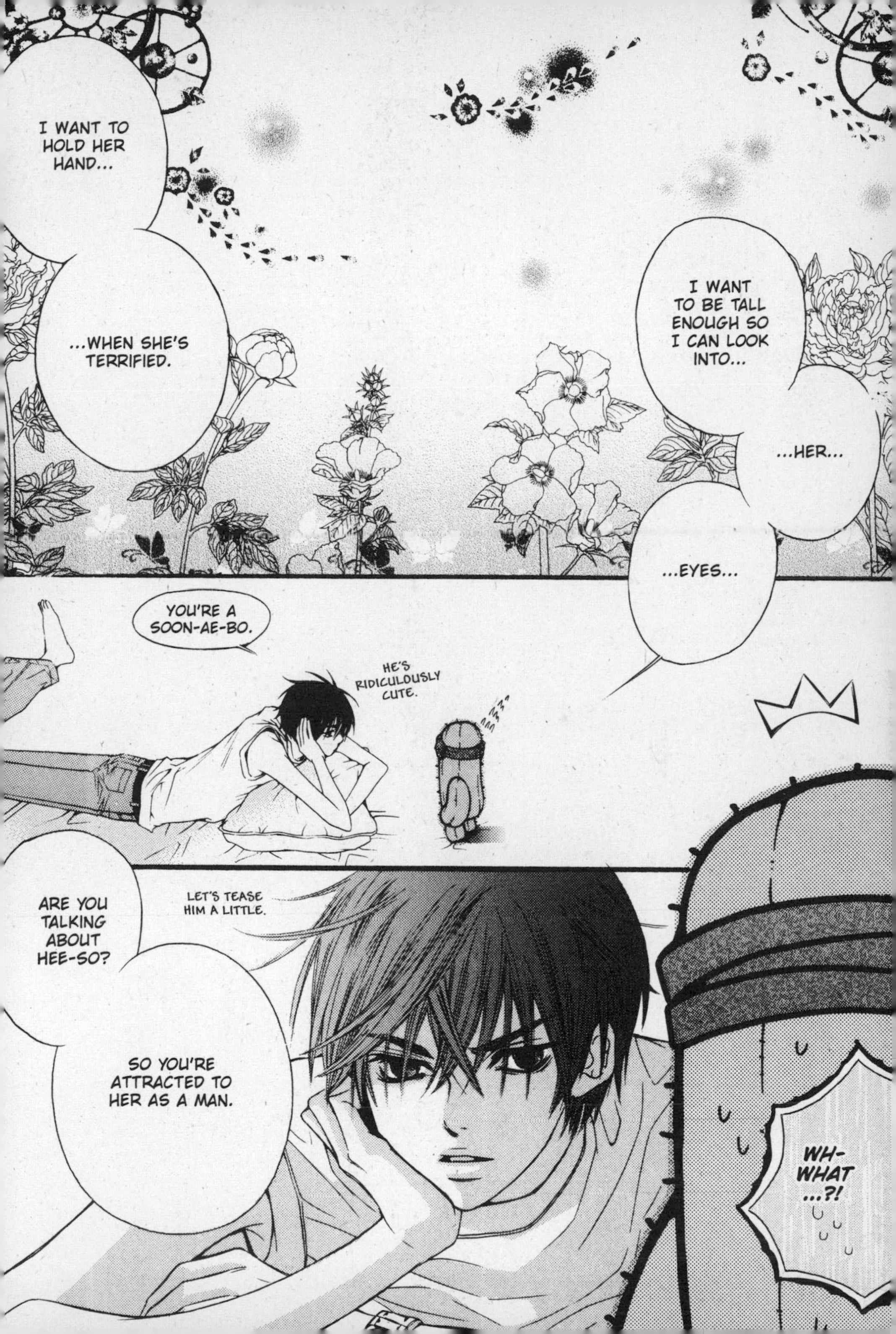
I WANT TO HOLD HER HAND...
...WHEN SHE'S TERRIFIED.
I WANT TO BE TALL ENOUGH SO I CAN LOOK INTO...
...HER...
...EYES...
YOU'RE A SOON-AE-BO.
HE'S RIDICULOUSLY CUTE.
ARE YOU TALKING ABOUT HEE-SO?
LET'S TEASE HIM A LITTLE.
SO YOU'RE ATTRACTED TO HER AS A MAN.
WH-WHAT...?!

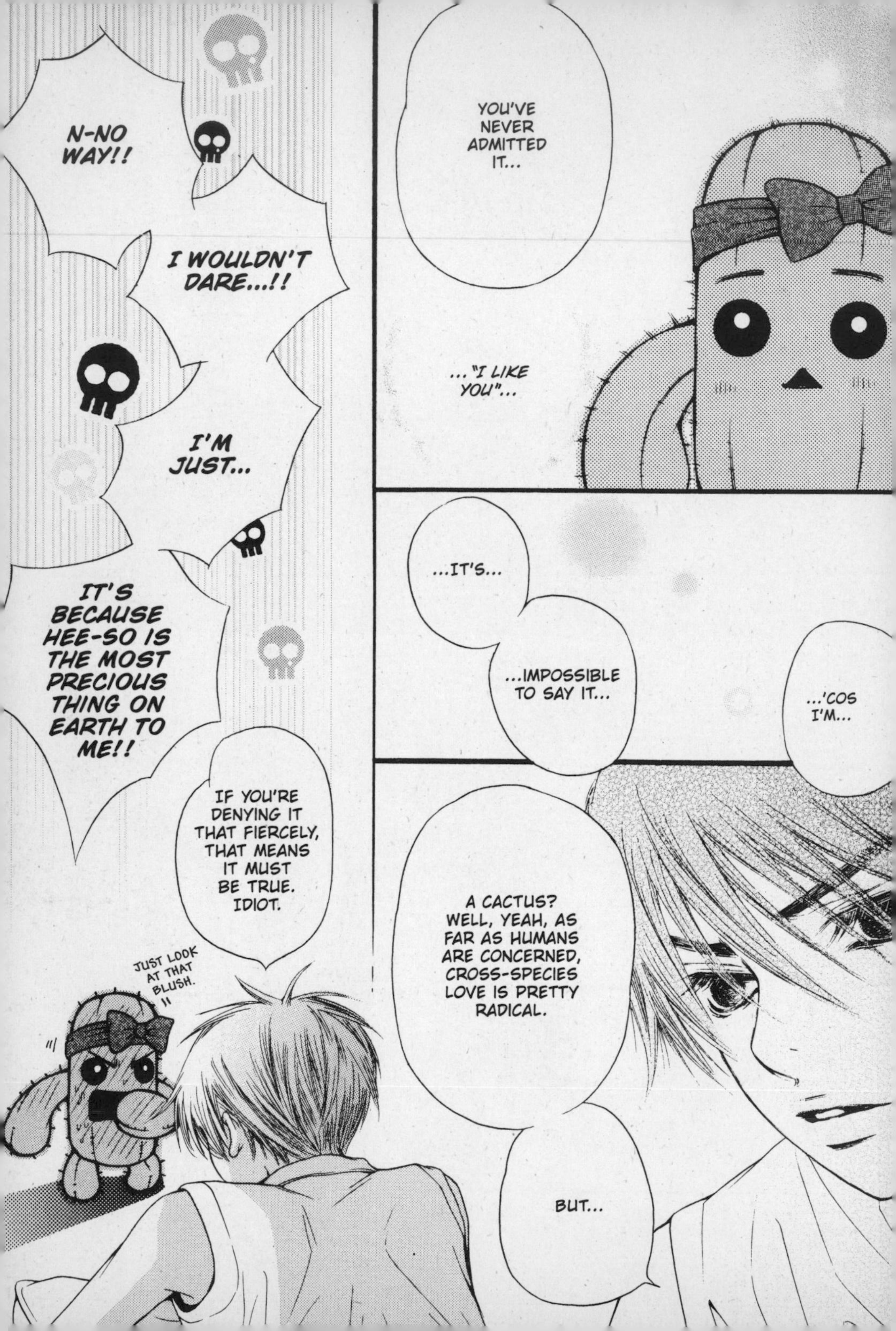

N-NO WAY!!
I WOULDN'T DARE...!!
I'M JUST...
IT'S BECAUSE HEE-SO IS THE MOST PRECIOUS THING ON EARTH TO ME!!
IF YOU'RE DENYING IT THAT FIERCELY, THAT MEANS IT MUST BE TRUE. IDIOT.
JUST LOOK AT THAT BLUSH.
YOU'VE NEVER ADMITTED IT...
..."I LIKE YOU"...
...IT'S...
...IMPOSSIBLE TO SAY IT...
...'COS I'M...
A CACTUS? WELL, YEAH, AS FAR AS HUMANS ARE CONCERNED, CROSS-SPECIES LOVE IS PRETTY RADICAL.
BUT...

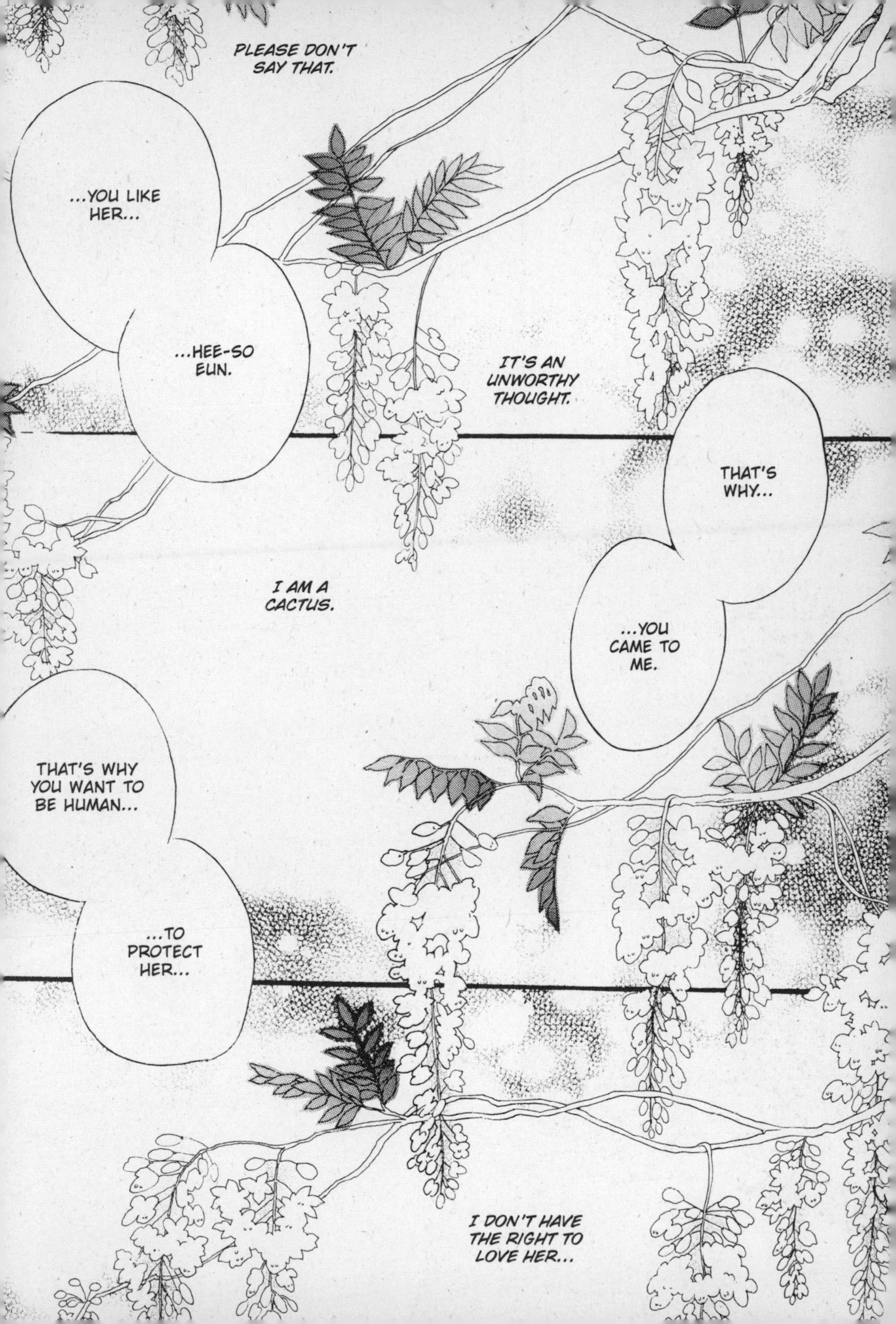
...YOU LIKE HER...
...HEE-SO EUN.
PLEASE DON'T SAY THAT.
IT'S AN UNWORTHY THOUGHT.
I AM A CACTUS.
THAT'S WHY...
...YOU CAME TO ME.
THAT'S WHY YOU WANT TO BE HUMAN...
...TO PROTECT HER...
I DON'T HAVE THE RIGHT TO LOVE HER...

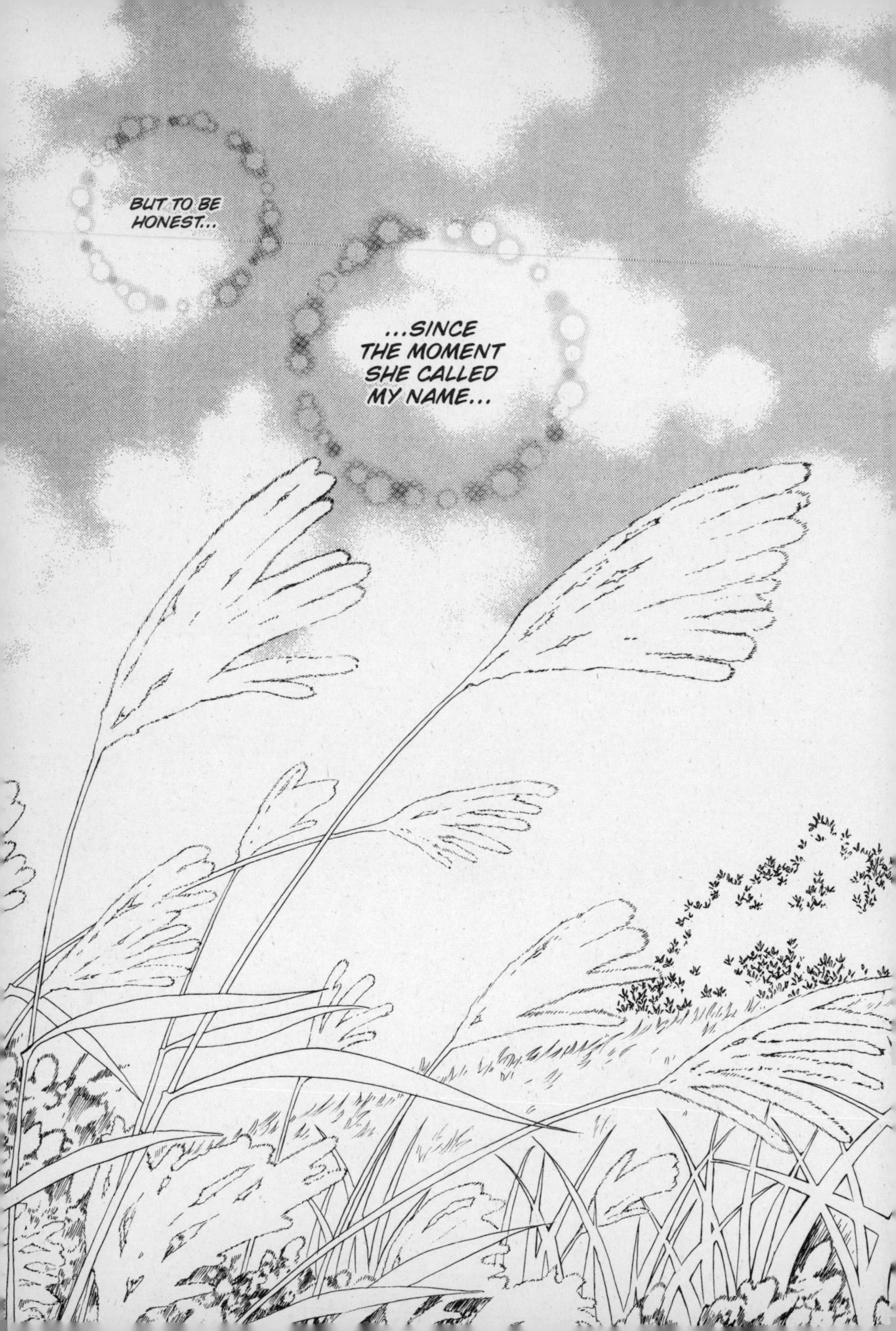
BUT TO BE HONEST...
...SINCE THE MOMENT SHE CALLED MY NAME...

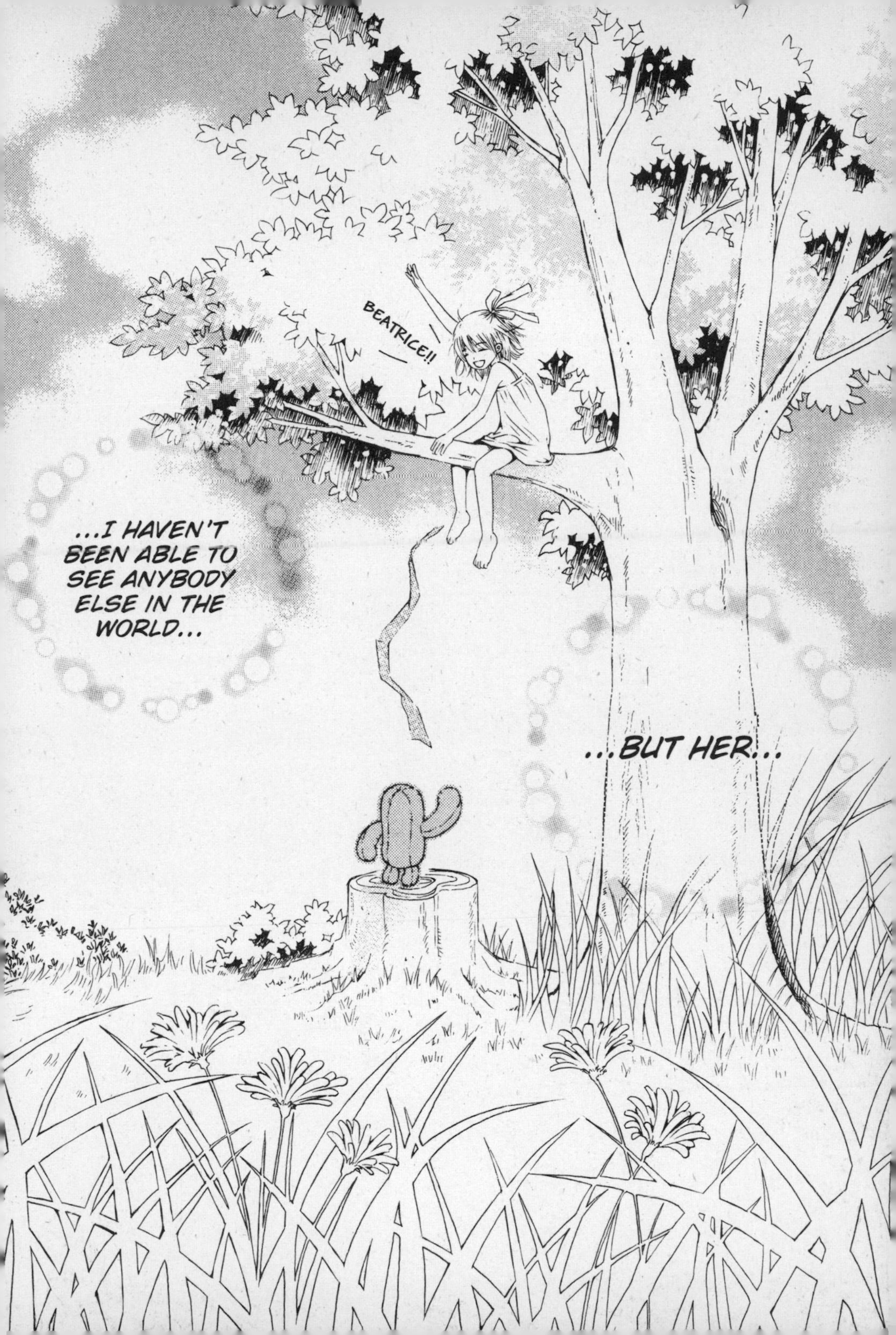
BEATRICE!!
...I HAVEN'T BEEN ABLE TO SEE ANYBODY ELSE IN THE WORLD...
...BUT HER...

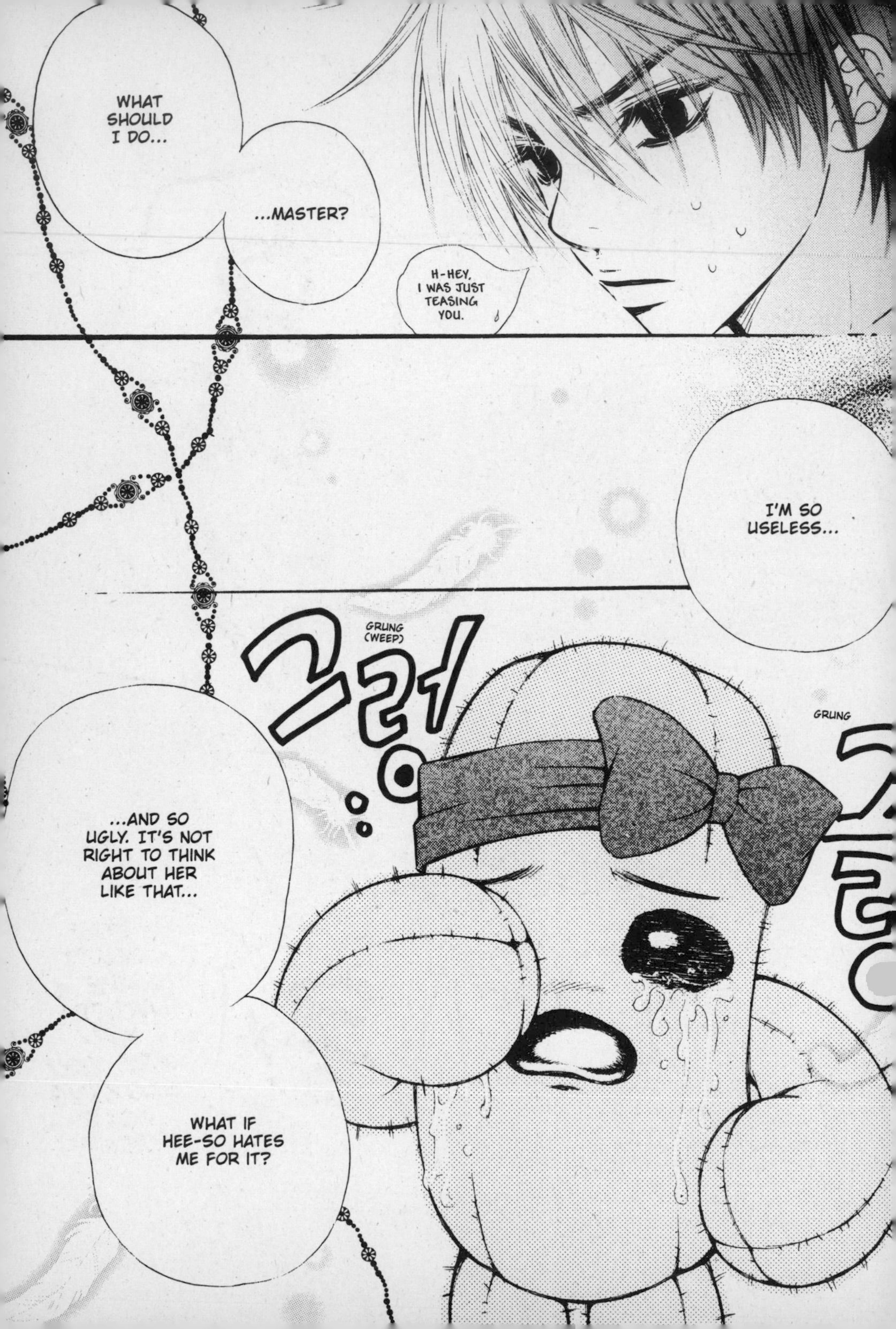
WHAT SHOULD I DO...
...MASTER?
H-HEY, I WAS JUST TEASING YOU.
I'M SO USELESS...
GRUNG (WEEP)
...AND SO UGLY. IT'S NOT RIGHT TO THINK ABOUT HER LIKE THAT...
WHAT IF HEE-SO HATES ME FOR IT?
GRUNG

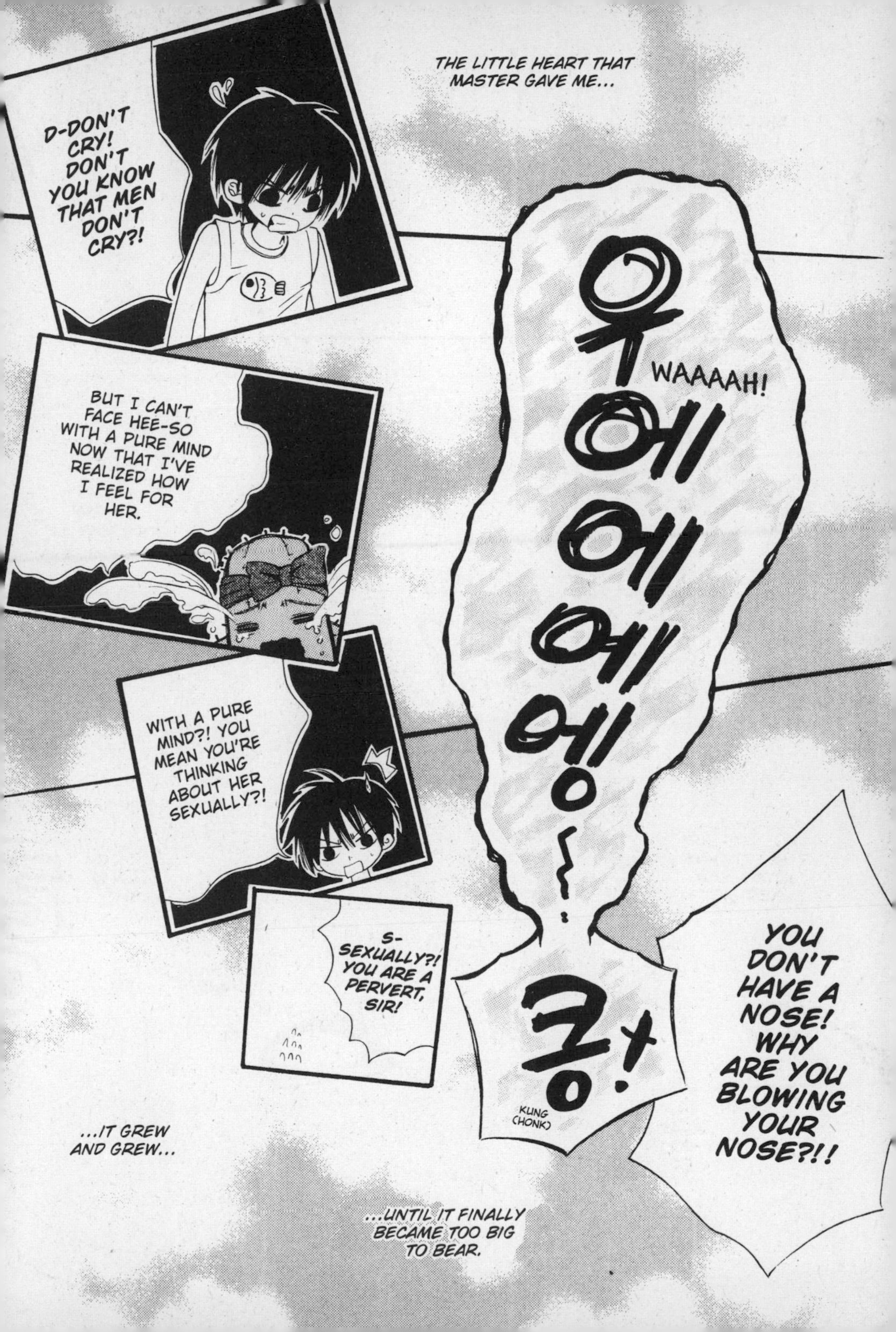
THE LITTLE HEART THAT MASTER GAVE ME...
D-DON'T CRY! DON'T YOU KNOW THAT MEN DON'T CRY?!
BUT I CAN'T FACE HEE-SO WITH A PURE MIND NOW THAT I'VE REALIZED HOW I FEEL FOR HER.
WITH A PURE MIND?! YOU MEAN YOU'RE THINKING ABOUT HER SEXUALLY?!
S-SEXUALLY?! YOU ARE A PERVERT, SIR!
우에에에엥~
WAAAAH!
킁!
KUNG (HONK)
YOU DON'T HAVE A NOSE! WHY ARE YOU BLOWING YOUR NOSE?!!
...IT GREW AND GREW...
...UNTIL IT FINALLY BECAME TOO BIG TO BEAR.

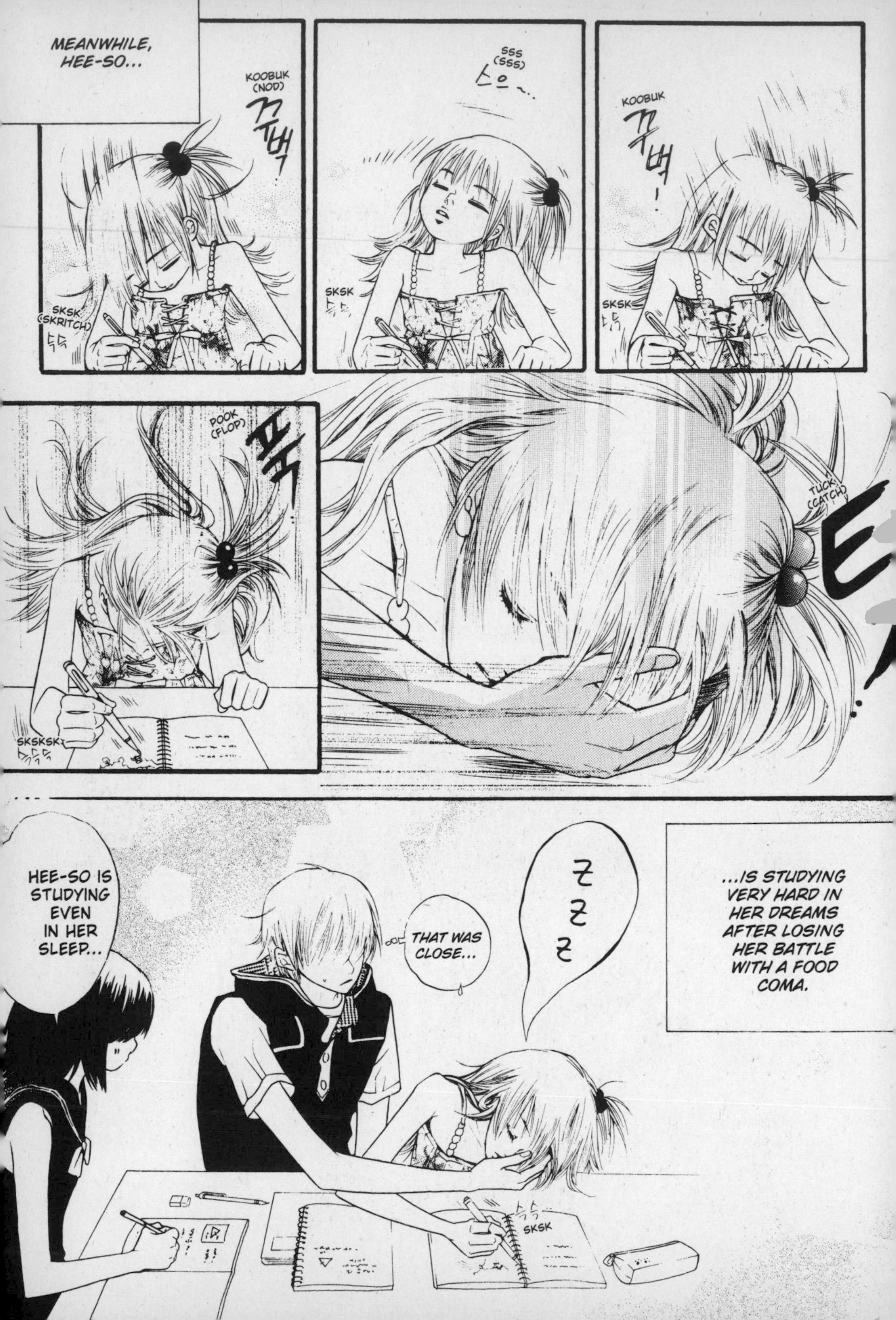

MEANWHILE, HEE-SO...
KOOBUK (NOD)
꾸벅
SKSK (SKRITCH)
SSS (SSS)
스으~..
SKSK
KOOBUK
꾸벅
SKSK
POOK (FLOP)
푹
SKSKSK
TUCK (CATCH)
HEE-SO IS STUDYING EVEN IN HER SLEEP...
THAT WAS CLOSE...
...IS STUDYING VERY HARD IN HER DREAMS AFTER LOSING HER BATTLE WITH A FOOD COMA.
SKSK

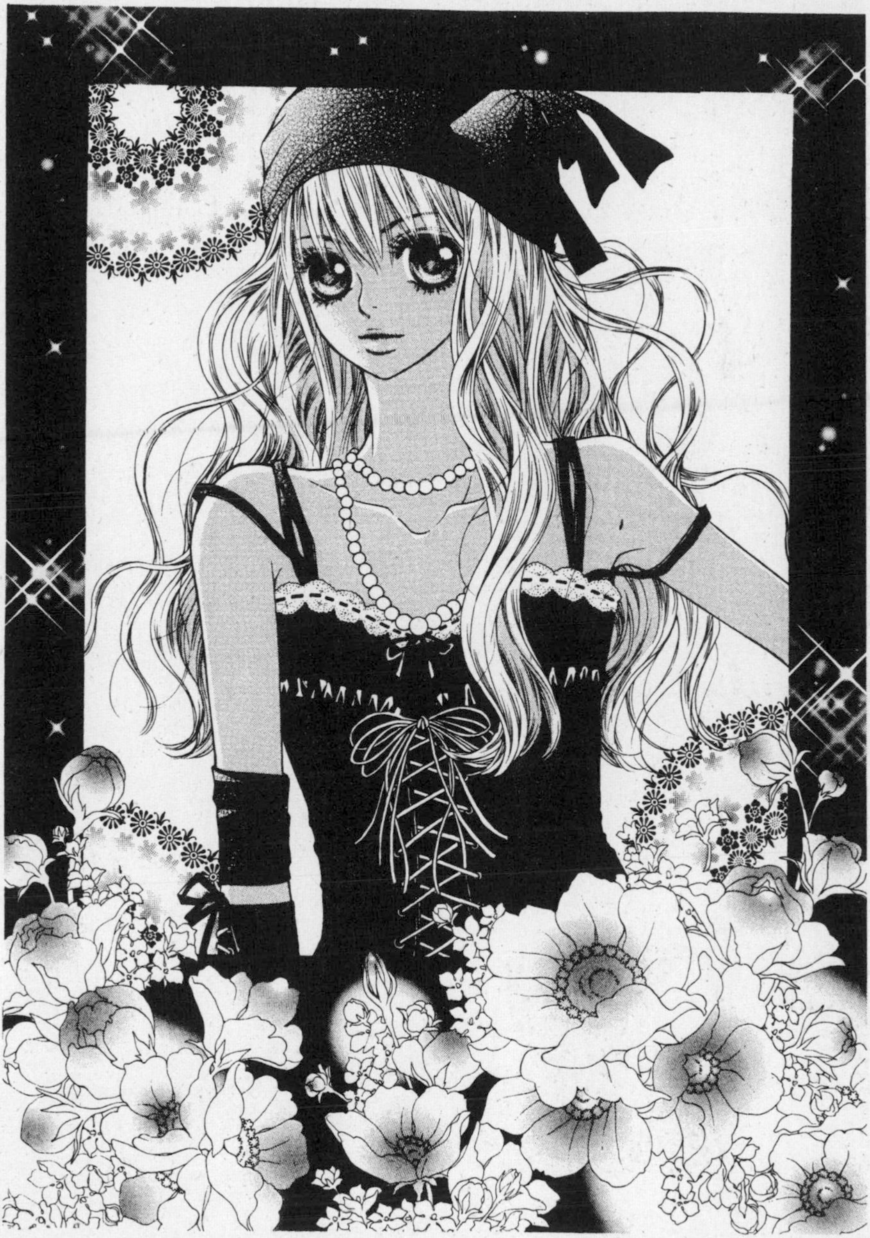

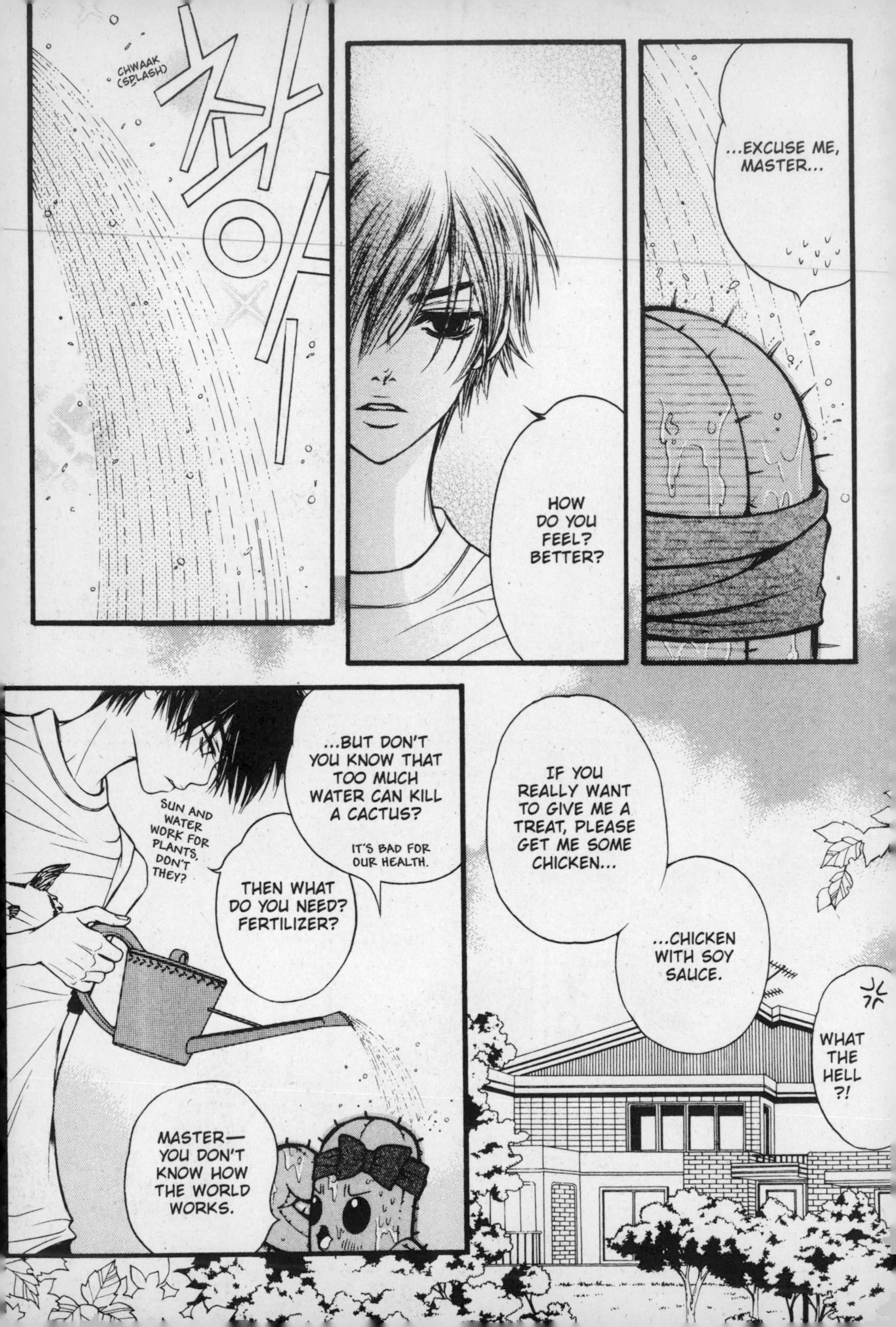
CHWAAK (SPLASH)
HOW DO YOU FEEL? BETTER?
...EXCUSE ME, MASTER...
SUN AND WATER WORK FOR PLANTS, DON'T THEY?
...BUT DON'T YOU KNOW THAT TOO MUCH WATER CAN KILL A CACTUS?
IT'S BAD FOR OUR HEALTH.
THEN WHAT DO YOU NEED? FERTILIZER?
MASTER— YOU DON'T KNOW HOW THE WORLD WORKS.
IF YOU REALLY WANT TO GIVE ME A TREAT, PLEASE GET ME SOME CHICKEN...
...CHICKEN WITH SOY SAUCE.
WHAT THE HELL ?!

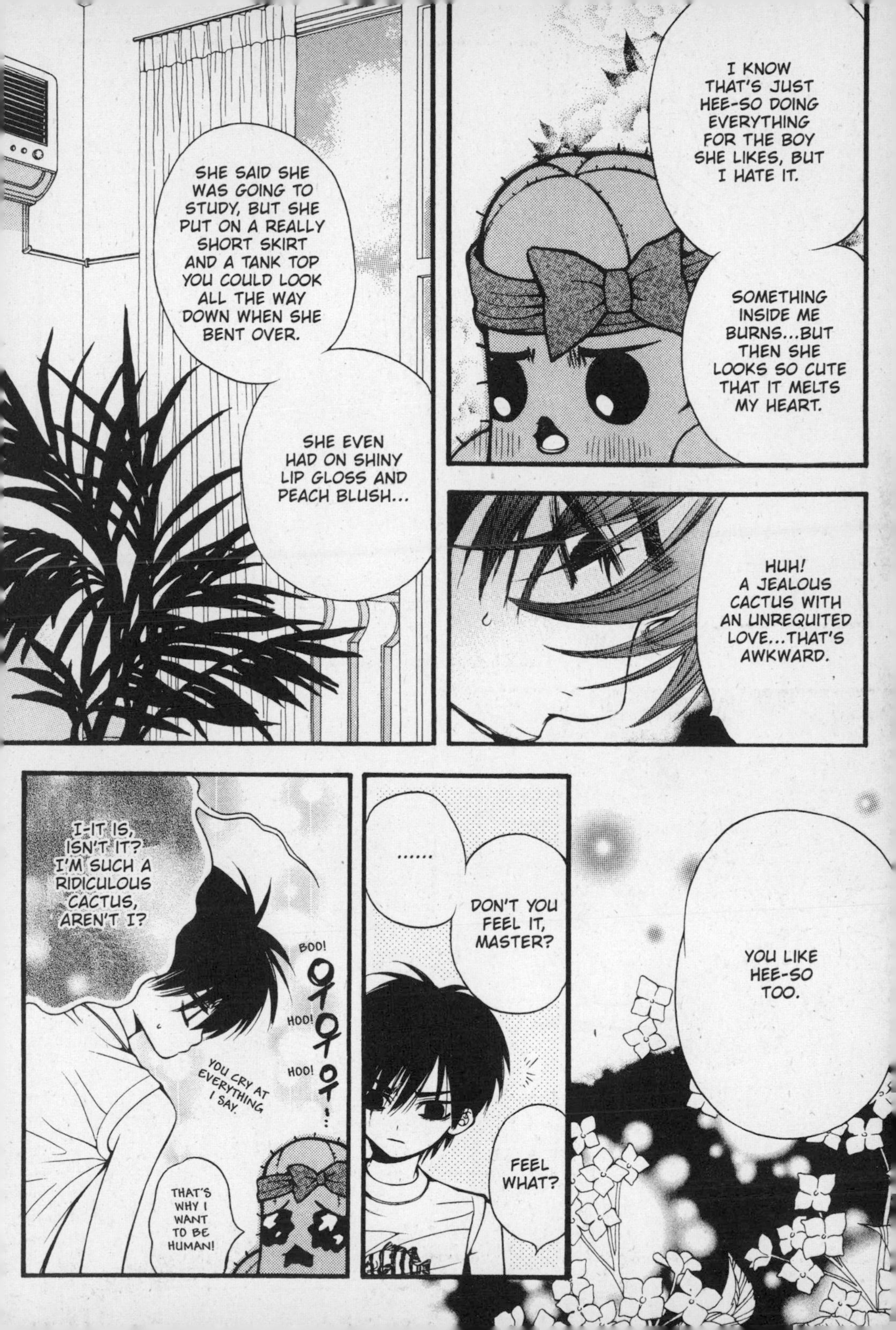
SHE SAID SHE WAS GOING TO STUDY, BUT SHE PUT ON A REALLY SHORT SKIRT AND A TANK TOP YOU COULD LOOK ALL THE WAY DOWN WHEN SHE BENT OVER.
SHE EVEN HAD ON SHINY LIP GLOSS AND PEACH BLUSH...
I KNOW THAT'S JUST HEE-SO DOING EVERYTHING FOR THE BOY SHE LIKES, BUT I HATE IT.
SOMETHING INSIDE ME BURNS...BUT THEN SHE LOOKS SO CUTE THAT IT MELTS MY HEART.
HUH! A JEALOUS CACTUS WITH AN UNREQUITED LOVE...THAT'S AWKWARD.
I-IT IS, ISN'T IT? I'M SUCH A RIDICULOUS CACTUS, AREN'T I?
BOO!
HOO!
HOO!
YOU CRY AT EVERYTHING I SAY.
THAT'S WHY I WANT TO BE HUMAN!
......
DON'T YOU FEEL IT, MASTER?
FEEL WHAT?
YOU LIKE HEE-SO TOO.

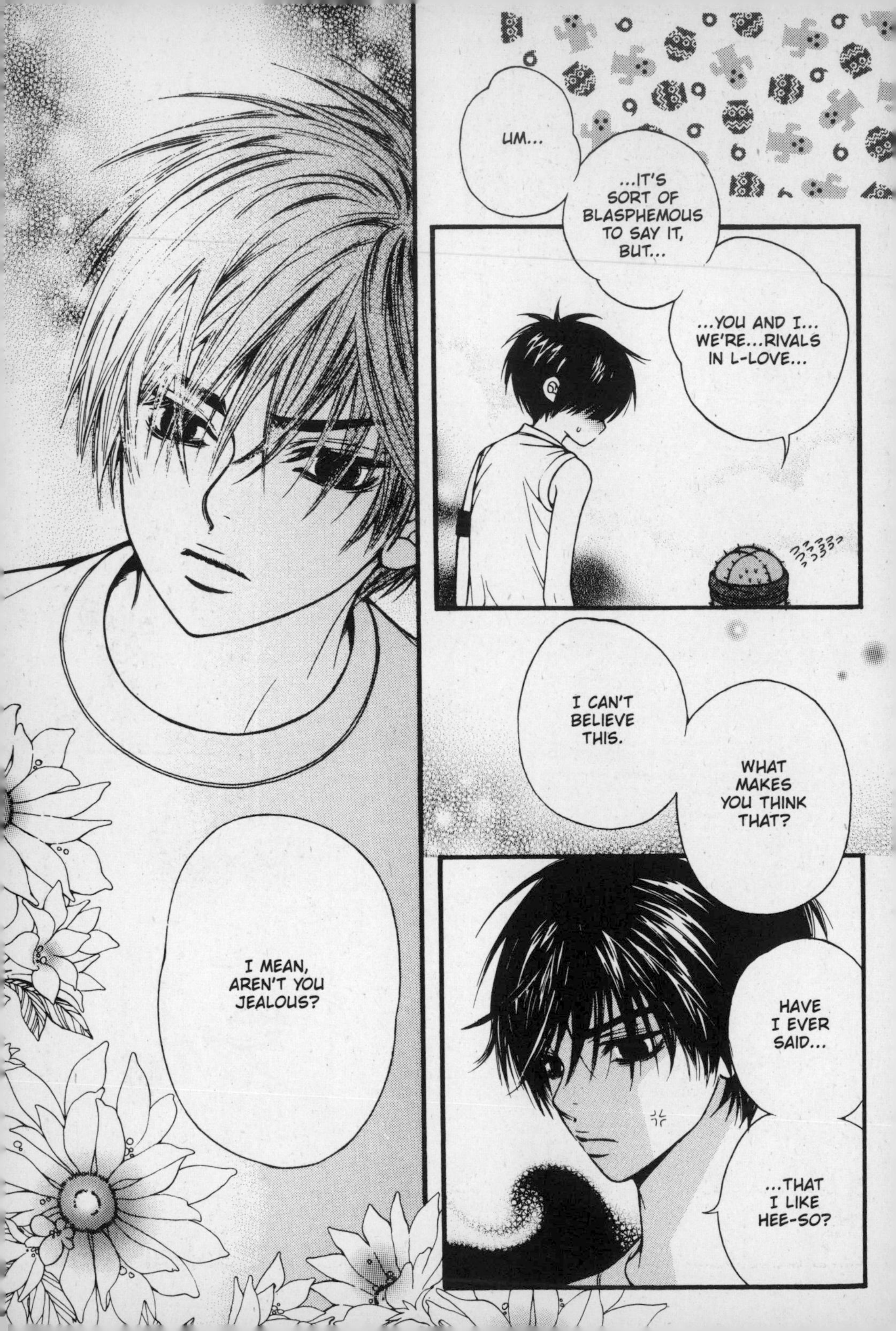
I MEAN, AREN'T YOU JEALOUS?
UM...
...IT'S SORT OF BLASPHEMOUS TO SAY IT, BUT...
...YOU AND I... WE'RE...RIVALS IN L-LOVE...
I CAN'T BELIEVE THIS.
WHAT MAKES YOU THINK THAT?
HAVE I EVER SAID...
...THAT I LIKE HEE-SO?

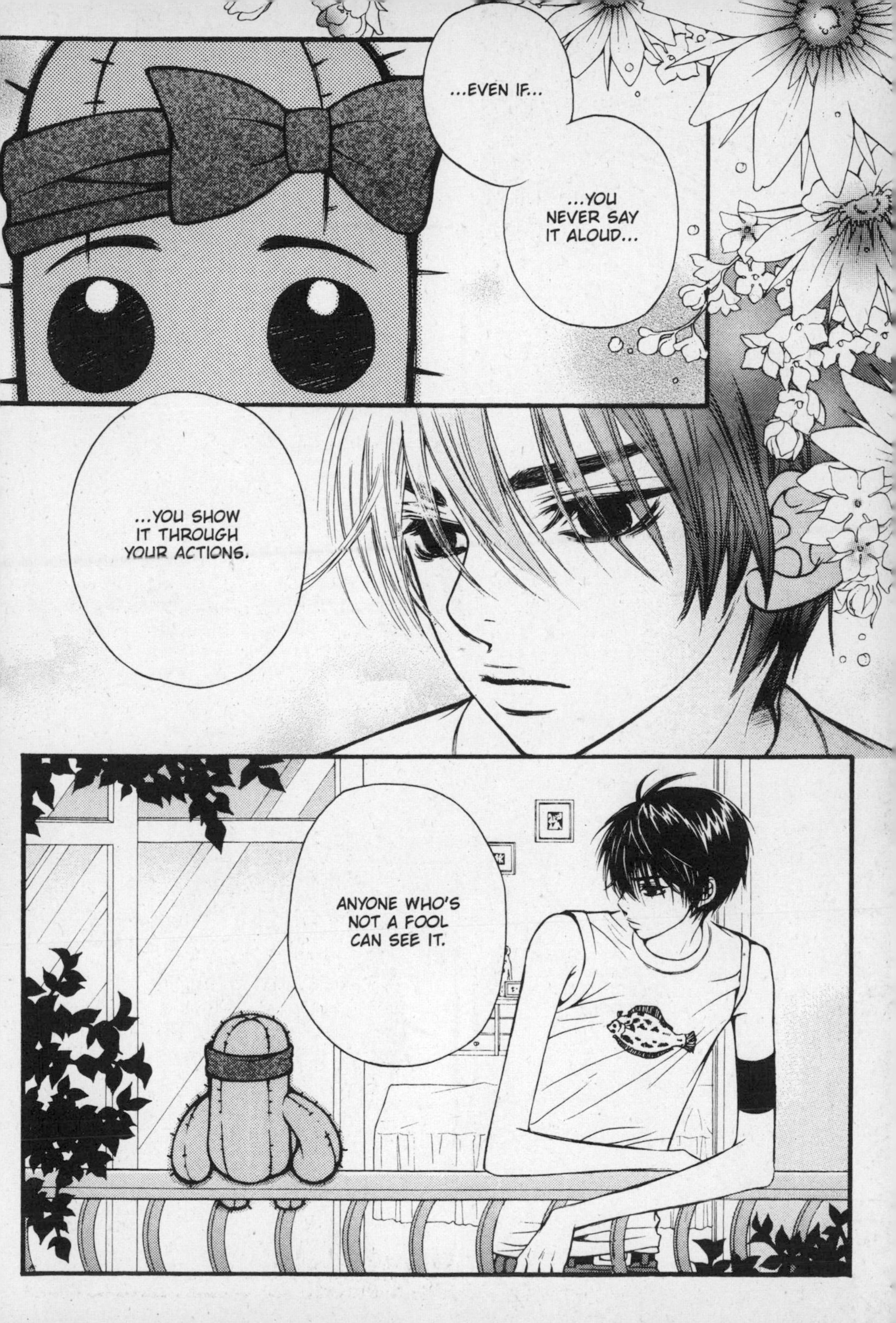
...EVEN IF...
...YOU NEVER SAY IT ALOUD...
...YOU SHOW IT THROUGH YOUR ACTIONS.
ANYONE WHO'S NOT A FOOL CAN SEE IT.

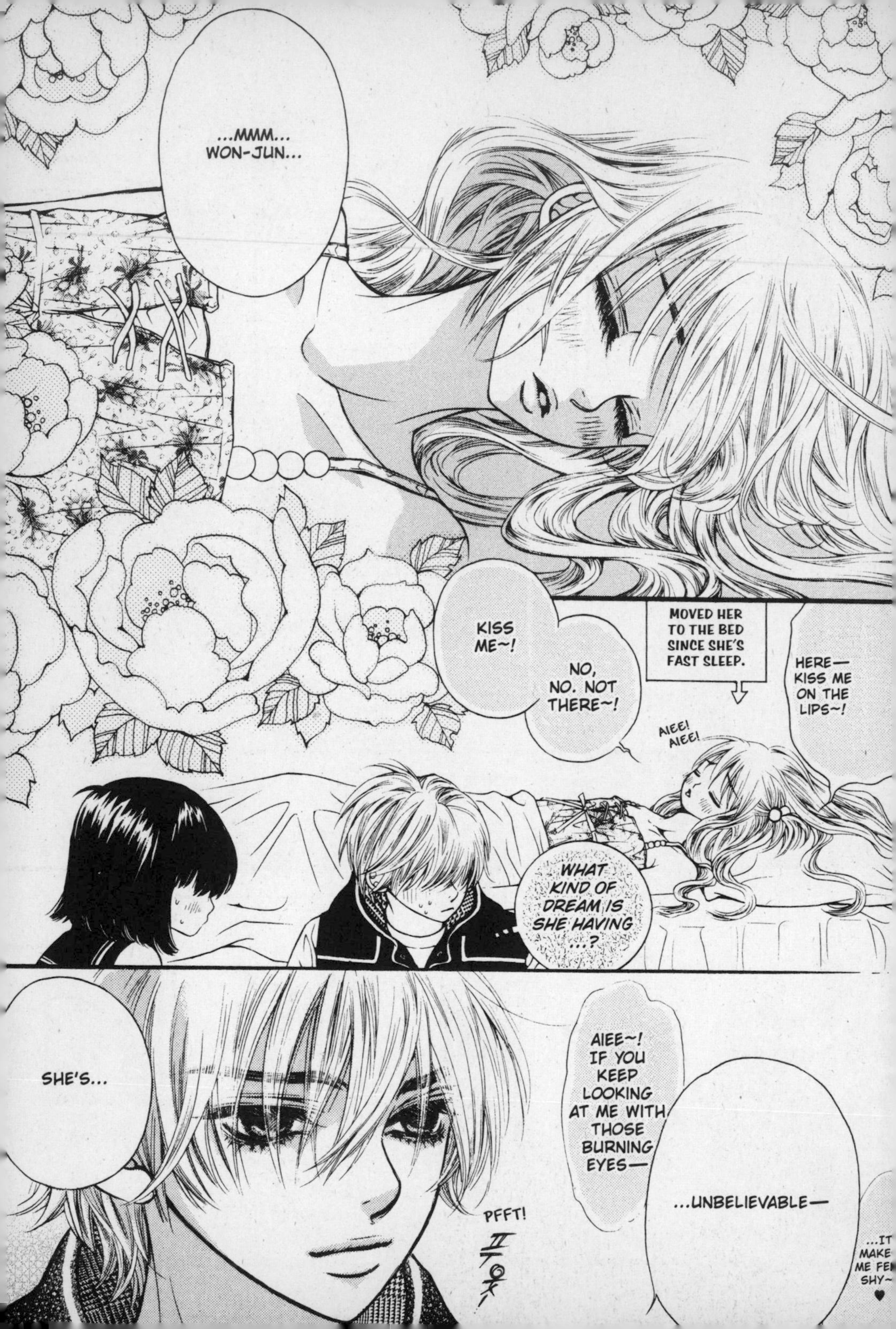
...MMM... WON-JUN...
KISS ME~!
NO, NO. NOT THERE~!
MOVED HER TO THE BED SINCE SHE'S FAST SLEEP.
HERE— KISS ME ON THE LIPS~!
AIEE! AIEE!
WHAT KIND OF DREAM IS SHE HAVING ...?
SHE'S...
AIEE~! IF YOU KEEP LOOKING AT ME WITH THOSE BURNING EYES—
PFFT!
...UNBELIEVABLE—
...IT MAKE ME FE SHY~ ♥

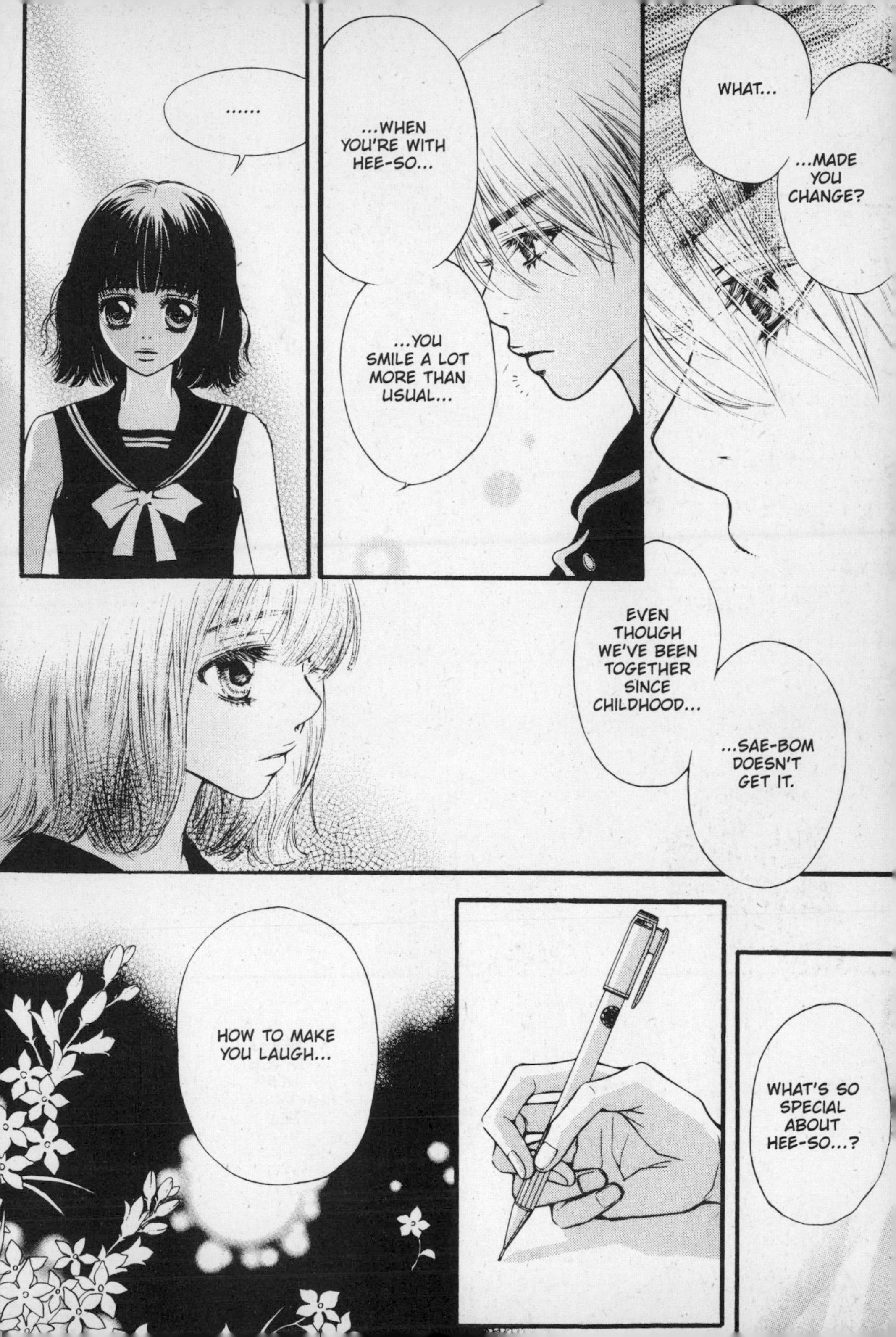
......
...WHEN YOU'RE WITH HEE-SO...
...YOU SMILE A LOT MORE THAN USUAL...
WHAT...
...MADE YOU CHANGE?
EVEN THOUGH WE'VE BEEN TOGETHER SINCE CHILDHOOD...
...SAE-BOM DOESN'T GET IT.
HOW TO MAKE YOU LAUGH...
WHAT'S SO SPECIAL ABOUT HEE-SO...?

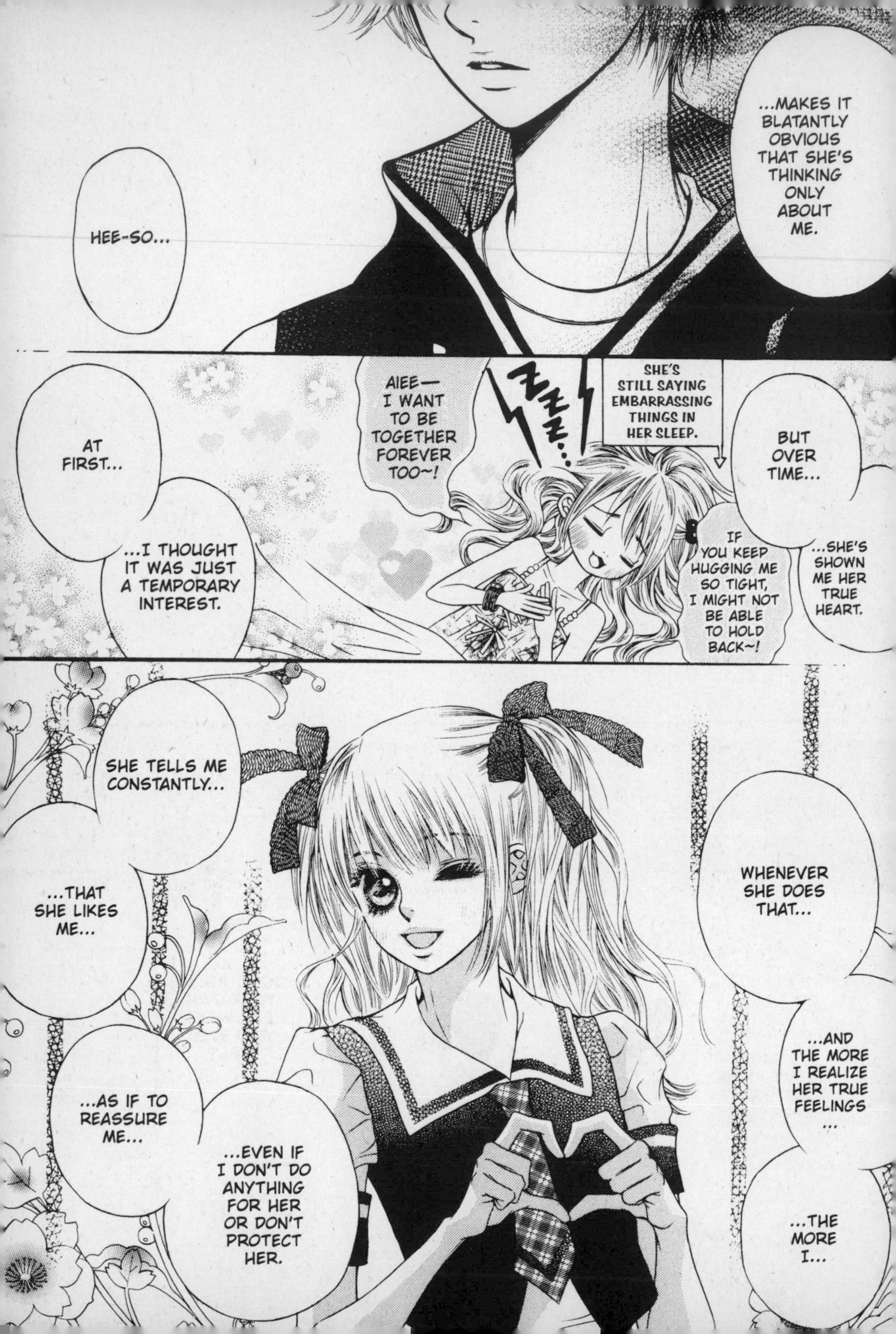
HEE-SO...
...MAKES IT BLATANTLY OBVIOUS THAT SHE'S THINKING ONLY ABOUT ME.
AT FIRST...
...I THOUGHT IT WAS JUST A TEMPORARY INTEREST.
AIEE— I WANT TO BE TOGETHER FOREVER TOO~!
ZZZ...
SHE'S STILL SAYING EMBARRASSING THINGS IN HER SLEEP.
BUT OVER TIME...
IF YOU KEEP HUGGING ME SO TIGHT, I MIGHT NOT BE ABLE TO HOLD BACK~!
...SHE'S SHOWN ME HER TRUE HEART.
SHE TELLS ME CONSTANTLY...
...THAT SHE LIKES ME...
...AS IF TO REASSURE ME...
...EVEN IF I DON'T DO ANYTHING FOR HER OR DON'T PROTECT HER.
WHENEVER SHE DOES THAT...
...AND THE MORE I REALIZE HER TRUE FEELINGS...
...THE MORE I...

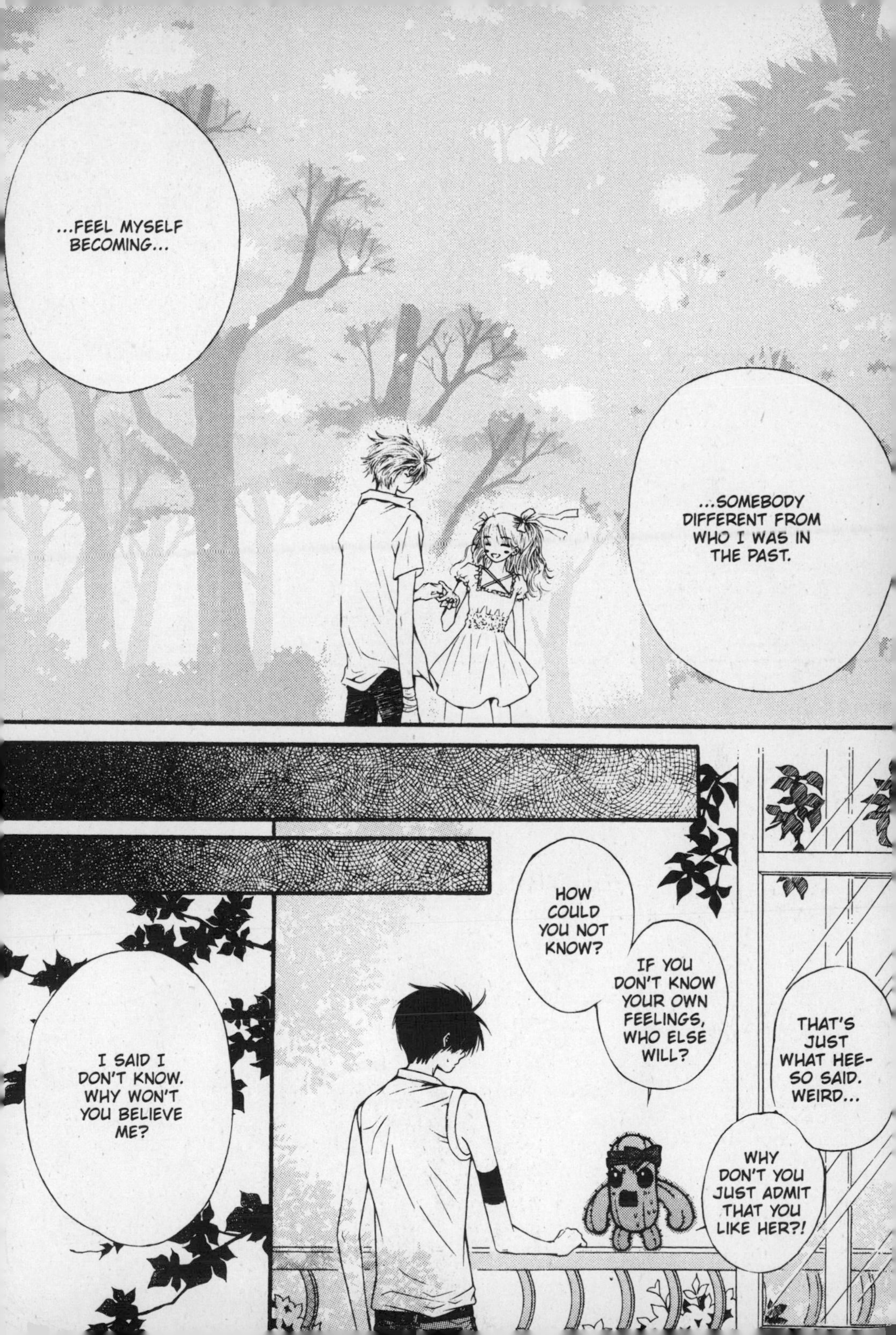
...FEEL MYSELF BECOMING...
...SOMEBODY DIFFERENT FROM WHO I WAS IN THE PAST.
I SAID I DON'T KNOW. WHY WON'T YOU BELIEVE ME?
HOW COULD YOU NOT KNOW?
IF YOU DON'T KNOW YOUR OWN FEELINGS, WHO ELSE WILL?
THAT'S JUST WHAT HEE-SO SAID. WEIRD...
WHY DON'T YOU JUST ADMIT THAT YOU LIKE HER?!

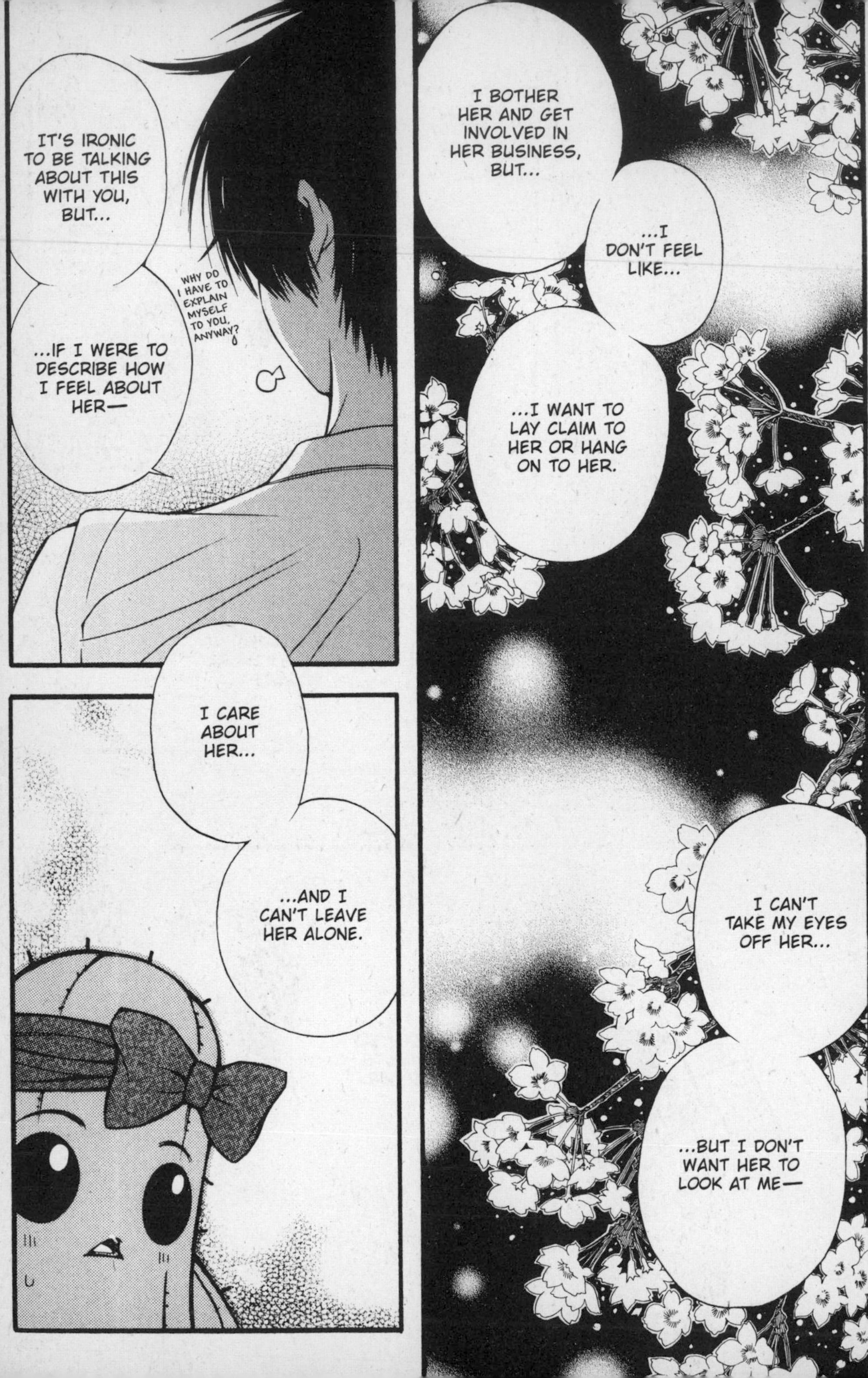
IT'S IRONIC TO BE TALKING ABOUT THIS WITH YOU, BUT...
...IF I WERE TO DESCRIBE HOW I FEEL ABOUT HER—
WHY DO I HAVE TO EXPLAIN MYSELF TO YOU, ANYWAY?
I CARE ABOUT HER...
...AND I CAN'T LEAVE HER ALONE.
I BOTHER HER AND GET INVOLVED IN HER BUSINESS, BUT...
...I DON'T FEEL LIKE...
...I WANT TO LAY CLAIM TO HER OR HANG ON TO HER.
I CAN'T TAKE MY EYES OFF HER...
...BUT I DON'T WANT HER TO LOOK AT ME—

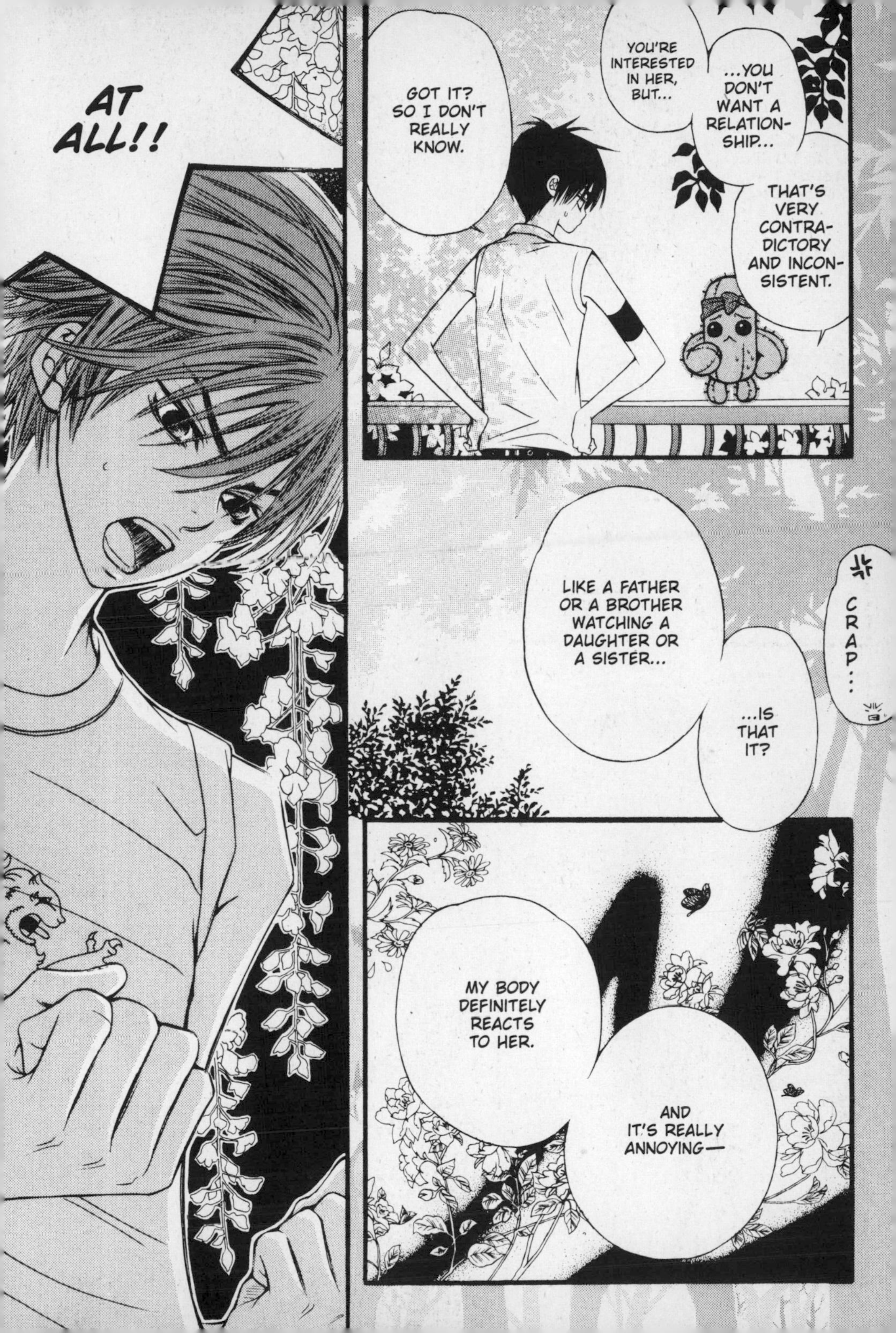
AT ALL!!
GOT IT? SO I DON'T REALLY KNOW.
YOU'RE INTERESTED IN HER, BUT...
...YOU DON'T WANT A RELATIONSHIP...
THAT'S VERY CONTRADICTORY AND INCONSISTENT.
LIKE A FATHER OR A BROTHER WATCHING A DAUGHTER OR A SISTER...
...IS THAT IT?
CRAP...
MY BODY DEFINITELY REACTS TO HER.
AND IT'S REALLY ANNOYING—

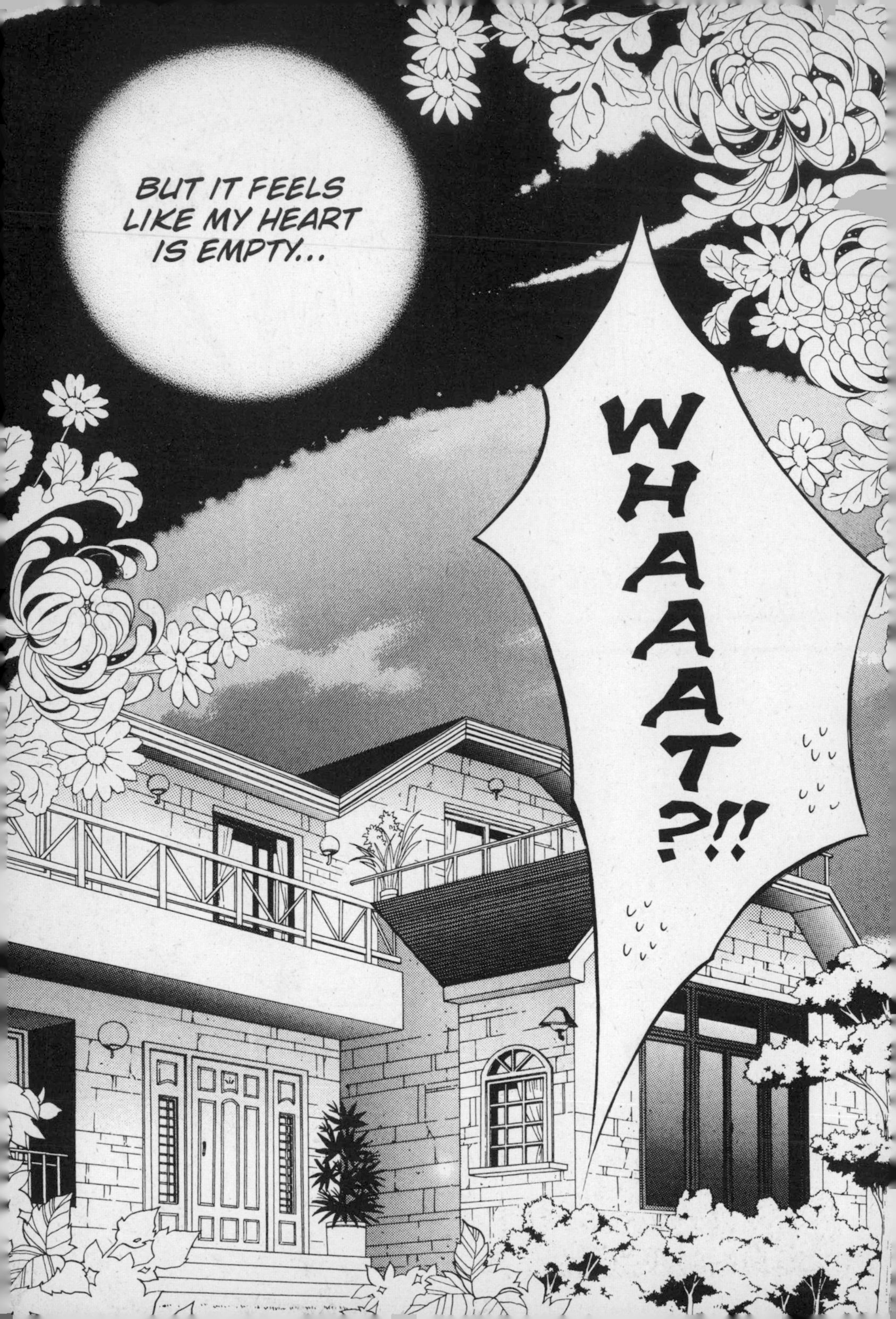
BUT IT FEELS LIKE MY HEART IS EMPTY...
WHAAAT?!!

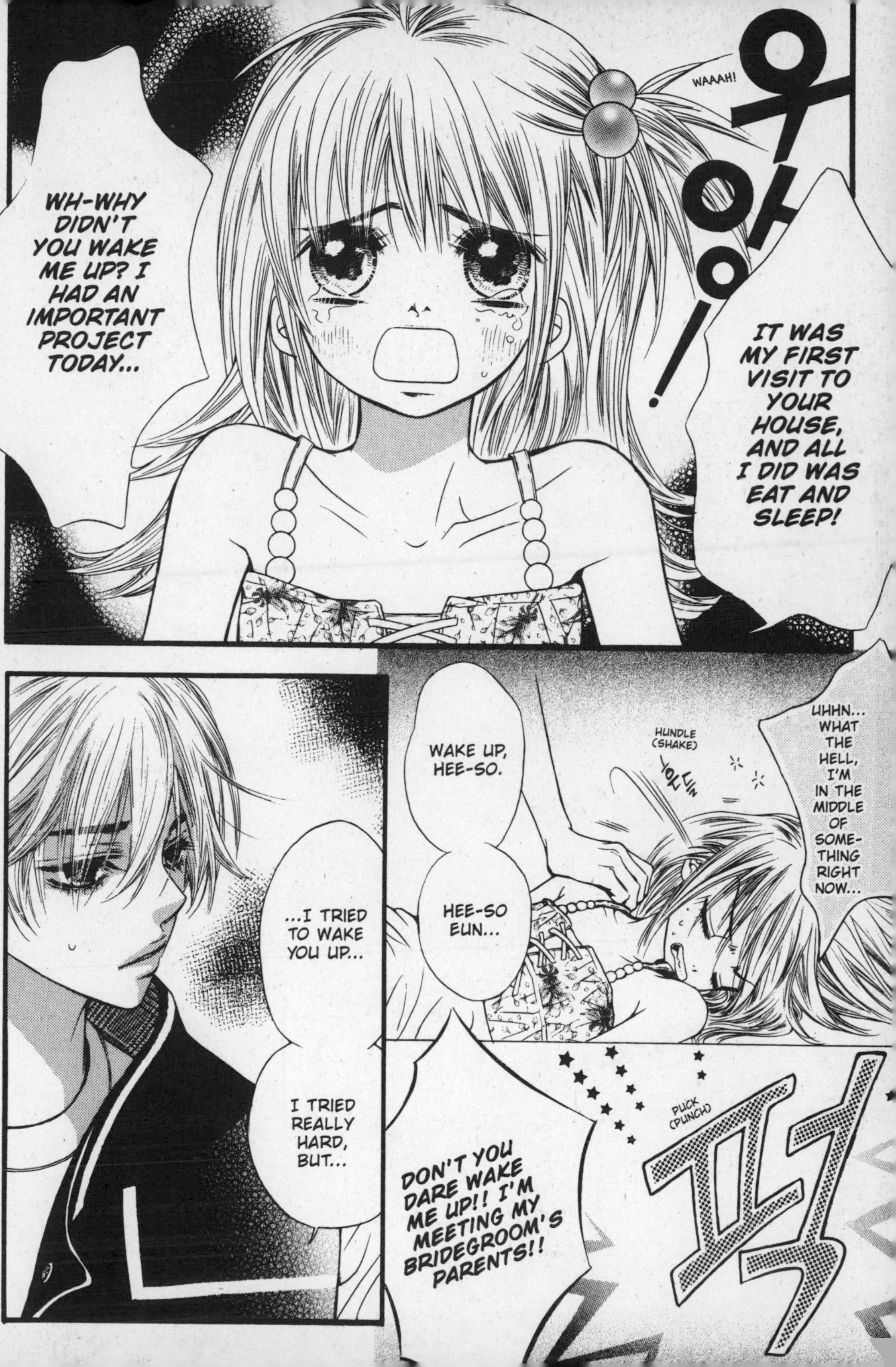
WH-WHY DIDN'T YOU WAKE ME UP? I HAD AN IMPORTANT PROJECT TODAY...
WAAAH!
IT WAS MY FIRST VISIT TO YOUR HOUSE, AND ALL I DID WAS EAT AND SLEEP!
...I TRIED TO WAKE YOU UP...
I TRIED REALLY HARD, BUT...
WAKE UP, HEE-SO.
HUNDLE (SHAKE)
HEE-SO EUN...
UHHN... WHAT THE HELL, I'M IN THE MIDDLE OF SOMETHING RIGHT NOW...
DON'T YOU DARE WAKE ME UP!! I'M MEETING MY BRIDEGROOM'S PARENTS!!
PUCK (PUNCH)

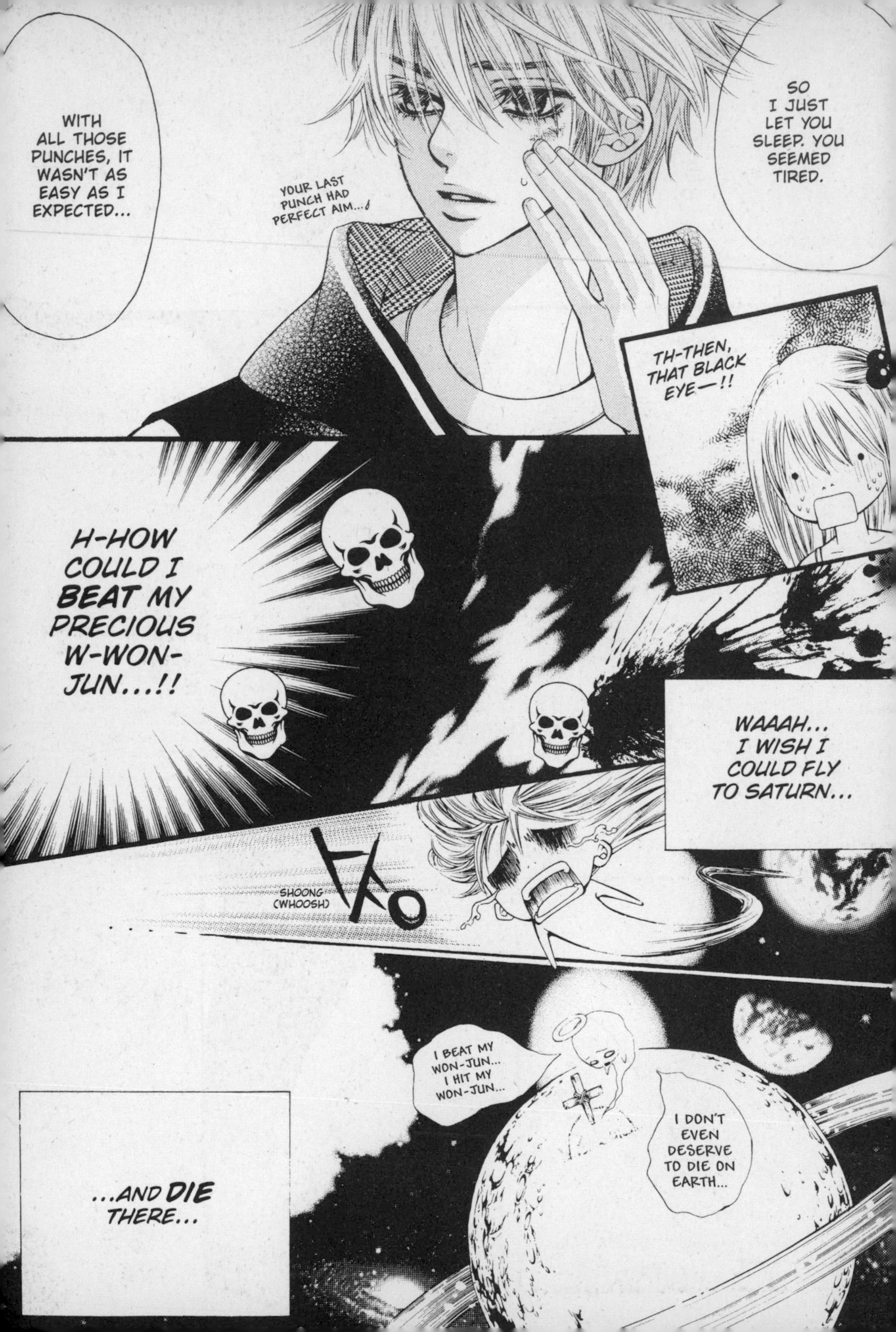
WITH ALL THOSE PUNCHES, IT WASN'T AS EASY AS I EXPECTED...
YOUR LAST PUNCH HAD PERFECT AIM...
SO I JUST LET YOU SLEEP. YOU SEEMED TIRED.
TH-THEN, THAT BLACK EYE—!!
H-HOW COULD I BEAT MY PRECIOUS W-WON-JUN...!!
WAAAH... I WISH I COULD FLY TO SATURN...
SHOONG (WHOOSH)
...AND DIE THERE...
I BEAT MY WON-JUN... I HIT MY WON-JUN...
I DON'T EVEN DESERVE TO DIE ON EARTH...

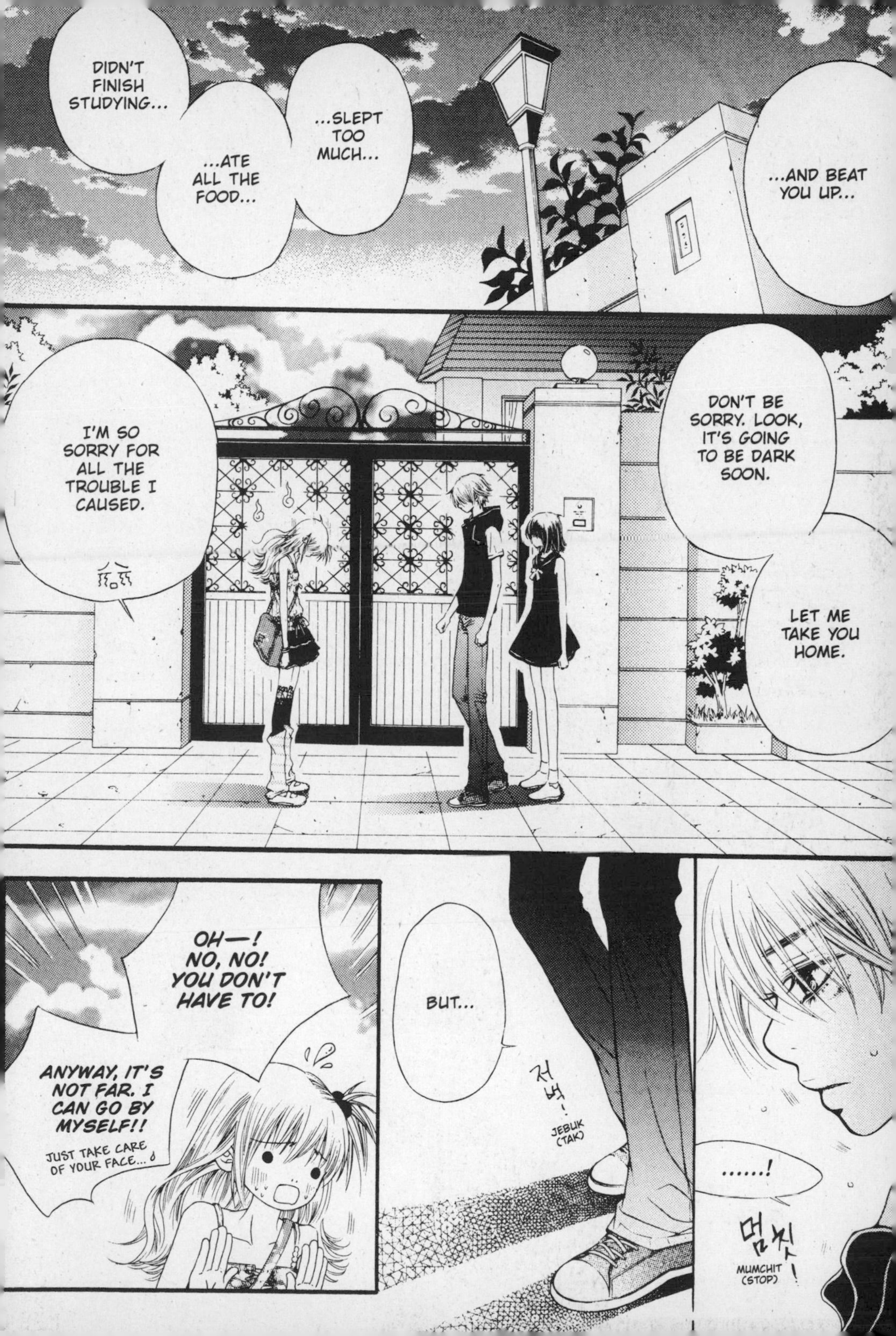
DIDN'T FINISH STUDYING...
...ATE ALL THE FOOD...
...SLEPT TOO MUCH...
...AND BEAT YOU UP...
I'M SO SORRY FOR ALL THE TROUBLE I CAUSED.
DON'T BE SORRY. LOOK, IT'S GOING TO BE DARK SOON.
LET ME TAKE YOU HOME.
OH—! NO, NO! YOU DON'T HAVE TO!
ANYWAY, IT'S NOT FAR. I CAN GO BY MYSELF!!
JUST TAKE CARE OF YOUR FACE...
BUT...
저벅!
JEBUK (TAK)
......!
멈칫!
MUMCHIT (STOP)

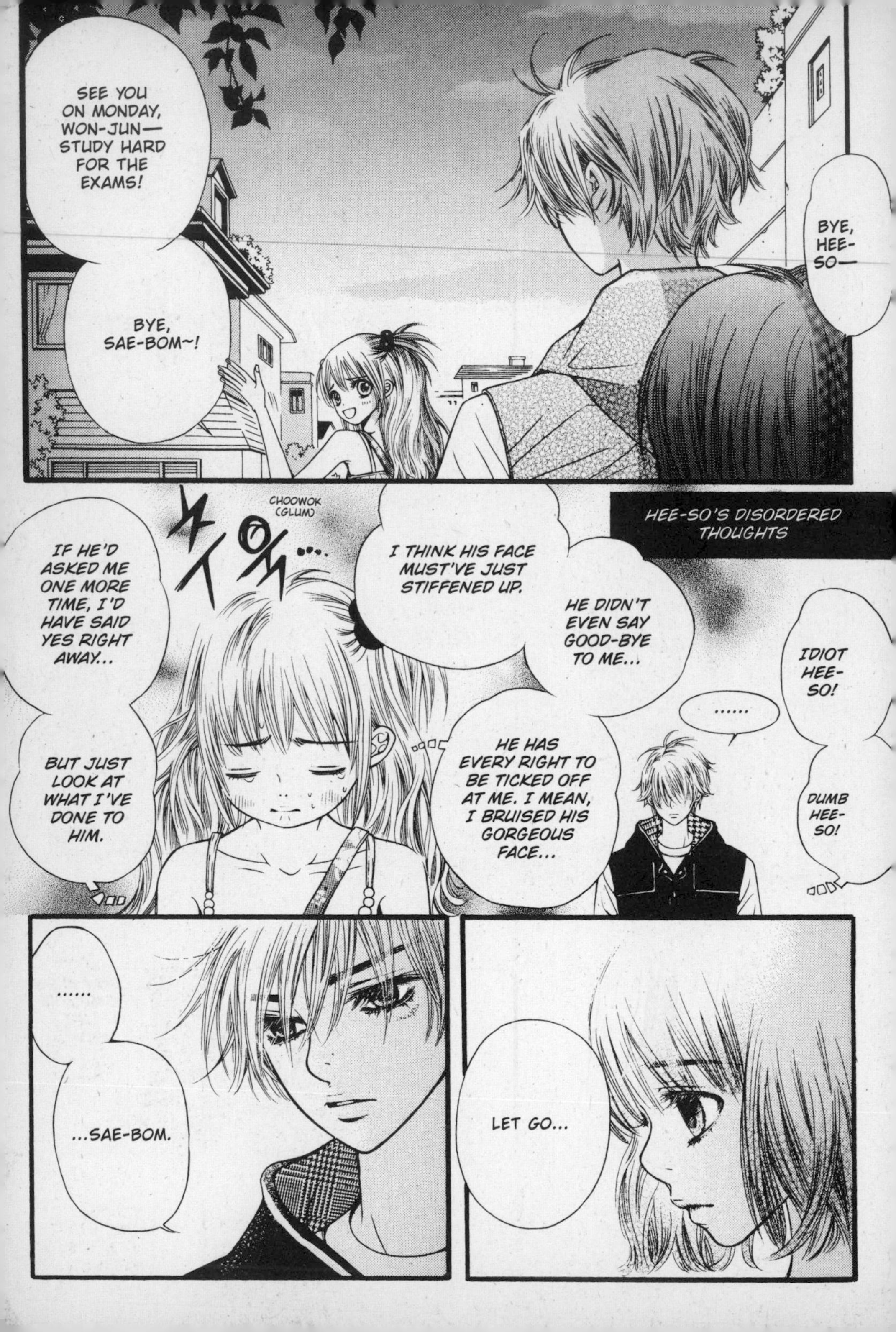

SEE YOU ON MONDAY, WON-JUN— STUDY HARD FOR THE EXAMS!
BYE, SAE-BOM~!
BYE, HEE-SO—
IF HE'D ASKED ME ONE MORE TIME, I'D HAVE SAID YES RIGHT AWAY...
BUT JUST LOOK AT WHAT I'VE DONE TO HIM.
CHOOWOK (GLUM)
I THINK HIS FACE MUST'VE JUST STIFFENED UP.
HE DIDN'T EVEN SAY GOOD-BYE TO ME...
HE HAS EVERY RIGHT TO BE TICKED OFF AT ME. I MEAN, I BRUISED HIS GORGEOUS FACE...
HEE-SO'S DISORDERED THOUGHTS
......
IDIOT HEE-SO!
DUMB HEE-SO!
......
...SAE-BOM.
LET GO...

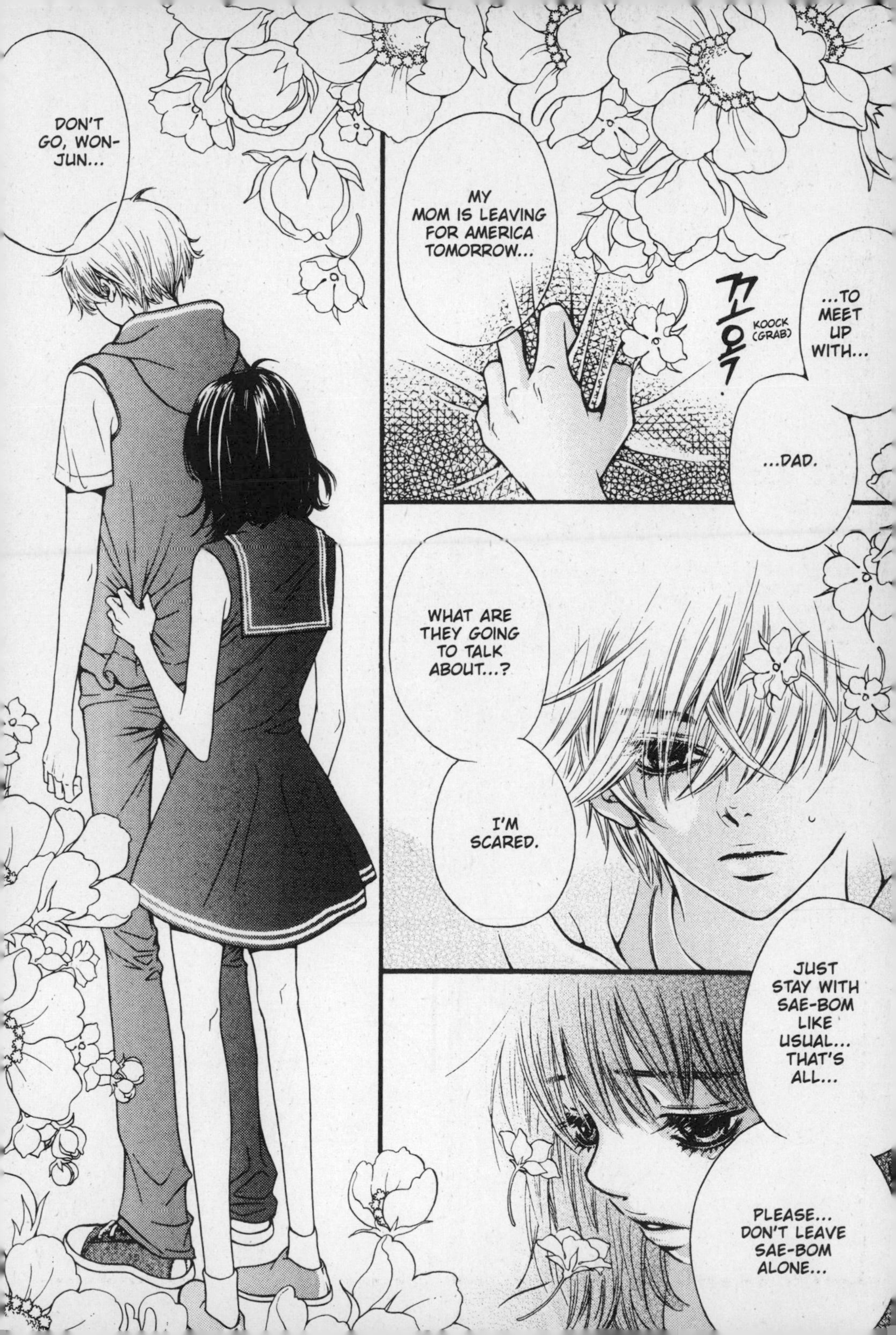
DON'T GO, WON-JUN...
MY MOM IS LEAVING FOR AMERICA TOMORROW...
KOOCK (GRAB)
...TO MEET UP WITH...
...DAD.
WHAT ARE THEY GOING TO TALK ABOUT...?
I'M SCARED.
JUST STAY WITH SAE-BOM LIKE USUAL... THAT'S ALL...
PLEASE... DON'T LEAVE SAE-BOM ALONE...

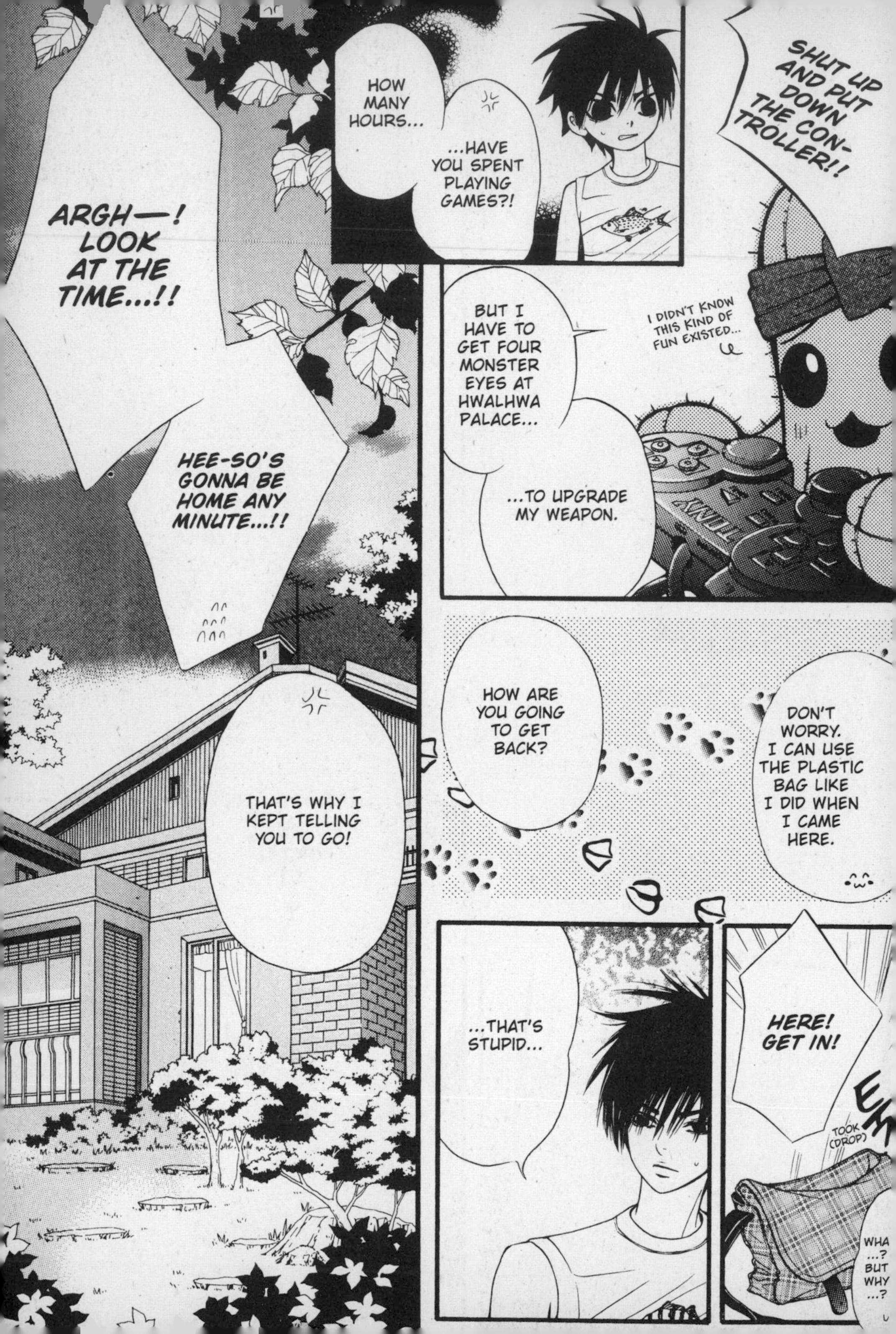
HOW MANY HOURS...
...HAVE YOU SPENT PLAYING GAMES?!
SHUT UP AND PUT DOWN THE CON-TROLLER!!
BUT I HAVE TO GET FOUR MONSTER EYES AT HWALHWA PALACE...
...TO UPGRADE MY WEAPON.
I DIDN'T KNOW THIS KIND OF FUN EXISTED...
ARGH—! LOOK AT THE TIME...!!
HEE-SO'S GONNA BE HOME ANY MINUTE...!!
THAT'S WHY I KEPT TELLING YOU TO GO!
HOW ARE YOU GOING TO GET BACK?
DON'T WORRY. I CAN USE THE PLASTIC BAG LIKE I DID WHEN I CAME HERE.
...THAT'S STUPID...
HERE! GET IN!
TOOK (DROP)
WHA ...? BUT WHY ...?

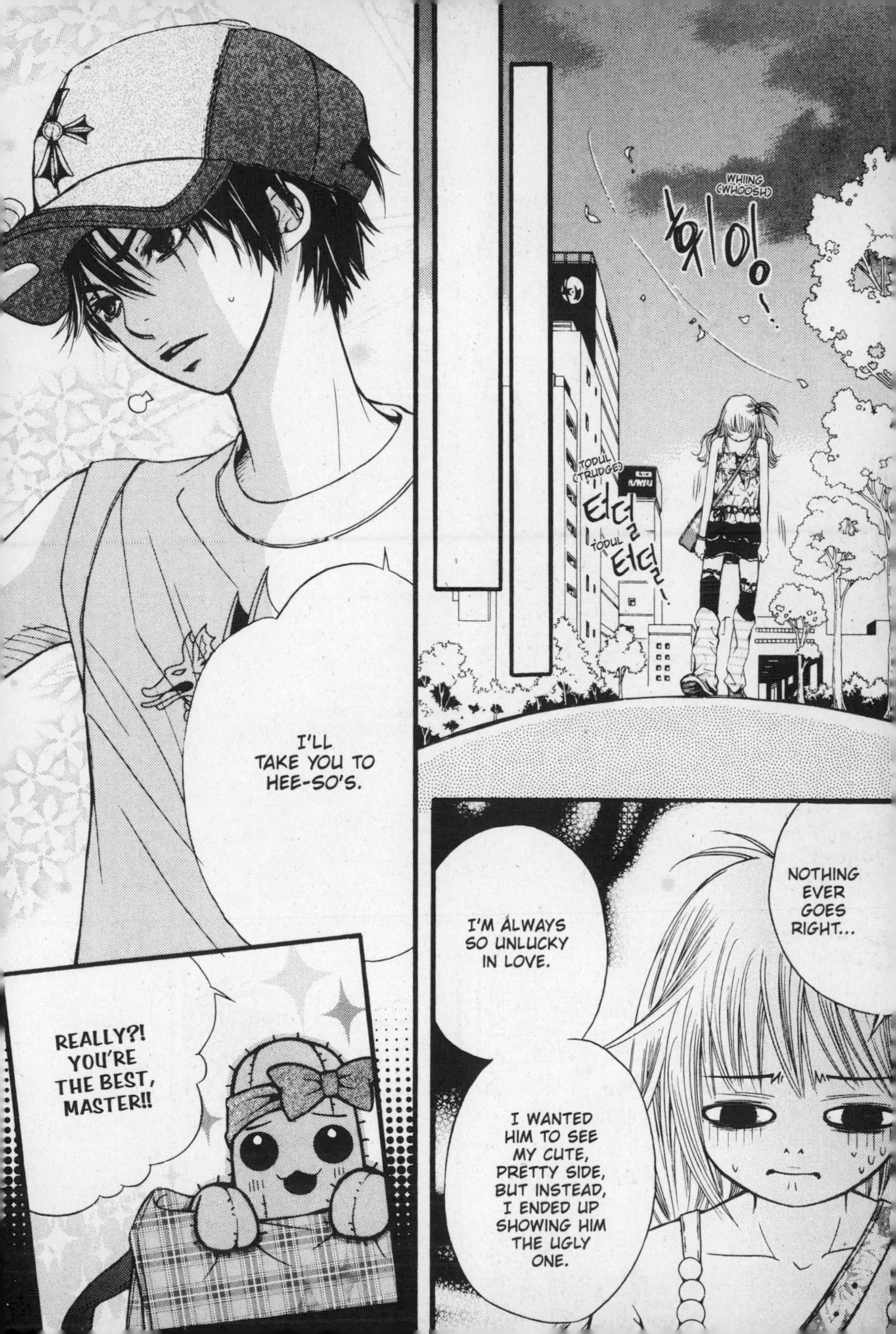
I'LL TAKE YOU TO HEE-SO'S.
REALLY?! YOU'RE THE BEST, MASTER!!
WHIING (WHOOSH)
TODUL (TRUDGE)
터덜
TODUL
터덜
I'M ALWAYS SO UNLUCKY IN LOVE.
NOTHING EVER GOES RIGHT...
I WANTED HIM TO SEE MY CUTE, PRETTY SIDE, BUT INSTEAD, I ENDED UP SHOWING HIM THE UGLY ONE.

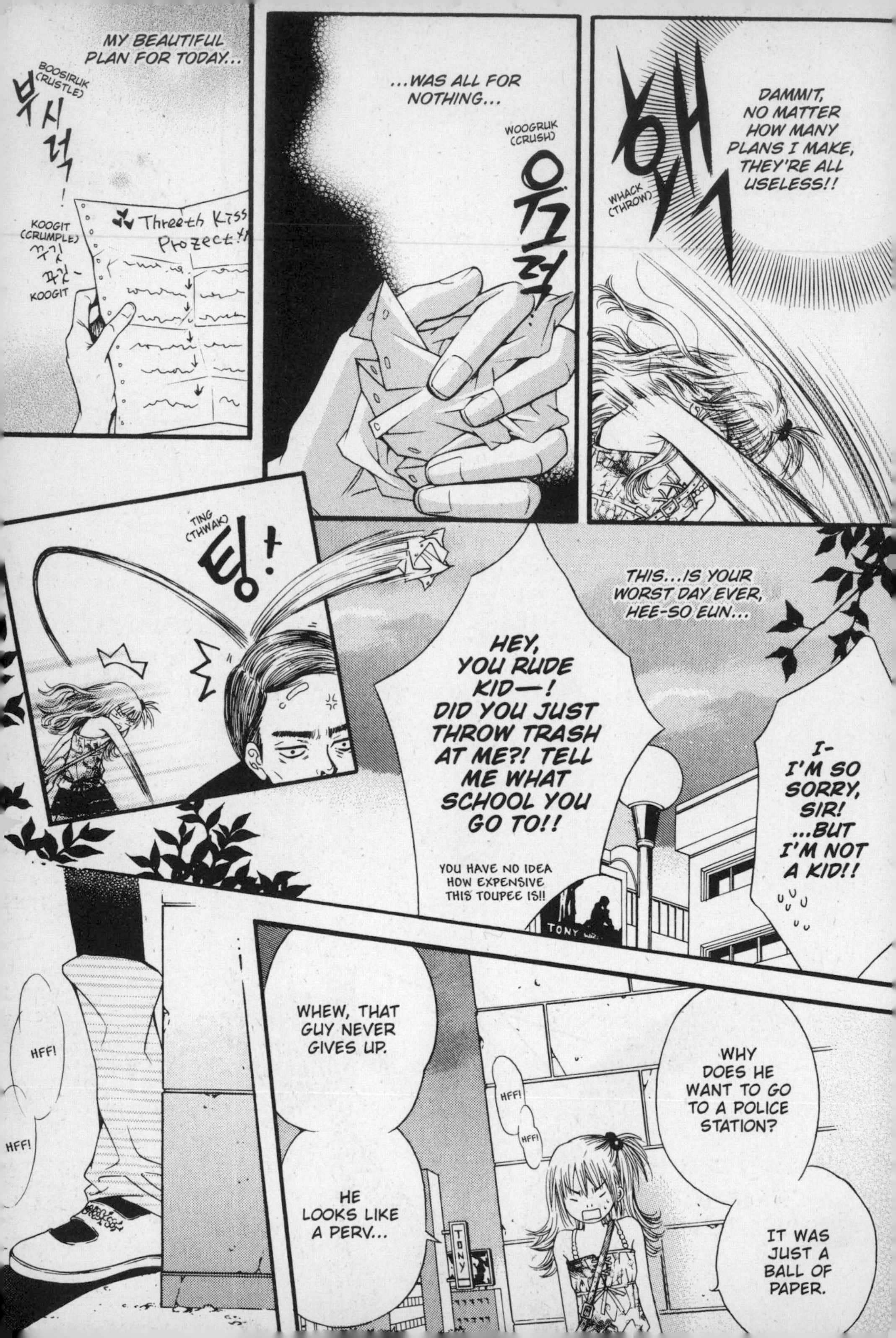
MY BEAUTIFUL PLAN FOR TODAY...
BOOSIRUK (RUSTLE)
부시럭
KOOGIT (CRUMPLE)
꾸깃 꾸깃
KOOGIT
Threeth Kiss Prozect
...WAS ALL FOR NOTHING...
WOOGRUK (CRUSH)
우그럭
홱
WHACK (THROW)
DAMMIT, NO MATTER HOW MANY PLANS I MAKE, THEY'RE ALL USELESS!!
TING (THWAK)
팅!
THIS...IS YOUR WORST DAY EVER, HEE-SO EUN...
HEY, YOU RUDE KID—! DID YOU JUST THROW TRASH AT ME?! TELL ME WHAT SCHOOL YOU GO TO!!
YOU HAVE NO IDEA HOW EXPENSIVE THIS TOUPEE IS!!
I- I'M SO SORRY, SIR! ...BUT I'M NOT A KID!!
HFF!
HFF!
WHEW, THAT GUY NEVER GIVES UP.
HE LOOKS LIKE A PERV...
HFF!
HFF!
WHY DOES HE WANT TO GO TO A POLICE STATION?
IT WAS JUST A BALL OF PAPER.

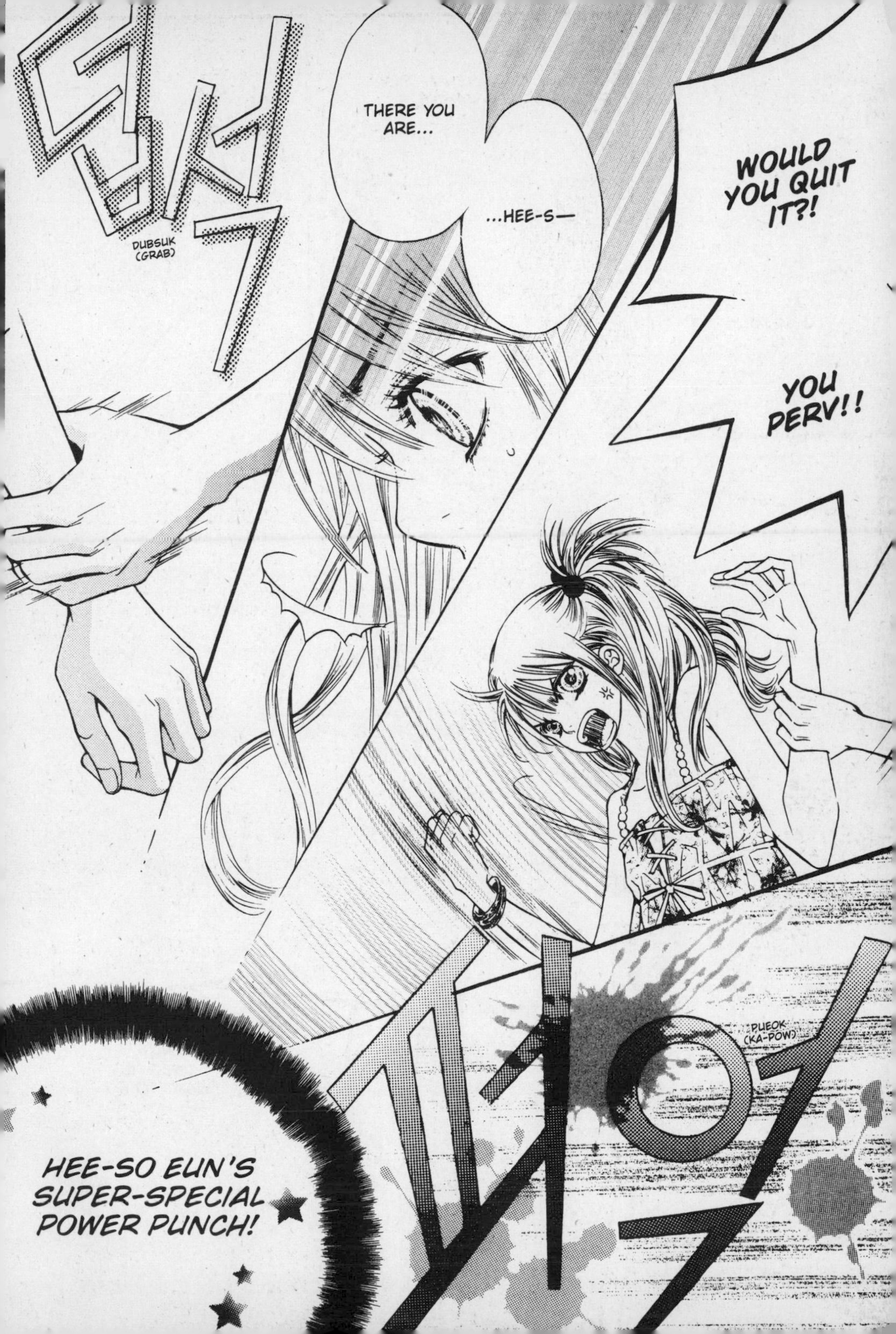

DUBSUK (GRAB)
THERE YOU ARE...
...HEE-S—
WOULD YOU QUIT IT?!
YOU PERV!!
PUEOK (KA-POW)
HEE-SO EUN'S SUPER-SPECIAL POWER PUNCH!

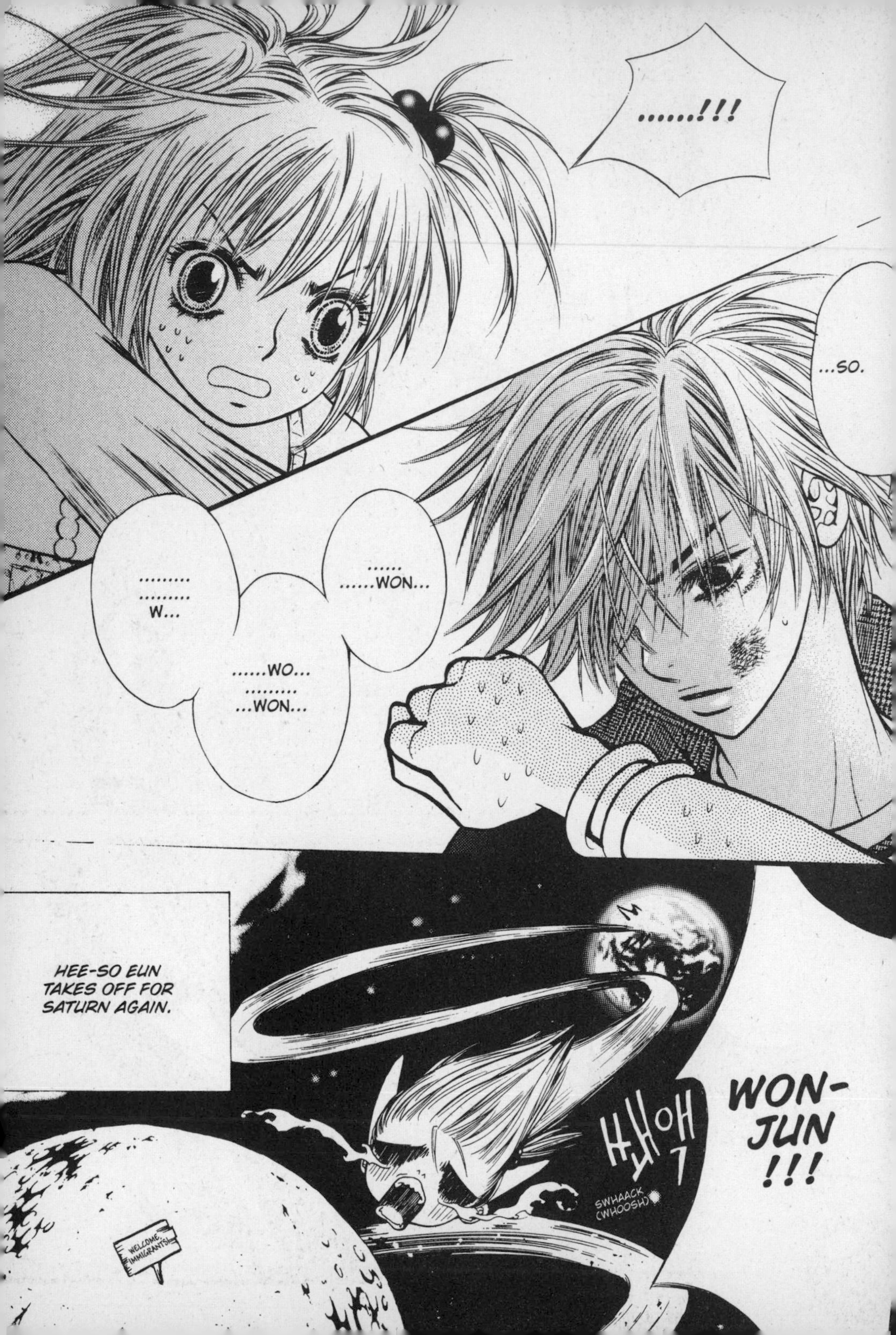
......!!!
...SO.
....
....
W...
......
......WON...
......WO...
....
...WON...
HEE-SO EUN TAKES OFF FOR SATURN AGAIN.
WON-JUN!!!
SWHAACK (WHOOSH)
WELCOME IMMIGRANTS!

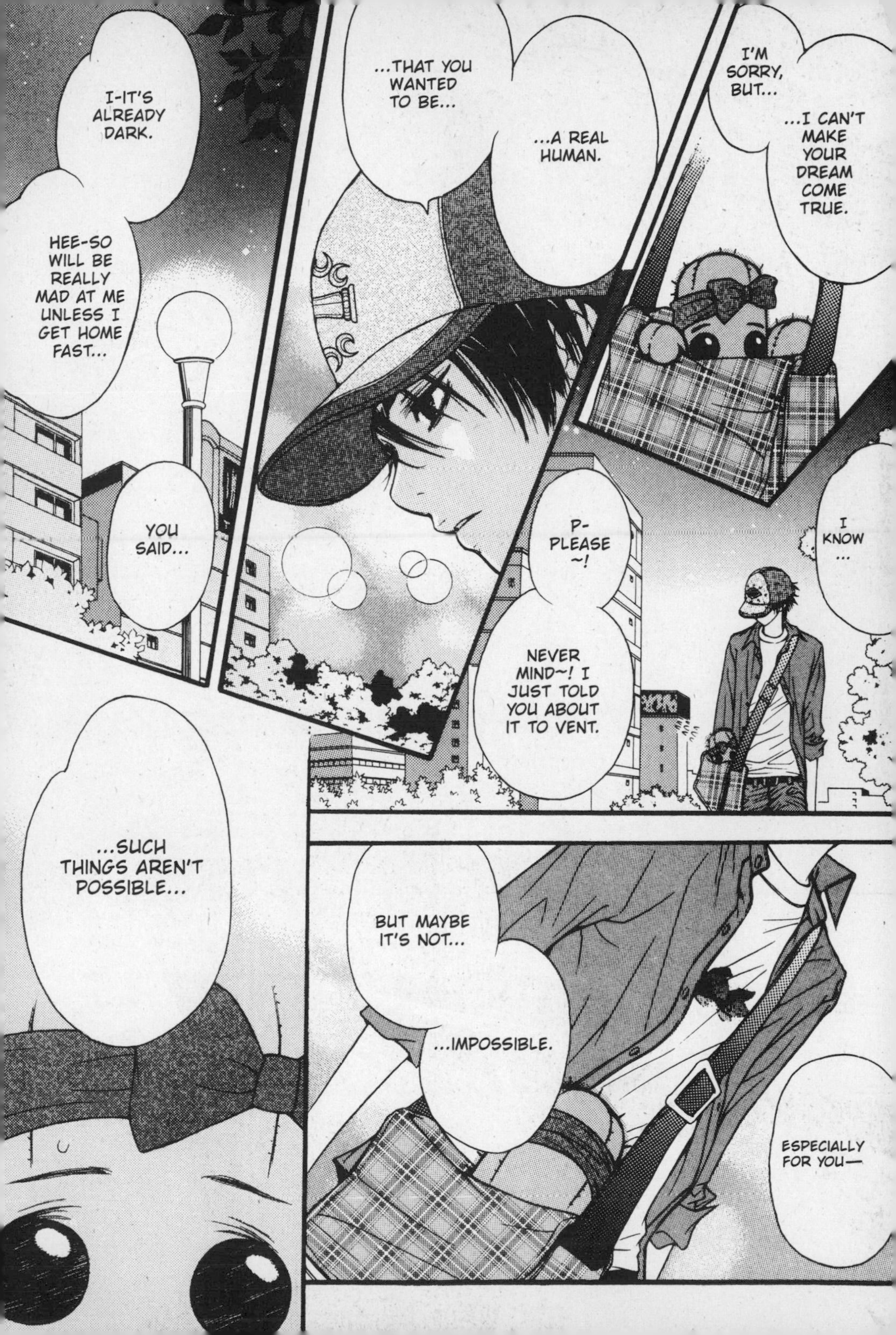
I-IT'S ALREADY DARK.
HEE-SO WILL BE REALLY MAD AT ME UNLESS I GET HOME FAST...
YOU SAID...
...THAT YOU WANTED TO BE...
...A REAL HUMAN.
I'M SORRY, BUT...
...I CAN'T MAKE YOUR DREAM COME TRUE.
P-PLEASE ~!
NEVER MIND~! I JUST TOLD YOU ABOUT IT TO VENT.
I KNOW...
...SUCH THINGS AREN'T POSSIBLE...
BUT MAYBE IT'S NOT...
...IMPOSSIBLE.
ESPECIALLY FOR YOU—

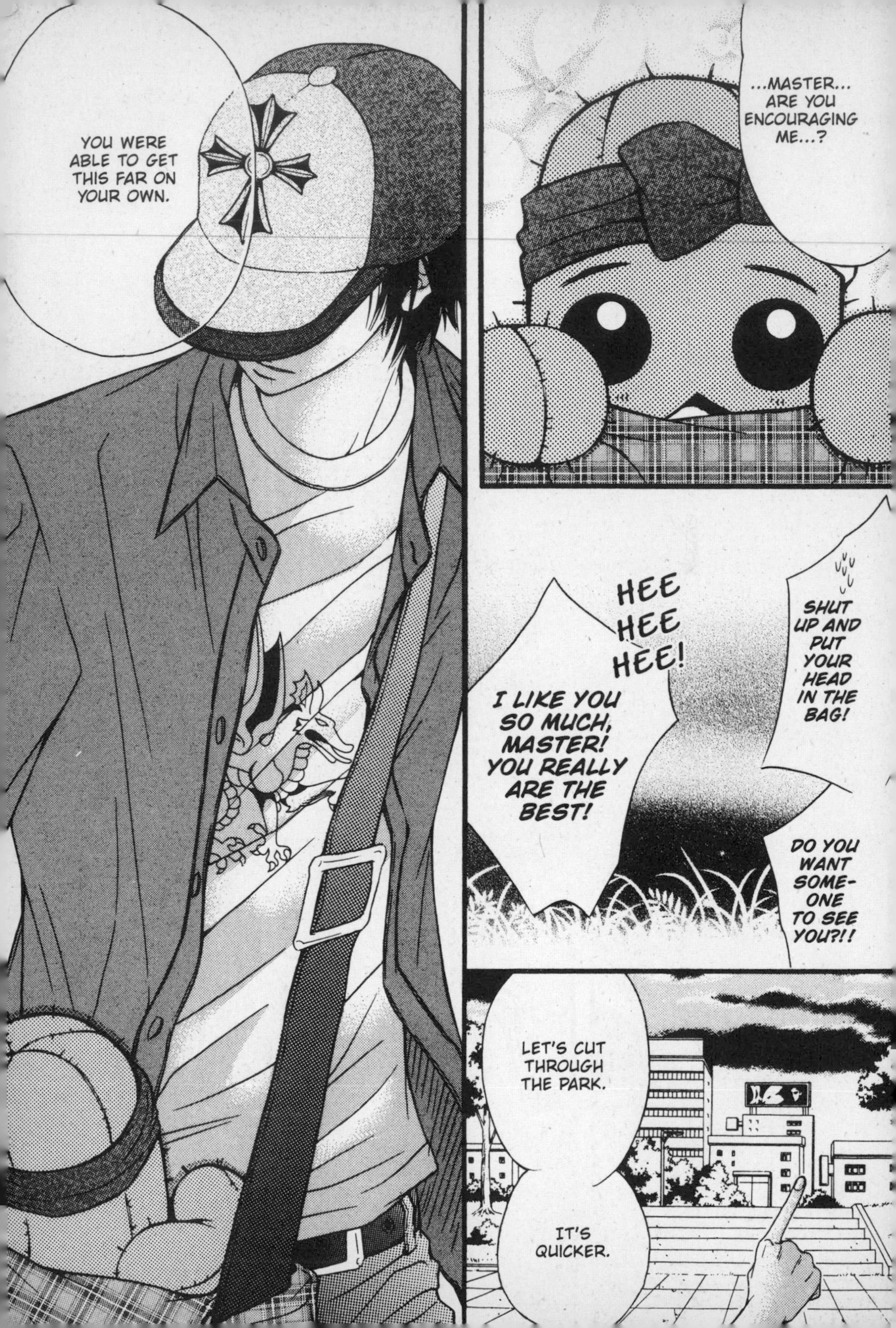
YOU WERE ABLE TO GET THIS FAR ON YOUR OWN.
...MASTER... ARE YOU ENCOURAGING ME...?
HEE HEE HEE!
I LIKE YOU SO MUCH, MASTER! YOU REALLY ARE THE BEST!
SHUT UP AND PUT YOUR HEAD IN THE BAG!
DO YOU WANT SOME-ONE TO SEE YOU?!!
LET'S CUT THROUGH THE PARK.
IT'S QUICKER.

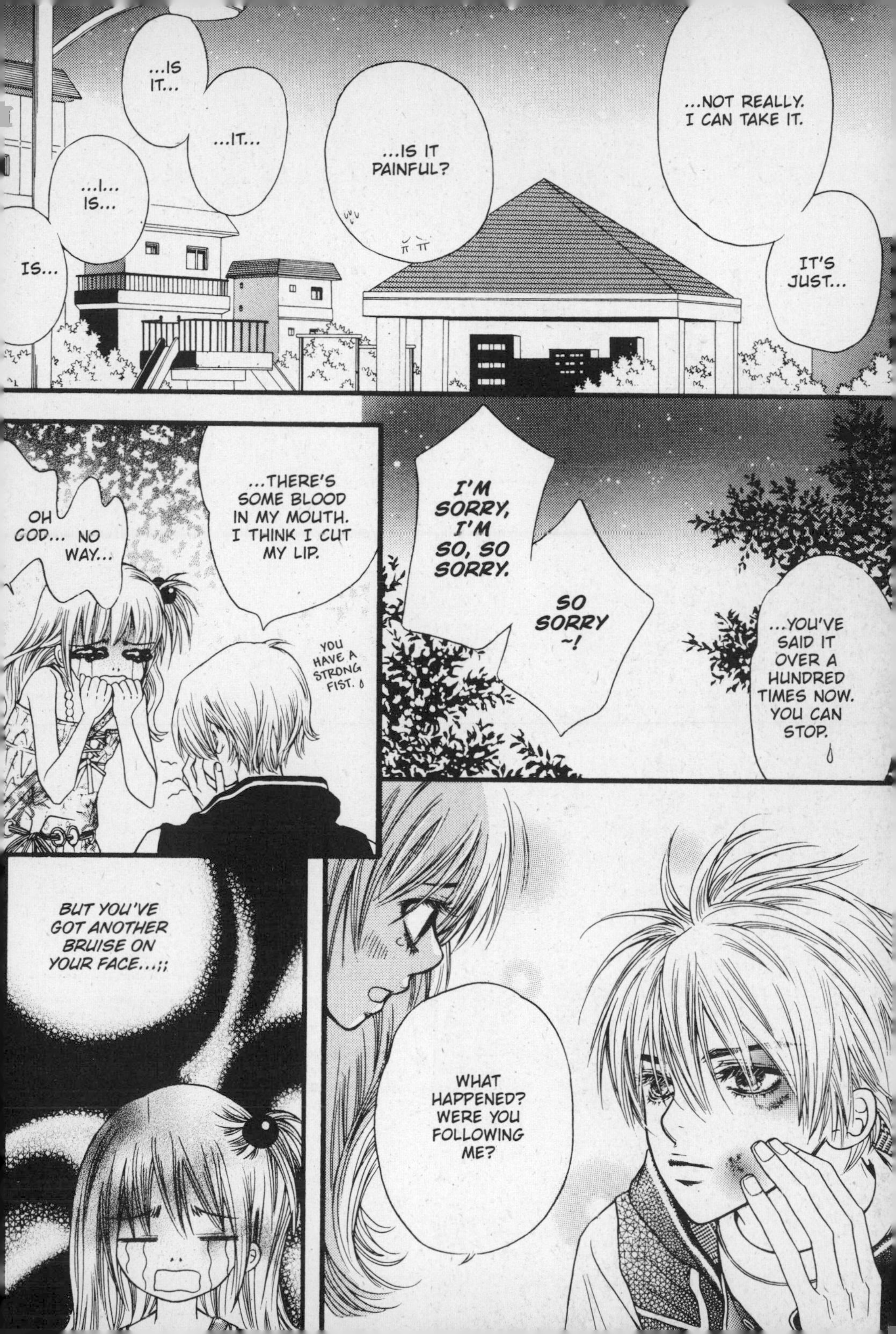
...IS IT...
...IT...
...I... IS...
IS...
...IS IT PAINFUL?
...NOT REALLY. I CAN TAKE IT.
IT'S JUST...
OH GOD... NO WAY...
...THERE'S SOME BLOOD IN MY MOUTH. I THINK I CUT MY LIP.
YOU HAVE A STRONG FIST.
I'M SORRY, I'M SO, SO SORRY.
SO SORRY ~!
...YOU'VE SAID IT OVER A HUNDRED TIMES NOW. YOU CAN STOP.
BUT YOU'VE GOT ANOTHER BRUISE ON YOUR FACE...;;
WHAT HAPPENED? WERE YOU FOLLOWING ME?

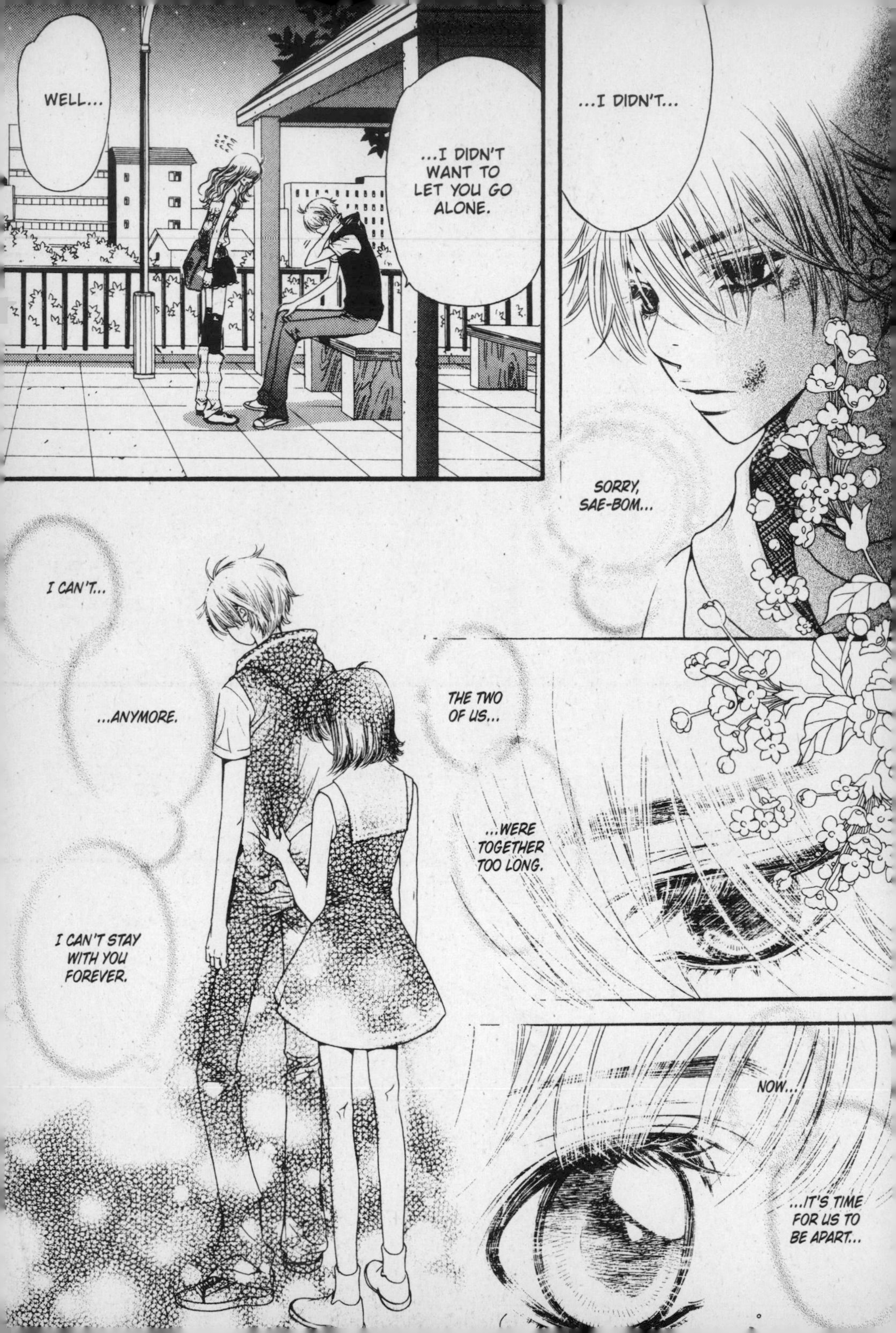
WELL...
...I DIDN'T WANT TO LET YOU GO ALONE.
...I DIDN'T...
SORRY, SAE-BOM...
I CAN'T...
...ANYMORE.
I CAN'T STAY WITH YOU FOREVER.
THE TWO OF US...
...WERE TOGETHER TOO LONG.
NOW...
...IT'S TIME FOR US TO BE APART...

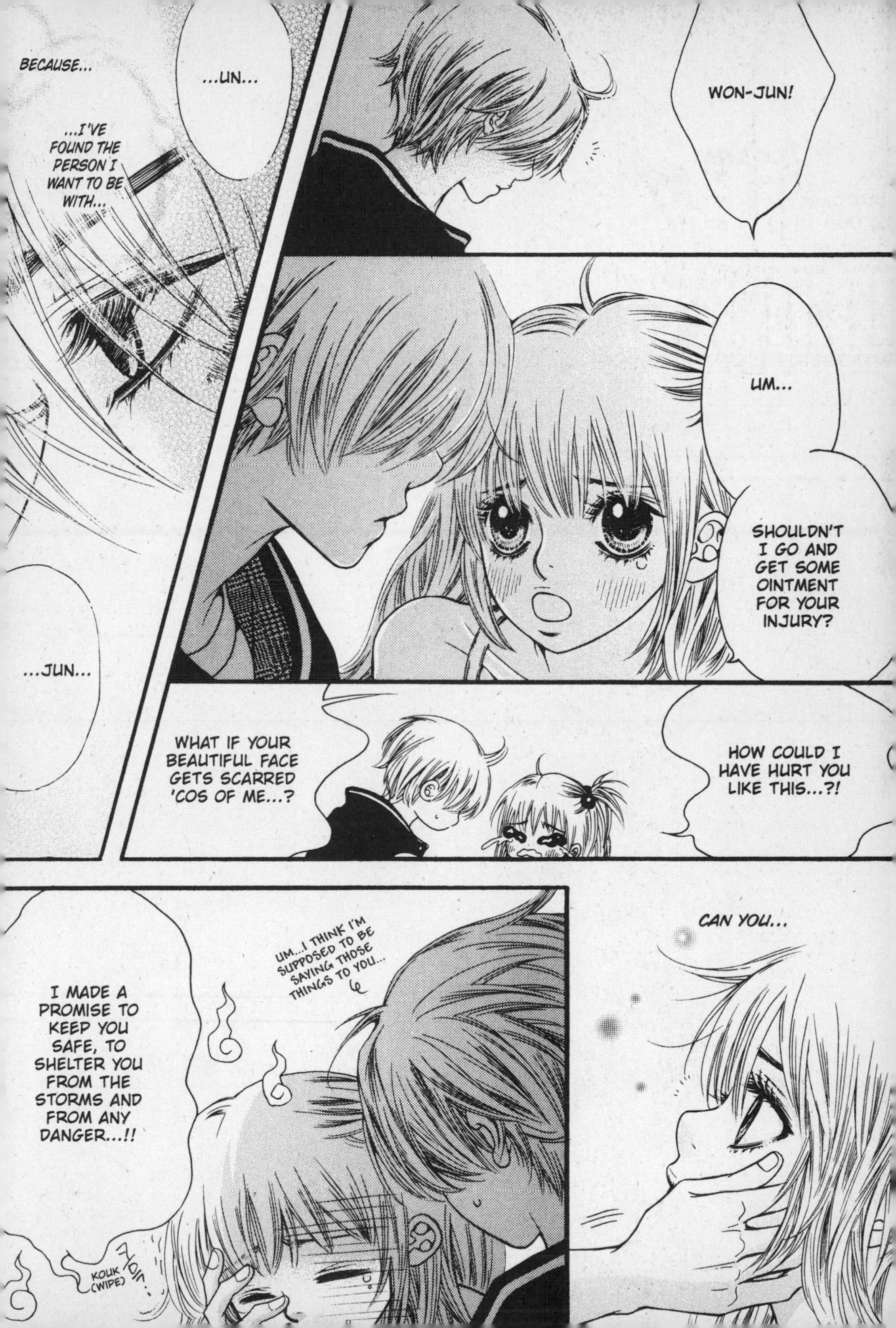
BECAUSE...
...UN...
...I'VE FOUND THE PERSON I WANT TO BE WITH...
...JUN...
WON-JUN!
UM...
SHOULDN'T I GO AND GET SOME OINTMENT FOR YOUR INJURY?
WHAT IF YOUR BEAUTIFUL FACE GETS SCARRED 'COS OF ME...?
HOW COULD I HAVE HURT YOU LIKE THIS...?!
I MADE A PROMISE TO KEEP YOU SAFE, TO SHELTER YOU FROM THE STORMS AND FROM ANY DANGER...!!
UM...I THINK I'M SUPPOSED TO BE SAYING THOSE THINGS TO YOU...
KOUIK (WIPE)
CAN YOU...

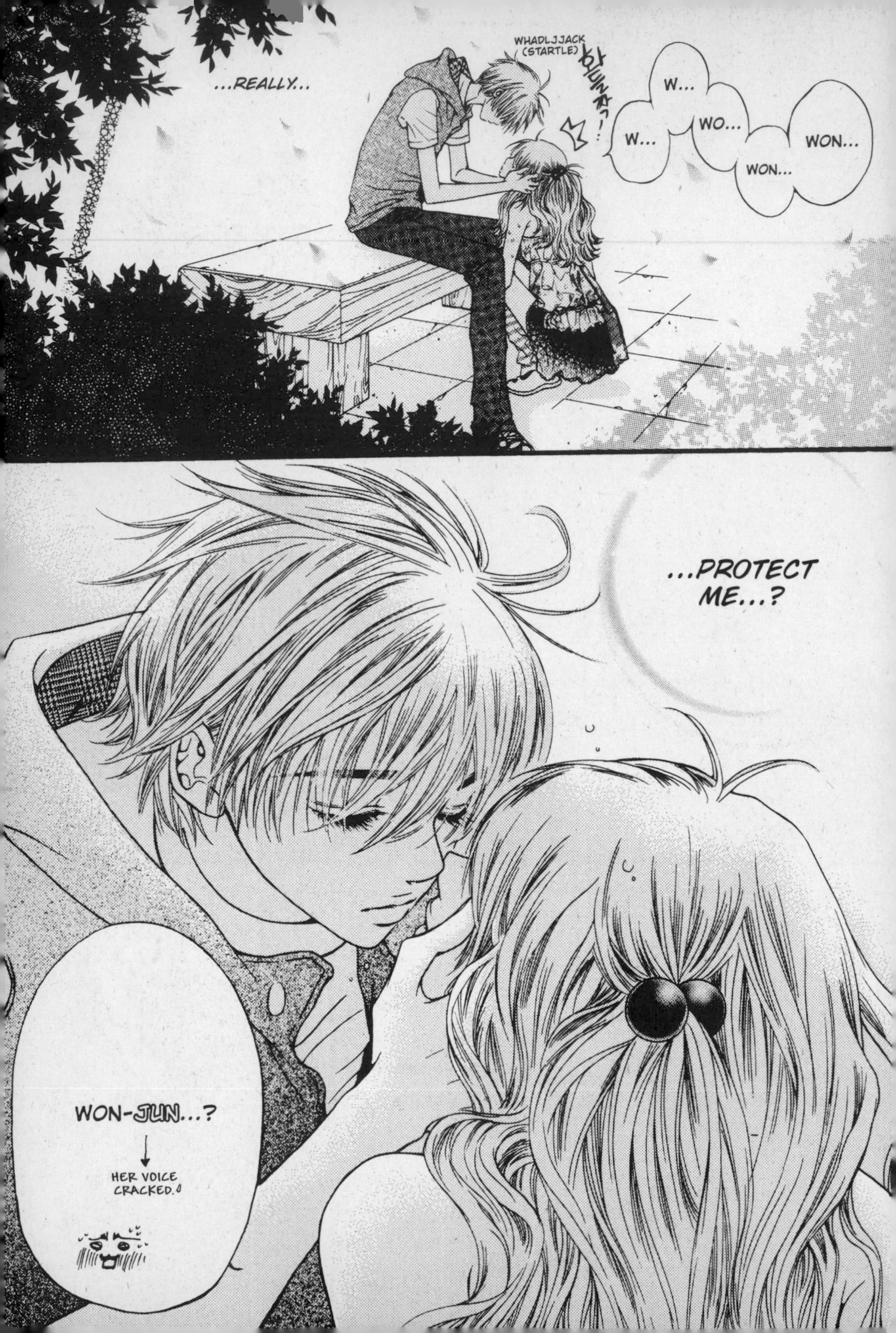

...REALLY...
WHADLJJACK (STARTLE)
W... W... WO... WON... WON...
...PROTECT ME...?
WON-JUN...?
HER VOICE CRACKED.

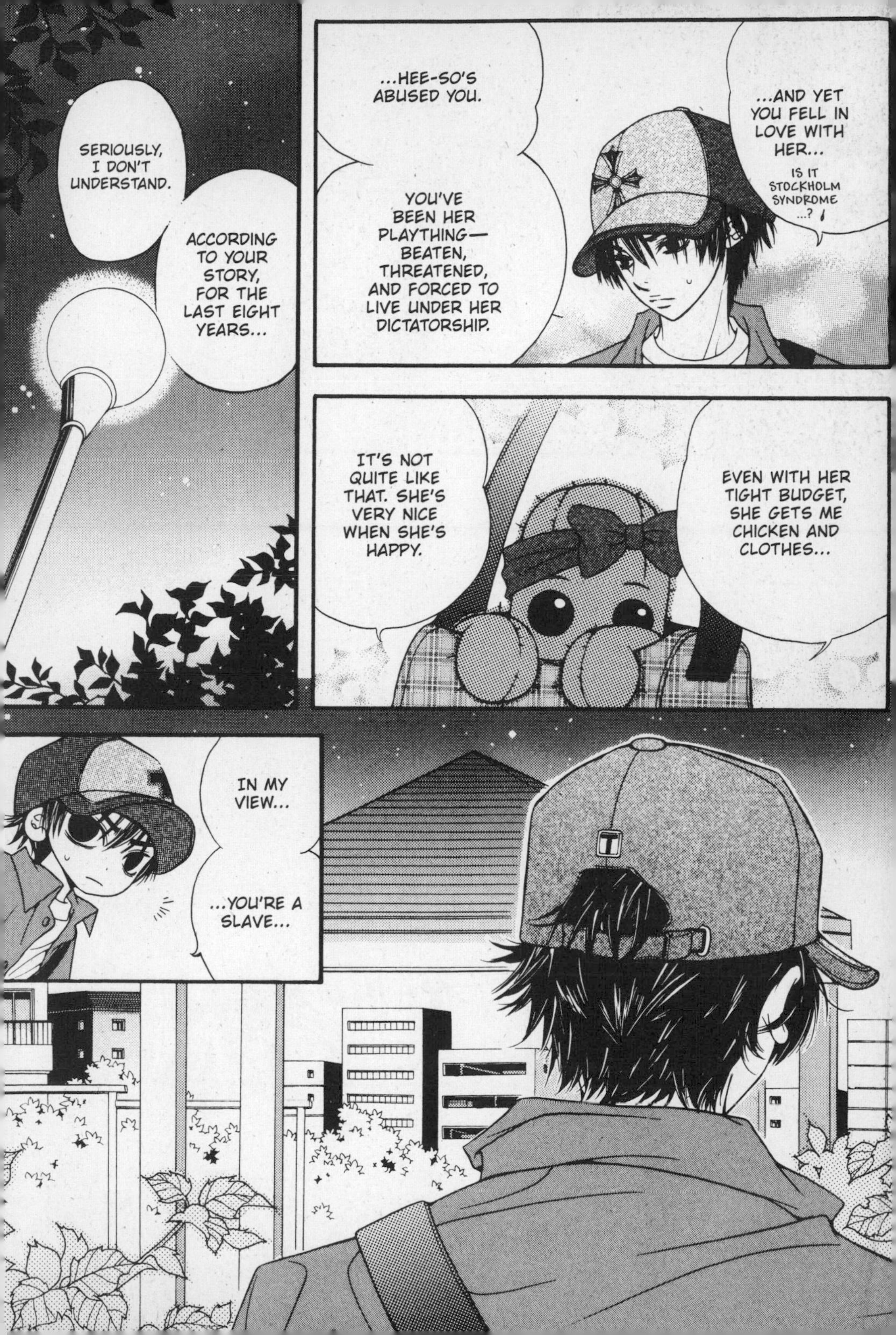
SERIOUSLY, I DON'T UNDERSTAND.
ACCORDING TO YOUR STORY, FOR THE LAST EIGHT YEARS...
...HEE-SO'S ABUSED YOU.
YOU'VE BEEN HER PLAYTHING— BEATEN, THREATENED, AND FORCED TO LIVE UNDER HER DICTATORSHIP.
...AND YET YOU FELL IN LOVE WITH HER...
IS IT STOCKHOLM SYNDROME ...?
IT'S NOT QUITE LIKE THAT. SHE'S VERY NICE WHEN SHE'S HAPPY.
EVEN WITH HER TIGHT BUDGET, SHE GETS ME CHICKEN AND CLOTHES...
IN MY VIEW...
...YOU'RE A SLAVE...

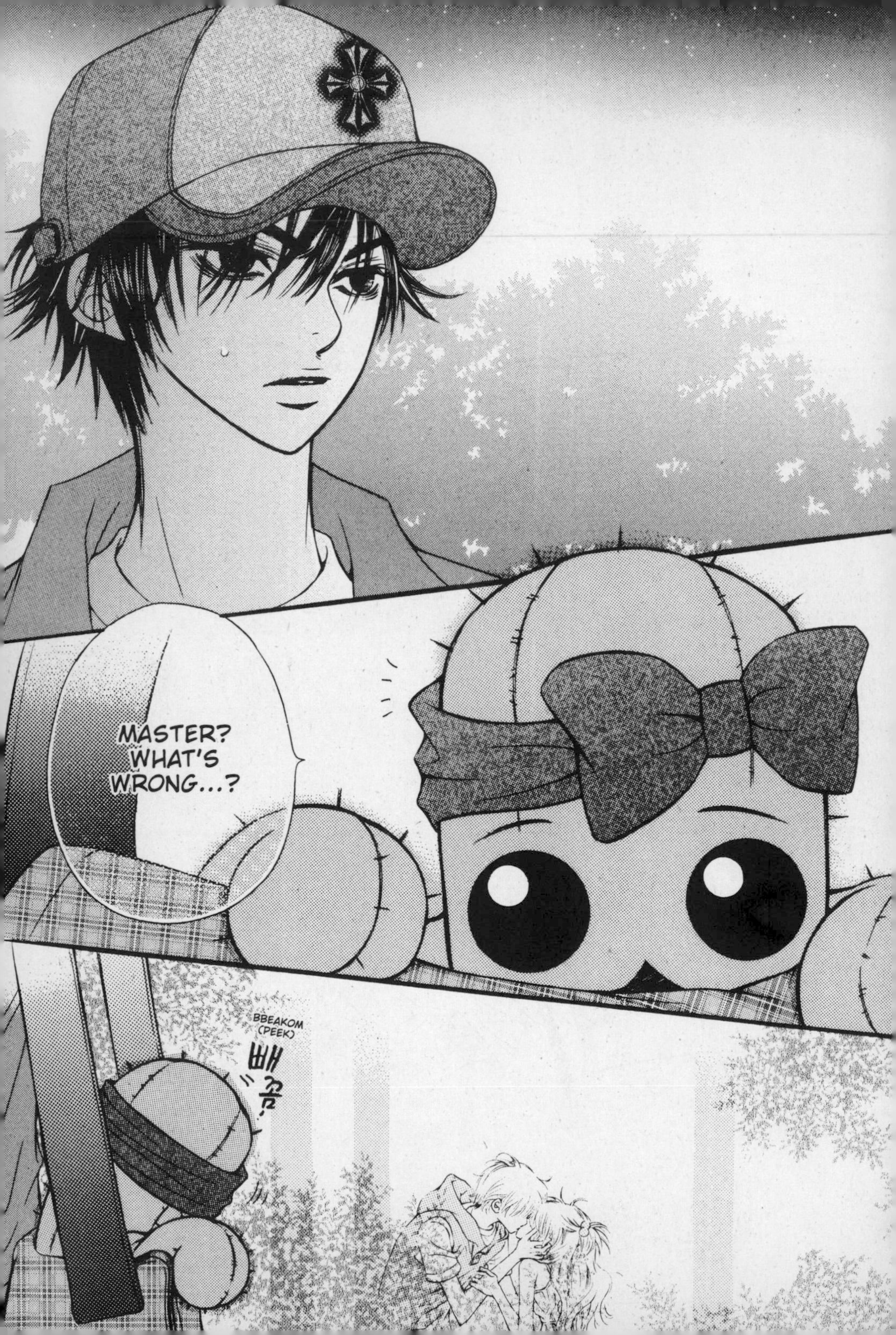
MASTER? WHAT'S WRONG...?
BBEAKOM (PEEK)
빼꼼

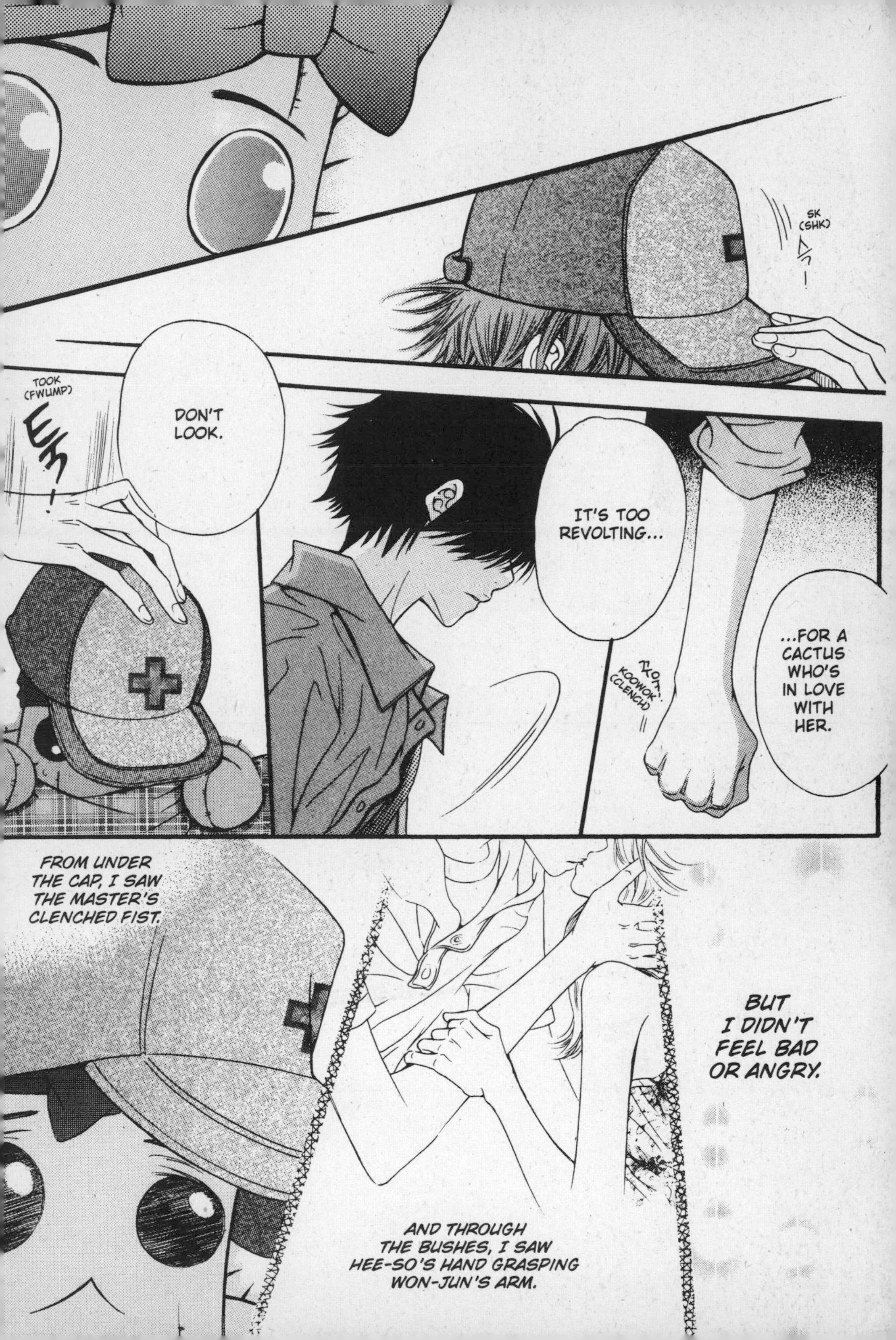
SK (SHK)
TOOK (FWUMP)
DON'T LOOK.
IT'S TOO REVOLTING...
KOOWOK (CLENCH)
...FOR A CACTUS WHO'S IN LOVE WITH HER.
FROM UNDER THE CAP, I SAW THE MASTER'S CLENCHED FIST.
BUT I DIDN'T FEEL BAD OR ANGRY.
AND THROUGH THE BUSHES, I SAW HEE-SO'S HAND GRASPING WON-JUN'S ARM.

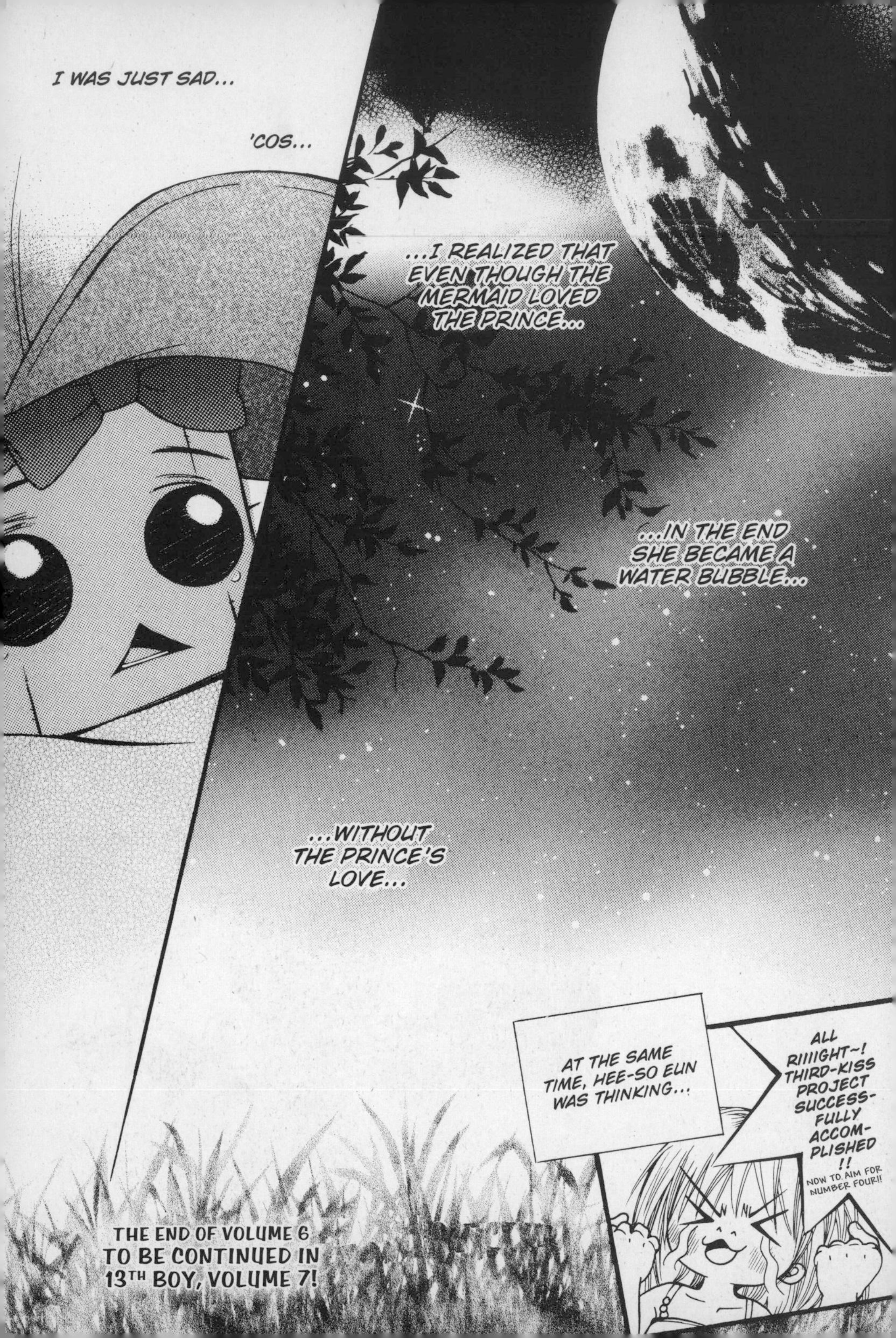
I WAS JUST SAD...
'COS...
...I REALIZED THAT EVEN THOUGH THE MERMAID LOVED THE PRINCE...
...IN THE END SHE BECAME A WATER BUBBLE...
...WITHOUT THE PRINCE'S LOVE...
AT THE SAME TIME, HEE-SO EUN WAS THINKING...
ALL RIIIGHT~! THIRD-KISS PROJECT SUCCESS-FULLY ACCOM-PLISHED!!
NOW TO AIM FOR NUMBER FOUR!!
THE END OF VOLUME 6
TO BE CONTINUED IN 13TH BOY, VOLUME 7!

13th Boy

THE FAMOUS BONUS FEATURE~!! LET'S TAKE A LOOK AT HEE-SO'S STORMY RELATIONSHIPS~!! THE THIRD EPISODE~!!

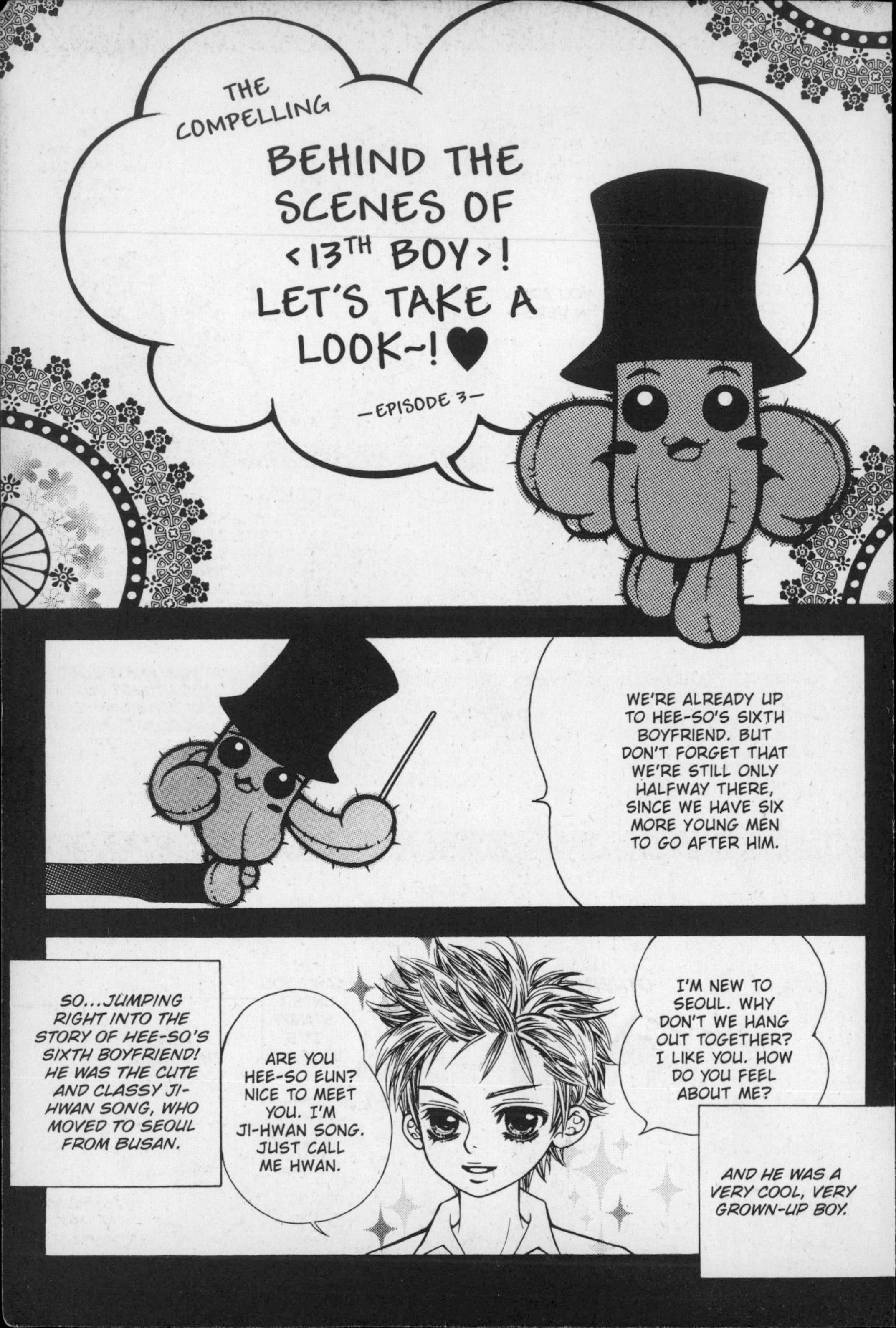
THE COMPELLING
BEHIND THE SCENES OF <13TH BOY>! LET'S TAKE A LOOK~! ♥
—EPISODE 3—
WE'RE ALREADY UP TO HEE-SO'S SIXTH BOYFRIEND. BUT DON'T FORGET THAT WE'RE STILL ONLY HALFWAY THERE, SINCE WE HAVE SIX MORE YOUNG MEN TO GO AFTER HIM.
SO...JUMPING RIGHT INTO THE STORY OF HEE-SO'S SIXTH BOYFRIEND! HE WAS THE CUTE AND CLASSY JI-HWAN SONG, WHO MOVED TO SEOUL FROM BUSAN.
ARE YOU HEE-SO EUN? NICE TO MEET YOU. I'M JI-HWAN SONG. JUST CALL ME HWAN.
I'M NEW TO SEOUL. WHY DON'T WE HANG OUT TOGETHER? I LIKE YOU. HOW DO YOU FEEL ABOUT ME?
AND HE WAS A VERY COOL, VERY GROWN-UP BOY.

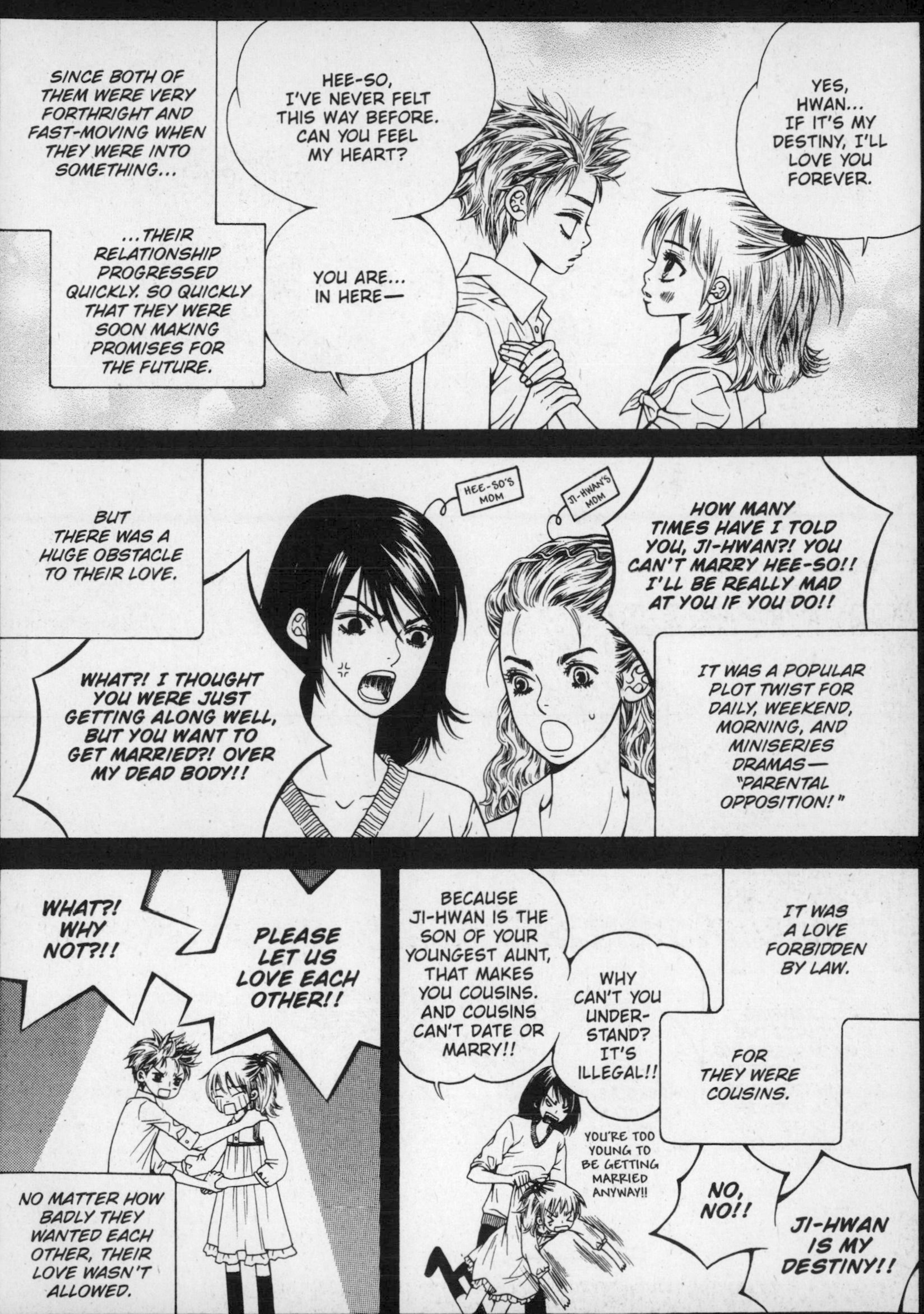
SINCE BOTH OF THEM WERE VERY FORTHRIGHT AND FAST-MOVING WHEN THEY WERE INTO SOMETHING...
HEE-SO, I'VE NEVER FELT THIS WAY BEFORE. CAN YOU FEEL MY HEART?
...THEIR RELATIONSHIP PROGRESSED QUICKLY. SO QUICKLY THAT THEY WERE SOON MAKING PROMISES FOR THE FUTURE.
YOU ARE... IN HERE—
YES, HWAN... IF IT'S MY DESTINY, I'LL LOVE YOU FOREVER.
BUT THERE WAS A HUGE OBSTACLE TO THEIR LOVE.
HEE-SO'S MOM
JI-HWAN'S MOM
WHAT?! I THOUGHT YOU WERE JUST GETTING ALONG WELL, BUT YOU WANT TO GET MARRIED?! OVER MY DEAD BODY!!
HOW MANY TIMES HAVE I TOLD YOU, JI-HWAN?! YOU CAN'T MARRY HEE-SO!! I'LL BE REALLY MAD AT YOU IF YOU DO!!
IT WAS A POPULAR PLOT TWIST FOR DAILY, WEEKEND, MORNING, AND MINISERIES DRAMAS— "PARENTAL OPPOSITION!"
WHAT?! WHY NOT?!!
PLEASE LET US LOVE EACH OTHER!!
NO MATTER HOW BADLY THEY WANTED EACH OTHER, THEIR LOVE WASN'T ALLOWED.
BECAUSE JI-HWAN IS THE SON OF YOUR YOUNGEST AUNT, THAT MAKES YOU COUSINS. AND COUSINS CAN'T DATE OR MARRY!!
WHY CAN'T YOU UNDER-STAND? IT'S ILLEGAL!!
IT WAS A LOVE FORBIDDEN BY LAW.
FOR THEY WERE COUSINS.
YOU'RE TOO YOUNG TO BE GETTING MARRIED ANYWAY!!
NO, NO!!
JI-HWAN IS MY DESTINY!!

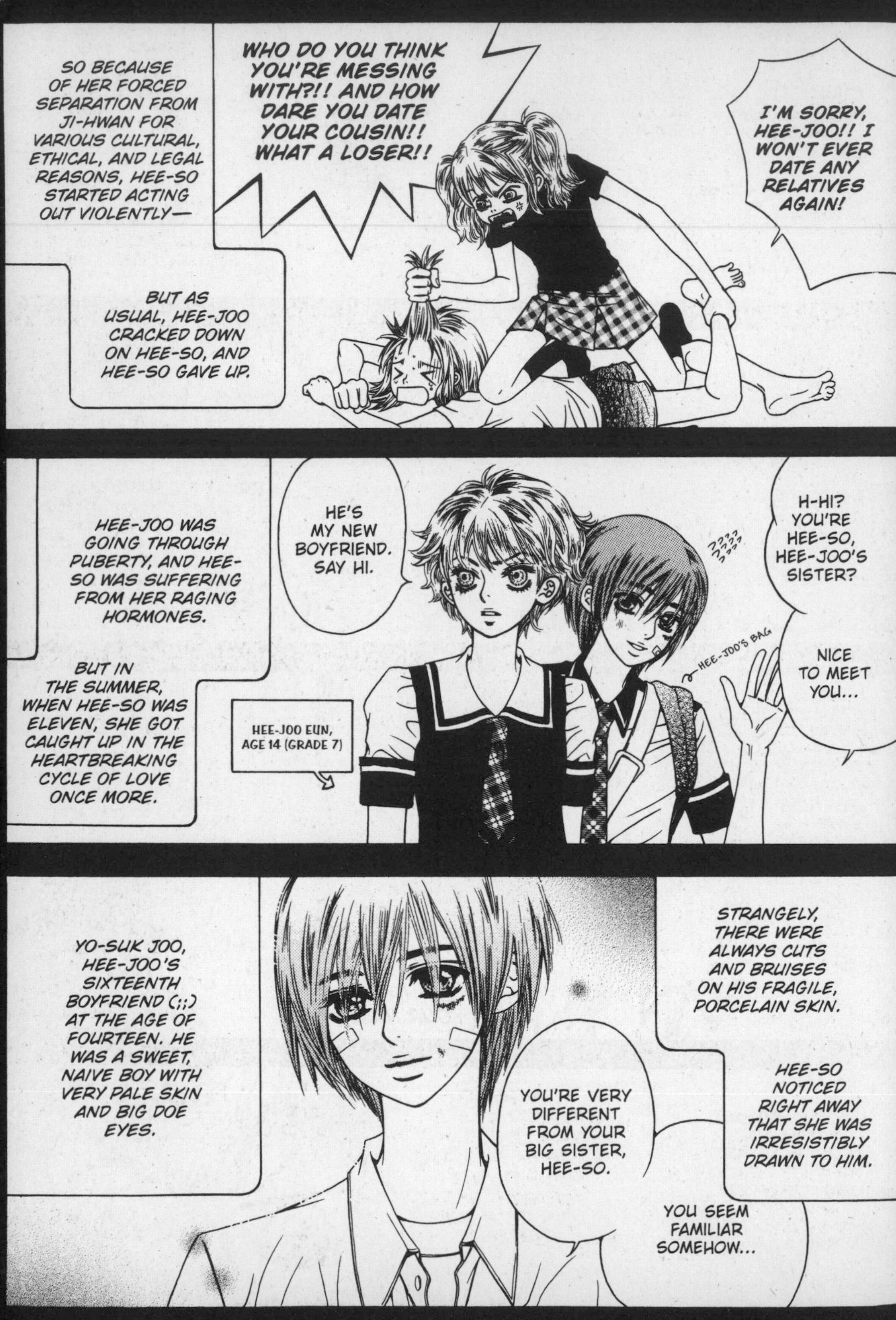
SO BECAUSE OF HER FORCED SEPARATION FROM JI-HWAN FOR VARIOUS CULTURAL, ETHICAL, AND LEGAL REASONS, HEE-SO STARTED ACTING OUT VIOLENTLY—
WHO DO YOU THINK YOU'RE MESSING WITH?!! AND HOW DARE YOU DATE YOUR COUSIN!! WHAT A LOSER!!
I'M SORRY, HEE-JOO!! I WON'T EVER DATE ANY RELATIVES AGAIN!
BUT AS USUAL, HEE-JOO CRACKED DOWN ON HEE-SO, AND HEE-SO GAVE UP.
HEE-JOO WAS GOING THROUGH PUBERTY, AND HEE-SO WAS SUFFERING FROM HER RAGING HORMONES.
HE'S MY NEW BOYFRIEND. SAY HI.
H-HI? YOU'RE HEE-SO, HEE-JOO'S SISTER?
HEE-JOO'S BAG
NICE TO MEET YOU...
BUT IN THE SUMMER, WHEN HEE-SO WAS ELEVEN, SHE GOT CAUGHT UP IN THE HEARTBREAKING CYCLE OF LOVE ONCE MORE.
HEE-JOO EUN, AGE 14 (GRADE 7)
YO-SUK JOO, HEE-JOO'S SIXTEENTH BOYFRIEND (;;) AT THE AGE OF FOURTEEN. HE WAS A SWEET, NAIVE BOY WITH VERY PALE SKIN AND BIG DOE EYES.
STRANGELY, THERE WERE ALWAYS CUTS AND BRUISES ON HIS FRAGILE, PORCELAIN SKIN.
YOU'RE VERY DIFFERENT FROM YOUR BIG SISTER, HEE-SO.
HEE-SO NOTICED RIGHT AWAY THAT SHE WAS IRRESISTIBLY DRAWN TO HIM.
YOU SEEM FAMILIAR SOMEHOW...

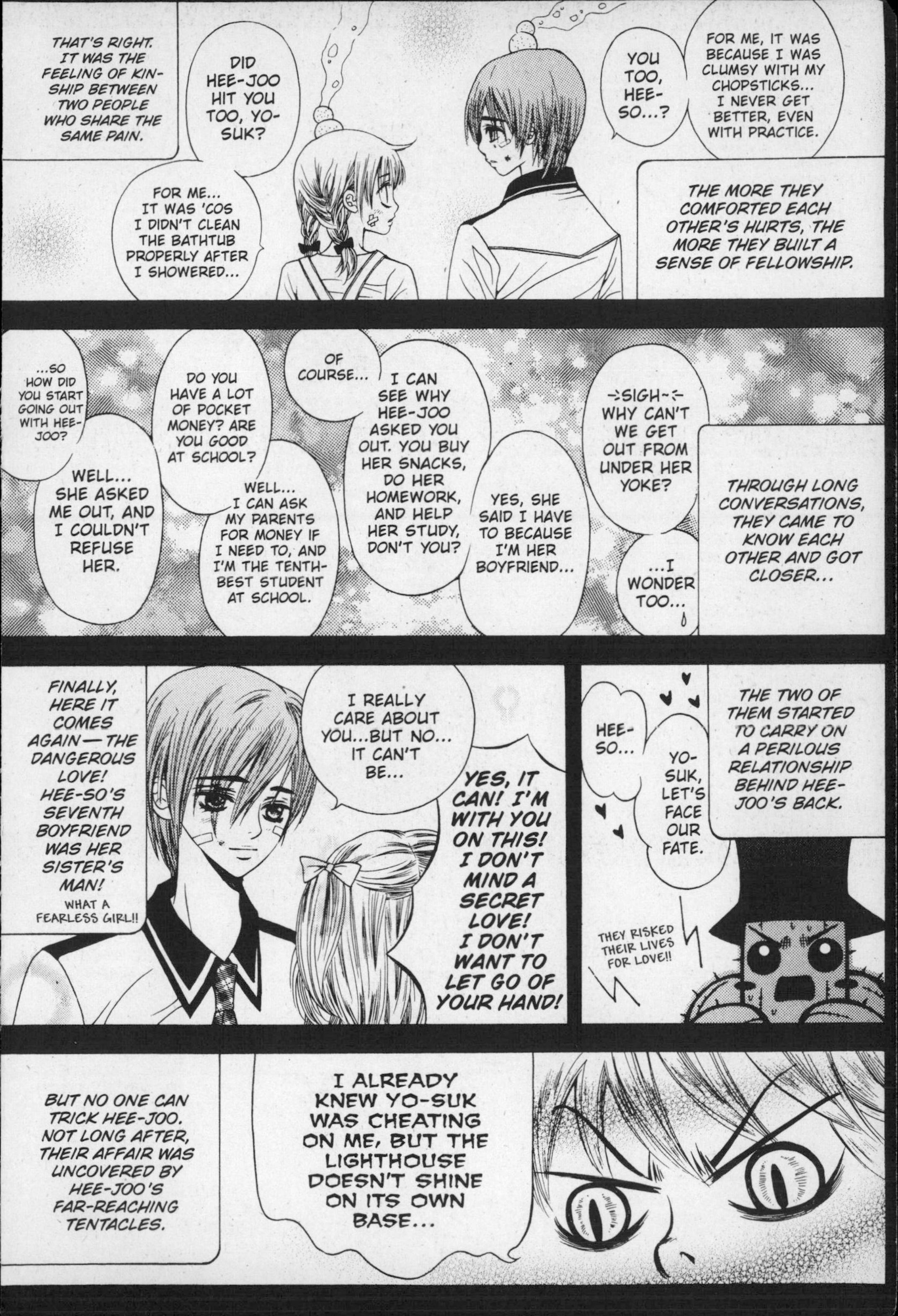
THAT'S RIGHT. IT WAS THE FEELING OF KIN-SHIP BETWEEN TWO PEOPLE WHO SHARE THE SAME PAIN.
DID HEE-JOO HIT YOU TOO, YO-SUK?
FOR ME... IT WAS 'COS I DIDN'T CLEAN THE BATHTUB PROPERLY AFTER I SHOWERED...
YOU TOO, HEE-SO...?
FOR ME, IT WAS BECAUSE I WAS CLUMSY WITH MY CHOPSTICKS... I NEVER GET BETTER, EVEN WITH PRACTICE.
THE MORE THEY COMFORTED EACH OTHER'S HURTS, THE MORE THEY BUILT A SENSE OF FELLOWSHIP.
...SO HOW DID YOU START GOING OUT WITH HEE-JOO?
WELL... SHE ASKED ME OUT, AND I COULDN'T REFUSE HER.
DO YOU HAVE A LOT OF POCKET MONEY? ARE YOU GOOD AT SCHOOL?
WELL... I CAN ASK MY PARENTS FOR MONEY IF I NEED TO, AND I'M THE TENTH-BEST STUDENT AT SCHOOL.
OF COURSE...
I CAN SEE WHY HEE-JOO ASKED YOU OUT. YOU BUY HER SNACKS, DO HER HOMEWORK, AND HELP HER STUDY, DON'T YOU?
YES, SHE SAID I HAVE TO BECAUSE I'M HER BOYFRIEND...
-SIGH- WHY CAN'T WE GET OUT FROM UNDER HER YOKE?
...I WONDER TOO...
THROUGH LONG CONVERSATIONS, THEY CAME TO KNOW EACH OTHER AND GOT CLOSER...
FINALLY, HERE IT COMES AGAIN—THE DANGEROUS LOVE! HEE-SO'S SEVENTH BOYFRIEND WAS HER SISTER'S MAN!
WHAT A FEARLESS GIRL!!
I REALLY CARE ABOUT YOU...BUT NO... IT CAN'T BE...
YES, IT CAN! I'M WITH YOU ON THIS! I DON'T MIND A SECRET LOVE! I DON'T WANT TO LET GO OF YOUR HAND!
HEE-SO...
YO-SUK, LET'S FACE OUR FATE.
THEY RISKED THEIR LIVES FOR LOVE!!
THE TWO OF THEM STARTED TO CARRY ON A PERILOUS RELATIONSHIP BEHIND HEE-JOO'S BACK.
BUT NO ONE CAN TRICK HEE-JOO. NOT LONG AFTER, THEIR AFFAIR WAS UNCOVERED BY HEE-JOO'S FAR-REACHING TENTACLES.
I ALREADY KNEW YO-SUK WAS CHEATING ON ME, BUT THE LIGHTHOUSE DOESN'T SHINE ON ITS OWN BASE...

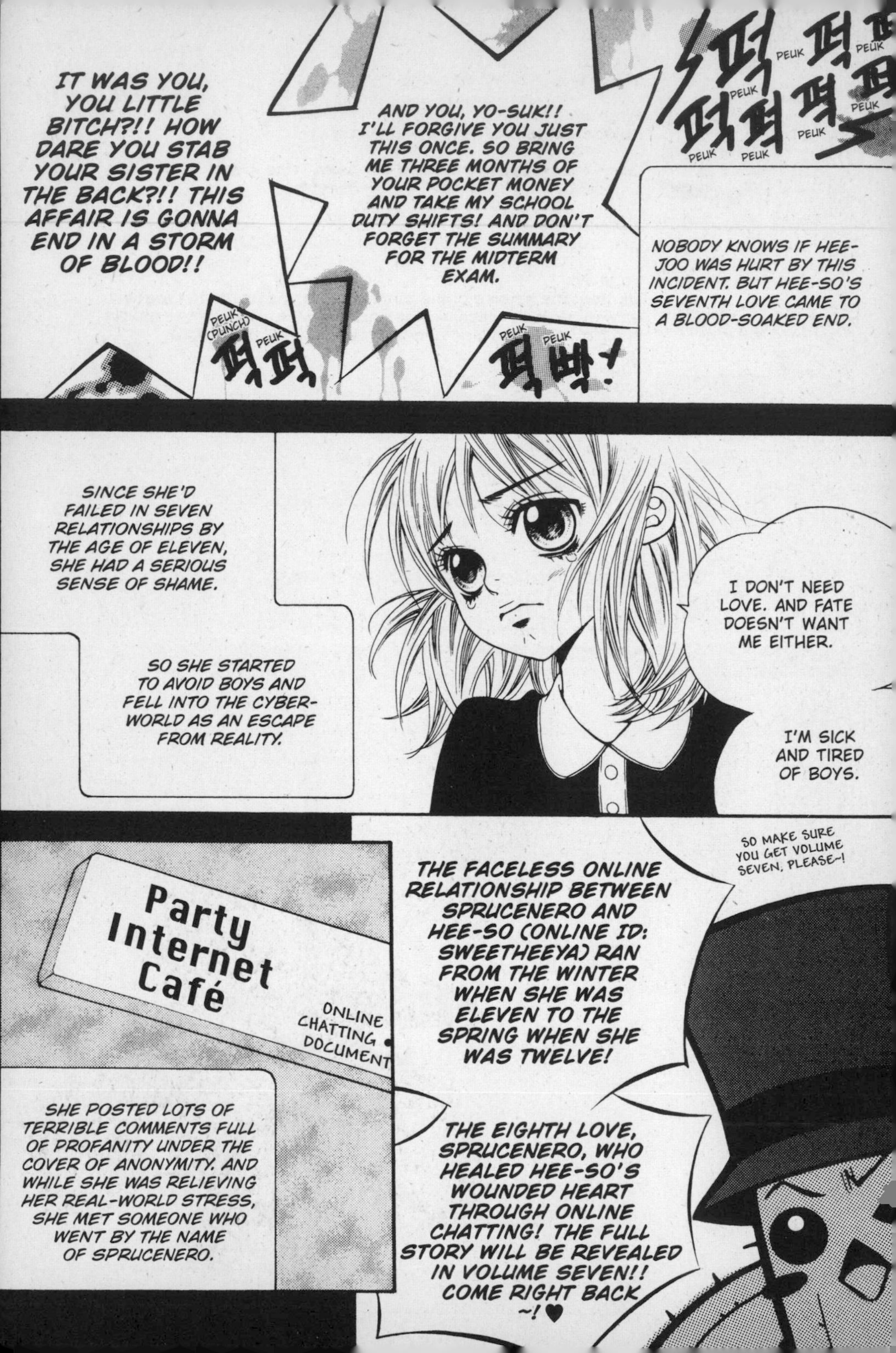
IT WAS YOU, YOU LITTLE BITCH?!! HOW DARE YOU STAB YOUR SISTER IN THE BACK?!! THIS AFFAIR IS GONNA END IN A STORM OF BLOOD!!
PEUK (PUNCH)
PEUK
퍽퍽
AND YOU, YO-SUK!! I'LL FORGIVE YOU JUST THIS ONCE. SO BRING ME THREE MONTHS OF YOUR POCKET MONEY AND TAKE MY SCHOOL DUTY SHIFTS! AND DON'T FORGET THE SUMMARY FOR THE MIDTERM EXAM.
PEUK PEUK
퍽빡!
퍽 퍽 퍽
퍽퍽퍽퍽
PEUK PEUK PEUK PEUK PEUK PEUK PEUK PEUK
NOBODY KNOWS IF HEE-JOO WAS HURT BY THIS INCIDENT. BUT HEE-SO'S SEVENTH LOVE CAME TO A BLOOD-SOAKED END.
SINCE SHE'D FAILED IN SEVEN RELATIONSHIPS BY THE AGE OF ELEVEN, SHE HAD A SERIOUS SENSE OF SHAME.
SO SHE STARTED TO AVOID BOYS AND FELL INTO THE CYBER-WORLD AS AN ESCAPE FROM REALITY.
I DON'T NEED LOVE. AND FATE DOESN'T WANT ME EITHER.
I'M SICK AND TIRED OF BOYS.
Party Internet Café
ONLINE CHATTING DOCUMENT
SHE POSTED LOTS OF TERRIBLE COMMENTS FULL OF PROFANITY UNDER THE COVER OF ANONYMITY. AND WHILE SHE WAS RELIEVING HER REAL-WORLD STRESS, SHE MET SOMEONE WHO WENT BY THE NAME OF SPRUCENERO.
THE FACELESS ONLINE RELATIONSHIP BETWEEN SPRUCENERO AND HEE-SO (ONLINE ID: SWEETHEEYA) RAN FROM THE WINTER WHEN SHE WAS ELEVEN TO THE SPRING WHEN SHE WAS TWELVE!
SO MAKE SURE YOU GET VOLUME SEVEN, PLEASE~!
THE EIGHTH LOVE, SPRUCENERO, WHO HEALED HEE-SO'S WOUNDED HEART THROUGH ONLINE CHATTING! THE FULL STORY WILL BE REVEALED IN VOLUME SEVEN!! COME RIGHT BACK ~!♥

Page 55
63 Building: It's the tallest building in Korea.

Page 56
Duksoo-dong: A famous tourist place.

Country boy (or girl) from Seoul: A person who lives in Seoul but has never seen any of its sights.

Page 58
Won: Korean monetary unit. It's worth about US$2.50

Page 59
Ok-Hee: The heroine of the famous Korean novel *The Houseguest and My Mother*, which was also adapted into film. Ok-Hee speaks in a high-pitched voice and sounds very weak and fragile.

Page 128
Toryong-tang: Earthworm soup.

Yongbong-tang: Carp and chicken soup.

Bundeki: Steamed silkworm chrysalis.

Page 133
Soon-ae-bo: A person who's willing to lay down his or her life for the love of one person.

Page 174
Busan: The second largest city in South Korea.

Page 175
"You are...in here—": Famous line from a well-known Korean drama.

SEE YOU IN 13ᵀᴴ BOY VOLUME 7~!

13th BOY ⑥

SANGEUN LEE

Translation: JiEun Park
English Adaptation: Natalie Baan

Lettering: Terri Delgado

13th Boy, Vol. 6 © 2006 SangEun Lee. All rights reserved. First published in Korea in 2006 by Haksan Publishing Co., Ltd. English translation rights in U.S.A., Canada, UK, and Republic of Ireland arranged with Haksan Publishing Co., Ltd.

English translation © 2010 Hachette Book Group, Inc.

The characters and events in this book are fictitious. Any similarity to real persons, living or dead, is coincidental and not intended by the author.

Yen Press
Hachette Book Group
237 Park Avenue, New York, NY 10017

www.HachetteBookGroup.com
www.YenPress.com

Yen Press is an imprint of Hachette Book Group, Inc.
The Yen Press name and logo are trademarks of Hachette Book Group, Inc.

First Yen Press Edition: February 2011

ISBN: 978-0-7595-2999-1

10 9 8 7 6 5 4 3 2 1

BVG

Printed in the United States of America